Policy and practice in primary education

Local initiative, national agenda

below.

Robin Alexander's report on primary education in Leeds, one of Britain's largest cities, provoked considerable interest and controversy when it was first published in 1991. Hailed as 'seminal', it has since been quoted – and misquoted – in support of widely-opposing political and educational agendas. It was also a catalyst for the government's 1992 'three wise men' enquiry, in which Robin Alexander was also involved and which proved no less controversial.

This book is a study of these two policy initiatives in primary education, one local and the other national, and of the lessons we can learn from them. Part I documents in detail the impact on schools, teachers and children of Leeds LEA's ambitious programme for educational reform, raising in the process important questions about children's needs, the curriculum, teaching methods, classroom relationships, school management, and the role of the LEA itself. Part II provides an insider's account of the sequel to the Leeds report, the government's 1992 primary discussion paper, showing the tense and complex interplay of political, media, academic and professional interests which influenced its writing and reception, and tracing its impact into the mid-1990s. Both studies are then used as a springboard for reflecting on the wider debate about standards and quality in primary education.

Of the first edition of this book one reviewer wrote: 'This book will be the benchmark against which new contributions to this debate will be measured ... the most important and distinctive study of primary education since Blyth's ground-breaking *English Primary Education* published in 1965'. This revision of *Policy and Practice in Primary Education* retains Part I from the first edition, but provides a totally new and much extended Part II, together with a new introduction and bibliography. In its first edition the book covered the period 1986–90; it now spans the decade 1986–96.

Robin Alexander is Professor of Primary Education and Director of the Centre for Research in Elementary and Primary Education at the University of Warwick.

Policy and practice in primary education

Local initiative, national agenda

Robin Alexander

Second edition

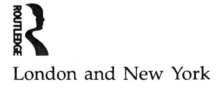

London and New York

First published 1997
by Routledge
2 Park Square, Milton Park, Abingdon, Oxon, OX14 4RN

Transferred to Digital Printing 2005

Simultaneously published in the USA and Canada
by Routledge
270 Madison Ave, New York NY 10016

© 1992 and 1997 Robin Alexander
The moral rights of the author have been asserted.

Typeset in Palatino by
Florencetype Ltd, Stoodleigh, Devon

British Library Cataloguing in Publication Data
A catalogue record for this book is available from the British Library

Library of Congress Cataloguing in Publication Data
Alexander, Robin J.
  Policy and practice in primary education: local initiative, national
  agenda/Robin Alexander. – 2nd ed.
  p. cm.
  Includes bibliographical references (p.   ) and index
  1. Education, Elementary – England – Leeds – Case studies
  2. Education, Elementary – England. I. Title
  LA633.A585 1997
  372.942–dc20 96–28529

ISBN 0–415–12837–4 (pbk)

Contents

Figures

Tables

Acknowledgements

Leeds City Council commissioned and funded the evaluation of which the first part of this book gives an account. They deserve not merely the conventional thanks but also credit for making public the outcome of what was, after all, a purely internal affair – especially in view of the way sections of the national press so cynically distorted some of the report's main findings.

This double acknowledgement – for taking part and for suffering the political and media fall-out – must extend to the staff of the 230 or so primary schools which took part in the evaluation. All schools in the city were involved at the minimum level of completing annual questionnaires, but many submitted to a much more searching programme of observation and interviews.

The Leeds evaluation was undertaken by a team, the individual and collective contributions of whose members I would like to acknowledge with gratitude. For part of each of the four years of data collection we were supported by a succession of teachers seconded by the LEA: Gwyneth Christie, Elizabeth Emery, Keith Goulding, Adrianne Harker, Jill Herron, Denise Nathan, Maggie Robson, Veronica Sawyer, Bob Shelton, Brian Taylor, Colleen Torcasio and Kevin Walker. The Leeds University members of the team included, besides myself, Steve Conway, Martin Ripley and Val Carroll, who succeeded each other as research assistants; Kay Kinder, who served for three years as research fellow; Elizabeth Willcocks, who helped with data analysis in the project's closing stages; and John Willcocks, who as senior research fellow/coordinator stayed with the project from beginning to end. Especially I would like to thank Kay and John, whose analytical perspectives are very evident in many of the project's reports, not least the final one on which this book's first part is based. John's role in the preparation of the final report was critical, and he made significant contributions to what have become Chapters 2, 4, 5 and 7 of this book.

Jim Campbell and Martin Merson made helpful suggestions about drafts of Chapters 10 and 11, and Karen gave me much-needed support first in 1992 when I was enjoying – if that is the word – the privileges or penalties of being dubbed a wise man, and again in 1996 when, in difficult circumstances, I was struggling to make sense of the experience in order to write Part II.

Abbreviations

AMMA	Assistant Masters and Mistresses Association
APU	Assessment of Performance Unit
AT	Attainment Target
ATL	Association of Teachers and Lecturers
BBC	British Broadcasting Corporation
CACE	Central Advisory Council for Education (England)
CATE	Council for the Accreditation of Teacher Education
CPS	Centre for Policy Studies
DES	Department of Education and Science
DFE	Department for Education
DFEE	Department for Education and Employment
EESA	Early Education Support Agency
EPFAS	Educational Psychology and Family Advisory Service
ERA	Education Reform Act
ESG	Education Support Grant
GEST	Grants for Education, Support and Training
GRIST	Grant-Related In-Service Training
HE	Higher education
HMCI	Her Majesty's Chief Inspector of Schools
HMI	Her Majesty's Inspector/Inspectorate of Schools
HSLO	Home–School Liaison Officer
IEA	International Association for the Evaluation of Educational Achievement
INRS	Individual Needs Recording System
INSET	In-service education of teachers
ITT	Initial teacher training
LEA	Local education authority
LEATGS	Local Education Authority Training Grant Scheme
LISSEN	Leeds In-Service for Special Educational Needs
LMS	Local management of schools
MPG	Main professional grade
NAHT	National Association of Head Teachers

NCB	National Children's Bureau
NCC	National Curriculum Council
NFER	National Foundation for Educational Research
OFSTED	Office for Standards in Education
PGCE	Post Graduate Certificate in Education
PNP	Primary Needs Programme
PrIME	Primary Initiatives in Mathematics Education
PRINDEP	Primary Needs Independent Evaluation Project
SAT	Standard Assessment Task
SCAA	School Curriculum and Assessment Authority
SD	Standard deviation
SEAC	School Examinations and Assessment Council
SEN	Special Educational Needs
SOA	Statement of Attainment
TA	Teacher Assessment
TTA	Teacher Training Agency
TTT	Teachers Teaching Together

Introduction

THE BOOK IN CONTEXT

In the summer and autumn of 1991 a rash of newspaper headlines proclaimed – not for the first time, or the last – that all was not well with British primary education: 'Progressive teaching in schools was £14 million failure' ... 'Leeds £14 million project fails to improve teaching' ... 'Reading standards fall at city schools' ... 'Good practice under siege' ... '£14 million project fails to focus on pupil needs' ... 'Very peculiar practice for state schools' ... 'Doomed by the experts' ... 'A generation of wasted time: the education of millions of primary school children has been blighted in the name of an anarchic ideology, says a new study' ... 'Happiness but little learning'.

The 1992 edition of this book gave itself two main purposes: to make available to a wider audience the evaluation report *Primary Education in Leeds* which 'when it was first published, attracted considerable publicity ... and comment ... much of it on the basis of press accounts which ranged from the merely selective to the blatantly distorted'; and 'to use the Leeds material as a basis for reflecting more generally on policy and practice in primary education'.

The book went to press in October 1991, too soon for me to refer to its sequel, though already there were indications from the political interest in the Leeds report and the continuing media attention that a sequel of some kind was a strong possibility. In December, Secretary of State Kenneth Clarke revealed all: 'Back to basics: Clarke shuts the classroom door on 25 years of trendy teaching' ... 'Clarke announces inquiry into progressive teaching' ... 'Three wise men with a Christmas deadline' ... 'Professor heads crusade against trendy teaching' ... 'Clarke backs return to formal lessons' ... 'Back to the blackboard at primaries' ... 'Sir gets a lesson from Ken' ... 'Go back to old ways, Clarke tells teachers' ... and, with the 1992 general election only a few months away, 'Clarke pins a blue rosette on new inquiry'.

In January 1992 the result of the 'inquiry' in question (*Curriculum*

Organisation and Classroom Practice in Primary Schools: a Discussion Paper)
was published to yet another clutch of headlines in the by now familiar
vein: 'Primary school dogma should be abandoned' . . . 'Teachers told to
rethink methods' . . . 'Clarke backs calls for common-sense primary teaching' . . . . 'Wise men bring gifts to Clarke' . . . . 'A heave on the primary
tiller' . . . . 'Call for return to traditional school lessons' . . . 'The great
betrayal: after affecting our schools for 25 years, the Plowden Report has
been laid to rest without mourners'.

Though some newspapers had hinted that the 'back to basics' treatment of the document in question may not have been entirely justified
– 'School inquiry challenges Clarke's plans' . . . 'Child-based style chalks
up a victory' . . . 'Schools inquiry rejects shake-up' . . . 'Teaching study
takes middle line' – the momentum gained was too great to allow such
doubts to register as more than a blip, and indeed, one newspaper made
doubly sure by seeking to discredit the offending doubter: 'Wise men
split over teachers' . . . 'Rewriting the message' . . . 'One rather unwise
man'.

What events lay behind all these headlines? In 1986, while on the staff
of Leeds University, I had been invited to devise and direct an independent evaluation of Leeds City Council's Primary Needs Programme
(PNP), a £14 million initiative which had been launched the previous
year to improve the quality of primary education in the city and address
in particular the needs of inner-city children and those with learning
difficulties. Untroubled by even the smallest hint of media or government interest, our team undertook a detailed study which through
regular surveys brought us into contact with all 230 of the city's primary
schools and entailed intensive programmes of interviews and classroom
observation in ninety of them. Between 1986 and 1990 we produced a
series of eleven interim reports on what we found (PRINDEP
1986a–1990) and then, in July 1991, published our final report (Alexander
1991a), provoking the media response illustrated above.

In November 1991, as a direct consequence of the final Leeds report,
I was invited by Secretary of State for Education Kenneth Clarke to
work with Jim Rose, at that time HM Chief Inspector of Primary Schools,
to prepare a brief discussion paper for primary teachers and heads,
grounded in available evidence from research and inspection, on the
kinds of professional issues which they might address in the context of
the education of pupils in Key Stage 2 (aged 7–11). We were some way
into this task when Clarke decided that the team should also include
Chris Woodhead, who was at that time Chief Executive of the National
Curriculum Council (NCC), the body which was later combined with
the School Examinations and Assessment Council (SEAC) to form the
School Curriculum and Assessment Authority (SCAA). There now being
three of us, all male, and with Christmas approaching, someone coined

the rather obvious sobriquet 'three wise men', and it stuck. Our discussion paper was published at the end of January 1992.

The newly established Office for Standards in Education (OFSTED) then decided to monitor the impact of the Clarke initiative, and published a succession of follow-up reports (OFSTED 1993a, 1993b, 1994). Woodhead's move from SCAA to the position of HM Chief Inspector at OFSTED, of which Rose had already become a senior member, sustained the interest of that body in the debate about teaching in primary schools and led to further publications, each rather more personalised and less corporate than the last (OFSTED 1995b; Woodhead 1995a, 1995b), and each prompting a recycling of the shock-horror headlines about plummeting standards and trendy teachers, especially when allied to evidence from national tests. Thus, from 1995–1996 for example, to bring us up to date: 'Dogma teachers are danger says schools chief' . . . 'Schools chief attacks progressive teachers' . . . 'Timewarp teachers' . . . 'Trendies in class who harm pupils' . . . 'Progressive teaching gets a caning' . . . 'Back to the blackboard' . . . 'Teachers must take blame over slump in standards' . . . 'Uproar over test failures by 11-year-olds' . . . 'Children of nine still counting on fingers' . . . ' Results expose junior schools as weak link' . . . 'Trendies produce a lesson in failure'.

At the same time, several related stories were unfolding. The 1992 discussion paper's concern about the disparity in funding between primary and secondary schools was picked up by the House of Commons Committee on Education, which after a lengthy enquiry concluded that the primary/secondary funding anomaly was indefensible and that primary schools were seriously under-funded (House of Commons 1994a, 1994b). The squeeze on educational funding exacerbated the sensitive issue of primary school class sizes, though the outcome of studies of the relationship between class size and pupil achievement was not as conclusive as teachers and parents believed it deserved to be (Mortimore and Blatchford 1993, Bennett 1994, OFSTED 1995c).

Meanwhile, the problems in the 1989–90 version of the National Curriculum – especially acute at Key Stage 2 – which were signalled in the 1992 primary discussion paper but for various reasons were not adequately explored there, had reached such a pitch that John Patten, Clarke's successor as Secretary of State, was forced to commission the review which led to a new, relatively slimmer version of the National Curriculum being introduced from 1995 and to a five-year moratorium on further changes in the statutory curriculum requirements (Dearing 1993a, 1993b).

In parallel, the Council for the Accreditation of Teacher Education (CATE), the teacher training quango of which I was a member from 1989 to 1994 and which in the latter year was dissolved and replaced by the

Teacher Training Agency (TTA), was asked to bring forward recommendations on the reform of primary teacher training in the light of the 1992 primary discussion paper. These, much modified by ministers and officials, were published as formal requirements in 1993 (DFE 1993).

Finally, there was the running battle over the mandatory assessment of children aged 7 and 11, which had produced a dramatic confrontation between teachers and the government in 1993 and culminated (as the final newspaper quotations above illustrate) in the publication of the first test results for both age groups in January 1996. These appeared to show that while the performance of 7-year-olds had improved since the first Key Stage 1 tests in 1991, over half of 11-year-olds were not reaching the defined norms in English and mathematics. Stretching credibility somewhat, the government – now in its seventeenth year of office – sought to pin the blame on the opposition's commitment to equality of educational opportunity. A few months later, the government eagerly exploited an OFSTED report claiming that eight out of ten 7-year-olds in three London boroughs were below their age norms in reading (OFSTED 1996a), a failure which the Chief Inspector attributed to 'progressive' teaching and inadequate training.

This was not all. Indeed, the first half of the twentieth century's final decade saw education established firmly at the head of the political agenda as the critically important but relatively narrow concern with primary education with which we started broadened to encompass school effectiveness and school improvement, failing schools and failing teachers, pre-school and nursery provision and their impact on the child's subsequent educational career and personal development, Britain's economic and educational performance relative to other industrialised countries, especially those on the East Asian Pacific rim, the 'standards' achieved (or, more commonly, not achieved) in British schools, the role of teachers as moral agents in an apparently amoral society, and indeed the core questions about the proper purposes and character of a state system of education which government policy since the early 1980s, reinforced by the Dearing moratorium, had so effectively pre-empted. Not surprisingly, therefore, others besides the government of the day, both inside and outside Parliament, sought to influence the way such questions were asked and answered (for example, Labour Party 1995; National Commission on Education 1993, 1995).

Most of these latter developments, of course, are well beyond the scope of the present book, though they are hinted at here as a reminder of the complexity of the context within which primary education, and discussion of primary education, must now take place. My task here, as in 1992, can be defined more precisely, though it goes much further now than it did then.

The book is an exploration of the policy/practice relationship in primary education at four levels: national, local, school and classroom. Part I presents, in the form of the Leeds report, a detailed analysis of the condition of a complete local system of primary education, from town hall to classroom, as studied over a five-year period, and considers the lessons which can be drawn from what was found. Part II then explores the origins, circumstances and outcomes of the government initiative which was stimulated by the Leeds report and purportedly shared with the Leeds initiative a concern to raise educational standards in primary schools. It then traces the legacy of these events through to 1996 and explores some of the wider issues, focusing in particular on a running theme of both accounts: the problematic notion of quality in primary education, or, in professional parlance, 'good primary practice'.

In its first edition, the book covered the period 1986–90. In its second edition it spans the decade 1986–96. It focuses on policy for primary education, and the relationship between policy and practice, at both local and national levels; and there is a tidy symmetry to the way that both editions have caught English primary education in the glare of political and media attention just before a general election.

EVALUATING PRIMARY EDUCATION IN LEEDS: A NOTE ON STRATEGY

Leeds Local Education Authority (LEA) initiated its Primary Needs Programme in 1985 and a year later commissioned the evaluation. This familiar but methodologically unsatisfactory sequence was not, as Galton (1995: 80) suggests, the fault of the evaluation team: the LEA's invitation to the university to prepare a bid for the evaluation was not made until well into the first year of PNP. But, the question of responsibility for the delay apart, it meant that there was no possibility of deploying purpose-designed baseline measures to assess the gains made by schools, teachers and children from the period preceding PNP, even though the question of gains would inevitably be of interest to the LEA, given its considerable financial and political investment in the programme. Instead, the evaluation would need to rely for its examination of the impact of the programme on a combination of existing LEA measures going back to before 1985 (notably, annual reading test scores for all 7- and 9-year-olds), a range of procedures for eliciting the views of the programme's main protagonists and participants on the extent and character of its impact, and close observation of those aspects of school and classroom life which the PNP initiative was most concerned to transform.

However, summative judgement was not the only, or even the main interest of the LEA when it commissioned the evaluation. In the first instance it was to be formative, raising issues and questions, and providing information and insights, in order to help the programme's participants understand and improve their work. To meet this objective two conditions were required: first, the focus and conduct of the evaluation would need to be negotiated with those involved; second, there would need to be a regular flow of interim reports back from the evaluation team to school governors, teachers and heads, and to LEA advisers, officers and elected members, coupled with ample opportunity for comment and discussion.

The chosen strategy and foci for the evaluation arose from discussions held during 1985–86, the outcomes of which were incorporated into the contract between Leeds City Council and Leeds University.

A first series of meetings, involving LEA advisers, officers and members, and representatives of the main teaching unions, negotiated the scope and style of the evaluation programme. It was to be formative as well as summative, as indicated. It was to be selective and sharply focused on a number of core themes. It was to be flexible and responsive, able to accommodate to issues and practices as these emerged. It was to be methodologically diverse and eclectic. It would protect the identity of individuals and schools, being an evaluation of a programme rather than an appraisal of specific people or institutions. It would be open: there would be no secret or restricted reports and all findings from the evaluation would be disseminated widely across the city and would be freely available to all. Finally, these findings would be presented in a style which made them accessible to a diverse readership, both lay and professional, without prejudicing the complexity of the issues and arguments which needed to be addressed.

A second series of meetings, with teachers and heads from schools in the Primary Needs Programme's first phase, led to the identification of the six specific themes to be examined by the evaluation team. These were:

- children's needs: definition, identification, diagnosis and provision;
- curriculum: content, development, management and evaluation;
- teaching strategies and classroom practice, including collaborative teaching;
- links between home, school and community;
- staff roles and relationships, and the management context of PNP schools;
- professional support and development, with particular reference to the LEA.

The first four of these themes derived from the four aims of the Primary Needs Programme. The last two were concerned with the strategies adopted by the LEA and its schools for making the programme aims a reality.

The focus of the evaluation in respect of the practice of primary education in the LEA was thus very broad, despite its intention to be selective. It was broad, too, in the way it included the three levels of a local system of primary education: LEA, school and classroom. We were aware of an assumption that the evaluation should be concerned only with the extent to which the LEA's policies were being implemented and that it should therefore be confined to examining what went on in schools and classrooms. As evaluators, we believed this to be an understandable standpoint for policy-makers but on several counts an unacceptable starting point for an evaluation. The success of a programme like PNP depended not only on what heads and teachers did with the resources they were given in order to implement LEA policies, but also on the character and quality of the policies themselves. To have focused on schools and classrooms alone would have been to imply that the LEA bore no responsibility for what we found there and to deny us access to important areas of insight and explanation about the programme's strengths and weaknesses. It might also have implied to the teachers and heads with whom we needed to work, and on whose confidence and goodwill we depended, that rather than being the impartial, independent researchers we (and the LEA) claimed, we were in fact agents of LEA policy. The middle word in our project title (Primary Needs Independent Evaluation Project) had to be more than rhetoric.

In the event, as the book shows, the relationship between the three levels of the system – classroom, school and LEA – was a powerful one, and the evaluation was able to show the considerable extent to which individual classroom teachers can be constrained as well as enabled by the climate, actions and policies of the school and LEA within which they work.

There were seven methodological strands to the evaluation:

- annual questionnaire surveys of the main groups of participants in all schools in the LEA: heads, PNP appointees, non-PNP appointees, advisory staff, and various other groups;
- a longitudinal analysis of change and development in a representative sample of thirty schools, ten from each of the three phases of PNP, incorporating a combination of interview and observation;
- a three-level observational study of classroom practice in sixty schools, ten of them from the sample drawn for the longitudinal study, the remainder from the group of schools ostensibly most affected by PNP in terms of additional resourcing and involvement in in-service courses;
- fieldwork involving observation and/or interviews in a further ten schools (making a combined fieldwork total of ninety schools) identified by advisers or the schools themselves as displaying interesting or significant practice as a consequence of PNP;

- observation of and/or interviews with participants involved in contingent activities such as in-service courses, LEA meetings, support services and so on, and with leading LEA players like advisers;
- examination of a large range and quantity of documentary material from both schools and the LEA;
- collection and analysis of all 7+ and 9+ reading scores over a six-year period, starting two years before the Primary Needs Programme's introduction.

The Appendix gives fuller details of these methods and lists all the research instruments used. These are described in detail in the eleven interim reports, all but three of which were subsequently published outside Leeds, as detailed below.

REPORTING EVALUATION

Each of the interim reports was sent in draft form to relevant LEA advisers for comment on matters of fact before, duly modified, the final version was presented to the evaluation programme's steering group, a sub-committee of the city council's Education Committee. This group authorised dissemination, identified action which needed to be taken in the light of the report, and monitored progress on decisions taken about earlier reports. Multiple copies of each interim report were sent to the city's schools, governing bodies and (for parents and the community) public libraries. Schools were invited to forward their comments on the reports to the evaluation team.

The procedure for the final report was somewhat more protracted, and considerably less straightforward, for the stance had perforce shifted from the formative to the summative and judgemental. The final report, as was expected, contained firm conclusions about the Primary Needs Programme as a whole, identified what we perceived to be its strengths and weaknesses, and set out recommendations for future development. In March 1991 the LEA was told that a draft was ready for discussion and was invited to nominate individuals to comment on it. Copies were then sent to a small but diverse selection of LEA officers, elected members, heads, teachers and external consultants, all of whom were invited to comment freely on matters of both style and substance. The latter three groups responded in writing. The LEA recipients preferred to identify their concerns about the draft face-to-face, and in a series of meetings with the Chief Education Officer and other senior administrative and advisory staff, held during April, May and June 1991, intensive negotiation over the paragraph-by-paragraph details of the report led first to a modified final draft and finally to an agreed version for publication.

It would be foolish to pretend that this was an easy process, or that everyone concerned was entirely happy with what was published. Negotiation over the way unpalatable findings are presented cannot really make them any less palatable, and the bruising treatment which the LEA received from the press and the Conservative Party in 1991–92 made the situation a very difficult one to handle and created both a mythology and a legacy of bitterness for the main actors which were not readily dispelled. Indeed, as this revision is being prepared, certain newspapers are once again dusting down and tracing back to Leeds three of the most carefully nurtured of the images they promulgated in 1991–92: of dictatorial LEAs operating on the basis of dogma and patronage, of teachers driven by fashion and fear rather than reason, and of primary pupils, nation-wide, wasting 40 per cent of the school day as a result (see, for example, *Daily Telegraph*, 26 January 1996).

Nevertheless, a final version of the report *was* agreed, and on 30 July 1991 Leeds City Council accepted it in full and agreed an action plan which attended to its fifty-five recommendations. A joint Leeds City Council/Leeds University press release was then issued, and the report was distributed to schools, governing bodies and other interested parties.

Several of the interim reports were edited for publication in Alexander *et al.* (1989), and the two very substantial reports dealing with the study of teaching in sixty classrooms, which were arguably the core of the evaluation and contained extensive observational material and analyses of classroom behaviour and discourse, now form the basis of two chapters in Alexander (1995). The twelfth and final report (Alexander 1991a) has become Part I of this book. The features which identify it as a formal report – numbered paragraphs, extensive cross-references, generous use of bullets to mark significant points – have mostly been removed to enable the present version to flow. There have been some minor revisions and additions, though none of them such as to alter the text's character or message, and the original report's final chapter, which discussed follow-up within the LEA, seemed too parochial for inclusion here. The style of the nine chapters in Part I, therefore, is that of a document prepared for teachers, heads, advisers and LEA officers and members. It is direct and to the point, it avoids technical detail and since much of it synthesises material which, through the interim reports, was already available to its original readers, it is rarely discursive.

At the end of the introduction to the 1992 edition of *Policy and Practice in Primary Education* I wrote:

> As this book goes to press, a major debate about primary education appears to be under way. Those of us who have made it our business to work to raise the profile and standing of this most vital yet

undervalued phase of education will be pleased that at last it is getting the scale of attention it deserves. The quality of that attention, however, is another matter, and it is to be hoped that both the profession and the public will insist that in place of trial by tabloid we achieve a level of debate which reflects the true seriousness and complexity of the issues which confront us.

This proved to be somewhat optimistic. As I have illustrated above, little has changed, and given this country's political culture it was perhaps naïve to expect that it would. The newspaper headlines in 1996, the stories, the ministerial soundbites, the distortion and manipulation of research evidence, the abuse and point-scoring in what passes for parliamentary debate, are all pretty well as they were in 1991–92, not merely in their tone, but also – virtually word for word – in their substance (or lack of it). True, some members of that parliament themselves occasionally voice despair at this state of affairs – for example, MP Denis MacShane in *The Times* of 26 January 1996:

> A visitor from the Continent or Asia would simply blink with amazement at the posturing from all political sides and ask when the English were going to stop shouting slogans at each other and get down to serious debate. . . . No other country would allow education to be reduced to the chanting of slogans about 'choice' versus 'comprehensives'.

The latter assertion may not be true, either. However, what must surely be acknowledged is that responsibility for the failure to shift public discourse on education in this country out of the crudely adversarial rut of the past two decades lies far more with government than with the professionals whom government and its agents deride as the 'educational establishment'. The very fact that ministers are happy to use this term, and with such frequency, indicates the depth of the malaise. The more telling comparison, therefore, is between those countries (most of our partners in the European Union, for example) whose governments believe in the need for policy-makers and education professionals to work together, and those, like Britain, where during the 1980s and early 1990s government preferred to pursue a strategy of attacking teachers and marginalising other professionals like advisers, teacher trainers and researchers. Viewing this sorry state of affairs MacShane's visitor might well wonder whether Britain's national education system functions in spite of government rather than because of it.

Part I

Classroom, school and LEA: the Leeds report

Chapter 1

The Primary Needs Programme: overview

ORIGINS

After the 1974 local government reorganisation Leeds became the third largest city, by population, in England. To many, this is a surprising statistic, since even now, in the 1990s, when it is enjoying an economic boom which has placed it ahead of most of its northern rivals, Leeds has far less of the appearance or feel of a big city than, say, Liverpool or Manchester: but while after 1974 these two cities lost population to the satellite towns of Merseyside and Greater Manchester, Leeds gained a substantial part of the old West Riding county.

For the new LEA, the result was a mixture both of educational traditions and of patterns of school organisation. The West Riding, under its former Chief Education Officer Alec Clegg, had been one of England's showcases for progressive primary education and for experiments in organisation (middle schools) and social intervention (educational priority areas). Leeds, though not untouched by these ideas, had remained, in contrast, educationally – and for some of the time politically – conservative. At the start of Leeds City Council's Primary Needs Programme (PNP), the initiative which forms the subject of this study, the 230 Leeds primary schools ranged in size from former West Riding village schools with a handful of children to large inner-city schools with up to 600 on roll. Their pupil age-spans included 5–7, 5–8, 5–9, 5–11, 5–12 and 7–11. By 1988, the average primary school size in Leeds was 191 (close to the then national average), with a school population of 48,000 pupils and 2,400 teachers.

For many years before the inception of the Primary Needs Programme, Leeds was consistently low in LEA league tables of primary school per capita educational spending and pupil–teacher ratios. The Authority operated a 'ring-fence' policy on new primary teacher appointments, and advisory and support services were, by comparison with many other LEAs, very thinly spread. These factors, combined with a relatively low rate of teacher mobility, generated a primary schooling system which by 1985 was perceived by the local politicians who inherited it to be stagnant and old-fashioned, though it also had, as do all LEAs, its pockets of excellence.

The Primary Needs Programme originated against this background, and should be seen first and foremost as a serious attempt to shift resources on a large scale towards the city's primary sector in order to reverse years of decline. Primary education, at last, was deemed to be an area of high priority. (For a more detailed discussion of the background to PNP, see Alexander *et al.* 1989: 1–7.)

In 1984, the Department of Education and Science invited bids from LEAs, under its Education Support Grant (ESG) scheme, for funding to improve the quality of education provided in primary schools in urban areas. Leeds LEA made a successful application for a five-year project which started in April 1985 (Leeds City Council 1984a). Though the ESG project was rapidly overtaken and indeed submerged by PNP, it served as the latter's prototype and provided a legitimation, if one was needed, for the Authority's 1985 decision to increase its own resources for inner-city primary education. The goals and strategy for the ESG programme, as proposed to DES, were very similar to those which emerged a few months later as the Primary Needs Programme (Lawler 1988).

The inception of PNP was complicated by the fact that there were four competing views of the nature of the 'primary needs' which were to be addressed. These are mentioned here because their persistence generated ambiguities in policy and confusion in teachers' understandings of PNP which caused serious difficulties at first, especially in Phase I schools, and indeed continued to generate tensions for the entire five-year period of our evaluation. The competing priorities were:

- provision for children with special educational needs in mainstream primary schools;
- provision for children in inner-city primary schools suffering social and/or material disadvantage;
- the improvement of standards of literacy and numeracy (especially reading) among inner-city children;
- the improvement of the quality of primary education across the city as a whole.

These priorities were not in themselves incompatible, but because they had different points of origin in the LEA and reflected competing territorial and political ambitions, teachers found themselves being offered varying and sometimes conflicting versions of PNP's nature and purposes.

AIMS

The aims of PNP, as they were published by the City Council in 1985, sought to reconcile these views. There was one overarching aim:

- to meet the educational needs of all children, and in particular those children experiencing learning difficulties;

and three specific goals by which this aim would be realised:

- developing a curriculum which is broadly based, with a stimulating and challenging learning environment;
- developing flexible teaching strategies to meet the identified needs of individual pupils, including specific practical help for individuals and small groups, within the context of general classroom provision;
- developing productive links with parents and the community.

(Leeds City Council 1985a)

Three problems were provoked by these frequently quoted statements. First, the problem of ambiguity: from the outset, and for much of the programme's duration, many school staff were uncertain whether PNP was about the special educational needs of certain children or the provision of 'good primary practice' for all. Second, the problem of amorphousness: even assuming the first matter was clarified, few of the phrases in the three enabling or subsidiary goals conveyed any clearly defined meaning. Finally, the problem of application: it was difficult to see what practical function, if any, aims expressed in this way could usefully fulfil.

Despite such difficulties, these remained the Primary Needs Programme's officially endorsed goals. They featured in numerous documents, job specifications, courses and other LEA statements and provided the framework within which heads and teachers were expected to work. Necessarily, of course, they were also the starting point and continuing point of reference for the evaluation which the Council commissioned from Leeds University in 1986.

Whatever its subsequent achievements, the lack of carefully worked-out, clearly expressed or seriously regarded aims represents a basic weakness of the Primary Needs Programme as educational policy. The programme lacked the precision of focus and direction which would have enabled the substantial resourcing to be exactly targeted. Our data show that as a consequence these resources, especially the PNP coordinators, were in some schools channelled into activities which bore little relation to the programme's goals as officially interpreted, yet which could nevertheless be justified in terms of the goals as stated because of their ambiguity.

The problem of amorphous language in the Authority's policy statements on primary education was not limited to the PNP aims, as we show both in our interim reports and in this book. Indeed, if this had been a feature of the aims alone its consequences would have been considerably less serious, since aims by their nature tend to be somewhat broad and sweeping, and need to be given operational meaning through objectives and strategies. Nor is this a problem peculiar to Leeds. It is in fact a characteristic of much of the post-war professional discourse in English primary education, and the case for many of the ideas and practices prominent during this period was often weakened by the way they were expressed and discussed. Equally, professional dialogue of the kind required for the improvement of practice was sometimes frustrated by the absence of shared or precise meanings (Alexander 1984, 1988). There is no reason, however, why an LEA cannot give a lead in its own documents and courses in promoting greater clarity and precision about the purposes and processes of primary education.

The tension between the 'special needs' and 'good primary practice' views of PNP persisted partly because of an institutional separation and indeed rivalry between the departments responsible within the Authority for primary education and children with special educational needs. Moreover, major components of PNP, like the 7+ and 9+ reading tests used to determine PNP phasing and levels of resourcing, were administered from outside the Primary Education Division. Such separation is common in English LEAs and has been criticised by HMI as likely to frustrate the integrative goals of the 1981 Education Act (DES 1989a). The LEA took note of our earlier comments on this matter (in the seventh interim report – Alexander *et al.* 1989, ch. 2) and from May 1990 the integration of the Authority's advisory services had begun to produce much more effective inter-divisional consultation.

Many of these problems stemmed from the speed with which PNP was conceived and introduced. To achieve such a radical shift in policy and resources in so short a time was impressive, but against this should be set the confusion referred to above and the professional disaffection discussed in later chapters. The Authority itself recognised and acknowledged the latter, and in subsequent policy matters was more scrupulous in consulting interested parties.

PHASES AND CRITERIA

PNP was introduced in three phases. The seventy-one Phase I schools were identified by reference to two criteria: educational need and social need. The measure of educational need was an analysis of each school's scores on the Authority's 7+ and 9+ reading screening tests. The extent of social need was determined by the proportion of children in each school qualifying for free school meals. The process was designed to ensure that those schools with the greatest need received the earliest and most substantial resourcing, starting in September 1985. The fifty-six Phase II schools were introduced on a similar basis in January 1987, and the remaining 103 schools entered the programme, with a rather smaller budget spread more thinly, in September 1988.

Crude though the phasing measures may seem, our analysis shows them to have been, by and large, reasonably accurate indicators of schools' needs in respect of the two criteria in question. However, there were a number of anomalies, among which the most notable and contentious were the several small Phase I schools in affluent areas where low pupil numbers produced distortion in the reading score analysis. This generated a certain amount of resentment among staff in other schools, partly because they felt they had manifestly greater problems than some of the schools selected for Phase I, and partly because they felt that some of the anomalies were tantamount to a reward for professional inadequacy, or that, conversely, they themselves were being penalised for professional competence.

In a sector as resource-starved as primary education, especially given the particular situation in Leeds referred to above, such reactions are inevitable. The important issue here would seem to be that at least the Council was prepared to commit substantial additional funds to primary education and to seek to devise a fair scheme for ensuring that these were targeted in accordance with policy. However, it is worth noting that such crude measures for selective targeting are bound to produce anomalies, and the government's scheme for the local management of schools (LMS) may well, on a much larger and more complex scale, introduce similar difficulties and reactions, since the approved LMS formula for Leeds includes weightings for needs derived directly from those used in the Primary Needs Programme (Leeds City Council 1989c).

RESOURCES

Between 1985 and 1989, the Council invested nearly £14 million in its Primary Needs Programme. The main areas for expenditure were:

- additional staff;
- increased capitation;
- refurbished buildings;
- in-service support.

The 530 additional staff appointed between 1985 and 1989 under PNP, at a cost of £11,428,000, comprised the following:

- 103 PNP Coordinators (Scale II/III, MPG with/without allowance after 1988);
- 213 PNP Support Teachers (Scale I, MPG after 1988);

- 54 Probationers;
- 21 Nursery Nurses;
- 12 Home–School Liaison Assistants (later called Liaison Officers);
- 120 Ancillary Assistants;
- 1 Coordinator of the Primary Needs Programme;
- 1 Head of the Primary Schools Centre;
- 1 Primary Support Teacher (Equal Opportunities);
- 1 Teacher in Charge of the Multicultural Resource Centre;
- 3 Administrative Staff.

The year-by-year breakdown is shown in Table 1.1.

The senior and most innovative of the PNP school-based appointments were the PNP coordinators, most of whom had a general, cross-school developmental brief, but a small number of whom were appointed with a multicultural brief only. The assimilation of pre-1988 coordinator appointees to the 1988 salary scales gave rise to difficulties in some schools in terms of each school's quota of above-MPG allowances. Similarly, the later appointees could find themselves undertaking a job defined as senior and responsible but being paid the same as ostensibly junior colleagues. This problem was not of the Authority's making, and it did its best to resolve it equitably. The role of PNP coordinator is discussed in Chapter 6, and in greater detail in our fifth interim report (Alexander *et al.* 1989: ch. 5).

Table 1.1 Appointments to the Primary Needs Programme, 1985–89

	1985–86	1986–87	1987–88	1988–89	Total
School-based staff					
Coordinators	53	28	18	4	103
Scale I/MPG	54	36[a]	35	88[b]	213
Probationers	6	29	5	14	54
Nursery Nurses	17	4	–	–	21
Home–School Liaison Officers	–	10	–	2	12
Ancillary Assistants	–	–	120	–	120
Support Staff					
Coordinator	1[c]	–	–	–	1
Head of Primary Schools Centre	–	1[d]	–	–	1
Equal Opportunities Support Teacher	–	1	–	–	1
Teacher in charge of Multi-cultural Resource Centre	1	–	–	–	1
Administrative Staff	2[d]	1[d]	–	–	3
Total					530

Notes: [a] Includes five half-time appointments
[b] Includes twenty-eight half-time appointments
[c] For one year only
[d] Until 1987–88, when absorbed into central administration

Each PNP appointee worked to a job specification. At first, the brief for the PNP coordinator was unrealistic in terms of the time available and the wide range of expertise required: it was subsequently modified by the Authority.

The appointments of the 120 ancillary assistants in 1987–88 were anomalous in the sense that they were mainly of staff redeployed from other Council departments as a result of financial cuts rather than part of the original conception of PNP; they were none the less useful for that.

Between 1985 and 1989 the Council allocated a total of £461,000 to enhance schools' existing capitation. Schools prepared bids specifying and costing their requirements which were then vetted by advisers before being forwarded to the Special Programmes Steering Group for formal approval. A detailed analysis of this spending is contained in our eighth interim report (Alexander et al. 1989: ch.4) and is referred to in later chapters.

PNP incorporated a £1.9 million Minor Works Programme of refurbishment to some of the least satisfactory buildings – other than those whose state was such as to warrant replacement – in each phase. Each school was tackled differently, but the refurbishment could include some or all of the following:

- new furniture;
- provision of display boards and curtains;
- repainting;
- carpeting;
- lowering ceilings;
- removing walls and changing layout.

The number of refurbished schools in each PNP Phase, to 1989, was as follows:

- Phase I: 16
- Phase II: 6
- Phase III: 3

The fourth major area of investment under PNP was in the in-service education of teachers (INSET). Because of the separate funding arrangements for LEA in-service activities, the way these changed even during the short lifetime of PNP, and the fact that the distinction between PNP courses and ordinary courses for primary teachers became increasingly blurred after the first year of PNP, it is not possible to cost them as a PNP expenditure item. The important statistics in this regard concern the types of courses and the attendances they achieved, and these are discussed in Chapter 7. However, it should be noted that centralised courses for primary teachers expanded dramatically with the arrival of PNP and that they became a most important tool in the

Authority's strategy for transmitting and fostering its versions of good primary practice.

The venue for the majority of LEA courses for primary teachers was the Primary Centre, established as part of PNP, first on the upper floor of St Charles RC Primary School and later in the redundant Elmete Middle School. Since its inception, the Centre has diversified to include a range of other activities besides courses, and without doubt came to represent a most valuable additional resource for the Authority and its primary teachers.

The year-by-year breakdown of PNP expenditure between 1985 and 1989 is shown in Table 1.2.

This, then, is the background to the initiative whose development, impact and implications is considered in the chapters which follow. The particular package of goals, philosophy, strategies and resources provided the framework and starting point for our evaluation. We needed to establish how the goals were being interpreted, how far the philosophy was sustainable and in practice viable, the way the resources were deployed, and the impact on children and teachers of the various strategies commended and adopted. We now take each PNP goal in turn, starting with the overarching commitment to address the needs of all the city's primary children, especially those seen as meriting particular attention.

Table 1.2 Summary of expenditure on the Primary Needs Programme, 1985–89

	1985–86	1986–87	1987–88	1988–89	Total
Extra school staff	1,217,000	2,301,000	3,109,000	4,623,000	11,250,000
Extra support staff	52,000	53,000	35,000	38,000	178,000
Increased capitation	119,023	125,704	97,762	79,120	421,609
Refurbishment/ minor works		600,000	650,000	650,000	1,900,000
Major works			8,200	17,200	25,400
Total	1,388,023	3,079,704	3,899,962	5,407,320	13,775,009

Chapter 2

Defining and meeting children's needs

POLICY

The notion of needs is central to any educational activity or programme, a fact which the Primary Needs Programme underlined admirably not only in its name but also in its resource investment. To be complete and useful, a policy directed at meeting children's needs should specify:

- the nature of the needs in question;
- the means of identifying the children who have them;
- the procedures for diagnosing these children's specific requirements;
- the appropriate forms of educational provision.

Thus, it should include, at the very least, matters of *definition, identification, diagnosis* and *provision*.

Our evaluation of this aspect of PNP was framed in terms of these four elements and through a combination of survey, interview and observation studied the way the core goal of the Primary Needs Programme was interpreted and enacted at the three levels of LEA, school and classroom (the analytical framework is explained in the interim report on this theme in Alexander *et al.* 1989, ch. 2).

A brief treatment of the needs which all children might be thought to share appears in the Authority's *Primary Education: a Policy Statement* (Leeds City Council 1988: 3, section b). However, this document is of limited relevance to the present evaluation since it was not issued until three years after PNP began. In any case, the section in question is couched in terms too general to meet the criteria listed above or to offer specific guidance for practice.

Indeed, needs were never defined or discussed at length in any statement of PNP policy, although certain assumptions can reasonably be made from the wording of the PNP aims. For example, the flexible teaching strategies of the third aim were *'to meet the identified needs of individual pupils'*, and this clearly implies some kind of identification process, however informal. It may also be inferred that such needs as were identified were to be tackled by the provision of a broadly based curriculum, a stimulating and challenging learning environment, the flexible teaching strategies already mentioned, and specific practical help for individuals and small groups.

In the field of Special Educational Needs and 'statementing', the Authority's policy was implicit in the detailed system devised by the Special Services Division for the recording of individual needs.

In the early days of PNP, the Authority's policy in relation to the particular needs of other specific groups or categories tended to be piece-meal and reactive, and had to be inferred from memoranda, minutes, job descriptions and daily practice – a task which we undertook, and summarised in our seventh report. The Education Committee approved policy statements on equal opportunities and anti-racist education soon after the start of PNP, and followed these with more specific primary guidelines (Leeds City Council 1986, 1987a, 1989f).

PRACTICE

Children with special educational needs

At both LEA and individual school levels, needs policies were more comprehensive in the area of special educational needs than in any other. Against the background of the national working definitions laid down by the 1981 Education Act and Circular 1/83 (DES/DHSS 1983), the Special Services Division of the LEA developed a local procedure for teachers to identify children who might fall into the various categories of special need, and to begin the process of more precise diagnosis. This Individual Needs Recording System (INRS) (Leeds City Council 1984b) was a comprehensive instrument whose application introduced rigour and thoroughness into the identification and diagnosis stages, and went considerably further than the reading screening tests on which some other LEAs have relied (Gipps *et al.* 1987).

To train teachers in the use of INRS and help them devise educational programmes and evaluate children's progress, the Authority mounted a highly successful and very popular in-service programme, Leeds In-service for Special Educational Needs (LISSEN) (Leeds City Council 1985b). In addition, the Educational Psychology and Family Advisory Service (EPFAS) provided specialist guidance and support, and centrally monitored both general trends and individual cases. 'Statementing' then introduced a wider array of medical and social expertise. The proced-ures themselves were subjected to internal evaluation, and have acquired national recognition, not least because the Leeds initiative stands in marked contrast to the known failure of a number of other LEAs to implement the 1981 Act in full (Wolfendale 1987).

The number of statemented children in our representative sample of schools was, at 0.5 per cent, very much lower than would have been predicted on the basis of Warnock's figure of 2 per cent of the school population (DES 1978a), and this low proportion remained fairly constant across the PNP phases. It might be supposed that the discrepancy arose from the efficiency of the INRS procedures in preventing children from reaching a stage where statementing became necessary. However, such an interpretation would be convincing only if large numbers of children were subjected to the earlier stages of INRS, and if their educational needs were subsequently met without recourse to formal statementing. The relevant figures do not support such a notion.

The overall proportion of children who were not statemented but who were nevertheless perceived as having special needs of some kind was only 11 per cent as against Warnock's notional 20 per cent of the school population. As would be expected from the way in which schools were selected for the first two phases of PNP, the proportions were systematically related to PNP Phases, being highest in Phase I and lowest in Phase III.

The INRS package earned a high reputation in the areas of definition, identification and diagnosis, but our evidence suggests that many teachers did not use the system to the full, possibly because it carried no guarantees about educational provision. By July 1988, three years into PNP, heads were reporting that their requests for extra staffing to implement agreed programmes for statemented children were being met by the response that this was the job of PNP coordinators and that no further support was available. Such a trend would seem to represent a return on the part of the Authority to a very early model of PNP – PNP coordinators as *special needs* coordinators – which it had later taken pains to modify: an apparent shift of attitude which we charted in our fifth report, and which is illustrated in the comments of a Phase I coordinator quoted among others in that report: 'The information I received with the application form and the style of interviews led me to believe I would be dealing with special needs. This emphasis changed between my appointment in May and my taking up the post in September' (Alexander *et al.* 1989: 166). By 1989, our annual surveys of heads and PNP coordinators were finding that the apparent return to the special needs role had become even more marked, and subsequently some heads expressed anxiety that despite its good intentions in this regard the Authority's LMS formula might erode further the ability of schools to deploy staff with the flexibility required for children's special educational needs fully to be met. Clearly, this is a problem which will need careful monitoring during the period of transition to full delegation under LMS in 1994 (DES 1991d).

There can be no doubt that over the years the lack of both clarity and consistency in coordinators' terms of reference led to a certain amount of confusion as they and their colleagues sensed an uncomfortable discrepancy between, on the one hand, the advisory team's messages about the 'broadly-based curriculum' with its emphasis on first-hand experience and outside visits, and, on the other hand, the precision teaching strategies which are normally associated with special educational needs (SEN) provision and which were part and parcel of the INRS procedures.

From the beginning, only a few coordinators (usually those in larger schools with several PNP appointments) defined their role solely in terms of special educational needs. Indeed, throughout the history of the programme it was unusual for coordinators to have only a single role of any kind, most of them undertaking three or four simultaneously. Many PNP coordinators combined work in the area of special educational needs with other responsibilities, and a few also supported the work of their schools' existing SEN coordinators, perhaps taking responsibility for children on Stage One of INRS, or for those with learning difficulties in a particular age group.

From year to year, the involvement of PNP coordinators in the area of special educational needs steadily declined as they increasingly undertook senior managerial roles or found themselves used as class teachers. This trend, and other aspects of the PNP coordinator role, are discussed more fully in Chapter 6. During the same period fewer and fewer heads deployed their PNP staff on special educational needs. It should be noted, however, that even in 1989 about a half of PNP coordinators were still involved in this work, and responses to our survey of all local primary heads in the summer of that year indicated that the major perceived impact of PNP on special educational needs had been at the level of provision rather than at the levels of definition, identification or diagnosis. Extra PNP staffing and resources brought about a significant increase in the amount of individual and small group work in this area.

Thus, in relation to special educational needs, the requirement we set out under 'Policy' above seems to have been met. Leeds LEA made available the mechanisms and resources for SEN *definition*, *identification* and *diagnosis*, and increased staffing – backed by INSET and central support services – offered appropriate *provision*. However, more recent events, and notably the impact of LMS on school staffing, should caution us against complacency here. By 1990, schools were claiming increasing difficulties in continuing the extent of SEN provision which had been possible in 1985–88.

Children from ethnic minority groups

Leeds City Council developed policies at various levels, not only for education, in an attempt to meet the aspirations and needs of ethnic minorities and to improve relationships between all groups in the wider community. A policy on anti-racist education was approved by the City Council in 1987 (Leeds City Council 1987a) and distributed to schools along with guidelines on *Combating Racist Behaviour in Educational Institutions*. All schools, not merely those with children from ethnic minority groups, were instructed to produce their own policy statements on anti-racism for discussion and adoption by their respective governing bodies.

For its part, the Authority launched a number of initiatives in relation to the particular social and linguistic needs of children from ethnic minority groups, who tended to be concentrated in certain areas of the city, and hence in certain schools where they might form anything from a substantial minority to well over 90 per cent of the children on roll. Among these initiatives were:

- a multicultural centre;
- in-service courses to enhance professional skills and understanding;
- a primary adviser with multicultural responsibilities;
- advisory teachers;
- multicultural coordinators;
- second language teachers;
- home–school liaison officers;
- bilingual and cultural development assistants.

The help and support most frequently mentioned to us in relation to children from ethnic minorities came in the form of courses offered jointly by the multicultural advisory teacher and the equal opportunities support teacher. These courses were challenging in content and highly interactive in their style, and hence made heavy personal demands on organisers and participants alike. However, courses on racial issues during the evaluation period accounted for only 39.5 teacher-days a year on average, an allocation of time which, if shared equally among the primary teachers of Leeds, would have given them only about six minutes a year each. In their responses to our 1989 survey of all primary heads, respondents also made frequent mention of extra language support, and the provision of role models (in the form of teachers, nursery nurses and bilingual assistants who were appointed as a direct result of PNP and who were themselves members of ethnic minority groups).

Quantitatively, however, the level of support for professional development in this area during the Primary Needs Programme remained inadequate to the task. Our evidence showed the extent of the ground to be covered, in terms of the frustrations of some heads and teachers who wished but were unable to do more, and the persistently ethno-centric attitudes of others.

Part of the problem, in Leeds as – even more markedly – elsewhere, was that in many primary schools the education of children from ethnic minority groups is simply not part of everyday experience. That being so, some of these schools, adopting the common fallacy of equating *multicultural* and *multi-ethnic* (Lynch 1983), asserted that in their schools multicultural education was not on the agenda because it did not need to be. At the same time, other all-white schools articulated policies and introduced innovative practices in multicultural education, recognising that this is quite a separate thing from ethnic minority provision, and that although they have no need for the latter, the former is re-levant and important whatever the ethnic composition of their own catchment area. However, even where there was a good deal of sym-pathetic awareness in matters of definition, identification and diagnosis, and even where long-term goals were relatively clear, there was often vagueness about the practicalities of provision.

If this matter is one of an Authority's priorities, substantial changes in the amount, content and balance of current guidance and support to schools may be necessary. As a start, and as a simple minimum, these matters could and should be openly and seriously discussed in schools. The extra staffing which PNP brought in its wake could have greatly facilitated such discussion, but its use for such purposes, like multicul-tural provision generally, was extremely patchy.

Generally, it has to be said, the task in the area of multicultural educa-tion in primary schools remained a long way from completion, despite well-publicised policies and a generous allocation of resources. It is not just that provision on the ground was uneven and in some schools inad-equate. For schools to take seriously their responsibilities in this regard, attitudes and perceptions at the level of individual teachers have to change, sometimes radically, and for this to happen the teachers concerned have to become much more knowledgeable about societal and cultural matters and about the nature and causes of prejudice. This, for the time being, is where the main thrust of initiatives must continue to be concentrated.

At the same time, the initiatives taken in many of the schools that chose to confront this issue directly were both imaginative and greatly facilitated by the PNP staffing enhancement.

Girls, equal opportunities and gender

In relation to gender issues, as in multicultural education, teachers are confronted with a matter which does not seem to all of them to be directly related to their traditional task of handing on acquired skills or information, but which depends on their own understanding of, and sympathy for, a major contemporary issue and the ways in which they can do something positive about it. Well over a quarter of our respondents completely rejected the idea of special gender-related provision in their schools. One head commented, 'I don't understand what all the fuss is about,' and a very common response was, 'We treat everybody equally here' – an assertion which was hard to reconcile with our own systematic observation of teachers and children, reported in detail in our tenth and eleventh interim reports, and summarised in Chapter 4 below.

This discrepancy between stated beliefs and observed behaviour may be easier to understand in the light of the manifest, yet widely ignored, gender-related inequality of opportunity which runs through our society as a whole. Within this context, primary teachers' own opportunities for both promotion and subject specialisation are very closely related to their gender, the relatively small number of men in the profession occupying a disproportionately large number of headships, deputy headships and posts of special responsibility in specific, high-status curricular areas. In this matter, as we illustrated with a detailed analysis of local data in our eighth report (Alexander *et al.* 1989: 128–35), Leeds was no exception to the national trend. The educational and professional implications of the gender discrepancies in school and curriculum management are also discussed in Chapter 3 of the present volume.

In situations of such widespread and generalised discrimination, two quite separate factors impede change. The first is the tendency for what is very common to seem normal or natural, so that many people remain genuinely unaware of the extent of the discrimination. The second is the fact that among the comparatively few people who are alert to the problem, those who are in the most favourable position to implement change are nearly always those who are deriving benefit from the discrimination in question. Against this background it is scarcely surprising that some of the heads and class teachers with whom we spoke were blandly dismissive of gender issues.

Those of our respondents who were sympathetic to the topic mentioned only one source of help or support in their attempts to clarify their ideas about gender issues or to make appropriate provision for the particular needs of girls, and this was the primary support teacher seconded by the Authority. All the respondents who mentioned her work spoke with unreserved enthusiasm of her visits to their schools, the books she had lent and the courses she had run both on her own and in conjunction with the multicultural advisory teacher. Because of her other commitments, these courses were necessarily few in number, accounting for only sixty-nine teacher-days a year on average, the equivalent of about ten minutes per teacher per year throughout Leeds as a whole.

Mainly through the efforts of this teacher, the major gender-related impact of PNP reported by heads in the 1989 survey was increased awareness of the issues involved and the formulation of school policy documents. It should be added that a substantial minority of heads reported no change, making such comments as, 'It's never been a problem. We've always had strong feelings and positive policies in this area.'

As with multicultural education, however, we have to report that in gender matters policy and school practice remained a long way apart throughout the period under review. Partly this was a matter of resources, as we have shown, and it was encouraging to be able to note that by 1990 the Authority had extended and rationalised these so that there would be not only an increase in support staff dealing with gender issues but also a new Equal Opportunities Unit could develop a coherent and coordinated approach to the whole field of equal opportunities, of which gender is only one part. But resources alone, even on this increased scale, will make limited headway in an area like this where gender-related ways of thinking, seeing and acting are so deeply embedded in the consciousness of individuals and groups. This is a long-term problem, not resolvable simply by spending money. The main thrust of initiatives, in gender as in multiculturalism, has to be in the area of the professional education of teachers.

Social and material disadvantage

In a sense, by far the largest proportion of PNP funding was dedicated to the needs of socially and materially disadvantaged children, since extra staffing and refurbishment, which together accounted for 97 per cent of the total cost of the programme, had their greatest concentration in schools with very large numbers of children in this category.

However, the root causes of social and material disadvantage are, both in their scale and their nature, such as to place much of the problem beyond the range of practical competence of teachers. If we ask what a child from a family which is poor, hungry, homeless and ill-clad needs, the list of answers is obvious, but no class teacher can hope to meet those requirements in her role as a teacher. It was perhaps for this reason that the Authority issued no policy statement, no formal definition of its term 'social need', and no practical guidelines on procedures for the identification of individual cases, ways of diagnosing their specific educational needs, or appropriate provision.

This was in marked contrast with its strategy in relation to special educational needs, where teachers could reasonably be expected to tackle problems with some hope of success and where consequently it was a realistic proposition to devise systematic procedures for identification and diagnosis, backed by clear guidance on the classroom provision to be made in individual cases.

In relation to social and material disadvantage, the strategy was extremely basic. It was not to single out particular disadvantaged children for special or different treatment, but simply to give to the schools in which most of them were located the first and largest share of a package of resources which was intended in the long run to benefit everybody. In this way, if PNP succeeded in raising educational standards and helping children throughout the city's primary schools as a whole, the chances were that it would help the socially and materially disadvantaged more (and more quickly) than anyone else.

This policy might seem to be the only one possible in the circumstances, but as with several other aspects of PNP it is open to question on the grounds of its diffuseness and lack of precise targeting or follow-up. Thus, schools had little choice other than to employ mainly rule-of-thumb methods for identifying socially and materially disadvantaged children, and to use some of their PNP resources to make what provision they could in the light of the advisory team's general advocacy of a stimulating and challenging learning environment. No guidance of a more exact kind was available.

This emphasis on milieu is in marked contrast to strategies adopted elsewhere, not only through the community curriculum which was such an important part of the Educational Priority programme of the 1970s (DES 1972) but more straightforwardly through a direct, sustained emphasis on the basic skills of literacy and numeracy, on the grounds that in the end these skills are what school-leavers seeking jobs are judged by, and that without them they are far more disadvantaged than they would be if they had missed other kinds of experience at the primary stage. This quite widely held view is implicit in the comment from a Leeds primary teacher which we have quoted elsewhere: 'If a child leaves my class and can't paint, that's a pity; if he leaves and can't read, that's a problem' (Alexander *et al.* 1989: 284).

These are admittedly contentious issues, but for that very reason they may be thought to have merited a fuller and more balanced public discussion under the umbrella of PNP. Whatever the achievements of the programme may have been in terms of improved working conditions, the fact remains that after an additional expenditure of nearly £14 million in four years to identify and tackle the educational needs of the city's primary school children and to regenerate schools in socially disadvantaged areas, not only did overall reading standards fail to rise by so much as a single point on either of the two measures used annually by the Authority, but the very wide discrepancy between the standards of reading in inner-city and suburban schools did not diminish in the smallest degree (see Chapter 3).

The central problem here, as will become increasingly apparent in this volume, is that curriculum was a major and persistent point of weakness in the Primary Needs Programme as a whole. Where the Authority took the lead in identifying socially and materially disadvantaged children as deserving positive discrimination, primary professional staff failed to address the question of precisely what, in curricular terms, these children needed from schools in order to give them the best possible chance of surmounting the adverse social, educational and occupational consequences of their situation. Instead it was assumed – though never demonstrated – that an upgraded learning environment would somehow deliver what was required. The rhetoric of the 'broadly-based curriculum' and the constant reiteration of 1960s-style exhortations about 'good' classroom practice were a poor substitute for the close analysis of curriculum provision which was needed. In this respect, by failing to consider more radical solutions, the Authority perhaps risked being accused of simply 'throwing money' at the problem, and of confirming in some schools the very 'curriculum for disadvantage' so heavily criticised in the 1960s and 1970s (for example Merson and Campbell 1974; Sharp and Green 1975).

When this book's first edition went to press, in 1991, we noted that the government's recently announced programme of Grants for Education Support and Training (GEST) for 1992–93 included 'a major new initiative for the inner cities ... to raise standards in identified schools facing severe problems' (DES 1991e). We expressed the hope that if Leeds LEA were to bid for funding under this scheme, it would heed our commentary on this particular aspect of PNP. Equally, we hoped that DES, in considering the bids from LEAs, would look carefully at any proposals on *curriculum* which they contain.

Children with very high ability

A final category of need must be mentioned before we turn to other matters. We occasionally encountered a particular concern with the needs of children of very high ability. It seems clear from all the written evidence that this topic did not feature at all in the thinking which led to the setting up of PNP, and we found no examples of schools with systematic procedures for identifying such pupils or diagnosing their individual needs.

This is a disturbing situation, since even gross underachievement in exceptionally able children can all too easily go undetected. Work which by no means reflects the full extent of their abilities may still be well up to the standard of their fellow pupils.

A major difficulty in formulating guidelines for practice is that discussion of high ability often becomes bogged down with talk of elitism and privilege. However, it is decidedly and demonstrably not the case that exceptional ability is to be found only in the children of highly educated and well-off parents, although such an assumption is still widely held. Yet some teachers also hold extremely low expectations of children from materially less advantaged backgrounds, a situation which actively encourages underachievement (Tizard *et al.* 1988; Maltby 1984).

The full range of human potential is, of course, to be found in every social context. Therefore we have to ask whether Leeds LEA gave sufficiently broad attention in its policies to the full range of ability-related needs. There is surely a strong case for concentrating quite specific attention on other levels of ability and attainment in addition to the lowest.

CONCLUSION

There are two quite distinct ways to evaluate a policy and its related programmes and practices. One is in its own terms – to accept the policy as it stands and then consider how successful it has been. The other is to stand back from the policy as such and ask questions about its validity as well as about its success in practice.

So far we have concentrated mainly on the first of these. Though PNP was a programme nominally concerned with the needs of every child, its resourcing and support were directed at particular categories of need and at children identified as coming into those categories. In terms of the four-part framework described in detail in our seventh report (Alexander *et al.* 1989: 68–9) and referred to briefly at the start of this chapter, we found that as a category of need, SEN was the most comprehensively served. That is to say, there were clear *definitions* of the needs in question, explicit procedures for the *identification* of children having the needs so defined, procedures (INRS) for the *diagnosis* of what those needs might be, and a range of *provision* at the level of both LEA and school.

The other three categories in the programme were rather less comprehensively covered. The disentangling of ethnic minority needs from the multicultural needs of all children – an essential preliminary to defining needs in this area – happened rather belatedly, and some schools persisted in confusing the two. In this they were perhaps reinforced by the way provision concentrated more on the minority needs aspect than on the broader task of multicultural education, and in any case questions of diagnosis and provision overall were not tackled with anything like the same rigour that obtained in the area of special needs. Gender presented a similar picture, with a comparable confusion for many between the specific challenge of giving girls and boys equal opportunities and the broader task of developing gender awareness among all children and their teachers. In these cases, the paucity and unevenness in provision were exacerbated by the rather modest level of resourcing.

Finally, when we came to socially disadvantaged children we found that, while provision was in one sense very generous, in some cases it may have been inappropriately used and thus wasted, since there was a general tendency to avoid addressing afresh the question of what precisely the educational needs of these children are, and how in curriculum terms they can best be met.

Heads viewed staffing enhancement as the most valuable resource for meeting the designated categories of need. However, such a global view takes us only so far. In fact, the 'needs' part of PNP had highly variable and in some cases rather limited impact. This was due partly to resource limitations (in the cases of multicultural education and equal opportunities); partly to a failure to give sufficient attention to all four components of each policy, from clear definitions through to carefully devised and precisely targeted provision; partly to a neglect of the curriculum questions which must lie at the heart of all educational provision, of whatever kind, for whatever children; and partly to the way that most if not all of the needs in question require a substantial increase in teachers' professional knowledge and understanding, coupled in some cases with a major shift in attitudes: such attributes are not easily developed.

At the same time, there are considerable strengths in the Leeds approach. The policy of discriminating positively in favour of particular categories of need and of those children who are identified as being in them represented a dramatic change in policy, particularly as the Authority was prepared to go well beyond mere words and back its commitments with a substantial resource investment. Where the resources were located in schools with committed staff having an intelligent and sensitive grasp of the issues and possibilities, the impact of the resources and central support could be considerable, as our interim reports showed.

However, basic questions remain, and here we move to the other dimension of policy evaluation mentioned above. The policy was essentially grounded in a deficit view of children's needs. That is to say, it concentrated more on what children could *not* do than what they were capable of. The most obvious casualties of this approach were those children defined as socially disadvantaged and children who were very able. In the former case, the tendency was to seek to make good a perceived social or material deficit in social or material rather than in educational or curricular terms. In the latter case, able children simply did not feature in the educational rationales and policies to which schools were expected to attend.

Relatedly, PNP illustrated a view of children's educational needs which was very problem-centred. That is to say, although it was asserted that all children have needs which it is the obligation of primary schools to meet, only when those needs presented schools with some kind of problem were they defined with anything approaching precision, or allocated resources in anything like a specific way. For the rest – in other words, for the majority of primary school children – it was enough to assert that teachers could meet their needs simply by purveying a partly updated version of the post-Plowden model of 'good primary practice'.

Such a basis for policy is both pessimistic and highly selective. In this sense, it ran contrary to the claim that PNP was about the needs of *all* children, since no attempt was made to help teachers to discover what this potentially limitless diversity of needs and talents might be.

Moreover, the policy had its counterpart in classroom practice. As we show in Chapter 4, some teachers consciously adopted strategies of giving certain groups of children – classically defined by one respondent as 'the undemanding ones' – less attention in order to concentrate on others. At any given point in time, selectivity of teacher attention is an essential response to the demands of the task. However, if it leads to the persistent neglect of some children, then the consequences are likely to be serious, and the strategy must be called into question, especially if, as we found, there is a tendency for 'undemanding' children to be given undemanding work.

The failure to engage properly with needs was coupled with a reluctance to grasp the essential connection between a teacher's ability to diagnose a child's needs and the educational opportunities with which that child is provided – in other words, the curriculum. Children will begin to show what they are capable of if they are offered curricular tasks which absorb and challenge them, and if their teachers hold, and make it clear that they hold, high expectations of them. As we have seen, such questions were not really addressed in the Primary Needs Programme, though there were many individual schools and teachers who understood these matters very well. But elsewhere, as we showed in our discussion of needs in the seventh report, and in our accounts of curriculum and classroom practice in Reports 8, 10 and 11 (Alexander *et al.* 1989: ch. 4; Alexander 1995: chs. 3 and 4), low expectations might be combined with curriculum experiences and teaching strategies which demanded relatively little, or which frustrated rather than enabled children to pursue the questions they wanted and needed to answer. Thus, while PNP policy on needs was in general terms an enabling one, in so far as diagnosing and meeting needs are bound up with the child's curriculum experiences and the teacher's curriculum understanding, it could also be somewhat debilitating.

Now that the National Curriculum and National Curriculum Assessment are in place, many of these problems have to be looked at in a different light. There may be grounds for optimism in the way the formal assessment requirements have encouraged LEAs and schools systematically to confront questions about children's difficulties and achievements, and to develop ways of recording and building on the diagnoses and assessments which they make. In this matter, Leeds may have progressed faster and further than some other LEAs in its setting up of an assessment unit and its production of documentary and other support (Leeds City Council 1990b). Similarly, the attainment targets, statements of attainment, programmes of study and non-statutory guidance present curriculum possibilities of which many primary teachers may have been unaware – especially in areas like science and technology, but also perhaps in fields like speaking, listening and writing.

However, though the National Curriculum opens up possibilities and provides the spur for teachers to develop new kinds of professional skill and understanding, these consequences are by no means inevitable. Increased curriculum understanding does not come from reading the National Curriculum statutory orders alone, nor does increased diagnostic skill come merely from having to keep records. Each of these attributes requires a positive programme of professional development.

We have argued that it is only when the staff of a school individually and collectively confront their assumptions about children – their identities, their needs and their potential – and it is only when the question of needs-related provision is tackled in day-to-day curricular terms, that an LEA's commitment to meeting each child's needs can become a reality. The professional climate of primary schools – in Leeds partly because of PNP and generally as a necessary response to the National Curriculum – seems more conducive to such exploration than it used to be. Where schools commit themselves to such reassessment and realignment, they can be greatly aided by national and local policies of school-devolved INSET. However, where attitudes are entrenched, knowledge is limited, or commitment to change is low, devolved INSET may do nothing to overcome the problem, and children will suffer. Indeed, devolved INSET in such circumstances could well reinforce a school's inadequacies. It seems essential, therefore, that LEAs maintain a significant stake in centralised INSET and support, and the power to intervene in those schools which show signs of becoming locked into a cycle of self-reinforcing inadequacy. But in doing so, the LEAs must examine the same assumptions about children, their learning and the curriculum to which teachers need to attend, and which lie behind the consistently noted pattern of underexpectation and underachievement in primary schools (for example, Sharp and Green 1975; Nash 1976; Tizard et al. 1988; King 1978; DES 1978b, 1982a, 1989g, 1990e, 1991a).

This, it should be noted, is a matter as much for central government as for LEAs and schools.

It is interesting to note that the DES Education Support Grant Urban Primary Schools Scheme, to which we referred in the first chapter and which in some respects served as a prototype for PNP, had a very explicit emphasis on raising teachers' expectations which was grounded in over a decade of concern flagged fairly persistently by HMI and successive governments. Somehow that goal, to which the Authority's successful ESG application also subscribed, became dissipated, and indeed PNP itself may have encouraged this. Where the Authority's ESG proposal sought 'to raise pupil performance and levels of expectation' (Leeds City Council 1984a) the PNP aims and subsequent documents referred merely to meeting pupils' 'identified needs'. Thus, where the Authority's ESG statement implied that we should rethink what children's needs and capabilities are, the PNP rationale seemed to suggest that we already know, and that the problem is simply one of provision. The initial emphasis was more apposite and should perhaps have been pursued further.

We argued above that future initiatives concerned with inner-city education ought to give close attention to curriculum issues. These, in turn, are inseparable from the even more fundamental matter of teachers' expectations of their pupils, by common consent much more likely to be pitched too low than too high. It is to be hoped that initiatives like the government's 1992–93 inner-city GEST programme referred to earlier (DES 1991e) will seek to ensure that the rhetoric of raising expectations and standards is translated into kinds of policy and INSET which probe the vital relationship between teacher expectations and classroom provision much more searchingly than has been the case hitherto.

Beyond these issues is a more fundamental question. To what extent are some of the problems we have identified here intrinsic to the primary class teacher system and therefore only to a limited degree thus capable of redress? It is one thing to argue that primary teachers need skill and support in order to identify and address the wide range of individual needs and potentialities with which they are daily confronted. It is another to demonstrate convincingly that one person can achieve the level of knowledge and skill required to do this.

We have suggested here, and in greater detail elsewhere (Alexander 1984: ch. 2), that although the class-teacher system is frequently justified on the grounds that it provides the teacher with a deeper understanding of the child than is possible under the secondary specialist model, this argument is in certain respects flawed. For a start, to know someone in any meaningful sense demands far more of the knower than of the setting, and merely being with a person over a long period of time does not of itself generate such insight. Moreover, much depends on the conditions within which that most elusive yet overworked of educational notions, human potential, is evoked. Here there would seem to be a necessary link between the teacher's own level of knowledge or skill and his or her capacity to recognise such knowledge or skill, or its potential, in the child.

How, for example, can one identify a child's potential in mathematics if one's own mathematical understanding is limited? Or in music? Or in any other area of human learning? Each of these acts of recognition or diagnosis surely requires appropriate knowledge on the part of the teacher. To recognise something, arguably, you need to know it.

Similarly, we should consider how far a child's potential, or needs, can be manifested with anything approaching precision unless the teacher provides the kinds of educational tasks which will challenge the child to the extent required. Without appropriate *opportunities for learning and assessment* the child's potential may remain undiscovered; but without appropriate *curriculum knowledge* on the part of the teacher, the provision of such opportunities may be beyond that teacher's competence.

We need to ask, therefore, how far it is useful constantly to stress the need for primary teachers to have higher expectations of the children they teach without also addressing the need for such expectations to be specifically focused rather than generalised.

There are thus at least two missing ingredients in conventional discussion of the relationship between teacher expectations and pupil performance: first, the curriculum experiences which the teacher provides; and second, the knowledge and skill which the teacher needs in order to do so. To this extent children's needs and teacher expertise are linked, for in the end it is the teacher, and not the child, who defines what those needs are.

For as long as these ingredients are neglected we shall continue to encounter a model of educational needs couched, as it was in Leeds, more in terms of children's manifested problems than their latent potential. Yet as soon as we address the curricular and pedagogical issues with any seriousness we shall have to confront the question of the extent to which the generalist class-teacher system is capable of delivering either the professional expertise or the classroom experiences which are required if the full diversity and depth of individual needs and potentialities in a typical class of primary school children are to be identified with precision and addressed with reasonable hope of success. As I have attempted to show elsewhere (Alexander 1984), far from vouchsafing special insights into what children are capable of, as is frequently claimed, the class-teacher system may sometimes do the exact opposite.

Chapter 3

The curriculum

THE LEA AND THE CURRICULUM

The curriculum was treated prominently from the outset of the Primary Needs Programme. A 'broadly-based curriculum, with a stimulating and challenging learning environment' was to be both a major aim in its own right and one of the three routes to achieving the programme's goal of meeting the needs of every child in the city's primary schools.

LEA curriculum policies, some of them specific to PNP, but most intended to apply across the board, were contained in various documents, notably the Education Committee papers of 1985 and 1986, the job specifications for PNP appointees, and the draft and final versions of *Primary Education: a Policy Statement* (Leeds City Council 1988) and *The Curriculum 5–16: a Statement of Policy* (Leeds City Council 1990a). Another source, providing not so much formally approved curriculum policy as preferred curriculum sentiments or interpretations, were the various talks given by members of the advisory team at the Authority's in-service courses, and the important compendium of such interpretations contained in the autumn 1989 *PNP Conference Report* (Leeds City Council 1989a). The LEA also produced a number of subject documents, though most of them post-dated the period in question.

Our content analysis of all this material showed that it tended to focus on the broad purposes and character of curriculum rather than its operational detail. At first sight it was also fairly eclectic, drawing on a variety of (mainly official) sources. In fact, these appear to have been selected not so much to present alternatives as to buttress or legitimate a particular value-position. Moreover, justifications for the particular views and practices espoused were rare, and the documents were essentially vehicles for the transmission of beliefs and values. This in itself is entirely legitimate, were it not for the authority which the documents carried as prescriptions for day-to-day classroom practice (rather than merely statements of principle or ideal), and their implicit message that they were to be regarded as incontrovertible by virtue of their source rather than their substance.

In fact, the curriculum statements most influential in the Primary Needs Programme espoused values of a particular persuasion – that of what one might call neo-Plowden progressivism (CACE 1967; Cunningham 1988) – whose defensibility as educational principles and viability as educational practice had begun seriously to be challenged long before the start of PNP (for example, Dearden 1968, 1976; Peters 1969; Entwistle 1970; Bennett 1976; Galton and Simon 1980; Simon 1992; Alexander 1984). Given the quasi-legal status of such statements in the eyes of many of our teacher respondents, therefore, it is a matter for some concern that while curriculum and classroom practice were prescribed in terms which were manifestly in need of debate, no such debate was initiated or encouraged.

The authority of the LEA's curriculum statements, and the dangers inherent in their lacking any explicit justification, were somewhat blunted by their tendency to impreciseness and ambiguity. Thus, as was shown in Interim Reports 6, 8 and 10 (Alexander et al. 1989: chs 2, 3 and 5), schools were confronted by the dilemma (or opportunity) of being required to implement policies whose exact meaning they could not always grasp. Nowhere was this problem more acute than in respect of the PNP goal of 'the broadly-based curriculum', as originally set out and as subsequently elaborated in a variety of contexts.

Within certain limits, therefore, centrally devised curriculum statements meant what schools wanted them to mean. The limits in question were those set by the basic 'progressive' tenets of thematic inquiry, curriculum integration, a learning environment strong on visual impact, an 'exploratory' pedagogy, group work, and the other patterns of classroom organisation discussed in Reports 6, 10 and 11 and in our next chapter. These, at least, were viewed by many teachers as non-negotiable. This is an important distinction – vagueness on curriculum and precision on pedagogy. We argue later that perhaps it should have been the other way round, and it is worth noting that in specifying curriculum content and leaving the manner of classroom implementation to heads and teachers, the government appeared to endorse this alternative principle in respect of the National Curriculum, initially at least.

PNP has now been superseded by the requirements of the 1988 Education Reform Act in respect of curriculum and delegated school budgets, yet although from 1988 to 1989 Leeds, like other LEAs, paid increasing and substantial attention to the INSET implications of the National Curriculum subject and assessment requirements, there was also a general tendency to attempt to accommodate these to the mainstream primary ideology referred to above. Thus, while some saw the

1988 Act as a vehicle for radical transformation of the school curriculum, others offered the reassurance of continuity, encouraging primary teachers in the belief that 'we do all this already' and that the once-condemned subject framework had become acceptable in so far as it was little more than a relabelling of 'good primary practice'.

Although the urge to reassure is understandable, longer-term problems may be generated by this short-term strategy if at the same time two points are not grasped and addressed. First, that the foundations upon which the National Curriculum has been constructed – established primary philosophy and practice – are at the very least somewhat problematic; second, that the new edifice and these foundations, far from providing a comfortable continuity, are in certain important respects in conflict. In particular, the systematisation of subject knowledge in the National Curriculum (DES 1989b, 1989c, 1990a, 1990b, 1991b, 1991c, 1991f, 1991g, 1991h) represents a version of curriculum sharply at variance with that espoused in the primary mainstream during the previous three decades (Kelly 1990).

As noted elsewhere, the Authority's primary education support services expanded dramatically as a direct consequence of PNP. In the case of curriculum, we witnessed a shift from an exclusively generalist advisory brief to a partly specialist one, mirroring the development of curriculum consultancy in schools. Simultaneously, as our analysis of primary INSET in the Authority will show, curriculum became an increasingly prominent INSET focus, with courses related to the National Curriculum showing the sharpest increase of all after 1987.

Alongside LEA curriculum policy and INSET were several specific initiatives bearing directly on curriculum. These included commitments in the fields of special needs, gender and multiculturalism, discussed in Chapter 2 under 'needs' but all with a necessary (though not always manifest) curriculum dimension; and participation in two National Curriculum initiatives, in science and mathematics. The first of these drew on DES Education Support Grant (ESG) funding; the second was funded by the LEA, but in association with the national PrIME project. Feedback from schools testifies to the perceived positive impact on curriculum of all these initiatives, particularly PrIME.

CURRICULUM IN THE SCHOOL: RESPONDING TO POLICY

PNP straddled the old and new dispensation in respect of curriculum control. Before the 1988 Act, the head was the main arbiter of the content and character of a primary school's curriculum, subject to LEA policy. Since 1988, the content of the larger part of this curriculum has been determined by central government and specified in statutory instruments, though in addition schools and LEAs have needed their own curriculum policies and development plans.

Despite this change, there were two constants throughout the PNP era: the existence and force of views on the curriculum emanating from the LEA and/or its officers, and the pivotal role of the primary school head in interpreting and acting on such views.

We found considerable variation in the latter. Heads interpreted LEA statements on curriculum in widely differing ways, partly – as we have already suggested – as a result of those statements' inherent ambiguities. Moreover, heads' attitudes to Authority curriculum statements ranged from acceptance to opposition, with a variety of uncertain or non-committal reactions in between.

Opposition in turn divided into what we termed 'traditionalist' and 'modernist'. 'Traditionalists' reacted to LEA curriculum policy as an encroachment on their autonomy, while the 'modernists' felt that it was they rather than the Authority who set the pace on curriculum thinking and practice and that the Authority's own prescriptions were in certain respects inadequate. 'Modernist' heads also valued dialogue and rigour in professional discourse and asserted the need for such discourse to be centred on the staff of the school, rather than conducted elsewhere and imposed on them.

Thus, the question of the character and interpretation of curriculum statements leads to the equally pressing issues of how these were evolved and of professional structures and relationships both within the school and between the school and LEA. Three matters became clear. First, heads had been needlessly antagonised by the LEA's failure to involve them in the development of policies, such as those on PNP and the curriculum, which intimately concerned them and their staff. Second, the LEA's ideas and recommendations on curriculum could have benefited greatly from open dialogue with primary heads, and in this sense the latter were an undervalued resource within PNP. Third, policies stand a better chance of being understood and implemented if those people most affected are involved in their formulation. This is a lesson which the LEA was keen to transmit in respect of schools' internal decision-making: the lesson could perhaps have been applied to the LEA's own practices. We note, however, that subsequent – post-PNP – curriculum initiatives (for example, Leeds City Council 1990b, 1990d) involved a greater measure of teacher participation.

Class teachers displayed similar diversity to heads in their interpretations of the 'broadly based curriculum', coupled with considerable consensus on what we termed earlier its 'non-negotiable' aspects like curriculum integration, experiential learning and group work. They felt themselves under a clear obligation to enact such policy, nevertheless.

The exclusion of class teachers from curriculum policy and decision-making is at least as counterproductive as the exclusion of heads. It has the added consequence of inducing dependence on others in respect of those aspects of professional life where teachers need to think for themselves. Indeed, our interview and questionnaire survey programmes provided clear evidence of a culture of professional dependency during this period.

However, there were three countervailing influences. One was enhanced staffing under PNP, which, when coupled with a properly worked-out structure for curriculum leadership, considerably increased professional discussion within many schools. The second was the National Curriculum, which teachers acknowledged to have shifted the climate of schools towards collective policy development, especially where curriculum and assessment were concerned. The third was the change in the balance of power, over matters like finance and staff appointments, from the LEA to school governing bodies and heads. The net result was a wider involvement of heads and teachers in the discussion of those issues and policies which concerned them, together with membership of the various LEA working groups – for example, on science, technology, history, geography and assessment – set up in the context of the National Curriculum. This was a welcome trend in view of the severity of the problems directly attributable to a failure to consult and involve teachers during the PNP period. However, membership by a small minority of teachers on LEA working groups neither proves nor secures the necessary democratisation of professional discourse for the majority (a problem replicated at the national level since the early 1980s in the proliferation of educational quangos filled on the basis of ministerial patronage and, arguably, political affiliation rather than professional expertise).

CURRICULUM IN THE SCHOOL: EXPLOITING PNP ENHANCED STAFFING FOR CURRICULUM REVIEW AND DEVELOPMENT

Our annual surveys of primary heads reinforced the view that of the various PNP resources, enhanced staffing had a particularly important impact on the curriculum. It enabled schools, as we have said, to rationalise curriculum responsibilities, often moving away from a situation where curriculum review and development were undertaken on the basis of 'one subject per year' (and perhaps, in small schools, 'four subjects per teacher') to one where several major areas could be kept under review simultaneously, each the responsibility of a specialist committed to building on his or her existing knowledge by studying the professional literature and attending courses.

PNP coordinators became especially prominent in curriculum review and development. Our annual coordinator surveys showed curriculum moving into first place among coordinator responsibilities after 1987, overtaking special needs.

In our fifth report (Alexander *et al.* 1989: 169–73), we identified four distinct ways in which PNP coordinators were undertaking their curriculum responsibilities:

- as *Curriculum Managers* involved in overall school curriculum policy as part of a senior management team;
- as *Curriculum Consultants* responsible for the school-wide review and development of a specific subject or subjects (in our fifth report we termed these 'specialists');
- as *Curriculum Enhancers* working collaboratively with other staff in a class or year group to support development, inject new ideas and serve as a catalyst for change;
- as *Curriculum Facilitators* having no direct engagement in curriculum development processes themselves, but releasing other staff to undertake this work.

Each of these is a valid strategy for curriculum improvement – and there could well be others. It is important, however, that schools recognise that such alternatives are not only possible but also that they can coexist in any one school. In some schools only one such role might be taken, and where, for example, it was that of Curriculum Facilitator, this might seem a waste of the curriculum expertise of the coordinator.

Another powerful device for promoting curriculum improvement, also directly attributable to PNP resourcing, was collaborative teaching, or what we termed Teachers Teaching Together (abbreviated to TTT). A fuller discussion of TTT appears elsewhere in this volume (see Chapter 4), but we can note here certain points about its potential within the arena of curriculum review and development.

Our fourth report analysed and discussed four key aspects of each TTT arrangement, based on observation and interviews in PNP classrooms:

- participants;
- purposes;
- collaborative style;
- pupil organisation.

Of the various *purposes* which TTT could serve, we identified three which were widespread:

- special educational needs;
- curriculum enhancement;
- professional development.

It is the second such purpose, curriculum enhancement, which concerns us here.

As defined on the basis of the first stage of our study of TTT the term 'curriculum enhancement' referred particularly to those activities where teachers shared and exploited each other's curriculum strengths, often, though not exclusively, in the context of thematic inquiry. The follow-up studies (hitherto unpublished) showed such enhancement to be taking a number of forms beyond this specific focus.

First, a team of teachers would work together for the *shared delivery of the whole curriculum*. In larger schools these might be members of a year-group; in smaller schools they could be most or even all of the staff. Enhanced staffing under PNP would then enable flexibility in staff deployment to allow for the disposition of curriculum expertise where at any one time it was most needed. The essential prerequisite in such arrangements, which could be logistically quite complex, was collaborative *planning*: this arrangement was essentially about the open pooling of individual ideas and strengths for the benefit of all.

Second, PNP support staff might be deployed to provide (or to enable others to provide) regular tuition, usually in language or mathematics, for particular groups of children, often though not necessarily the less able. Such teaching often utilised a structured scheme or programme, and its purpose is best described as *curriculum intensification*.

Third, PNP support staff might be used to facilitate *curriculum invigoration*. Where the focus in curriculum intensification was on the curriculum needs of specific groups of *children*, curriculum invigoration was designed to meet the needs of their *teachers*. It is thus best seen as a device for the remediation of curriculum deficiency. Characteristically, the curriculum areas concentrated on tended to be those other than the 'basics' of mathematics and language: areas like art or environmental studies which, under solo teaching arrangements and in the context of the very unequal distribution of curriculum resources within the Authority and its primary schools, were more commonly left to fend for themselves, with adverse consequences which are now well documented in HMI surveys and elsewhere.

Finally, the simplest form of curriculum enhancement was one where PNP support staff were used merely to release a class teacher to undertake curriculum-related work elsewhere within the school. We have already termed this *curriculum facilitation*.

Each of these arrangements presented challenges for those concerned – team dynamics, problems of status, problems of ownership and difficulties in planning.

However, our TTT follow-up studies confirmed and strengthened two views we set out in our earlier reports. First, that TTT was one of the most significant consequences of PNP resourcing, with the potential in this case to provide a corrective to the inconsistencies in curriculum expertise and delivery which are an inevitable hazard of the primary school class-teacher system. Second, that the realisation of this potential was by no means an inevitable consequence of enhanced staffing (or, to put it another way, there were many schools where enhanced staffing, in respect of its TTT potential at least, was wasted).

It will be seen that our studies of the work of PNP coordinators and of TTT combine to produce a repertoire of roles and strategies for using teacher collaboration to promote curriculum improvement:

- The Curriculum Manager;
- The Curriculum Consultant;
- The Curriculum Enhancer:
  (a) Shared Delivery of the Whole Curriculum
  (b) Curriculum Intensification
  (c) Curriculum Invigoration
- The Curriculum Facilitator.

Of these, the first two are school-wide roles, while the last two are classroom-based roles involving TTT. The most productive and successful use of PNP staff resources occurred in those schools which realised and exploited all of these. In contrast, some schools failed to grasp that enhanced staffing provided a chance to go well beyond the two established ways of using extra staff: for 'remedial' attention to certain children (one, but only one, aspect of curriculum intensification); and for providing cover for staff needed elsewhere (possibly for curriculum facilitation, but sometimes for more mundane purposes).

With the familiar exceptions of music and physical education (where, unlike subjects like mathematics, English and art primary teachers have always found it acceptable to admit to insecurity or ignorance), we came across no examples of PNP coordinators serving as fully specialist subject teachers, despite the fact that the level of staffing enhancement frequently permitted this. The strength of professional loyalty to the class-teacher system seems to have prevented this from even being considered.

CURRICULUM IN THE SCHOOL: EXPLOITING THE PNP DEVELOPMENT FUND AND INSET FOR CURRICULUM REVIEW AND DEVELOPMENT

The PNP development fund of just under £500,000 between 1985 and 1989 was a useful device for extending curriculum resources. Of the many and varied bids coming through the LEA's Special Programmes Committee during this period, the largest proportion by far were for mathematics and language resources, followed some way behind by computing and science. The lowest call on the fund was made for design and technology, PE, art and craft, humanities and drama, though of these, design and technology's share increased throughout the period in question, in line with its emergence as an important curriculum area, confirmed in the National Curriculum subject hierarchy from 1988.

Chapter 7 contains an analysis of LEA-mounted INSET in support of PNP from 1985–89, though in focusing on courses mounted at the Primary Schools Centre it does not claim to cover the full range of INSET on offer during that period. Overall, 31 per cent of these courses dealt with curriculum. In terms of our formula for calculating INSET teacher-days, mathematics again predominated, taking 44 per cent of the curriculum time, with English receiving 30 per cent, science 13 per cent, and all other curriculum areas sharing the remaining 13 per cent.

Given the needs of the National Curriculum core subjects, the considerable maths/English/science discrepancy might seem unsatisfactory. However, two points should be noted. First, PNP preceded the National Curriculum and thus the confirmation of science's status as a new 'basic'. Second, analysis of changing INSET priorities showed a sharp increase in the number of INSET teacher-days devoted to English after 1987. However, during the same period the increased science INSET commitment was not maintained.

There were clearly anomalies in schools' use of the very full and varied INSET curriculum support programme provided centrally. However, it should be noted that, though the Authority mounted these courses, heads and teachers decided whether or not to attend them. The issue, then, is one of *take-up* rather than *provision*, and indeed to some extent take-up in one year determines provision the next. In any case, Leeds LEA has for several years asked teachers to identify their INSET preferences and the programme has been constructed partly by reference to their views.

Global analysis of courses and attendances provides only part of the picture of how school curriculum development was supported by LEA INSET. Our analysis showed considerable variation between schools in the extent of their use of such courses, with, as a general tendency, large inner-city schools making most use, and small or outlying schools least. Heads and staff identified a number of factors; frequently cited were the lack of sufficient staff in small schools to cope with cover problems, and the time taken to travel to the Primary Centre. However, our comparison of schools having similar staffing levels and access shows that this, too, is not the whole story. Clearly, some schools which could make use of curriculum courses were not doing so, as a consequence of deliberate choice rather than accidental circumstance. In such cases, the attitudes and management styles of heads were crucial factors, as we show in Chapter 6.

Alongside centrally provided courses on aspects of the curriculum, schools undertook their own INSET. The process of school-led INSET was boosted by the arrival of Grant-Related In-Service Training (GRIST) in 1987 (to which Leeds LEA responded with a pilot scheme of devolved INSET budgets for 30 per cent of primary schools) and its successors, the LEA Training Grant Scheme (LEATGS), and Grants for Educational Support and Training (GEST). Since then, budgetary devolution for INSET in Leeds primary schools has been greatly extended.

The limited resources made available to our evaluation project and the requirements of its existing programme made it impossible to include all these school-led INSET developments in the evaluation of PNP. However, we understand that the Authority undertook its own evaluation of the GRIST pilot scheme, and to gain a more complete picture of schools' use of INSET to enhance curriculum provision and development it would be useful to juxtapose the LEA study and our own.

CURRICULUM IN THE SCHOOL: OTHER DEVELOPMENT STRATEGIES

Review and development are both essential aspects of curriculum improvement. In the period immediately prior to the introduction of the National Curriculum, we gathered data on these processes from our sample schools. The lists of subjects under review in the two years in question were dominated by mathematics and language, with science increasing in prominence though still some way behind. This closely mirrors the use of INSET and the PNP development fund discussed above. The list of reviewed subjects across all the schools covers the full gamut of the primary curriculum, which indicates that schools, regardless of external pressures, were identifying and attempting to remedy their particular curricular needs.

However, such league tables are less significant than study of the review processes themselves. Here, clear subject-related discrepancies emerged. Thus, school-based review of mathematics was strongly supported by the advisory service, both in person at the schools in question and through central courses. As a consequence the review process tended to be carefully thought out, and treated as a long-term programme of development rather than a one-off discussion. In contrast, external support for language review was rare, and for the first two years of PNP the INSET alternative was negligible, with no courses at all on reading. Science was even more patchy and homespun, despite the existence of the ESG team. For all other curriculum areas, the situation was even worse.

Many schools have considerable staff strengths in particular curriculum areas, and their capacity to engage in curriculum review and development can be independent of the availability of external support. However, because curriculum expertise is as yet disposed in such a random way across primary schools, particularly the smaller ones, it seems essential that an LEA provides some kind of development safety-net for those schools without the expertise or resources for independent curriculum development. The gross discrepancies between the 'basics' of mathematics, English and now science, and the rest of the curriculum, though scarcely defensible in educational terms, is at least understandable as a consequence of societal values. The discrepancy between mathematics and English is not so easy to understand, and may have an important negative bearing on the state of this subject in Leeds, as discussed towards the end of the present chapter.

Although curriculum consultants/coordinators/post-holders/leaders (the terms are still used interchangeably) were not specific to PNP, they were an important contingent aspect of the Authority's primary policy. Indeed, schools were expected to ensure that all teachers, other than probationers, had school-wide responsibility for a curriculum area, and it was a reasonable assumption that the enhanced staffing under PNP would enable this particular aspect of policy to be fulfilled.

We have seen that between 1985 and 1989 PNP coordinators themselves gave an increasing lead in curriculum development both within the classroom and across the school. Our annual returns made it clear that during the same period the numbers of curriculum leaders and curriculum areas covered also rose steadily. Curriculum consultancy in primary schools, at first resisted within some parts of the teaching profession, is now part of the normal fabric of school management, and PNP certainly helped to accelerate its institutionalisation in Leeds. The next stage – an even higher hurdle for the collective professional psyche – is an acknowledgement of the potential of specialist teaching in primary schools.

Despite the general acceptance of curriculum consultancy, a detailed study of such posts in the evaluation project's thirty 'Fieldwork B' sample schools once again reinforces the picture of anomaly and discrepancy in respect of curriculum review, support and development which emerged from our earlier discussion. A simple head count of subjects covered by curriculum posts suggests a reasonably satisfactory situation, in that mathematics, English, science, music, art and craft were all attended to in most schools. Leadership in computers, environmental studies, history, geography, drama and other subjects was more patchy. With these it was less a question of ensuring that they were covered as a matter of policy than of responding if people happened to express an interest in taking them on. With the Orders for all subjects now published, schools will need to look urgently at the level of support they provide for subjects like history and geography, especially in the light of HMI criticism of the quality of the teaching of these subjects in primary schools (DES 1989f). The same argument applies to the remaining National Curriculum foundation subjects of art, music and physical education, the Orders for which were due to be implemented in September 1992 (DES 1991k, 1991l, 1991m). [These references, left intact from the Leeds report as first published in 1991, relate to the pre-Dearing version of the National Curriculum. This has now been superseded by the 1995 requirements. However, though the report's bibliographic references have been overtaken by events, its arguments on this matter may still be valid.]

Matters are made even more problematic by the tendency for clear links to emerge between curriculum leadership, status and gender (Interim Report 8, Alexander *et al.* 1989: ch. 4). Thus, to take status, mathematics had the highest concentration of senior staff involved in curriculum leadership, then language (though with far fewer heads and deputies than mathematics). At the other end of the scale, art and music were mainly led by main professional grade (MPG) staff. Similar patterns emerged with gender: in relation to the overall male/female ratio in primary schools, mathematics, computing and environmental studies were disproportionately covered by men, while language, art, music and science were mainly covered by women.

There are two reasons why these patterns should give pause for thought. First, the linking of particular subjects to status and gender conveys, whether we like it or not, clear and questionable messages to children and their teachers about what subjects are most and least important, about where career advancement lies, and about which are 'male' and 'female'. Second, though there is no necessary connection between professional status and quality of work, there is certainly a connection between such status and the *opportunity* to undertake the kinds of work involved in curriculum leadership. Curriculum leadership requires time, and it requires access to classrooms and staff throughout the school: the MPG teacher with a full-time class-teaching commitment will have little of either. This last point is also strongly supported by the evidence from the AMMA/ATL study of teacher-time at Key Stage 1 (Campbell and Neill 1994a).

Thus, in a fairly subtle way, the disposition of curriculum posts among a school's staff may reinforce other discrepancies in curriculum provision and development of the kind that we have already noted. Equally, it can convey messages to children and their teachers which may be wholly inconsistent with the policies on gender and equal opportunities to which LEAs like Leeds are committed. But, it must be stressed, this is a complex matter and we are not saying that any of these consequences is inevitable: rather, that the whole question of status and gender in school and curriculum management deserves further attention.

Overall, schools used a wide range of strategies for curriculum development, of which the following were adopted most frequently:

- Defining school and teacher needs:
  staff meetings;
  GRIDS (McMahon et al. 1984);
  appraisal interviews.
- Delegating responsibility:
  establishing coordinating teams or working parties;
  drafting of guidelines or policy statement by staff member.
- Extending expertise:
  attending courses;
  requesting support from the advisory service;
  visiting other schools;
  inviting outside experts to talk to/work with staff.
- Staff discussion:
  staff meetings;
  workshops;
  training days;
  informal discussion;
  structured small group discussion;
  collective formulation of guidelines or policy statements.
- Classroom activity:
  collaborative teaching (TTT);
  year-group planning.

No school used all of these strategies. However, they (and others) constitute a repertoire for curriculum development, of each of which heads and staff need to understand the potential. A systematic exploration of all of these can provide a useful focus for both school-based INSET and the Authority's courses on management and curriculum leadership, and by the time our final report was published this had begun to happen.

Meetings – whether involving all the staff of a school, or a sub-set like a year-group – were and are a universal device in connection with curriculum review and development. They have an even more critical function in the context of the National Curriculum, now that schools have to respond to external initiatives at such great speed and with so little warning.

Though informal exchanges between staff are, and will remain, vital to the fabric of professional life in primary schools, staff are finding it increasingly necessary to operate within the framework of formal meetings. At the start of PNP these were a rarity in many schools; by the end of PNP they had become much more common, partly as a consequence of the opening up of professional discourse and decision-making which enhanced staffing and the PNP coordinator role permitted, but mainly in response to the arrival of the National Curriculum.

Running meetings is a considerable skill, especially against the background of low professional morale and rapid change. The most successful meetings we observed (in the Fieldwork B sample of schools) were those with the following characteristics:

- a clearly understood and stated purpose;
- an agreed focus and/or agenda;
- a clear structure, moving from analysis of a problem or need through to conclusion and decision;
- support from the head, whether or not the meeting is led by him or her;
- on complex issues, some kind of prepared oral or written input – if the latter, then preferably in advance;
- someone, not necessarily the head, taking a chairing or leading role;
- genuine rather than token involvement of all those attending, with particular attention paid to staff reluctant to press their case and to those inclined to view the proceedings with suspicion or disdain;
- individual preparedness to submit to the disciplines of
  (a) sticking to the point;
  (b) decentring from one's own particular preoccupations and situation to the wider issue at hand;
  (c) resisting the urge to hog the proceedings.
- a recognisable outcome in the form of action or documentation.

CURRICULUM IN THE CLASSROOM: THE PHYSICAL SETTING

Roles and strategies for curriculum review, development and management have little point unless they exert a positive influence on the quality of the curriculum experienced by the child in the classroom. Our evaluation of PNP culminated in a large-scale study of classroom practice in sixty (over a quarter) of the city's primary schools. This study, conducted at three levels, each one more concentrated than the last, is described in full in Reports 10 and 11 (Alexander 1995) and serves as the main basis for the present book's next chapter, 'Teaching Strategies'. Taking this study together with those described in Reports 4, 7 and 8, however, we encounter certain issues to do with curriculum in the classroom which can usefully be isolated at this point.

The first such issue is the relationship between curriculum and the physical appearance and layout of the classroom. The Leeds advisory team's views on classroom layout and appearance were a prominent aspect of its work, consistently purveyed to teachers through in-service courses, documents, and the work of individual advisers and advisory teachers. The physical character and arrangement of a classroom, it was asserted, should be a reflection and embodiment of two basic principles. One was that children learn best in what the second PNP aim terms 'a stimulating and challenging learning environment', hence the very strong emphasis on display and the visual appearance of the classroom. The other was that a thematically dominated integrated curriculum is best achieved through an 'integrated' arrangement of furniture. The advisory service went as far as to set up a model classroom to serve as the centrepiece of a number of its in-service courses and to project the image of that 'quality learning environment' to which teachers in Leeds were expected to aspire (for example, Leeds City Council 1988, 1989a, 1989d, 1989e, 1990a, 1990c).

Without doubt, the quality of classroom display in primary schools improved over the period of our evaluation of PNP. When such improvements were undertaken in the context of school refurbishment and the upgrading of furniture, the visual transformation of the physical context for learning could be dramatic.

The layout commended by advisory staff, and perceived by many of our interview and questionnaire respondents as being less a suggestion than a requirement, had work bays for each major area of the curriculum. These were intended to facilitate the patterns of curriculum provision generally denoted by terms like the 'flexible day' or 'integrated day', in which at any one time a classroom will contain children working on quite disparate tasks in different areas of the curriculum. Since some such tasks might involve children standing or working on the floor, advisory staff also encouraged teachers to make flexible use of furniture, some commending what was termed 'the concept of fewer chairs than children': the argument being that since the nature of the activity did not require one chair per child, more space for those activities could be created by dispensing with superfluous chairs.

In practice, we found a tendency for PNP classrooms to cluster round four layout types ranging from what in Report 10 we termed 'Type 1' classrooms with no work bays, through Types 2 and 3 with a limited number of work bays for certain activities, to Type 4 with a comprehensive arrangement of work bays for each curriculum area, as in the model classroom set up in connection with the primary INSET programme. Since the majority of classrooms were Types 2 or 3, with half of the total observed having just one curriculum-specific work bay (invariably a reading corner and/or class library), this particular message would seem to have had limited impact, in its pure form at least, though teachers were widely aware of what was preferred. At the same time, if we compare Leeds with, say, inner London at the time of Mortimore's study (Mortimore et al. 1988), the message was clearly influential. In

Leeds, some degree of curriculum-specificity in layout was a feature of most classrooms we visited, while in the London study it occurred in only a minority of classrooms. (We develop this point in the next chapter, where, in Figures 4.1–4.4, the four layout types are illustrated.)

Where there were several work bays, these were most commonly for reading, other language work, art/craft and mathematics. Science areas were less common, and our evidence from this and other studies suggested that the messages about the growing importance of science were taking some time to filter through into the classroom. The National Curriculum, clearly, will change this.

Teachers were similarly reluctant to adopt the 'fewer chairs than children' suggestion, on the grounds that it made for less rather than more flexibility.

These findings raise a number of issues. First, despite the high profile given to classroom appearance and layout in the Authority's courses and documents, the message was only selectively and partially responded to.

Second, both teachers and evaluation team members gained the strong impression that the concern with the visual dimension of primary teaching was sometimes pursued as an end in itself, rather than as a means to an end: what we call elsewhere 'surface rather than substance'.

Third, the classroom arrangements and curriculum patterns recommended, though arguable in terms of progressive ideology, have come in for increasing criticism as to their capacity to promote children's concentration and learning, and the effective management, interaction, diagnosis and assessment on which learning and progress depend (Galton and Simon 1980; Bennett et al. 1984; Alexander 1984; Delamont 1987; Mortimore et al. 1988; Galton 1989; DES 1990c).

Fourth, despite the existence of evidence of this kind, such arrangements continued to be commended as constituting 'good primary practice'.

Finally, far from promoting the 'flexibility' in teaching and learning espoused in the PNP goals and claimed for such arrangements on PNP courses and elsewhere, they may actually have had the opposite effect, since many teachers found that their practice was constrained or compromised, rather than facilitated, by their attempting to conform to what they took to be official requirements on such matters as layout, display, furniture and grouping. (The paradox of 'inflexible flexibility' in primary teaching is explored in Alexander 1988 and Alexander et al. 1989, ch. 8.)

CURRICULUM IN THE CLASSROOM: PLANNING AND RECORD-KEEPING

That curriculum planning is a prerequisite to effective teaching is not, publicly at least, disputed. We found that teachers' planning had three main dimensions:

- Time-scale:
  short/medium/long term;
  daily/weekly/half-termly/termly/yearly.
- Formality:
  elaborate and schematic written documents;
  brief written notes;
  planning 'in the head'.
- Structure:
  comprehensive planning of an entire programme;
  incremental planning, each stage building on the last;
  ad hoc planning according to circumstances and needs.

To a large extent, these dimensions operated independently of one another, different circumstances and needs dictating different approaches or combinations of approaches. Thus, even comprehensive and long-term planners were also at times *ad hoc* planners – out of necessity if not choice.

The majority of teachers made written plans of some kind. A sizeable minority appeared to undertake little written planning and to leave more than was defensible to the last minute. Such a response to the demands of teaching was sometimes defended on the grounds of 'flexibility', and indeed there is still a body of opinion in primary education which sees written planning as by definition the product of inflexible thinking and practice. However, the failure to engage in forward planning seemed to reflect anything but favourably on the commitment and capacities of some of the teachers concerned, and reinforces our view that 'flexibility' in the primary context is a word subject to a certain amount of abuse.

Similar variation marked teachers' approaches to record-keeping, though here school policy was as likely as individual preference to be a determining factor. Most teachers kept records of some kind, though many were fairly rudimentary. Further, there is a clear distinction to be made in record-keeping systems between a record of what a child has *encountered* and what he or she has *learned*. In many cases, records purporting to be the latter were in fact no more than lists of tasks undertaken.

The National Curriculum spurred schools to review policy and practice in both planning and record-keeping. The existence of age-related key stages and the amount and complexity of what had to be covered dictated a long-term approach to planning. The challenge of mapping subjects and attainment targets, statements of attainment and programmes of study on to themes and topics, required an approach which was comprehensive rather than incremental, and certainly not *ad hoc*; and planning on the scale required could no longer be held in the head.

Some schools were reviewing their approaches to record-keeping before the National Curriculum. Its arrival, coupled with the statutory requirements in respect of the provision of information to parents, accelerated the review process in these schools and encouraged its initiation in others. In these matters, the Authority's considerable investment after 1988 in subject-specific INSET and in support for assessment may have helped many teachers.

CURRICULUM IN THE CLASSROOM: CONTENT

We discussed earlier the many ways in which heads and teachers understood and interpreted statements and policies on the scope and character of the primary curriculum, while noting the pervasiveness of certain commitments: to holism, to integration, to thematic rather than subject-based activity, to different aspects of the curriculum being pursued at any one time, and so on.

In studying classroom practice in PNP classrooms, we found teachers using the term *curriculum* in three rather different ways. For some the term connoted the conventional *subjects* of mathematics, language, science, art and so on. A second group had in view not so much these familiar labels as particular *generic activities* like writing, reading, drawing, play, investigating and making which are not necessarily specific to a particular curriculum area as defined in subject terms. Others defined as curriculum areas what can only be described as *organisational strategies*: *choosing*, a term much favoured in this region from West Riding days, is a prime example, since what is indicated is neither a curriculum area nor a specific learning activity, but the teacher's mode of organising these – in which, characteristically, the element of choice is relatively constrained.

Such ambiguity about defining the curriculum, from broad policy down to everyday discourse and practice, has been a recurrent feature of recent primary education in this country and was certainly not confined to Leeds alone. In the present case, it provided the evaluation project with both difficulties and opportunities. The difficulties emerged when we attempted to calculate the proportions of time children and teachers were spending on different aspects of the curriculum, for teachers used different labels for the same area and frequently one area subsumed another. The opportunities had to do with shedding new light on the nature and scope of primary children's classroom experiences.

The detailed figures on the time spent by children and teachers on different areas of the curriculum were set out in Report 11 (Alexander 1995: 144–58) and are discussed, within the context of classroom practice as a whole, in the next chapter. At this point, however, it is pertinent to make three general observations.

First, our figures for time spent within the curriculum during 1986–90 are remarkably similar to those from other studies undertaken before the arrival of the National Curriculum – for example, DES 1978b; Galton *et al.* 1980. Despite the terminological confusion, there appears to be a fairly consistent national pattern. The league table in Leeds, as elsewhere, was dominated by language, which accounted for about a third of pupils' time, and mathematics, which accounted for a fifth. All other subjects came a long way behind: science (8.5 per cent), art (6.1 per cent), PE (5.4 per cent), topic (4.5 per cent), environmental studies (1.7 per cent), computing (under 1 per cent), and so on. It should be noted that since the arrival of the National Curriculum the overall picture has remained much as here; the notable exception is science, now a core subject, which has moved up the league table, thus squeezing still further the other subjects (Campbell 1993; Campbell and Neill 1994a, b).

Second, the large amounts of time allocated to language and mathematics were the least efficiently used, since children spent less of their time working and more of their time distracted in these subjects than in other areas given far less time. This somewhat undermines the conventional allocations of curriculum time in primary classrooms, and indeed the assumption (now embedded in official thinking about the National Curriculum as well as in teacher consciousness) that the quality of curriculum delivery depends directly on the amount of time allocated.

Third, we gained evidence of a tendency for some teachers to use certain aspects of the curriculum, notably art, craft and topic work, as a means of creating time for them to concentrate their attention on language and mathematics. The work set in art, craft and topic was sometimes of a very undemanding nature, and only spasmodically monitored. This is one of many ways in which in practice the lie is given to the rhetoric about curriculum breadth and balance. We return to this issue below.

We noted above that many teachers defined curriculum in action in terms of activities rather than the familiar subject labels. Detailed observation of children at work showed this to be a more valid alternative perception than perhaps even they realised, since it became clear that regardless of the task set and the subject labels used, children invariably tended to be undertaking one or more of a limited number of *generic activities*. Analysed in these terms, their curriculum was dominated by writing, with reading, the use of apparatus, and listening/looking also paramount, though some way behind. The list then tailed off through drawing and painting, collaborative activities with other children, and movement, to talking with the teacher and talking to the class as activities on which children were engaged for a very small proportion of their time. Thus, children were required to spend far more time writing than undertaking any other activity, and over half their time on reading and writing together.

These figures are shown in Table 3.1, which also indicates the value of juxtaposing two of the versions or definitions of curriculum we referred to above: teachers' own subject labels and the observed 'generic activities'. The result is not only a league table of such activities in terms of time spent by children overall, but also a profile of each subject showing the particular mix and proportion of generic activities which each contained. We stress that the curriculum labels were not ours but the teachers' own.

These figures prompt questions about the proper balance of activities both within the curriculum as a whole and within each of its constituent areas, to which we return below. They also suggest the need for a reassessment of the whole thrust of the 'activity-based learning' movement which has been so prominent in recent primary education. Was it really only the activities of writing and reading that the Hadow Committee of 1931 had in mind when it argued for the curriculum 'to be thought of in terms of activity and experience rather than knowledge to be acquired and facts to be stored' (Board of Education 1931)?

CURRICULUM IN THE CLASSROOM: CHILDREN'S NEEDS AND CURRICULUM DIFFERENTIATION

In Chapter 2 we set out a four-stage framework for investigating LEA policy and school practice in respect of the various categories of specific need given priority in the Primary Needs Programme and in related policies of the Authority. The fourth stage, 'provision', is to some extent a synonym for curriculum, our concern here. We therefore remind readers briefly of certain salient points from that analysis.

We noted how, in general terms, provision for children with special educational needs was relatively well supported and resourced, though school staff believed that provision had been squeezed during the later stages of PNP and again under LMS. In contrast, we expressed concern that apart from well-publicised schemes like second language support, provision in respect of ethnic minority groups seemed rather more patchy, and we were particularly concerned at the numbers of heads and teachers who appeared to assume that meeting the educational needs of ethnic minority groups and multicultural education were synonymous. We found an even greater discrepancy between policy and curriculum when we examined gender-related needs, once again underscored by inadequate understanding or dismissive attitudes by some heads and teachers. As far as socially and materially disadvantaged children were concerned – a major focus of PNP, it must be remembered – we found that the generosity of resourcing for the schools in

Table 3.1 Percentage of time spent by pupils on ten generic activities in different areas of the curriculum, as defined by their teachers

	Write	Apparatus	Read	Listen/ Look	Draw/ Paint	Collaborate	Move about	Talk to teacher	Construct	Talk to class
Language	56	4	39	24	17	9	5	9	0	1
Maths	55	37	42	7	21	14	4	2	0	0
Science	16	39	5	27	25	20	5	18	11	2
Admin	0	2	9	82	0	9	29	30	0	0
Art	0	57	3	3	55	7	4	0	6	0
PE	0	18	0	18	0	27	100	0	0	0
Topic	41	0	19	12	47	15	3	8	0	4
Play	0	87	2	0	0	42	47	4	21	0
CDT	5	84	5	0	0	56	0	0	95	0
Choosing	10	49	19	19	29	44	28	0	0	0
Music	0	12	10	21	0	88	12	0	0	0
Environmental Studies	44	0	0	44	33	0	0	22	0	0
Sewing	0	100	0	0	0	0	0	0	0	0
Table games	0	100	0	0	0	63	0	0	0	0
Computer	53	47	53	23	0	30	0	23	0	0
Cooking	0	100	0	0	0	0	100	0	0	0
Television	0	0	0	100	0	0	0	0	0	0
All curriculum areas %	33	28	24	20	19	18	14	8	6	1

Note: The values in this table are percentages of the total time spent in each curriculum area. The rows generally sum to considerably more than 100 because the listed activities are not mutually exclusive.

which many of them were concentrated (Phase I of PNP) had not been followed through into careful analysis of their curriculum needs. Instead, there was a widespread assumption that the problem was less a curricular than an affective or behavioural one, with emotional security the prime concern. Finally, we noted the absence of policy in relation to other definable categories of need – for example, very able children.

As we indicated in Chapter 2, the Authority subsequently extended some of its needs-related policies. However, our study of classroom practice showed that curriculum provision in respect of these children requires continued attention at every level of the system. There were significant differences in the work of certain groups of children: older and younger, girls and boys, and those perceived by their teachers to be of average, above average and below average ability. These differences concerned the amount of time such children spent on various kinds of task-related behaviour – working, performing routine activities, awaiting attention, being distracted – both overall and in relation to each area of the curriculum. Our eleventh report provides full details.

We suggested that while some of these discrepancies may be attributable to the many individual pupil differences which are wholly independent of the teacher, others may well be related directly to a teacher's assumptions and expectations about the children in question, in so far as there is an established relationship between a teacher's view of a child and that child's characteristic responses.

Given the kinds of assumptions and expectations about particular groups of children which emerged from our other studies, the concern expressed here remains a valid one. Teachers need both opportunities and procedures for ensuring that the evidence about children on which their diagnoses, curriculum provision and assessments are based is as secure and reliable as possible. This matter was given little attention within PNP, despite the rhetoric of individual needs and provision which was so prominent a feature of that programme. Subsequently, the National Curriculum dictated a concern with assessment to which the Authority responded through courses and documents and by setting up an assessment unit.

Yet assessment is not merely, or even mainly, about procedures. The quality of an assessment depends vitally upon the quality of the evidence on which it is based; in turn, such evidence depends on the knowledge and skills of the teacher and the nature and duration of the interactions with children and their work through which the evidence about their needs and attainments is obtained. However, since the central pupil–teacher and pupil–pupil interactions of which teaching is constituted were somewhat peripheral to the messages of the Primary Needs Programme, and the emphasis was more on aspects like display, resources, classroom layout and organisation, we can anticipate continuing problems of misdiagnosis and inaccurate assessment among those teachers whose view of their task has been unduly influenced by this emphasis.

In the context of the [pre-Dearing] National Curriculum, the Standard Assessment Tasks (SATs) provide a check on the teacher's judgements. However, SATs are used only twice in a child's primary schooling, at the ages of 7 and 11, and even then they provide only a small proportion of the evidence on which assessments are based, the majority coming from Teacher Assessment (TA). In any event, after the 1990 pilot for Key Stage 1 National Curriculum Assessment the government began a severe pruning exercise, cutting back first the number of attainment targets covered by the SATs and then, after the 1991 assessment run, the scope of the SATs themselves.

Thus, a national system of assessment notwithstanding, most decisions about children's learning and progress will be based, as they always have been, on *informal* assessments by their teachers. In no more than a limited sense, therefore, does National Curriculum Assessment resolve this problem. Though it is encouraging to note the Authority's investment in assessment policy, training and support (Leeds City Council 1990b) as a consequence of the 1988 legislation, it is important that what we have termed 'informal' assessment receives no less attention than the statutory requirements. Just as there is now a trend to defining 'generic' skills in management (DES 1990f), so there are generic skills in classroom assessment, and in turn these are vitally dependent upon classroom strategies which maximise teachers' opportunities for careful observation of and interaction with their pupils.

THE QUALITY OF THE PRIMARY CURRICULUM

In this final section of the present chapter we return to the 'broadly-based curriculum' – the goal of both PNP and the 1988 Education Reform Act. How far was it a reality in Leeds primary schools during the period in question? The first problem we encounter, rehearsed at several points in this and other chapters, was that the concept of curriculum breadth was ill-defined in Authority policy and multifariously interpreted in schools. Until the arrival of the National Curriculum, indeed, Leeds LEA had no meaningful conception of the primary curriculum as a whole. The eight contrasting versions of the Leeds 'broadly-based curriculum' in Alexander *et al.* (1989: 123–6) illustrate the extent of this problem.

Thus, whole curriculum thinking in the schools was highly variable in quality and widely divergent in emphasis. All too frequently, the ritual genuflection to 'wholeness' barely concealed an absence of hard thinking and planning in relation to whole curriculum matters, or discrepancies in provision across subjects which were so substantial and deeply ingrained that they invalidated even the vaguest of 'broadly-based curriculum' claims, let alone those involving contingent principles like balance, coherence, continuity and differentiation. In disentangling themselves from this legacy, it must be said, schools had little help from elsewhere.

Thus, at each level of the system we found claims to breadth and balance undermined by countervailing policies and practices: in Authority special projects; in central INSET provision; in PNP development fund allocations; in the allocation of posts of responsibility in schools; in school-based INSET programmes; in the status of post-holders and the time and support available to them to undertake their responsibilities; in the range of curriculum areas subjected to review and development and the time and support given to each; in teacher expertise; above all, and as a consequence of all this, in the quality of children's curriculum experiences in the classroom.

Equally, it must be stressed, for every school which neglected a given subject or treated it indifferently, there was another whose staff taught it with commitment, flair and challenge. The variables, then, were not merely LEA policy and support, but also school policy and priorities, and – always a critical factor – the availability and extent of staff curriculum expertise.

At the same time, our data tended to lead inexorably towards confirmation of the 'two curricula' thesis – the idea that the primary world's claims to curricular wholeness, balance and integration may be frustrated or even invalidated by a sharp divide, both quantitative (in terms of time spent and resources allocated) and qualitative (in terms of professional expertise, thinking and practice) between 'the basics' and the rest, or 'Curriculum I' and 'Curriculum II' (Alexander 1984). In this matter, the proposition that different aspects of the curriculum should receive different proportions of time in the classroom is not contested: a complete curriculum is necessarily one in which priorities have been clearly identified. What is not acceptable educationally, let alone compatible with ideas of curriculum breadth and balance, is that there should be such variation in the actual *quality* of what teachers offer and children experience in the classroom as between the different curriculum areas. Put another way, however much or little time the various subjects are allocated, each of them should be fully staffed and resourced, carefully planned, seriously treated, and delivered in the classroom in a convincing, stimulating and challenging manner.

The National Curriculum, far from eliminating this historical tendency, could well reinforce it, unless positive steps are taken by both LEAs and schools (and indeed by central government) to enhance the quality of support, expertise and provision in *every* subject, regardless of its status.

Putting together our data on policy, INSET, school management and classroom practice, we can present the following brief summary of the overall position in relation to five contrasting areas of the curriculum as they stood immediately prior to the introduction of the National Curriculum, always emphasising that there were many notable exceptions to each general trend. The areas are listed in the order of their apparent importance in the classroom as signalled by the proportion of overall curriculum time spent by pupils on the subject or area in question.

English

In the classrooms we observed, the average pupil time spent on English as a specific area of the curriculum was 31.5 per cent. English had some 30 per cent of the central LEA INSET teacher-days devoted to curriculum from 1985 to 1989. There were no special LEA support programmes, except in relation to second language learners. English had the second largest share of the PNP development fund. Curriculum leadership posts were allocated in most schools. These post-holders were mostly female; a relatively small proportion were senior staff. English was a high priority area for curriculum review in schools, but not as high as mathematics.

The priority accorded to English in the school was frequently reflected in classroom layout, with reading and/or language bays common, though less so for the 7–11 age group than for the 5–7. Pupils spent a lower proportion of time working and a higher proportion distracted than in most other subjects: English had the highest time allocation of all subjects, but the time was not always economically used. Girls spent more time on task than did boys. Older children spent more time on task than did younger. Pupils rated as above average by their teachers worked less hard and were much more likely to be distracted than those rated average or below.

Classroom activities were dominated by writing (56 per cent) and reading (39 per cent), with very little time devoted to the systematic fostering of children's speaking and listening. The quality of teacher-initiated classroom talk was not, in general, high. (For a more detailed discussion of trends in this subject across the Authority, see pp. 55–62.)

Mathematics

The average pupil time spent on mathematics in the classrooms we observed was 20.2 per cent. From 1985 to 1989, mathematics had by far the largest share – 44 per cent – of the central LEA INSET teacher-days devoted to curriculum. Mathematics had considerable LEA support through the advisory service and PrIME, and the largest share of PNP development fund. Curriculum leadership posts were allocated in nearly all schools – more than for English. These post-holders were, in terms of the overall staff gender balance in primary schools, disproportionately male; mathematics also had the highest proportion of senior staff in leadership roles. The subject was top of the list of priorities for curriculum review.

In the classroom, mathematics work bays were common, equally so for 5–7- and 7–11-year-olds, but less common than in English and art. As in English, pupils spent a lower proportion of their time working and a higher proportion distracted than in most other subjects: mathematics had the second highest time allocation, but the time was not always economically used. Girls and boys appeared to work equally hard. Older children spent more time on task than did younger. Pupils rated as above average ability spent more time working and less distracted or awaiting attention than those rated average or below.

Mathematics was more commonly taught as a separate subject than any other in the curriculum. Classroom activities were dominated by writing (55 per cent) and reading (42 per cent), with substantial amounts of time using apparatus (37 per cent) and drawing or other graphic activity (21 per cent). There was little collaborative activity between pupils, and little discussion with the teacher.

Science

In the classrooms we observed, the average pupil time spent on science was 8.5 per cent. Of the central LEA INSET teacher-days devoted to curriculum from 1985 to 1989, science had 13 per cent, though this figure fluctuated from one year to the next. Over the years in question, LEA support for primary science, from the advisory service and through programmes like ESG Science and collaborative projects with the University of Leeds, expanded considerably, yet it had a much smaller share of the PNP development fund than mathematics or English. Curriculum leadership posts were allocated in most schools. Post-holders were predominantly female and of low (that is, main professional grade) status. Science became a review priority in many schools, especially after its designation as a National Curriculum core subject.

Science work bays were not common, especially where older children were concerned. Children spent a significantly higher proportion of their time on task in science than in mathematics or English, though of course a much smaller proportion of their overall time was devoted to the subject. However, girls worked for more of the time than did boys and the latter spent a disproportionate amount of time awaiting the teacher's attention. Children of all ages worked equally hard. Pupils rated as above average by their teachers worked considerably harder and were much less likely to be distracted than those rated as below average.

During the period in question, the subject was in a state of transition from being treated as an aspect of environmental studies-based topic work, with a predominantly biological emphasis, to being identified as a specific curriculum area. Classroom activities were a mixture of working with apparatus, drawing and other graphic activity. They were much more collaborative and interactive than language or mathematics, but with little writing and hardly any reading.

Humanities/Environmental Studies

In the classrooms we observed, the average pupil time spent on humanities and/or environmental studies (the labels were used interchangeably) was 6.2 per cent. There was very little LEA INSET commitment in terms of teacher-days from 1985 to 1989, no specific support programmes, and the area had a very insignificant share of the PNP development fund (less even than art and craft). A minority of schools surveyed had curriculum leadership posts in this area, though the number was rising. The designation was often for environmental studies and might be combined with another area, notably science or PE. In terms of gender bias in curriculum posts, the area contrasted dramatically with art/craft, having a larger proportion of male post-holders than any other subject, with a significant number of these being senior staff. It was not given priority in review, however.

Classroom activities in this area were usually delivered through the medium of the topic, an approach in which children spent a fairly low proportion of their time actually on task (55 per cent – the same as in English). Against, the general trend, girls spent *less* time than boys on task. In topic work generally, pupils perceived by their teachers as above average worked hard, but in environmental studies (that is, a specific content area usually delivered through topics) those rated above average worked much less hard, and were much more frequently distracted than those rated average or below.

This area of the curriculum was dominated by writing, drawing and painting, with some collaborative activity, though considerably less so in topic-based approaches than advocates tend to claim. There was evidence of relatively undemanding work, sometimes used to free the teacher (as, sometimes, was art) to concentrate on other curriculum areas. Since the area in question nearly always subsumes the two National Curriculum subjects history and geography, schools and the LEA will need to attend carefully to ways of rationalising it and giving it greater rigour and challenge in the classroom (DES 1989f).

Art

In the classrooms we observed, pupil time devoted to art was 6.1 per cent. There was very little central LEA INSET commitment to art in terms of teacher-days during the period 1985–89, and no specific LEA support programmes, though plenty of advisory encouragement to teachers to improve the quality of the visual environment of schools and classrooms. Art had an insignificant share of the PNP development fund. There were curriculum leadership posts for art/craft in just over half of the schools surveyed. Of all areas of the primary curriculum, art had by far the highest proportion of female post-holders (followed by music), and by far the lowest proportion of senior staff involved in such roles. It was rarely the subject of curriculum review: curriculum leadership tended to have more to do with resources and display than with curriculum content and progression.

Children spent a fairly high proportion of time on task, though girls much more so than boys, who were rather more frequently distracted, and younger children tended to be more absorbed by their art activities than older. Pupils rated as above average spent less time working and more time distracted than did those rated average or below, and this confirms the other observational evidence of the lack of real challenge or interest in many tasks in art/craft. The activities were a combination of two- and three-dimensional work, with a predominance of the former, and little collaboration or discussion. Activities defined as art were frequently used to extend or round off other work ('Now do a picture.') and in this respect were sometimes little more than a time-filler. Moreover, some teachers consciously adopted the strategy of using art as an unsupervised activity which freed them to concentrate on groups undertaking mathematics and language tasks.

In this and various other respects, our evidence indicates that, primary rhetoric and the visual emphasis of PNP notwithstanding, art frequently lacked seriousness, integrity or challenge. The emergence of Design and Technology in the National Curriculum (DES 1990b; Leeds City Council 1990d) has led to a re-examination of aspects of art/craft. The two are clearly not synonymous, though there is an increasing tendency to treat them as such, thus quite erroneously implying that aesthetic judgement is a kind of technical problem-solving.

These five summaries indicate general trends, though of course they cannot do justice to significant variations between individual classrooms and schools. It will be noted that they represent the situation as it was in the last few months before the introduction of the National Curriculum. With that in mind, we can reasonably anticipate that the character of each area will begin to change as teachers adjust their practice to meet the statutory requirements. The most obvious change will be in time allocations, especially in the newer subjects like science. How much deeper change will penetrate is at present an open question, though one which a number of projects have begun to address (Campbell and Neill 1984a, b; Pollard *et al.* 1994; Alexander *et al.* 1996; Webb and Vulliamy 1996). For the moment we can note that the national evidence points to the long-term persistence of certain fundamental problems in the teaching of language, mathematics, science, history and geography (DES 1989d, 1989e, 1989f, 1990d). In any case, many of the tendencies we have noted are unrelated to the attainment target specifics of the National Curriculum. For all these reasons, we believe that the longer-term significance of the characterisations is considerable, and that they repay careful study.

THE QUALITY OF THE PRIMARY CURRICULUM: THE PARTICULAR CASE OF ENGLISH

The anomalous character of English in policy, school management and classroom practice will be readily apparent from the above comparisons. It is clear that during the PNP period the Authority, and in many cases schools, did not provide support commensurate with the subject's central place in the curriculum. Further grounds for concern about English emerged from two rather more specific studies which we undertook. One of these, dealing with teacher–pupil talk, was undertaken as part of Level Three of our study of classroom practice, described in full in our eleventh report. The other was a longitudinal analysis of all the Authority's 7+ and 9+ reading test scores between 1983 and 1989. The first part of the latter, dealing with the period 1983–88, is described in Report 9 (Alexander *et al.* 1989: ch. 3). The second part, extending the coverage to include 1988–91, and reworking the entire 1983–89 analysis in the light of new data, is presented here for the first time. While the studies do not claim to cover English comprehensively as an area of the curriculum, they do shed important additional light on two major aspects which, as pre-eminent National Curriculum Attainment Targets, are now of considerable public, as well as professional, concern.

Speaking and listening

Our combination of quantitative and qualitative analysis of classroom interactions (dealt with more fully in the next chapter) indicates practice which sometimes fell some way short of the requirements of the twenty-one National Curriculum Statements of Attainment for Speaking and Listening which at the time of this report's publication [before the implementation of the Dearing Report's recommended revisions] were applicable to the primary phase (DES 1990a). In saying this, we must emphasise that since part of the evaluation predated the imposition of these requirements there was no reason to expect otherwise: the point is made to indicate the extent of change which was needed in order to meet the letter and spirit of the statutory requirements.

Our analysis of the curriculum as both *generic activities* and *subjects* shows that English, as observed during our project, tended to be dominated by writing and reading with relatively little opportunity for structured teacher–pupil or pupil–pupil talk, especially among older children. Even accepting the argument that talk is cross-curricular rather than confined to an area labelled 'English' or 'Language', such opportunities were still surprisingly rare.

Teacher–pupil talk tended to be dominated by the teacher's questions, frequently of a rhetorical, closed or token kind. Questions inviting or encouraging the child to think were rather rarer. Questions were sometimes pitched low: while accessible to all, they then ceased to challenge more than a few. Answers to such questions might be accepted by the teacher, however incorrect or irrelevant.

The exaggerated or undiscriminating use of praise could deny children access to the kind of focused feedback they most needed. Conversely, pupils' unusual and thought-provoking statements and questions were sometimes blocked or ignored if they risked diverting the teacher from his or her agenda.

Much pupil–teacher discourse which had the appearance of being open-ended and exploratory was in fact closed and directive, providing little scope for children to extend their understanding beyond the sometimes very restricted goals set.

Pupil (and teacher) time could be wasted by what might be called 'pseudo-exploratory discourse'. There is a clear place in teaching for questions, statements and instructions, and for questions, statements and instructions of different kinds. Each should be used appropriately and discriminatingly.

Class size and the complexities of the job of whole-curriculum teaching in primary schools make one-to-one teacher–pupil talk a rare and precious commodity. Schools need to devote much more attention to ways of extending and refining professional skills in this area, and to upgrading pupil–pupil talk within small groups from random exchanges to a structured and genuinely collaborative programme of discourse designed to promote learning. (We further consider the unrealised potential of group work in the next chapter.)

Reading

Our study of reading standards was of a very different kind. Reading scores on the Authority's 7+ and 9+ tests had been used as one of the measures of schools' needs in respect of the PNP. In addition, the scores constituted a rare piece of consistent and objective data covering both the PNP period and that preceding it and thus provided a pertinent indicator of PNP's impact, though not, it must be emphasised, the only or even necessarily the best one. We collected and computer-analysed all available 7+ and 9+ test scores for the six years 1983–89 – some 85,000 in all – in order to gain a picture of trends in each PNP phase, across all 230 or so of the Authority's primary schools, and – for comparative purposes – across all middle schools. The first part of our analysis was presented in Report 9 (Alexander *et al.* 1989: ch. 3). What follows is taken from the re-analysis, which added the 1989 scores and some additional data from previous years to give a more comprehensive picture of trends during the six-year period.

We were also able to study four additional reports: the National Foundation for Educational Research in England and Wales (NFER) survey of LEA evidence on reading standards (Cato and Whetton 1990) undertaken on behalf of the School Examinations and Assessment Council (SEAC) (Leeds LEA was one of the twenty-six LEAs on which the NFER was able to report in some detail and it did so by drawing mainly on our own data); the HMI survey of the teaching of reading in 120 primary schools (DES 1990c) which, along with the SEAC/NFER study, was undertaken at the request of the Secretary of State following the controversy generated by Turner's analysis of reading test results in nine LEAs (Turner 1990); the Turner study itself; and Leeds LEA's own analysis of the figures for the two years following our own study, 1989–90 and 1990–91.

Tables 3.2 and 3.3 show means and standard deviations (SD) for each year and PNP phase. Figure 3.1 shows fluctuations in the mean reading ages, again by year and phase.

We now summarise our findings. Reading standards, in so far as they can be defined by test scores (a caveat of critical importance) both rose and fell very slightly during the period 1983–89. Combining the project and LEA data so as to encompass the period 1983–91 – though with due caution – we find a slight but discernible downward trend in the later years of the survey, notably in Phase II schools at 7+ and Phase I and III and middle schools at 9+.

However, this does not necessarily denote the beginning of a longer-term decline in reading standards. If the graph had stopped in 1987 the picture would have looked very different; likewise, perhaps, if it had been continued beyond our research period. To justify claims about whether standards in reading – or in education generally – are rising or declining, the time-scale needs to be sufficiently long for short-term fluctuations to be seen for what they are.

More significant is the variation within and between the three groups of primary schools and the middle schools. The fact that pre-1985 Phase

Table 3.2 Mean raw scores on the 7+ reading test (re-analysis incorporating additional data)

		1983–84	1984–85	1985–86	1986–87	1987–88	1988–89
Phase 1:	Mean	25.6	24.8	25.8	25.7	25.0	23.5
	SD	10.2	10.4	10.1	10.2	10.2	10.2
Phase 2:	Mean	29.0	29.1	29.0	29.1	28.6	27.3
	SD	9.4	9.5	9.5	9.6	9.6	9.5
Phase 3:	Mean	31.6	32.1	32.7	32.2	32.1	31.7
	SD	8.9	8.7	8.5	8.7	8.8	8.8

Table 3.3 Mean raw scores on the 9+ reading test (re-analysis incorporating additional data)

		1983–84	1984–85	1985–86	1986–87	1987–88	1988–89
Phase 1:	Mean	22.4	21.6	21.9	22.4	22.5	21.5
	SD	7.1	7.9	7.5	7.1	7.6	7.4
Phase 2:	Mean	22.2	23.0	22.4	22.2	23.4	23.0
	SD	7.4	7.0	7.2	7.4	7.1	7.2
Phase 3:	Mean	25.2	25.1	25.0	25.5	25.4	25.0
	SD	6.4	6.1	6.4	6.2	6.1	6.4
Middle	Mean	21.8	21.6	21.0	21.5	21.7	21.2
	SD	7.8	7.9	8.1	8.2	8.1	8.5

I scores are lowest and Phase III scores are highest is inevitable, since that is why the schools were allocated to those phases. The fact that middle school scores are lowest at 9+ might seem at first sight disturbing. However, it must be remembered that in Leeds the middle schools were mainly fed by inner-area primary schools and thus their scores should be examined in relation to those for Phase I and perhaps Phase II. In any event, children took the 9+ test so soon after entering their middle schools that it would have been impossible for those schools to have affected the outcomes of the 9+ tests.

Having entered these caveats, it is important to point out that although there is no firm evidence of an overall decline in reading standards at 7+ and 9+ in Leeds during the period 1983–89, neither is there evidence for an overall improvement, either differentially between phases, or across the board.

A further trend, shown in our ninth report, but not in Tables 3.2 and 3.3, is the slight rise in the proportion of children scoring low (with reading quotients of 80 or below) on the 7+ test. In contrast the proportion of children in the highest-scoring group has remained more or less stable.

The LEA's own analysis was undertaken on a different basis from ours, and we have not had access to their raw data or calculations.

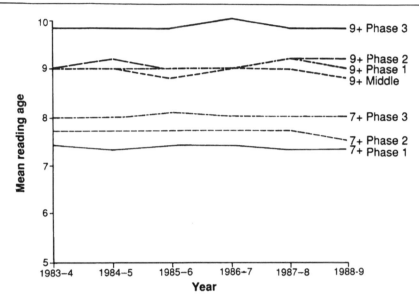

Figure 3.1 Reading standards: primary and middle schools, 1983–89

However, the analysis is useful because it brings us up to date in two important respects. First the apparent decline noted towards the end of our own data period of 1983–89 is continued into 1990 and 1991. Second, the increase in the proportion of 7+ low scorers is confirmed as a much longer-term trend, going back to 1983, and being particularly marked in PNP Phase I. The figures for 9+ remain less conclusive.

The figures in Table 3.2 show standard deviations to be largest in Phase I schools at 7+. Taken together with figures showing an increase in the proportion of Phase I children of 7+ with reading quotients of 80 or below, this means, first, that teachers of young children in the inner-city schools were facing wider gaps between their least and most able readers than were their colleagues elsewhere, and second that they had a particular and increasing challenge in respect of the least able readers. Staff in these schools were thus manifestly in greatest need of Authority support in the teaching of reading, and the inner-city weightings in the Leeds PNP and LMS policies would seem to have been vindicated.

However, it would seem that the substantial injection of extra staff and material resources under the Primary Needs Programme had no perceivable impact on reading test scores overall, though the school-by-school figures do show considerable improvements in some cases (and deterioration, PNP notwithstanding, in others). However, it is also possible that without PNP any downward trends would have been even more marked.

The lack of apparent impact of PNP on reading scores raises important questions about the focusing of the programme. If instead of the vagaries of the 'broadly-based curriculum' the Authority had systematically targeted PNP resources on very specific curriculum and school needs, and if reading had been one of them, the picture would almost certainly have been different. Thus, although our figures confirm the PNP policy of greatest support for inner-city schools, they also question the kind of support which was provided, with its emphasis on increasing staff and capitation rather than enhancing those professional skills which teachers need most if they are to cope successfully with the central challenges of inner-city teaching.

In our earlier comparison of five areas of the curriculum, we pointed to the inadequacy of LEA support for English in relation to its importance. In this respect it compared very unfavourably with mathematics. Our analysis of the reading scores underlines this point dramatically. Here was a need acknowledged by everyone (including the Authority itself, since it used reading scores in its allocation of PNP resources), yet having been identified, the need was simply not addressed by the Authority, and the resources were directed elsewhere. In this sense, the neglect might seem almost perverse. In any event it seems to underline two major criticisms we have made of PNP: its confusion and ambivalence of purpose, and its neglect of curriculum specifics.

The question of reading standards cannot be separated from consideration of the wider language environment of primary schools and classrooms. Our cumulative evidence – on reading test scores, on classroom practice, on curriculum development, on INSET and on LEA policy – indicates that language as a curriculum area was given surprisingly low priority during the PNP period. In any event, the evidence raises important questions about the overall language environment of primary classrooms which must be addressed as part of any serious attempt to improve reading standards.

The SEAC/NFER study (Cato and Whetton 1990) confirms that the position in Leeds during this period was comparable to that elsewhere in the country. In as far as a decline in measured reading standards was detectable in the late 1980s from the NFER data, it occurred mainly among lowest-scoring groups of children. However, while in Leeds deterioration in these scores was most marked in inner-city schools, NFER asserted that 'there is no evidence [nationally] . . . that decline is an inner-city phenomenon'.

Yet it is important to understand that the national evidence on this matter is far from conclusive. The SEAC/NFER study is extremely cautious in its conclusions, since it acquired usable data from a mere 26 of the 117 LEAs, and could report a decline in scores in only three quarters (19) of them. A study from Buckinghamshire, reported as this book's first edition went to press in 1991, seemed to contradict the NFER evidence and concur with our own, suggesting that the sharpest decline in test scores occurred in the most disadvantaged areas (Lake 1991). However, what is not in doubt is the need – voiced frequently in all our interim reports – for a much more focused approach to curriculum in inner-city schools than that offered under PNP, with literacy given very high priority.

At the same time, as we commented in Chapter 2, some of the root causes of the problem may well be beyond the reach of the educational system, and certainly of individual teachers. The impact of poverty on a child's life and educational prospects is far greater than the rather clinical phrase 'social and material disadvantage' can ever convey. The teaching of reading has been in the public arena for some time now, and the brunt of the political and media attack has been borne by primary teachers and teacher-trainers. While our evidence underlines the need for a considerable sharpening of the educational response, it also suggests that without a change in the political, social and economic circumstances which lead to poverty and social dislocation, teachers will continue to fight a losing battle.

There remains the question of what to do about the LEA's 7+ and 9+ reading testing programmes. Their prime function has been to identify children with learning difficulties. This screening function is now superseded, to some extent, by the introduction, from 1991, of National Curriculum Assessment at 7+, within which a formal assessment of reading is a compulsory part. Dealing with reading assessment in this context is much more satisfactory: the teacher is more involved in the assessment process and reading assessment is contextualised within the wider curriculum. But we have also seen that the testing of reading across the Authority can also yield valuable information about overall trends. The particular tests used in Leeds are by now somewhat dated, and if this kind of blanket testing is to continue, more up-to-date, comprehensive and sensitive tests need to be used.

Accordingly, we recommended the following to the LEA in advance of our report's publication: that the 7+ and 9+ tests should cease to have a screening function, and that this should henceforth be undertaken as part of each school's statutory assessment obligations; that the existing 7+ and 9+ tests should be phased out, and better tests should be phased in with the monitoring of standards firmly in mind; that to maximise the value of the data already gathered, the existing tests should be used for a further two years so that the Authority would gain, through the combination of PRINDEP and LEA data, an analysis for the decade 1983–93 – a period over which claims about longer-term trends may have a reasonable validity; and that the LEA should begin to make systematic monitoring of reading test scores, along the lines initiated by ourselves during the evaluation, part of its response to its statutory obligation to undertake curriculum monitoring and quality assurance.

Finally, it is important to note that the prioritisation of reading in the National Curriculum, and in the statutory assessment requirements for Key Stages 1 and 2, cannot of themselves guarantee higher standards. Reading needs closer attention in initial teacher-training and INSET – that much is evident – and in the summer of 1991 the Secretary of State instructed the Council for the Accreditation of Teacher Education (CATE) to undertake an inquiry into the initial training of teachers to teach reading (CATE 1992); but there is an equally important need to look searchingly at the classroom context within which the teaching of reading is located. The evidence when this report was first published was not encouraging. HMI (DES 1990c) reported a link between poor teaching of reading and the complex patterns of classroom organisation we consider in our next chapter. The Warwick study of teacher-time at Key Stage 1 (Campbell and Neill 1990) and the NCC (1991) study of National Curriculum implementation in 1989–90 showed how reading was one of the first casualties of the sheer volume of National Curriculum requirements, particularly those in mathematics and science, which the primary teacher was by then legally obliged by law to accommodate.

The National Curriculum was introduced subject by subject, with maximum pressure from the favoured subject lobbies and no serious acknowledgement of the fact that a curriculum cannot be indefinitely expandable. Primary teachers inevitably responded by concentrating on those subjects which were new or particularly demanding, putting other more familiar subjects on hold. This process had already begun during the PNP period 1985–90 and the problems we have reported – not just in reading but also in respect of wider issues of curriculum balance and consistency – may therefore have been exacerbated rather than remedied by the National Curriculum, since curriculum over-crowding and professional overload became, in a sense, statutory rather than accidental.

CONCLUSION

Notwithstanding its central place in the child's education, its conceptual and operational complexity, and the considerable demands it places on the expertise of primary teachers, and despite being highlighted in the initial aims of PNP, curriculum remained a kind of void in the Authority's policy until the arrival of the National Curriculum. The 'broadly-based curriculum' was elusive because it was never defined or argued through. The questions it invited about purposes, about scope, content and balance, about delivery and differentiation, about planning, management and assessment, were never addressed. Instead, teachers had to be content with recommendations about the physical and organisational context of curriculum, rather than its substance; about the 'learning environment' rather than learning itself.

Meanwhile, curriculum policies emerged *ad hoc*, in response more to the persuasiveness of this or that subject lobby, to community pressure and central government requirements than to any systematic local analysis of educational and professional need. Thus, mathematics, and increasingly science, fared well because they were powerful lobbies with central government policy on their side. In contrast, English, though arguably the most fundamental as well as the most extensive curriculum area at the primary stage, was left to its own devices, with consequences which are now only too apparent. Other curriculum areas – the arts, history, geography – having neither resources nor more than minority support, fared even worse. Although Leeds did far more in the fields of ethnicity and gender than some other LEAs, the *curriculum* applications of its policies were not always followed through, either – as in the case of gender and disadvantage – because of insufficient resources for teacher support and development, or as a consequence of the more general neglect of hard thinking about curriculum planning, content, differentiation and delivery.

The result was an array of confused and confusing messages, very uneven provision within both the LEA and its schools, a failure to provide support where it was most needed, and the general perpetuation or reinforcement of the very curriculum problems most in need of resolution. This, surely, was the worst possible way to construct a curriculum. The Authority needed people with educational vision and with detailed understanding of curriculum matters to map out a primary curriculum which was genuinely comprehensive, balanced, and relevant to the needs of both children and society. The National Curriculum may well have pre-empted the debate which ought to have taken place in LEAs like Leeds during the early and mid 1980s, but in doing so it has exacerbated rather than eliminated the problem.

Chapter 4

Teaching strategies

We consider now the fate of the third aim of the Primary Needs Programme – the promotion of 'flexible teaching strategies'. In doing so we should note the inevitable overlap with the previous chapter's discussion of curriculum management and content. It is not so much that curriculum is the 'what' of education and pedagogy the 'how', as that the teacher's classroom decisions and actions are what transforms curriculum from a mere bundle of inert ideas to experiences through which children learn. In this sense, therefore, the 'how' and 'what' of education are one.

The chapter has two main foci: the character and impact of teachers' classroom strategies as observed during the evaluation study; and the wider professional context within which such strategies were supported and developed.

POLICY

As we have seen, the Primary Needs Programme was based on a list of aims rather than a comprehensive statement of policy. The list referred only briefly and somewhat obliquely to classroom practice, recommending (but not defining): a stimulating and challenging learning environment; flexible teaching strategies to meet the identified needs of individual pupils; and specific practical help for individuals and small groups.

Subsequently the Authority issued more detailed and comprehensive statements of its policy in relation to primary education, notably in *Primary Education: a Policy Statement* (Leeds City Council 1988), and *The Curriculum 5–16: a Statement of Policy* (Leeds City Council 1990a). However, neither of these documents was available during the early years of PNP, and neither gives detailed guidance on classroom practice, being more concerned with underlying principles, aims and objectives.

Before the appearance of these two documents, teachers learned of the preferred modes of classroom practice in other, more informal ways:

from attendance at in-service courses or from discussions with advisers and advisory teachers, and conversations with their headteachers, PNP coordinators, and other colleagues. However, the main channel during the critical period when schools were being brought into the Primary Needs programme phase by phase (1985–88) was the Authority's substantial programme of in-service courses mounted at the Primary Schools Centre, and discussed in Chapter 7.

There was a certain lack of clarity about the status of the ideas which were introduced at the courses dealing with classroom practice. Some teachers saw them simply as points for discussion and considered themselves free to accept or reject them without prejudice to their professional future in the LEA. Others believed that practices described and demonstrated at length by persons of high status in the Authority must at the very least be strongly recommended and might even be – or become – mandatory.

In fact the central message of these courses, though diffuse, was consistent. Recommendations about classroom management, group work, the planning of projects, the fostering of pupils' self-reliance, the use of resources, classroom display and a number of other topics, reinforced by the powerful visual device of a model classroom, identified the various items on the advisory team's agenda for reforming classroom practice. Taken together, they conveyed a view of primary teaching which had a distinctive character. The physical and organisational settings in which children's learning took place were to be all-important, and the combination of PNP resourcing, advisory effort and enhanced school staffing were all to be directed to their improvement, or to establishing what advisory staff termed 'the quality learning environment'. The emphasis, then, was on the *context* rather than the *processes* or *content* of learning. Whatever the strengths of this approach as a way of giving teachers a practical basis for beginning to change their practice, it carried the risk that some might presume that changing the physical arrangements of a classroom would of itself produce improved learning.

Interviews and observations carried out during a long-term follow-up study in fifty classrooms revealed that the classroom practice of nearly 50 per cent of the respondents had not changed in any perceptible way as a result of their attendance at such courses. Of these, half had already been working along the lines advocated, and although some of them enjoyed the reassurance of seeing classroom practice like their own being commended to others, several expressed the view that such an experience did not merit time away from their classes. The other half of this group (about a quarter of the entire sample) either rejected the Authority's recommendations entirely or claimed that although they agreed with them in principle they were prevented from implementing them by unsuitable classroom conditions or other school circumstances.

On the other hand, for a little under a third of respondents the courses were highly successful, capturing their interest and provoking major changes in their thinking and classroom practice. A smaller group, comprising just under a quarter of the sample, spoke highly of such courses but had made only very superficial moves or token gestures in the direction of their recommendations. In this group there were some wide discrepancies between what teachers were doing in their classrooms and what they said – and seemed to believe – they were doing.

It is clear that this kind of INSET provision could have been much more effective if the membership of each course had been carefully targeted and hence more homogeneous; many of the teachers who attended would have been better served by a simpler, more sharply focused presentation of recommendations specifically relevant to their own current practice.

The complexity and diffuseness of the Authority's messages had a further effect. There was so much on offer that highly selective and incomplete incorporation of course recommendations was common. This sometimes led to productive and satisfactory change; but in some class-rooms it resulted in confusion as procedures became separated from their underlying objectives, and as teachers strove to balance the conflicting demands of a mixture of well-tried and untried practices, of a wide variety of grouping strategies, and of many different activities going on simultaneously in their classrooms. As a consequence, the complexity of some teachers' classroom organisation appeared greatly to increase the proportion of the time during which children were distracted, awaiting attention or working only sporadically.

There are, however, three overriding reservations about the approaches commended in Leeds during this period. First, although their ambience was ostensibly child-centred, they concentrated considerably more attention on teachers and classrooms than on children. Teachers had to take as self-evident what in fact needed to be closely questioned – namely, assumptions about how children learn and claims about the causal connection between such learning and the particular strategies for teaching and classroom organisation which the LEA commended.

Second, although much was made of the principle of 'flexibility' in both the PNP aims and its various courses and documents, there was an inherent contradiction in the notion of flexibility being mandated from above, especially given the didactic power of the model classroom. The message to teachers seemed to be that they could be flexible in the prescribed way but not in their own.

Third, the package of suggestions, recommendations and prescriptions was justified in terms of a notion of 'good primary practice' which was frequently provided as a validating label but never openly defined or explored. Consensus was assumed; the possibility that 'good practice' might be problematic was not.

We shall return to these points later.

PRACTICE

The classroom context: display and layout

Leaving aside for the moment the matter of the educational validity of the principles under discussion, their most immediately apparent influence – as might be expected – was on the physical appearance of PNP classrooms. The extent and quality of classroom display improved dramatically during the period of PRINDEP's evaluation, though we became increasingly aware of a tendency towards a certain repetitiveness in colour schemes and styles of mounting, conveying a sense of conformity rather than creativity. That teachers felt constrained in matters of display and layout by Authority guidelines (Leeds City Council 1989d) was confirmed in many interviews and questionnaire responses.

Of the teachers we interviewed, two-fifths reported that they had rearranged their furniture, and well over nine-tenths of them had made some kind of change to their classrooms as a direct consequence of suggestions or recommendations made to them as part of the Primary Needs Programme. We were able to corroborate such claims observationally. A few of the suggestions about the deployment of furniture were fairly generally rejected. For example, only a minority of respondents were willing to abolish the teacher's desk, and very few felt able to dispense with the convention that each pupil should have his or her own place, or to accept the idea of a classroom in which there were, as a matter of policy, fewer chairs than children.

A common response to the PNP messages was to convert at least a part of the room into work bays which were generally, though not invariably, dedicated to specific areas of the curriculum. Most classrooms had at least one such area, usually a reading or library corner, and a few teachers had organised their rooms entirely in this way, forming as many as six or seven work areas. A popular arrangement involved four areas, devoted to reading, art, maths and language. The area of the curriculum most commonly given a corner of its own was reading. Art came second, with more space devoted to it than either maths or language; it accounted for just over a quarter of all curriculum-specific work areas for younger pupils, and a fifth of those for older pupils. In contrast, only 4 per cent of curriculum-specific work areas were devoted to science.

In seeking to understand the extent of the LEA's influence on primary classrooms it is instructive, as we have already noted, to compare our own findings with those of Mortimore *et al.* (1988) from ILEA junior schools. In the London sample, one-tenth of classrooms had tables or desks arranged in rows: in Leeds we observed none (though that is not to say that none existed). In London, curriculum-specific layouts were rare: in Leeds they were the norm.

Our analysis produced four main classroom layout types (compared with Mortimore's three, and these are shown in Figures 4.1 to 4.4. The proportions in our sample were as follows: Type 1, 8 per cent; Type 2, 50 per cent; Type 3, 39 per cent; Type 4, 3 per cent. A more detailed analysis appears in Alexander *et al.* (1989: 247–54).

The strong emphasis on visual appeal and curriculum-specific class-room layout has a distinct local genealogy in the approaches inherited from the West Riding. However, not all teachers found curriculum-specific organisation easy to implement or operate, and it provides a good example of a practice commended in the name of 'flexibility' which makes the work of some teachers less flexible rather than more. Moreover, the practice has been shown by other studies, notably those of Mortimore *et al.* (1988) and HMI (DES 1990c), to reduce rather than enhance children's learning, in some situations, and in the hands of some teachers, at least. If the practice is introduced from a sense of obligation rather than conviction, the adverse effects on children are likely to be even greater.

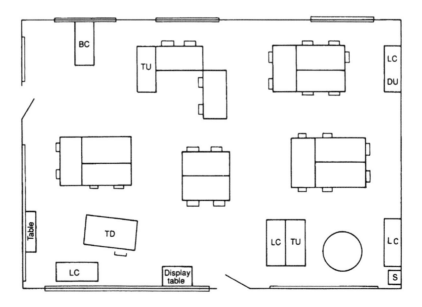

Figure 4.1 Type 1 classroom layout

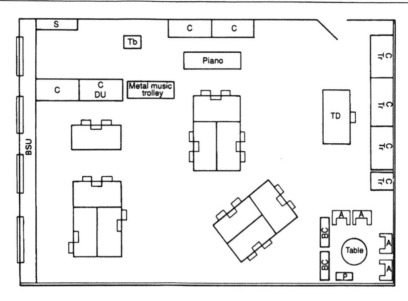

Figure 4.2 Type 2 classroom layout

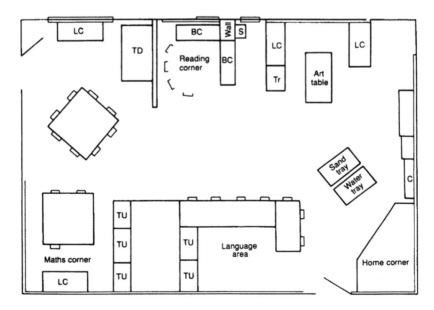

Figure 4.3 Type 3 classroom layout

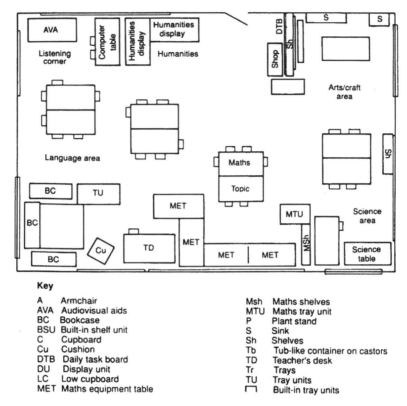

Key

A	Armchair	Msh	Maths shelves
AVA	Audiovisual aids	MTU	Maths tray unit
BC	Bookcase	P	Plant stand
BSU	Built-in shelf unit	S	Sink
C	Cupboard	Sh	Shelves
Cu	Cushion	Tb	Tub-like container on castors
DTB	Daily task board	TD	Teacher's desk
DU	Display unit	Tr	Trays
LC	Low cupboard	TU	Tray units
MET	Maths equipment table	⊓	Built-in tray units

Figure 4.4   Type 4 classroom layout

In view of the high incidence of these arrangements in Leeds, and their adoption and dissemination during a period when the massive resourcing of PNP appeared to have little impact on reading test scores, it might be worth carefully pondering HMI's finding, referred to towards the end of the previous chapter, that 'some of the poorest work in reading occurred where the organisation and management of the class were weak. Examples included too many groups of activities running at the same time and an emphasis on individual work which could not be sustained in sufficient depth for all the children in the class' (DES 1990c: 15).

The classroom context: grouping

The most obvious influence of PNP on teachers' approaches to the management of learning was the encouragement of group work. This was consistently commended by advisory staff throughout the period under review and still remains a central component of expected practice (for example, Leeds City Council 1989a, 1989e, 1990a, 1990c). The norm, as we have noted, was for different groups to be working in different curriculum areas simultaneously.

The most common way of grouping was to sort the children by ability (as informally rated by the teacher) and to make the groups as homogeneous as possible. Groups formed in this way tended to remain relatively stable, moving as a whole from one activity to another, although in a few classes they were formed only for specific activities (generally mathematics) and disbanded for the rest of the day. An alternative form of ability grouping was to aim for as wide a range of ability as possible in each group. A minority of teachers used other grouping criteria. An eighth of them opted for friendship groups for at least part of the time, and a few grouped their pupils by age.

We found that the larger the group, the less time its members tended to spend on task. However, against the obvious conclusion that small groups are more effective one must set the increased managerial challenges of having a larger number of groups.

It was by no means uncommon for teachers to switch from one type of grouping to another as the activities of individuals and groups of children changed. This fluidity of grouping practice, in classrooms dominated by curriculum-specific work areas in which a wide range of totally dissimilar tasks were simultaneously undertaken, occasionally led to extremely complex organisational problems and a good deal of confusion.

Though grouping of some kind was the norm in the classrooms we visited, our interview and observations data revealed it to be a somewhat problematic strategy for many teachers. Grouping children was an organisational device as much as a teaching approach, a way of maximising the opportunities for productive teacher–child interaction as well as a means of encouraging cooperation among the children and flexibility in curriculum.

However, as we show below, there could sometimes be a significant gap between intention and outcome. One-to-one teacher–child interactions were brief and (for most children) infrequent; and collaborative group work was rare (cf. Galton *et al.* 1980; Galton and Simon 1980).

As for the goal of flexibility, grouping can be distinctly double-edged, permitting teachers to concentrate as much *or as little* of their time on particular children or particular curriculum areas as they wish. The danger, witnessed sometimes in practice, is that certain children (notably the most able, the oldest, the best-behaved, and girls) are tacitly deemed 'undemanding' and may be left to their own devices for long periods, denied the kinds of challenging interaction which they, like all children, need. In turn these children may give no signals to a busy teacher 'scanning' the class while working with another group that they are other than fully and productively engaged in their learning tasks. Indeed, some will actively adopt strategies to convey this impression and secure a quiet life (Galton 1989; Bennett *et al.* 1984).

By the same token, certain curriculum areas (notably topic work and art) might be seen as of low priority and requiring little more than occasional and cursory monitoring by the teacher, with the result that unless the tasks set have an exceptionally high combination of challenge, motivating power and self-monitoring potential, children may spend excessive amounts of time either off-task or only partially engaged, or undertaking low-level learning.

In combination, this double neglect must mean that certain children, when working in certain areas of the curriculum, are getting a distinctly raw deal. Yet many of the teachers we interviewed, far from being unaware of this risk, perceived only too clearly that it was inherent to the LEA's preferred combination of group work and multiple curriculum focus teaching.

The dilemma can be expressed as follows: the more accessible teachers seek to make themselves to all their pupils as individuals, the less time they have for direct, extended and challenging interaction with any of them; but the more time they devote to such extended interaction with some children, the less demanding on them as teachers must be the activities they give to the rest; and the less demanding an activity is of their time and attention as teachers, the more the likelihood that the activity in question will demand little of the child.

The strategy of 'unequal investment' – deliberately concentrating attention on specific groups – was a conscious response to the dilemmas of grouping. In some cases a carefully monitored rolling programme ensured that over a given period of time, say a week or a fortnight, the teacher engaged directly with every child in every area of the curriculum; but in other cases the inequality of investment was not adjusted in this way, and the result was the persistent neglect of certain children and certain areas of the curriculum.

One way through, explored by researchers like Galton (1989) and Bennett (1987), is to exploit much more fully the potential of collaborative tasks within groups. In our own studies, the ostensibly collaborative setting of the group tended to be one in which children spent most of their time on essentially individual reading and writing tasks. Much of this time could be wasted while children awaited the teacher's attention or were simply distracted. The early findings from the Leverhulme Project (Wragg and Bennett 1990; Bennett and Dunne 1992) showed that where learning tasks are genuinely collaborative, children will use the group rather than the teacher as their main reference point, and the ratio of work to routine interactions will improve.

Collaborative group work is not a panacea, but it is certainly a strategy worth exploring. Equally important, as we urge later on, the kinds of dilemmas and compromises associated with all teaching strategies, and perhaps especially with group work, need to be admitted and addressed. Unfortunately, the climate of PNP did not encourage this.

A final point to note on grouping is the mismatch we frequently witnessed between the ostensibly *collective* strategy of grouping and the predominance of *individualised* work tasks. Common sense dictates that task and setting should as far as possible be consistent. Just as collaborative activity is difficult in a traditionally arranged classroom, so the concentration needed for individualised tasks may be difficult within a group. We gained the impression that – like several other practices in primary education – the strategy of grouping has become an end in itself rather than a device adopted for particular educational purposes; moreover, as a strategy grouping may have become so deeply ingrained in primary consciousness and practice that to ask questions about its educational purposes may seem, to some, almost impertinent.

Our data were gathered, as we have emphasised elsewhere, during the period immediately before the introduction of the National Curriculum. Since it was frequently predicted that the pressures of the latter would lead to an increase in whole-class teaching, it is useful to supplement our comments by reference to more recent data. In the national sample of primary classrooms used in the SEAC-funded evaluation of the 1991 Key Stage 1 National Curriculum Assessment (the ENCA project), four-fifths were divided into groups and the number of groups per class averaged four to five, with a mean group size of 6.1 (Shorrocks *et al.* 1993). Similarly, a national survey conducted as part of the ESRC-funded CICADA project found that the majority of the teachers surveyed believed they had not shifted significantly towards whole-class teaching, even though the National Curriculum had called into question the balance of whole-class, group and individual work (Alexander 1995: 220–69).

Although these findings appear to run counter to predictions that the National Curriculum would cause a wholesale shift away from group work, the matter is not that simple. The national sample of teachers in the ENCA project spent only a third of their time interacting with groups: the remaining two-thirds was divided between whole-class and individual interactions. Thus what the emerging national data seem to confirm is the Leeds data's sense of a pervasive incongruence in classroom strategies between pedagogic style and mode of organisation. The Leeds local data pointed up a mismatch between predominantly individualised learning tasks and the collaborative setting in which children were expected to undertake them. The national data suggest a further mismatch – between this same collaborative setting and the teacher's predominantly individual or whole-class mode of interaction.

Two interpretations are suggested. The first is that grouping is the ideal organisational arrangement in that it gives the teacher the flexibility to move freely between individual, group and whole-class activities in a way which the traditional arrangement of desks in rows does not. The second, however, is that the physical arrangement of grouping in primary classrooms has acquired such a powerful doctrinal status that no other arrangement is even entertained. Whatever the interpretation, the cumulative research and survey data since 1978 suggests an urgent need to look at the justifications, dynamics and effectiveness of grouping.

The classroom context: planning

Teachers' planning, as we showed in Chapter 3, varied greatly in its time-scale and degree of formality. The time-scale ranged from the very short-term to the comparatively long-term: from daily to yearly, with many intermediate steps. The degree of formality ranged from elaborate and schematic written documents to a simple mental rehearsal of what would happen next.

There was also considerable variation in the structure of teachers' planning. Some teachers showed a *comprehensive* awareness of the balance of different lessons and their place in the curriculum as a whole, as well as a very clear concern with progression, continuity, the acquisition of underlying skills and the achievement of goals. Others adopted a more *incremental* approach, planning as they went along (Clark and Yinger 1987). They were much less concerned with the details or wider context of future activities, and much more interested in trying out ideas in practice before moving on to further planning. There were also teachers in the sample who were grappling with several complex long-term and short-term schedules and forecasts at a time, and others whose only apparent work plan was to set up a succession of *ad hoc* activities with little long-term coherence or progression.

Methods of curriculum planning are inseparable from teachers' thinking about what has to be planned, and the arrival of the National Curriculum is dictating a much more considered and long-term approach than was adopted in at least some of the classrooms we visited (NCC 1989, 1991; Alexander *et al.* 1990).

The classroom context: record keeping

We found very few teachers who kept no records of any kind. The records which were kept varied from the elaborately formal and comprehensive, involving a good deal of detailed and meticulous clerical work, to the admittedly casual and labour-saving. Some teachers were chiefly concerned to chart the acquisition of underlying skills, but many were satisfied with checklists of tasks completed.

Only about one teacher in three had any kind of supervision in the matters of planning or record-keeping.

Again, the requirements of the National Curriculum will make minimalist approaches to record-keeping difficult to sustain, let alone justify to parents. The agenda of educational objectives to be charted – and perhaps the record-keeping format too – are now very clear.

The working day

In the third stage (Level Three) of the observational study of practice in sixty PNP classrooms reported in full in our final two interim reports (Alexander 1995: chs 3 and 4), we found that, on average, children spent

- 59 per cent of their time working;
- 11 per cent on associated routine activities (getting out and putting away books and apparatus, sharpening pencils and so on);
- 8 per cent waiting for attention from a teacher or other adult;
- 21 per cent distracted from the task which had been set;
- 1 per cent other (unclassified).

These figures are averages which cover a very wide variation between individual classes. They are broadly consistent with those from earlier studies carried out in other parts of the country (for example, Galton and Simon 1980), except that children in the Leeds study spent more time waiting for attention, in spite of the presence of an unprecedented number of support teachers and other ancillary staff and helpers.

[Figures like these were bound to provoke comment, and these particular figures featured prominently in the press coverage of the Leeds report, as we shall see in Part II. The journalistic and political inference was that children in primary classrooms do not work nearly hard enough; generally this was based on an aggregation of the percentages for 'routine', 'awaiting attention' and 'distracted' to produce the claim that 40 per cent of time was 'wasted'.

Though we would expect our findings to generate constructive discussion about the effective use of pupils' and teachers' time in primary schools, to base such discussion on these figures alone is unacceptable. Quite apart from questions of sample size and representativeness in the Leeds study (from which some journalists were happy to extrapolate to the country as a whole), this particular aggregation is wholly inappropriate. The more legitimate aggregation is of the 'working' and 'routine' categories, since both are necessary and contingent aspects of the learning task. Moreover, it is impossible to give mathematical precision to notions of what constitutes the 'appropriate' proportion of time which a 5-year-old, or an 11-year-old, should spend on task in a school day of some five and a half hours.

To set the issue in its proper perspective, we might care to consider the way time is used in *adult* work settings. Adults, too, spend much time distracted and on routine activities – indeed, even leaving aside the temporal curiosity of the business lunch – such time may even be dignified as 'incubation' or 'thinking time' – and few work for anything remotely approaching 100 per cent of the time they are employed. Indeed, we suspect that in many work settings – those of journalists or government ministers not excluded – 70 per cent of contracted time spent on task or on task-related activities would occasion little comment.]

Nevertheless, the figures give pause for thought. Clearly it is important to find strategies to reduce the proportion of time children spend awaiting attention and distracted. Whole-class teaching, usually seen as the device most likely to keep children on task, may well reduce distraction (or at least distraction of an undisguised kind) but it may also increase the time children spend awaiting attention, and indeed our own figures on group sizes tend to confirm this.

In any event, the aggregated figures above are less significant than variations which can be shown to relate to specific categories of children, kinds of learning and classroom contexts.

Thus, in Levels Two and Three of the classroom practice study, girls generally spent more of their time than boys on work and associated routine activities. Boys were more often distracted, and also spent more time waiting for attention from their teachers.

Older children were less inclined to wait for attention than younger children. In maths and language they were less distracted and spent more time on work and routine activities, although in art the pattern was reversed: older children were more often distracted and did less work.

Children whose teachers rated their ability as average tended to spend less time on work and routine activities and more time distracted or awaiting attention than either those who were thought to be above average in ability or those who were rated as below average. In the absence of any objective index of the children's true ability we cannot know the extent to which the teachers' ratings were themselves unduly influenced by the observed behaviour.

In classrooms where there were two adults, children were generally less distracted and spent more time working than in classrooms where there was only one. Beyond that point, however, there was no tendency for the presence of additional adults to bring about more work and less distraction, partly because extra adults tended to introduce extra challenges and more complex organisational structures. Moreover, as we shall see when we discuss collaborative teaching later in this chapter, it is much easier for two teachers than three or more to undertake the shared planning on which the success of classroom collaboration depends.

Children generally spent less time working and more time distracted as the size of their work groups increased from one to twenty. In even larger groups, however, this pattern was reversed, partly because of the nature of the tasks that were undertaken in large groups, but mainly because of the whole-class style of supervision to which they were subjected.

We noted in Chapter 3 that the large amounts of time allocated to language and mathematics were sometimes the least efficiently used. The overall percentages are shown in Table 4.1.

Such figures appear to challenge the conventional assumption that one way to improve standards is to give the subjects deemed most important more and more time. Perhaps familiarity breeds contempt – among teachers as well as children. Perhaps, too, there is a Parkinsonian effect at work here: the standard allocation for mathematics in primary schools, often regardless of the ground to be covered, has for decades been the equivalent of an hour a day.

A clearer understanding of such anomalies, however, comes from probing beneath the curriculum labels. In Chapter 3 we identified ten

Table 4.1 Percentage of time spent by pupils on task-related behaviour in different areas of the curriculum, as defined by their teachers

	Working	Routine	Awaiting attention	Distracted	Not observed
Language	55	11	7	26	<1
Maths	59	10	9	23	<1
Science	64	8	5	20	2
Admin.	64	5	11	18	1
Art	65	16	3	16	0
PE	51	21	18	10	0
Topic	55	21	6	16	3
Play	70	10	2	18	0
CDT	69	5	4	22	0
Choosing	63	16	7	14	0
Music	67	8	9	13	2
Environmental Studies	63	6	6	26	0
Sewing	57	20	14	8	0
Table games	69	13	6	13	0
Computer	51	19	26	5	0
Cooking	55	15	0	30	0
Television	58	0	32	11	0
All curriculum areas	59	11	8	21	1

'generic activities' which we found to underpin primary classroom practice regardless of the subject labels used by the teacher, and argued that
these activities therefore constitute at least as important a curriculum
reality – certainly for children – as terms like 'topic' or even 'language'.
Table 4.2 shows how each of these generic activities generates different
patterns of task-related behaviour.

Thus, children in our Level Three classroom practice sample spent a
high proportion of their time working when they were engaged in tasks
which involved talking to the class, talking to the teacher, construction,
listening or collaboration. Their work levels were lowest in writing, draw-
ing/painting, or tasks which involved movement from one part of the
room to another, and all three of these activities generated very high
levels of routine behaviour. For the most part, high levels of distraction
were found where work levels were low, and the highest distraction levels of all were in tasks involving writing, drawing/painting, and reading.

In general, the most work and the least distraction occurred in the
rarest activities. The striking feature of the activities at which children
worked for a high proportion of the time was involvement with other
people; conversely, most of the activities at which children worked for
the lowest proportion of time – writing, reading, drawing/painting –
involved no other people and could have been carried out most effectively in isolation. Thus, there could be a significant mismatch between
the tasks which children were given, and the setting in which they were
required to undertake them.

The importance of these variations in children's use of classroom time
lies less in the precise quantifications than the questions they provoke.
Why do such variations occur? To what extent are they inevitable? Does
the situation warrant improvement? If so, what?

Table 4.2 Task-related behaviour in different generic activities (percentage of
pupil time)

	Working	Routine	Awaiting attention	Distracted	Not observed
Writing	52	13	8	28	<1
Apparatus	65	12	6	17	<1
Reading	57	12	6	24	<1
Listening/looking	68	6	10	15	1
Drawing/painting	55	14	5	25	1
Collaboration	67	11	6	15	<1
Movement	54	15	14	17	<1
Talking to teacher	71	11	6	10	2
Construction	70	7	3	20	0
Talking to class	100	0	0	0	0
All activities	59	11	8	21	1

There was a common sequence to nearly every teaching session observed, at all three levels of the classroom practice study. The teacher settled the children down; explained the tasks; allocated children to groups; interacted with one or more groups while they worked; initiated finishing off or tidying up. Whole-class sessions were very rare, though many sessions had a whole-class element, usually at the beginning and/or end. Within this basic framework the amount of time allocated to each stage varied considerably. Thus the time spent on the settling-down and clearing-up stages varied from 7 to 45 per cent of the total session, and the introductory stage varied similarly, largely because some teachers treated it as a purely administrative matter to be dealt with as succinctly as possible, while others incorporated it into the session as the whole-class teaching in an arrangement otherwise dominated by group work. Three examples, taken from our eleventh report, show something of the variation.

A class of thirty-eight 5- and 6-year-olds:

2 minutes	teachers settles class down after playtime;
2 minutes	allocates tasks;
2 minutes	works with language group;
1 minute	gives a task to an unsupervised number group and asks the nursery nurse who should be with them how long she will be;
16 minutes	returns to work with language group;
2 minutes	monitors jig-saw group;
1 minute	gives new task to computer group whose supervising nursery nurse has given them a task which is too difficult;
5 minutes	works with writing group whose teacher has been called away;
5 minutes	supervises change-over of free-choice activities and then monitors maths group and two language groups;
3 minutes	supervises tidying up;
3 minutes	children sit and sing in the book corner;
9 minutes	teacher tells a story;
5 minutes	informal activities (e.g., clapping a rhythm).

A class of twenty-nine 8- and 9-year-olds:

3 minutes	teacher talks with class about a Victorian penny brought in by a child, and about penny-farthing bicycles;
7 minutes	sorts out group choices for the afternoon session;
11 minutes	allocates tasks for current session;
11 minutes	works with maths group;
16 minutes	monitors the work of all groups and responds to individuals seeking help;
7 minutes	supervises tidying up.

A class of thirty-six 7- to 8-year-olds:

8 minutes	teacher takes register and then describes and allocates tasks;
14 minutes	monitors the work of all groups and deals with individuals who seek help;
7 minutes	works with language group;
8 minutes	works with science group;
2 minutes	monitors work of language and maths groups;
7 minutes	gives new task to maths group;
11 minutes	works with science group and deals with individuals seeking help.

As Bennett (1978, 1991) points out, one of the most important determinants of pupils' learning is simply the amount of time they spend in it. In a class where almost half the time is spent on administrative matters, the time left over for active engagement in learning tasks is severely curtailed.

Though, the foregoing examples suggest a healthy diversity within the common framework, the questions they raise are common to all teachers:

● How can the time children spend in classrooms most effectively be used?
● How far is the fairly low proportion of time spent on task in some classrooms attributable to factors unique to those classrooms – the teacher's mode of organisation, the quality and appropriateness of the learning tasks he or she devises, the personalities of the children and adults present, and so on? How far is it attributable to more generally prevailing patterns of teaching and classroom organisation in primary schools, including those commended by Leeds LEA? We believe that our evidence suggests that the latter is indeed a critical factor.
● What can be learned from the differential figures for particular groups of children – boys and girls; older and younger children; those rated by their teachers as of average, above average and below average ability or attainment? How far are such differences inevitable? How far are they a consequence of the teacher's assumptions about and expectations of the children in question?
● Do the figures on the impact of increasing the number of adults in classrooms challenge the conventional assumption that the more adults there are, the better?
● Do the figures suggest that there is an optimum size for groups?

More generally we might ask the following:

● What is the best way to introduce and allocate learning tasks?
● How can the time and opportunities for children to engage in these tasks be maximised?

- What kinds of classroom environment will most support children's learning?
- What kinds of task is it most appropriate for groups to undertake?
- How can we achieve the best possible match not only between learner and task but also between task and classroom setting?

Classroom practice and the curriculum

In Chapter 3 we outlined the findings on curriculum in practice as they emerged from the quantitative data. We do not propose to repeat this material here. However, the questions and issues this material raises about the way primary classrooms are organised are worth presenting as an extension of those above.

- Is the balance of time between the various parts of the curriculum appropriate?
- Where teachers have sought to accommodate the subject requirements of the National Curriculum, have they achieved a better balance than that shown by our figures, or has the result been an imbalance even more marked than that which obtained previously?
- If it is indeed the case that time is used least economically in those subjects to which most time is allocated (see Table 4.1), should not schools [and indeed the current keepers of curriculum balance, the DFEE and SCAA] look afresh at their assumptions about how much time these subjects (that is, the National Curriculum core subjects) really need?

We found that regardless of the subject labels adopted, the curriculum in practice consisted of a further and perhaps more influential 'core' of ten *generic activities* (writing, using apparatus, reading, listening/looking, drawing/painting, collaboration, movement, talking to the teacher, construction, talking to the class – see Table 3.1). While there is some inconsistency within and between classrooms where subject labels and subject relationships are concerned, there is rather less inconsistency in this 'alternative curriculum', and for children it has a much more profound impact than the labels teachers use. In raising questions about curriculum content and balance, therefore, the balance and disposition of these generic activities must be looked at as searchingly as the balance of subject time. Indeed, it is very clear from our studies that to define curriculum balance solely in terms of subject time allocations is both superficial and misplaced. Yet this is precisely how the problem tends to be approached by official bodies.

Balance, in our alternative sense, needs to be tackled in two ways. One is to appraise the overall mix of generic activities undertaken by children during, say, a typical day or week. The other is to examine the mix within each curriculum area or subject. Our figures suggest that many of the subjects were neither what their proponents claimed, nor what their nature demanded that they should be. Particular concern is merited over the dominance of writing, especially where this is a low-level, time-filling activity; over the general failure to exploit the potential of collaborative activity – especially since every one of the sixty classrooms we visited in the classroom practice study used a grouping system of some kind; and over the limited opportunities given to children for work-related talk of a challenging kind.

This point is all the more necessary in view of our finding that collaborative, interactive tasks kept children's attention more effectively than solitary tasks – yet solitary tasks predominated. This does not mean that there is no place for the latter. Rather, we might infer first that the potential of collaborative tasks needs to be more fully exploited; second, that the conditions in which children are expected to undertake solitary tasks may frequently be inappropriate. Indeed, common sense must tell us that there is something paradoxical about setting up primary classrooms in which 'busyness', diversity, movement and activity are counted as virtues if within these classrooms children are mainly engaged in solitary activities requiring concentration. But then, common sense is usually one of ideology's earliest casualties, in education as in politics.

Teacher–pupil interaction

At all three levels of the classroom practice study, teachers spent a very high proportion of their time interacting with pupils. The type and frequency of teachers' interactions at Level Three are summarised in Table 4.3. Work and associated routine interactions accounted for nearly two-thirds of the total. Disciplinary interactions were comparatively rare because experienced primary teachers, particularly of younger children, have a repertoire of 'oblique' disciplinary strategies which avoid direct confrontation except in extreme cases (King 1978). Control tends to be exercised by means of work and monitoring interactions.

Although there were large differences between classes, in general individual children (as in other studies, notably Galton et al. 1980) were involved in very few interactions with their teachers. Table 4.4 clearly shows that in spite of all the additional resources of PNP, and in spite of the fact that, on average, their teachers were involved in more than three teacher–pupil interactions every minute, individual children took part in only eleven teacher–pupil interactions per hour, of which fewer than half were task-related: indeed in some classes the mean hourly rate of individual pupils' task-related interactions with their teachers was as low as two, and in no class was it higher than eleven.

Table 4.3 Type and frequency of teacher–pupil interaction (based on systematic observation of teachers)

Type of interaction	Frequency	%
Work	4,564	37
Monitoring	2,452	20
Routine	3,322	27
Disciplinary	1,260	10
Other	729	6
Total	12,327	100

Table 4.4 Rate of each type of teacher–pupil interaction (based on systematic observation of teachers and pupils separately)

Type of interaction	Teachers	Pupils
Work	58	5
Monitoring	43	2
Routine	58	2
Disciplinary	22	1
Other	10	1
Total	191	11

Note: Rate = mean number of interactions per hour.

These overall figures conceal considerable variation between classes, as the comparison of ten sample schools in Table 4.5 shows. The figures raise important issues. For instance, the considerable differences in the number of interactions (compare, for example, the pseudonymous Claybourn and Greystock) is partly a function of their length: a relatively low number of interactions does not indicate prolonged periods of silence, and most teachers were interacting with children most of the time. Fewer interactions, therefore, indicate more sustained conversations between teachers and their pupils. A very high interaction rate indicates a succession of extremely short interactions, characteristically in the context of brief and necessarily somewhat superficial monitorings of individual and groups. The two styles are – or should be – a conscious response to the question of whether the brief monitoring of many or even all the children in a class is more effective in promoting learning than more sustained interactions with a smaller proportion.

The question, however, may be about control as much as learning. Engaging in sustained interactions with a relatively small proportion of the class presupposes that the remainder are willing and able to work with little attention. Conversely, a very high rate of short interactions may sometimes reflect a poor level of control or a lack of structure in the tasks set. Having said that, it is important to add that interaction

Table 4.5 Rate of each type of teacher–pupil interaction in ten schools (based on systematic observation of teachers)

	Work	*Monitoring*	*Routine*	*Disciplinary*	*Other*	*Total*
Applegarth	67	56	88	26	8	245
Blakemore	44	31	40	19	11	145
Claybourn	54	35	131	22	15	257
Deacondale	52	26	52	47	14	191
Easterbrook	68	87	34	4	17	210
Freshwater	47	62	55	17	14	195
Greystock	48	15	41	23	4	131
Hartfield	59	40	28	19	4	150
Illingworth	61	31	45	7	4	148
Jeffcote	79	43	62	31	13	228
Mean rate	58	43	58	22	10	190

Note: Rate = mean number of interactions per hour.

rate is also related to children's age: older children are usually expected to sustain concentration for longer periods than are younger.

Another matter raised by these figures is that of the proportion of different kinds of interaction. Again, these vary considerably from one classroom to another. The challenge, clearly, is to reduce the proportion of 'routine' and 'disciplinary' interactions and increase the proportion concerned with work. A high proportion of disciplinary interactions may reflect (as in the case of Deacondale) a lack of 'oblique' disciplinary strategies and a tendency to adopt a more confrontational style; and a high proportion of routine interactions may stem from an excessively complex organisation or an inability to engage in depth with the content of the tasks given to one's pupils. Teachers, therefore, need to look both at the *frequency* and the *proportion* of their interactions in considering how to make the best use of the strictly limited time available for interacting with each of their pupils. This brings us to the more important underlying issue, that of the *quality* of teacher–pupil interaction, as revealed by the transcript data.

Though questioning was a prominent mode of teacher discourse, the full potential of questioning as a teaching strategy was not always exploited. Thus, questions might feature as little more than conversational or rhetorical devices; they might be more token than genuine; they might be predominantly closed; and they might lack cognitive challenge. Moreover, in some classrooms where teachers asked many questions, their pupils were able to ask relatively few, and having done so they might risk having their questions blocked or marginalised. Teachers were clearly conscious of the pressure of time and the need to cover the ground intended. Yet the urge to press on, paradoxically, could lead to questioning becoming not more but less effective and therefore a somewhat inefficient use of the time available.

Our eleventh interim report (Alexander 1995: ch. 4) contains many annotated examples from the considerable body of transcript material gathered at Level Three of the classroom practice study: they repay close analysis.

Here and at Levels One and Two, and reflecting perhaps a consciousness of the taboo on didacticism which was such a strong feature of primary education during the 1960s and 1970s, there was a tendency for teachers to ask questions rather than make statements or give instructions. In some circumstances this remained true even in straightforward administrative interactions where strings of questions about what was going to happen next sometimes led to complicated and unproductive guessing games, where the questioning stance appeared to offer no obvious gain in terms of the child's learning, and where a simple clear statement would have saved a great deal of time.

Teachers tried to strike a reasonable balance between the challenges they were setting and the skills of their pupils. Their ability to motivate children was heavily dependent upon the precision of this balance since tasks which are too difficult invariably generate frustration or anxiety while those which are too easy soon lead to boredom and a general sense of purposelessness. It is not always easy to balance challenges and skills even when working with a single child on a relatively straightforward task; for these class teachers working with mixed ability groups in settings where the normal practice was for several different tasks in different curriculum areas to be undertaken simultaneously, an adequate balance between challenges and skills throughout the group had to remain an aspiration rather than an achievement. Some children experienced the balance for some of the time; others inevitably did not.

Frequently strategies were adopted which camouflaged the intractability of this particular problem. A common device was to ask very large numbers of token questions (or pseudo-questions) which gave the illusion of educational dialogue without making any demands at all on the children's skills.

The imposition of a small amount of easy work was another popular strategy, particularly in situations where children were offered some degree of choice of activity. This reduction of demand to a very low level maximised the number of children who could proceed without assistance, and offered at least the illusion of motivation through enjoyment.

Some of the teachers observed at Levels Two and Three of the classroom practice study displayed a certain reluctance to say openly that a particular answer to a question was wrong. Incorrect answers were sometimes ignored; more often they were praised as if they were right, and then ignored. Conversely, correct answers were sometimes treated as if they were incorrect. The problem here was that genuine open dialogue is unpredictable and can lead anywhere; it is not consistent with the pursuit of a detailed prearranged plan of work, yet it is widely accepted as an appropriate medium for teaching. Consequently, the fate of children's contributions sometimes had less to do with their quality than with their ability to sustain the teacher's pre-existing intentions for the session as a whole.

The observed teachers showed a great deal of skill in dealing with the many interruptions of the classroom day, generally managing to neutralise them either by simply refusing to be distracted by them, or by transmuting them into a part of the teaching session.

However, more damaging to the continuity of sessions were the frequent occasions when teachers interrupted themselves, either because they did not have a very clear idea of what they were trying to say, or because their organisational structure was so complicated that they were trying to do too many things at once. The problem of time in primary classrooms does not arise solely from external pressures. It may in part be a function of the teacher's own practices, and when this is so an analysis of their use of time, from the broad organisational strategies right down to the minutiae of their moment-to-moment interactions with the children, could help both in creating more time and in making for a more effective and efficient context for learning.

The patterns of interaction explored and illustrated in detail in our eleventh report and briefly summarised here raise important issues for teachers, heads and advisory staff:

● Is the balance of questions and other kinds of utterance in primary classrooms right? Should we not be more discriminating in our use of questions, statements and instructions, being prepared to tell or instruct if the occasion warrants?
● What can be done to shift from pseudo-questions to those which genuinely invite an answer?
● What can be done to shift from closed questions to those which encourage children to reflect and solve problems rather than recall low-level information?
● Should children themselves be asking more of the questions?
● What are the contexts in which it is most appropriate to adopt a questioning stance?
● When is it appropriate to tell rather than ask?
● How can we strike the right balance between steering discussion down a prescribed path and recognising that apparently divergent responses may contain considerable learning potential?
● How can we learn to listen to children as well as get them to listen to us?

- How can we encourage them to talk and listen to each other?
- How can we make our use of praise discriminating and therefore meaningful, rather than profligate or ritualised?
- How can we balance praise and encouragement with clear and useful feedback?
- How can we use classroom dialogue to promote genuine learning and understanding?

In the context of these questions the rarity of genuinely collaborative group work in these classrooms seems unfortunate. It can be educational in itself, encouraging the kinds of interaction in which effective learning, arguably, is grounded. It can promote self-monitoring by encouraging children to use the group as well as the teacher as their point of reference. It can shift interaction between pupils away from casual social conversation in the direction of discussion about the task in hand, and in doing so it may reduce the amount of time spent by the teacher on matters of routine.

Although most teachers would recognise the desirability of appraising their classroom practice in terms of questions like those listed above, the difficulty of applying such a process to one's own discourse should not be underestimated. In the 1984 study by Bennett et al., teachers thought that their learning tasks were considerably more challenging than they were. In the evaluation of the 1991 Key Stage 1 National Curriculum Assessment, teachers rated the tasks they gave to children as rather more challenging than did observers, and were rather more generous than the observers in their estimates both of the frequency of open questions and of the opportunities they gave pupils to volunteer opinions. On the other hand, observers felt that teachers were needlessly pessimistic about the clarity of their explanations (Shorrocks et al. 1993).

Self-monitoring in a busy classroom is not easy, yet the need for training in the skills of classroom discourse is evident; as part of that training the trainee or serving teacher needs to be able to objectify his or her modes of discourse in order to begin to improve them. Video and audio recording are helpful in this matter, and the particular use of radio microphones in the Leeds study – less obtrusive and yet more effective than conventional microphones – deserves to be developed.

However, issues like those listed above can only begin to be seriously addressed if more fundamental assumptions about primary practice are challenged at the same time. We have indicated that the unthinking and undiscriminating use of questions – often closed or low-level – may reflect what we termed a 'taboo on didacticism', a sense that children at all costs must not be told. The result, as some of the Level Three transcripts show (Alexander 1995: 158–96), can be a charade of pseudo-inquiry which fools nobody, least of all the children, but which wastes a great deal of time. Similarly, the indiscriminate and thus unhelpful use of praise – rather than more judicious and exact feedback – may stem from a laudable concern that children should be encouraged and supported in their learning. Yet in the end this too can be counterproductive, with children becoming confused or cynical in the face of what they may begin to see as so much mere noise. Teachers' interactions with individual children – as is clear from other research as well as our own (notably Galton *et al.* 1980; Bennett *et al.* 1984; Mortimore *et al.* 1988; Galton 1989) – are rarer and much briefer than they may realise. Such interactions must never be other than supportive; yet they must also carry as much potency as possible for moving children's learning forward.

However, behind the tendencies we have charted lurks a more intractable problem, that of curriculum expertise. There may on occasions be sound educational reasons for adopting a style of interaction in which unfocused questions predominate. Equally, the strategy may serve as another of the various 'camouflaging' devices we have identified; in this case what remains disguised is the extent to which a class teacher's limited grasp of subject matter may make unavailable the options of adopting a more focused and challenging mode of questioning, or making judicious use of a didactic mode.

The same difficulty may discourage a teacher from permitting the children to ask too many questions themselves. To confine the interaction to what is known is the safest course, but not necessarily the best one educationally; and there are limits to the number of times a teacher can reply – as, to encourage autonomous learning and inquiry among their pupils primary teachers frequently do – 'I don't know, but let's find out, shall we?' without straining their credibility and generating frustration.

This particular problem emerged most tellingly in the context of our studies of TTT. Here, some teachers found themselves, often for the first time in their careers, with the opportunity to engage in depth with a small number of individuals, yet were not always able fully to exploit the possibilities because sustained questioning and discussion at that level required them to have a clear framework of the kinds of question they wished to promote and a grasp of the ways a sequence of such questions related to the wider map of the curriculum area in which a particular learning task was located. One of the preconditions for productive teacher–pupil interaction, therefore, must be curriculum mastery on the part of the teacher: keeping one step (or one statement of attainment) ahead of the children is not enough.

The matter bears as much on *assessment* as on learning, and indeed the two are intimately connected. Accurate diagnosis and assessment require two kinds of professional knowledge: knowledge of the child, and knowledge of the aspect of the curriculum in which evidence about the child's capacities and progress is sought. To form judgements about a child we need evidence. Posing questions is one of the most powerful tools at the teacher's disposal for establishing the nature and extent of a child's understanding; providing feedback is a necessary way of registering whether that understanding is correct or complete. Both questions and feedback have a *prospective* as well as a *retrospective* function: they enable the child to build on present understanding and to move forward into new areas of learning.

The urge to question and praise are deeply embedded in the conventional wisdom about what constitutes 'good practice' in primary education. Despite the growing weight of conceptual and empirical evidence (Dearden 1968, 1976; Bennett 1976; Bennett *et al.* 1984; Galton *et al.* 1980; Galton and Simon 1980; Galton 1989; Alexander 1984; DES 1978b, 1982a, 1983, 1985; Mortimore *et al.* 1988; Tizard *et al.* 1988, and so on), there was a tendency to acquiesce in this conventional wisdom and what, all too often, went with it: the reduction of what ought to be a complex and multifaceted debate to the simple adversarialism of 'formal' versus 'informal', 'didactic' versus 'exploratory', teacher as 'instructor' versus teacher as 'facilitator', rote learning versus 'discovery', 'subjects' versus 'integration', class teaching versus group work, 'traditional' versus 'progressive'. This primitive style of discourse, in which complex issues are reduced to simple polarities, was a powerful and persistent feature of English primary education at the start of PNP.

The need for a review of teaching strategies in the light of the National Curriculum requirements is evident. However, the vocabulary for such a review will need to be more subtle and precise, and much less polarised, than that which has dominated discussion of such matters in primary education for the last two decades or so (Alexander 1984, 1989).

At the same time, we may have to accept that the National Curriculum finally forces us to address the question of how far the polarisation of the discourse, and the adopting of classroom strategies which celebrate something called 'process' at the expense of content, may both stem in part from a posture of defensiveness in the face of the problem of the primary class teacher's curriculum knowledge. (This hypothesis is explored more fully in Alexander 1984: 74–5.) In turn, to open up these issues to honest and realistic scrutiny must entail our preparedness to challenge the ultimate article of faith in primary education: the inviolability of the class-teacher system.

[Here I must deviate from the principle of interfering as little as possible with the report's original text and make two points. First, the review which is argued for above has now taken place (Alexander *et al.* 1992 – see Part II of this book), partly in response to the Leeds report and its attendant publicity. Whether the 1992 primary discussion paper and its follow-up reports (OFSTED 1993b, 1994, 1995b) managed to counter the polarisation of pedagogic discourse is another matter, however. Second, my monitoring of these matters since 1991 strongly suggests that it is now the press and right-wing politicians – sustained, at the time of this book's second edition, by the head of OFSTED (Woodhead 1996) – rather than teachers, who keep alive the primitive polarities of traditional/progressive, subject/topic, whole class teaching/ group work and so on. The profession itself would seem to have moved on. These matters are discussed more fully in Part II.]

TEACHERS TEACHING TOGETHER

Before PNP, Leeds primary schools were staffed on the conventional basis of a head plus a teacher for each registration group, and in the national league table many Leeds primary classes were very large. Enhanced staffing under PNP gave schools two broad possibilities: to continue the traditional arrangement of one teacher per class, but with smaller classes; or to maintain class sizes but have more than one teacher working in some of them.

Advisory staff encouraged the latter, using labels like 'support teacher', 'collaborative teaching' and 'working alongside' and arguing in courses and documentation that enhanced staffing used in this way would enable the central goal of PNP – to meet the needs of each and every child – to be achieved. Schools responded variously, some taking up the opportunity, or challenge, of collaborative teaching while others seized the chance to reduce class sizes, for decades a source of frustration and complaint in the primary profession. In this section we summarise our findings on what we termed 'Teachers Teaching Together' or TTT – a label we introduced as being as neutral as possible and free of the particular value-orientations of 'team' or 'collaborative' teaching. This label allowed us to start from the simple proposition that in some classrooms more than one teacher was present and to explore without preconception what they were doing. Others adopted the term, sometimes using it more prescriptively than we had intended.

Our original analysis, outlined in the fourth report, showed that TTT involved four main dimensions or areas of decision-making:

● Participants (who the collaborating teachers are);
● Purposes of the collaboration;
● Collaborative style of the teachers concerned;
● Pupil organisation (the ways pupils worked with each teacher).

Our fieldwork revealed a number of emerging possibilities, practices and issues in respect of each of these.

Participants

Most collaborations involved the class teacher and one other: a PNP appointee (coordinator or Scale I/MPG teacher) or an existing colleague released from his/her own class duties by PNP staffing.

Much depended on the relationship participants were able to establish, and in this any status differential could prove problematic. Traditionally, primary class teachers attach much importance to having 'their' class, and notions of territory, ownership and autonomy are deeply embedded in professional consciousness. TTT could threaten these, especially if the visiting teacher had higher status than the class teacher. The issue called for a great deal of understanding on both sides, which inevitably in many cases could not be guaranteed. Yet at the same time the question of who was in charge had to be addressed, in the interests of effective planning and action, and to avoid any later confusion. Both partners could find the situation difficult, for different reasons. For the class teacher the problem was one of territory and ownership. For the visiting teacher it was one of access.

Purposes

Three main purposes for TTT emerged:

- special educational needs;
- curriculum enhancement;
- professional development.

Given the strong emphasis on children with special educational needs during the early days of PNP it was not surprising that many collaborations concentrated their attention on these children. However, there was a clear distinction between those schools which used TTT to achieve greater *integration* of SEN children into a class, and those in which there was *segregation*, with one or other of the participating teachers adopting the traditional 'remedial group' model of SEN provision.

By 'curriculum enhancement' we meant initially the use of TTT to spread the specialist curriculum expertise of individual members of staff, along the lines commended by HMI since 1978 (DES 1978b; House of Commons 1986). Our later fieldwork showed three variants of curriculum enhancement (discussed in more detail in Chapter 3): *shared delivery of the whole curriculum* (the use of specialist expertise across the school in pursuit of whole-school curriculum policies), *curriculum intensification* (support for specific groups of children in particular areas of the curriculum) and *curriculum invigoration* (meeting the subject needs of particular teachers on an *ad hoc* basis).

The boundary between curriculum enhancement and the third TTT purpose, professional development, is not clear-cut: curriculum enhancement necessarily involves professional development, but TTT of this kind acquires the latter label when its purposes are quite explicitly directed at improving teacher competence. Moreover, the focus for the professional development purpose of TTT can be aspects of teaching other than curriculum expertise and delivery.

However, making the intention explicit meant that the dynamics of collaboration had to be handled very carefully. With the goal of *curriculum enhancement* it was possible for a junior member of staff with specific subject expertise to support a senior colleague without such expertise; but when the goal was *professional development* it required a clear status differential between senior partner as trainer or consultant and junior partner as trainee or client. Yet even in these cases the situation could be an awkward one: senior partners needed both credibility and backing from the head; they also needed tact and skill in the development enterprise, and such attributes are not an automatic concomitant of experience; and client teachers needed to be able to accept that their practice needed such attention.

Collaborative style

There were two main forms that TTT collaborations could take in the classroom: *working alongside* and *withdrawal*. The first was the advisory team's preference when the Authority introduced enhanced staffing as a strategy, while the second, being the traditional way of using extra pairs of hands in most contexts other than nursery, was the initial preference of many schools.

Clearly, it is far less problematic for the teachers involved if they each take full responsibility for separate groups of children and work independently – especially when their independence is underlined by physical separateness. Moreover, there is no doubt that in large classes this practice can ease the burden on the class teacher. But the strategy of working alongside is more likely to bring about significant change in professional thinking and classroom practice, because the partners have no alternative but to confront questions of planning and organisation, and hence to explore each other's ideas.

However, we came across many examples of teachers who had failed to tackle the imperative of genuinely shared planning ostensibly working alongside each other in pursuit of shared goals. As a result the climate of collaboration could be full of unresolved questions and tensions, children could be confused about what was going on and the potential of the collaboration could be subverted. In some of these cases the collaborative style was really withdrawal, and such was the tension and confusion generated by the participants claiming to be working together but not really doing so that it would have been better to drop the pretence and designate the practice withdrawal.

The prerequisite for successful collaboration, therefore, was *shared planning*; the precondition for such planning to be coherent was *shared values*. In turn, both of these required that the participants were open and honest in presenting and discussing their individual value-positions on matters of curriculum and classroom organisation.

Pupil organisation

There were three patterns of pupil organisation:

- equal division;
- no division;
- small group/rest of class.

Where the class was equally divided, two mini-classes were in effect created, each teacher taking responsibility for one of them. Where there was no division, one or both teachers started the session off, then both moved freely round the whole class. In the third case, one teacher took responsibility for the majority, while the other looked after a small group, or even an individual. The latter was particularly favoured as a strategy for dealing with children with special needs.

It is our contention that each of these dimensions – participants, purposes, collaborative style and pupil organisation – is intrinsic to TTT, wherever it takes place. Moreover, the dimensions can be variously combined, producing a wide range of ways of exploiting the potential of TTT. We also believe that the dimensions constitute an essential discussion agenda for the teachers concerned. Both parties need to be absolutely clear about the purposes of the collaboration; they need to resolve matters of leadership, status and responsibility; they need to plan together in order to sort out these matters and practical questions to do with who is responsible for what activities and which children. Only then will the potential of TTT be fully realised.

As PNP progressed, we came across many examples of collaborations which were clearly working well and which had liberated staff to work in new ways, to increase their understanding and skill, and to attend more closely to the needs of particular groups and individuals. We were also aware that 'TTT' began to be in danger of becoming yet another over-used and under-defined primary slogan and all kinds of claims were being made for its educational efficacy for *children* simply because of the novelty, stimulus and enjoyment which it could give to their *teachers*. Such self-indulgence needs to be guarded against: what is pleasurable for teachers is not necessarily beneficial to children. TTT at best is a complex and sophisticated way of working. When the participants fail to address the agenda referred to above, it may do more harm than good. Flooding schools with teachers of itself solves nothing, and may merely disrupt effective solo teaching. Indeed, as our data on adult–pupil ratios showed, increasing the number of adults in a classroom can sometimes detrimentally affect children's task-related behaviour. TTT has considerable potential, but it is not a panacea.

CONCLUSION: THE PROFESSIONAL CONTEXT OF CLASSROOM PRACTICE

The Authority recognised that classroom practice would not improve without a considerable investment in INSET and in professional support at both LEA and school level. In this chapter and others, we describe and comment on the strategies for professional development adopted and/or commended, ranging from day-to-day collaboration in the class-room, as discussed above, to whole-school strategies such as those explored in Chapters 3 and 6, and LEA courses and the work of advisers which we consider in Chapter 7. In this final section of the present chapter we pull together some important issues relating to the context within which the LEA sought to improve the classroom practice of its primary teachers.

Versions of 'good practice'

As we have shown, the prevailing model of 'good practice' was in certain important respects incomplete. In focusing on the physical and organ-isational features of the 'quality learning environment' it neglected the necessary questions about the purposes and content of primary educa-tion on which decisions about layout, organisation, grouping and so on should be contingent. Equally serious was its neglect of the issue of children's learning.

It should go without saying that questions about the purposes and character of children's learning are of fundamental importance not just to teachers but also to those who undertake the task of constructing the policies and strategies through which teachers' ideas and practices are shaped. To neglect these questions and concentrate instead on the 'envi-ronment' of learning, however important that might be, is to risk encouraging the belief that teachers are judged and advanced on the basis of how their classrooms look rather than how and what their pupils learn; consequently, some may feel that it is strategically sensible to concentrate on surface at the expense of substance. The implied agenda is in any event back-to-front. Questions about purposes, content and learning are logically prior to questions about layout and organisation:

the latter should be set up to implement goals set out on the basis of attention to the former. Learning is both the end and the means, organisation the means only. Teaching strategies and classroom organisation should never be viewed as ends in themselves.

There was an even more profound sense in which the prevailing version of good practice was deficient. Nowhere in our considerable quantity of data is there any sense that the notion of 'good practice' was presented to teachers as problematic. Nowhere were teachers invited to note that 'good' implies questions and judgements of *value*, and that the whole issue of good practice might raise controversial yet essential questions about the claims made for particular approaches, the arguments and evidence for and against them, the educational values they represented, or the practical problems of implementing them. Instead, despite the ostensible commitment to 'flexibility' there was apparently just one version of good practice, presented as a package of recommendations and principles and exemplified in the model classroom. This was viewed by teachers as having the force of policy and therefore not open to challenge.

Further, it has to be asked whether in any event layout, display, grouping and organisation are proper subjects for central policy or prescription. Clearly, an LEA has an obligation in the words of a recent Audit Commission report (Audit Commission 1989a) to 'articulate a vision of what the education service is trying to achieve' and to 'support schools and help them to fulfil this vision', but it could be argued that the most appropriate focus for such a vision, necessarily generalised because of the range of institutional contexts and pupil needs involved, should be on identifying broad goals and the kinds of learning which schools might seek to promote. It might also be suggested that for officers of an LEA to concentrate time and resources on prescribing how the physical arrangements of classrooms should be attended to represents a rather demeaning view of teachers and heads, whose proper concern such matters undoubtedly are.

Responding to officially commended versions of 'good practice'

Many teachers had difficulty accommodating what they thought others expected to see in their classrooms, partly because they were frequently unclear about what was expected, and partly because of practical and personal difficulties. Some ignored the recommendations; others implemented them wholeheartedly; others changed – as they were implicitly invited to do – the surface of their practice without engaging with deeper issues about what purposes such practice might serve.

For many, the sense of having to adopt a preferred version of practice accentuated the dilemmas which are always part of everyday teaching. Our reports provide many examples; for the present we note three which were both prominent and recurrent. In these cases the pressures and dilemmas could not only prove intractable but might also have adverse consequences for the children.

The first example is the view that it is good primary practice to have children working in groups. For some teachers, problems arose when they sought to reconcile this expectation with their simultaneous sense of obligation to monitor, diagnose, assess and interact at the level of the individual child. In this case a solution was at hand, although it helped the teacher rather more than the children: it was to neglect those children working in curriculum areas perceived to be relatively unimportant (such as art and topic work), to devise for them low-level activities which could be tackled with minimal teacher intervention, and to focus attention on those children who demanded it. The strategy was deliberate, and indeed was often referred to as focused, or unequal, investment. Yet as we noted in our tenth report: 'The price that some children may pay for demanding little of the teacher may be that they are given work which demands little of them' (Alexander et al. 1989: 284).

The second example, a frequent concomitant of the first, is the notion that it is good primary practice to have the different groups pursuing different areas of the curriculum at any one time, because only thus can the goals of 'seamlessness' and 'flexibility' in curriculum and learning be achieved. For some teachers not only was this difficult to plan and implement as an organisational strategy per se, but the increased demands imposed on them by the strategy meant that their opportunities for systematic and sustained monitoring of children's progress were further reduced, while at the same time the increased levels of movement and disturbance in the classroom might adversely affect children's concentration and time on task.

The third example is the view that it is good primary practice to adopt a predominantly 'inquiry' or 'exploratory' mode of teacher–pupil interaction and to couple this with plenty of encouragement and support for children's responses. We discussed in our eleventh report (Alexander 1995: 103–219) the way this can be taken to excess by those teachers who couch the majority of their utterances in the form of questions, even when statements or instructions are more appropriate, and how such questioning can then become further debased by being low-level or closed. We also showed how the indiscriminate use of praise is a poor substitute for positive and specific feedback. We believe that many teachers who adopt such modes of interaction, though they do so partly as a matter of habit, are also responding to what they feel is expected of them. Though they might thereby earn their spurs as 'good practitioners', their children might gain rather less than if they had experienced a more varied and exact mode of discourse.

These are just three examples. Our reports contain many others. The general principle they all provoke is this: all teaching involves dilemmas which arise when teachers seek to reconcile the various circumstances, contingencies and expectations of which the job, by its nature, is constituted (Berlak and Berlak 1981; Nias 1989; Alexander 1988). No approach to professional support and development, still less an account of 'good practice', can afford not to identify and confront these. Yet many teachers clearly feel that to admit to facing dilemmas is somehow an admission of weakness, and that at all costs a front of professional equanimity and consensus must be maintained in respect of the validity and practical viability of mainstream primary orthodoxies. In suppressing their dilemmas and in failing to challenge the orthodoxies they help neither themselves nor the children they teach.

Lest we be misinterpreted on this matter, we are not advocating the abolition of grouping or the withdrawal of encouragement. Far from it: encouragement is essential and grouping, appropriately used, is a highly effective classroom strategy. We are arguing, on the basis of what actually happens in classrooms, that a purist adherence to any methodological orthodoxy can generate considerable problems, that these need openly to be addressed, and that in any event the notion that the act of teaching can be made the subject of procedural mandates is suspect and unrealistic.

Strategies for improving practice

Leeds LEA sought to improve classroom practice by a combination of two main strategies:

- enhanced staffing, and the exploitation of its potential to encourage classroom-based professional development;
- the work of the advisory service in general, and of adviser-led INSET in particular.

Schools recognised the potential of these strategies, and our discussions elsewhere of PNP coordinators and TTT explore some of the possibilities and problems of having staff work together with the improvement of classroom practice in view.

However, in this chapter we have identified certain reservations about the models of teaching commended during the period under discussion, and to the extent that teachers felt obliged to implement these the effectiveness of enhanced staffing must have been blunted. A strategy for improving teaching has not one but two components: not only must there be an effective means for helping teachers to change their practice along the lines required, but the preferred approaches to teaching must be coherent, defensible and demonstrably capable of securing a quality of learning superior to that available previously. On this latter aspect, regardless of the successes claimed for enhanced staffing, we are less sanguine.

Three fundamental changes are called for in this regard. First, it is clear that the way classroom practice is defined and talked about must change. The quasi-consensus of 'good primary practice' must be replaced by a mode of professional discourse in which the difficulties of determining what practice is good must be addressed. The focus of discussion must be greatly extended to take in more issues to do with learning and with educational purposes and content. The day-to-day challenges and dilemmas of practitioners must be explored much more openly and honestly.

Moreover, and this concerns policy-makers at least as much as teachers themselves, where certain dilemmas remain unresolvable because they are rooted not so much in particular classroom strategies as the in-built limitations of the system within which teaching decisions are made, the professional, political and resource implications must be squarely faced.

Second, there needs to be a shift away from judgements of quality based mainly on visual cues to one based on engagement with what and how children learn. What we called in our tenth report 'the inviolability of practice' needs to be breached. Such a shift needs to take place in two contexts – one, as we have said, is professional discourse; the other is the strategies adopted by those responsible for promoting and encouraging teachers' development.

Finally, the idea that an LEA – let alone a national government – should be the sole definer, arbiter and guardian of good practice cannot be defended. The assumption is offensive to teachers; it discourages professional autonomy and self-motivated development and encourages instead an excess of dependency; and it is in any case empirically unsustainable.

These have far-reaching implications, especially for the strategies and styles adopted by advisory staff and heads, and for the ways class teachers view themselves as professionals. They are particularly important – and problematic – at a time when government policy seems to be introducing a serious tension into the local administration of the education service. On the one hand, advisory roles are shifting more towards inspection and quality control, and the accountability of advisers and inspectors to their employing LEAs is being more firmly underscored (Audit Commission 1989b). On the other hand, schools are being encouraged in a much greater degree of financial and professional self-determination. At the same time, the rhetoric of 'partnership' has never been stronger: used by educational policy-makers it is a device to disguise the true extent of central control; used by professionals it smacks of a desperate clinging to more liberal values. These matters will not easily be resolved.

Chapter 5

Links with parents and
the community

At the time of our third report, in May 1987, the LEA had no written policy on home–school links, and no officer carried overall responsibility in this area. It is fair to add that Leeds does not seem to have been unique in this respect: reporting on an inspection carried out in 'ethnically diverse areas within three LEAs' (including five Leeds Phase I PNP schools) in March 1988, HMI remarked that 'none of the three LEAs had specific policies for parent school liaison' (DES 1988a). However, the HMI report sampled only three LEAs, and we are aware of others which have been considerably more proactive and inventive in the area of home–school links. Frequently, such LEAs operate at two levels simultaneously: at the school level fostering and encouraging changes in attitude and practice, while at LEA level opening up direct two-way communication with parents through a variety of channels.

By the end of the project we could report that there had been some changes and developments in practice. Many of them were initiated independently by the schools, and some were a direct consequence of national legislation, but the Authority's own profile in this area continued to be remarkably restrained. There was still no official home–school links policy document to which interested parties might turn for clear and authoritative guidance.

However, in April 1989 an advisory teacher attached to the Primary Division was given responsibility for 'parents and community' along with her existing workload. At an in-service course which she led three months later it was proposed and agreed that a working party should be set up to produce a draft policy for links with parents and the community. Nine more months passed before the group convened. It consisted of the advisory teacher, an educational psychologist and sixteen of the teachers who had been at the course. At the time of going to press the working party's document is still awaited.

In view of the level at which responsibility for parents and the community was allocated, the pace at which action was taken, the apparently arbitrary way in which membership of the working party was decidedand the omission from its membership of key figures in the area of home–school links, it must be assumed that the formulation of an LEA policy in this area was a matter to which the Authority attached a rather low priority during this period. The situation contrasted sharply with the high profile initiatives taken in relation to the other three PNP aims.

PRACTICE

Our third report outlined a number of schemes and initiatives which were intended to further the general aim of closer links with parents and the community: the appointment of a team of home–school liaison assistants (later redesignated home–school liaison officers); the Portage scheme, described in more detail below; in-service support courses; and a wide range of everyday practice, including a great diversity of activities (forty-seven in all) which are listed in Table 5.1.

The report also examined the very real difficulties which sometimes beset home–school links, suggesting that a clash of basic objectives between teachers and parents may sometimes lead to a confrontation between widely differing models of home–school links. We identified four pairs of complementary roles commonly adopted by teachers and parents in their encounters with each other:

- consultant and client;
- bureaucrat and claimant;
- equal partners;
- casual acquaintances.

Problems arise when there is a mismatch between the models adopted by the teacher and the parent – when, for example, one wants to make a complaint while the other wants to give advice. With only four models in operation (and of course in reality there are many more) this kind of mismatch can take no fewer than twelve possible forms. When any one of them occurs, the teacher and the parent are likely to experience each other's behaviour as inappropriate and hence strange and uncooperative, and both may leave the encounter bewildered and disappointed.

Through comparison with an earlier survey undertaken by Leeds LEA itself, it was possible to report:

> that most of the present range of home–school links was already to be found in local primary schools well before PNP, and that activity in this field since 1985 has involved the further development and dissemination of existing practice rather than the devising of innovative techniques.

> Even so, PNP has clearly brought along with it a few entirely new initiatives. The 1985 study reports no examples of parents teaching

Table 5.1 Strategies for home–school links in thirty Leeds primary schools

	Phase I (n = 10)	Phase II (n = 10)	Phase III (n = 10)
Transmitting information			
Booklets about the school	6	9	6
Letters and notes	10	10	10
Regular newsletters	5	6	9
School magazines	0	2	1
Articles in parish magazine	1	1	0
Formal meetings	7	9	9
Informal meetings	9	9	9
Talks on curriculum/education	4	6	4
Notices pinned up in school	6	9	10
Admission of new pupils			
Letters	10	8	10
Meeting pupils before admission	9	10	10
Home visits before admission	3	3	2
Pre-admission play sessions	7	7	5
Parents' and toddlers' groups	4	3	3
Activity packs	3	2	3
Parents involved in settling in	6	8	5
Involving parents in school life			
Home–school liaison assistant(s)	2	0	0
Secondary/junior/infant liaison teacher	0	1	0
Home visits	6	3	2
Parents' assemblies	6	7	6
Parents' room	1	1	1
Parents' self-run support groups	1	1	2
Coffee mornings	2	4	6
Crèches	3	1	0
Open days	10	8	9
PTAs	3	8	4
Invitations to concerts/sports/plays	10	10	10
Shared church activities	1	0	1
Book sales	4	9	7
Parents helping			
Teaching their children at home	6	6	8
Parents' workshops	2	1	3
Portage	2	0	2
Helping in class with reading/number	5	2	5
Helping in class with cooking/sewing	9	6	8
Helping in class with art/craft	4	5	5
Helping in class with music	2	0	2
Helping in class with the computer	4	2	4
Helping with structured play sessions	4	1	1
Helping with stories/library sessions	4	4	5
Helping with games/swimming	3	3	6
Helping run school library	0	3	2
Making costumes/scenery for plays	7	7	7
Helping with general repairs	2	3	7
Fund-raising	8	9	8
Parents' dances	3	2	5
Family discos	4	5	6
Christmas parties/trips, etc.	10	9	9

their children at home under the guidance of a teacher; no activity packs for use at the time of the children's first admission to school; no parents helping in the classroom with music, and no home–school liaison assistants or secondary/junior/infant liaison teachers.

(PRINDEP 1987a: 9–11)

The questionnaire sent to all primary heads in July 1989 revealed that the combined resources of PNP were thought to have had far less impact on home–school links than on any of the programme's other objectives. Few heads had allocated any of their extra capitation to the development of productive links with parents and the community, while nearly all of them considered that such PNP resources as the Authority's advisory and support staff, the INSET programme and even the refurbishment of their own schools had made little or no impact on home–school links, however effective they may have been in furthering the programme's other objectives.

Only enhanced staffing and, in particular, the PNP coordinators were thought to have made a slight to moderate impact. By far the most widespread activity of PNP staff in the general area of home–school links involved reading or other language work with parents and their children. Number work was also common, as were programmes of home visiting and initiatives involving the parents of children with special educational needs. In all, well over sixty different specific activities were listed by heads in this context, including cooking for special occasions, a paired play project with a neighbouring special school, and the development of links with local elderly people.

The Education Acts of the 1980s greatly increased the responsibilities and powers of school governors, including parent governors. In response to the introduction of the local management of schools the LEA organised a series of measures to train and inform governors on such topics as the appointment of staff, provision for children with special educational needs, and the formulation of school policy on discipline, equal opportunities, child protection and a number of other matters.

The Governors' Unit serviced by the Education Department also produced a news-sheet which contained updates on government and LEA reports and initiatives, and offered lists of issues for consideration.

The 1980s legislation also gave parents the legal right to be informed about, and involved in, certain aspects of school life. In the Summer term of 1989 the LEA published and distributed a short booklet (Leeds City Council 1989e) which was 'intended to help parents to appreciate what constitutes the best primary school practice and also to highlight aspects of education that the Authority wishes to promote'. Home–school links did not feature prominently in this booklet although its content clearly implied that the Authority wished to:

- provide parents with basic information about its schools;
- suggest the kinds of questions they should be asking about their children's education;
- encourage them to participate in their children's early reading experiences;
- urge them to seek regular discussions about their children's progress;
- help them to find their way around school buildings.

By 1991, when the first edition of this book went to press, the LEA had embarked on a programme of school reorganisation. In place of the historically determined mix of two-tier (primary and secondary) and three-tier (first, middle and upper) the city was to have just primary and secondary schools, with pupil transfer at age 11. To prepare for change of this order of magnitude, the LEA set up numerous meetings between its officials and the parents and governors of its schools.

Home–school liaison officers

The setting up, training and work practices of the home–school liaison team were described at length in our third report. There we noted that:

> as a matter of policy, all ten of the home–school liaison assistants are themselves members of ethnic minority groups. The reasoning behind this is clear. Any minority group is likely to include a substantial number of people who feel the need of . . . help and reassurance, . . . and many members of ethnic minorities suffer an additional persistent burden of racial discrimination which may well cause them to wonder what hope they could ever have of a fair hearing from a representative of the culture which treats them in this way. . . . Yet of course each of the schools in which the assistants work has pupils of many different ethnic origins, and in practice no single head has expressed any other intention than that assistants should work with families from all parts of the local community.
>
> (PRINDEP 1987a: 17)

After HMI's inspection in March 1988, a set of guidelines about the use and deployment of home–school liaison officers was produced by the LEA and distributed to the heads of primary schools concerned.

In May 1988, the team of home–school liaison officers was augmented by two additional members and the LEA applied to the Home Office for funding for three more posts under Section 11 of the Local Government Act of 1966.

March 1989 saw the formal appointment of a coordinator for home–school liaison officers and bilingual support assistants, who was to be responsible to 'the appropriate adviser in the Primary Division' and whose job description listed eight major duties including close liaison with the schools involved in the two projects, cooperation with heads to provide a positive and coherent service, and attendance at appropriate working parties and committees 'as agreed with the Primary Adviser'. Contact with the advisory teacher who was subsequently (April 1989) given responsibility for parents and the community was not written into the job description.

In keeping with the exclusive emphasis on racial and multicultural matters in the job descriptions, the entire team of officers and their coordinator were all members of ethnic minority communities.

Portage

Portage is a method of working with pre-school children whose development is delayed: parents teach their children at home under the guidance of a Portage worker who visits the family once a week. The worker also attends weekly meetings with a supervisor who provides help and support, records details of the teaching programmes, writes reports and helps the family with problems involving contact with other agencies.

The Leeds Portage Scheme serviced twenty families across the city. It was set up under Education Support Grant funding in 1986, but was financed by the City Council when the grant expired in April 1989. It was not part of the Primary Needs Programme but the method was advocated through PNP INSET.

Early education support agency

A broadly similar philosophy underlay the work of the Early Education Support Agency (EESA). Again, this was not a PNP initiative but is reported here because it concerned parents, children and schools and gives an example of the practice from which the LEA's unwritten policy on home–school links has to be inferred. It was set up in September 1987 under the Department of Education Special Services Division, and its brief was threefold:

> to find out the needs of parents of children under five and work with them to help facilitate those needs, ... to help parents help their children acquire useful skills and act as a bridge between home and school, ... and to increase a shared community spirit and foster an attitude of sharing and support between parents and other parents in the local neighbourhood, alongside the paid professionals and voluntary agencies.

> (Leeds City Council 1987b)

The EESA team consisted of the educational psychologist who originally proposed that the agency should be set up, a supervisor and eight workers who were selected for such qualities as their apparent ability to empathise with their clients without seeming patronising, and to deal with difficult situations.

After the initial training of staff, and discussion with other agencies, EESA's work began with a pilot project in two inner-city areas. The success of the pilot project led to a decision in principle that EESA should extend its activities throughout the city. In September 1989, with the existing funding and personnel, five school groups were set up, one in each inner area of the city, while the original groups still met and were run by parents with minimal support from the EESA workers.

By this time the formally stated aims of EESA were:

• To support children, parents and teachers to enable children to start at the same starting line.
• To help children to happily acquire useful skills in order that they might take full advantage of nursery provision and formal schooling when that time begins.
• To help raise parental esteem so that they become equal partners in this process; and so that young children are able to see their parents as problem solving, confident role models.

(Leeds City Council 1989b: 4)

Primary Needs Programme INSET

Our analysis in Chapter 7 will show that the LEA's programme of in-service training was much more concerned with the other objectives of PNP than with home–school links. We know also that according to the Authority's primary heads, PNP INSET made no impact on their practice in this area.

Nevertheless, there were some INSET initiatives in this area, and in particular the Special Services Division organised and ran a small number of very ambitious courses. Firmly based in the educational and psychological literature and on research findings on home–school links, these courses involved detailed planning, comprehensive support material, built-in evaluation techniques and follow-up meetings.

It must be emphasised, however, that whether the criterion be the number of courses or the number of teacher-days devoted to this topic, the development of productive links with parents and the community did not account for more than a one-hundredth part of the Authority's in-service programme during the evaluation period.

CONCLUSION

This brief chapter – whose length might fairly be said to be in inverse proportion to the importance of its theme – has included details of the major LEA and school initiatives in the home–school field between the start of PNP in 1985 and the end of our fieldwork in 1990. At that point, the Home–school Working Group was still in existence, and still apparently moving towards the eventual drafting of a policy document, though this was not yet available when the first edition of this book went to press over a year later, in October 1991. Although individual schools reported some degree of increased activity in this area, facilitated by extra staff, it was clear that except in certain well-known cases home–school links was not a PNP priority. Those schools which changed their outlook and practice in respect of relationships with parents and the community did so for their own reasons and in response to their own sense of priorities and needs.

Home–school links were the forgotten PNP aim. The fact that by 1991 the situation had begun more generally to change was due less to Authority initiatives – which remained on a relatively small scale – than to a combination of growing commitment at school level and the legislative requirements in respect of school governing bodies and the provision of information to parents about curriculum and assessment.

It could be argued that home–school links is precisely the kind of issue where a generalised LEA policy is least appropriate, since the chemistry of relationships between each school's staff and its parents is a unique and subtle matter, hardly conducive to centrally determined procedures. Equally, it could be argued that the promotion of a sense of community, of which the primary school is a vital part, can only be achieved by local commitment and action.

In a fundamental sense this is true. Each of the schools we visited pursued the matter differently, and in some the quality of relationships established with parents and the community was impressive, the more so for being the result of long and painstaking work by heads and teachers, often encountering frustrations and setbacks on the way to success. Yet questions remain about those many schools still locked in the traditional relationship of 'casual acquaintances' or 'bureaucrat and claimant' discussed earlier. In these schools, while national legislation might nudge staff to introduce procedures for involving and informing parents where this is required by law, it would not encourage them to go beyond such procedures to establish the kinds of voluntary open dialogue and day-to-day collaboration which can do so much to enhance the quality of a child's education.

We believe that an LEA has an important role to play here. Indeed, there is something distinctly paradoxical about the Leeds stance on this particular aspect of PNP in comparison with the others, during the period in question. For while the LEA was happy for the advisory team to devise policies which went into considerable detail about aspects of classroom practice which, arguably, are best left to teachers, it remained relatively aloof from one area of school life – home–school links – where policy might usefully and helpfully have stipulated not just goals and commitments but also a range of procedures from which schools could choose.

The LEA, then, appears to have been interventive on matters which schools themselves ought to have dealt with, and *laissez-faire* on at least one major issue in which it had a wholly legitimate interest. Perhaps this paradox suggests an unresolved tension in Leeds during this period between two basic notions of local government: controlling, ordering, and prescribing on the one hand, empowering and facilitating on the other. In developing and implementing its Primary Needs Programme, the LEA leant unambiguously towards the first of these, pushing its schools, and thus to some extent the parents of the children in those schools, into the bureaucrat/claimant relationship discussed on page 100. This relationship was underscored in a wide range of encounters and contexts as the programme evolved. It is hard to see, therefore, how genuine school–home partnership could have prevailed within such a culture, except at the instigation of parents and teachers themselves, operating in a manner which was consciously and deliberately at variance with the wider context of local educational governance.

Chapter 6

Managing reform within the school

Our discussion in the previous four chapters has focused in turn on the substance and implementation of each of the aims of the Primary Needs Programme as set out by Leeds LEA in 1985 and as reinforced in numerous contexts subsequently. Although management as such did not feature in these aims, the Authority perceived from the outset that their successful implementation would depend as much on schools' internal management styles and strategies as on external guidance, advice and support.

Accordingly, the PNP resource package included not merely extra staff of varying levels of experience and seniority, but also a *particular category* of extra staff – the PNP coordinator – appointed to a specific managerial role. Within each school, PNP coordinators were to be the LEA's main agent for interpreting, explaining and implementing the goals of the programme. They therefore featured prominently in our evaluation of PNP.

However, PNP coordinators could achieve little in isolation. They were introduced into established professional cultures, dominated – as are all primary schools – by the personality and outlook of the head. They had to work alongside deputy heads and post-holders who also had managerial responsibilities, some of which overlapped considerably with their own. Each school had its own unique circumstances, its particular history, strengths and weaknesses. Managing PNP in the school, therefore, could never be a one-person affair.

This presented us with a problem. Our task was to evaluate PNP. We recognised PNP's central managerial dimension – the coordinator role – and included that in our programme. Yet we also recognised that the success of PNP in general, and of the coordinator in particular, depended vitally on aspects of the professional workings of schools which PNP addressed neither explicitly nor implicitly, and which were therefore not really within our evaluation brief. Moreover, we had neither the resources nor the time to undertake a comprehensive anatomy of primary school management and professional relationships along the lines pursued, for example, by Nias *et al.* (1989).

Consequently, we took a middle course. We made PNP coordinators the object of the detailed study described in our fifth interim report (Alexander *et al.* 1989: ch. 5), but in addition we gathered data on the managerial and professional contexts within which coordinators and other PNP appointees worked, so that we could identify those contextual factors which bore most heavily on how, and with what success, schools implemented the programme's goals.

ENHANCED STAFFING AND THE MANAGEMENT OF CHANGE

Table 1.1 (see page 8) lists in full the various categories of PNP appointment and the numbers in each category, year by year. The staggered introduction of Phases II and III means that years and phases do not correspond, but it is evident that there were considerable differences in the overall numbers of extra teaching staff allocated to each phase. The seventy-one Phase I schools shared 178 extra staff – some gaining a substantial complement – with the allocation averaging 2.5 per school. In the larger proportion of Phase I schools there were two appointees – one coordinator and one Scale I teacher – although many schools had considerably larger PNP enhancements – up to 7.5 in two schools, or a staff increase of 38 per cent. In contrast, the PNP enhancements for Phases II and III were 96.5 and 92 (full-time equivalents), producing an average enhancement per school of 1.7 in Phase II and 0.9 in Phase III.

The disparity between PNP phases was accentuated by two factors. One was that in many Phase III schools with fewer than 150 pupils on roll the allocation was only 0.5, giving them a much smaller range of support and development possibilities than was open to those schools with a full-time enhancement. The second was the level of seniority at which appointments were made. The 1985–86 Phase I initial staffing profile shows a balance of senior and junior appointees – fifty-three coordinators and sixty Scale I teachers. This represents a senior/junior staffing enhancement ratio, in percentage terms, of 47:53. By Phase III, the balance had shifted to a preponderance of main professional grade teachers (11:89), and while in Phases I and II PNP coordinators were created from the PNP staffing enhancement, most Phase III schools had to appoint coordinators from their existing staff.

All these discrepancies, of course, were deliberate. PNP was a programme explicitly grounded in a philosophy of positive discrimination in favour of the schools with the greatest social and educational needs, as represented by free school meals and low reading scores. Assuming these measures to be fairly reliable indicators of the needs in question, the differential allocation of staffing was appropriate and just. However, while the LEA maintained, as was its obligation, a global view of primary schools' needs, heads and teachers in individual schools were less likely to do so. For them it was a matter of how many extra staff they received in comparison with a school down the road, and judged in these terms the disparities aroused great resentment, especially among Phase III heads.

The issue which these allocations does raise, however, is whether the level of Phase III resourcing was too low to have any significant impact. Primary schools are very tightly staffed, to the extent – as the 1986 Parliamentary Select Committee Report recognised – that an enhancement of less than one teacher above establishment can generally achieve relatively little (House of Commons 1986). Once the enhancement is one full-time teacher or more, then a whole range of managerial roles and strategies becomes available because it is possible to combine full-time class responsibility – which many heads see as vital to the integrity and continuity of children's education – with substantial cross-school management, development and support. When the appointment is of someone who is experienced and well-qualified in both teaching and professional leadership, as all coordinators were required to be, the potential of enhancement is even greater.

All PNP appointees had job specifications – a welcome and important innovation. Scales I/MPG appointees were recruited to a fairly open brief, which set out a number of options for negotiation between appointee and head: taking a class, releasing a teaching head, releasing other staff, working alongside colleagues in a 'support' role, facilitating and/or organising school visits, covering for colleagues, and so on. Probationers were expected to teach a class full-time, in order to meet DES requirements. Among the many statements about the character of PNP which were issued, orally and in writing, by officers and advisers in the early days of the programme, two points were particularly forcibly expressed. One was that PNP appointees were 'real' teachers, not supplies or ancillaries, and were to be treated as such, even though their roles might be more diverse than the traditional anchor of class-teaching. The other was that in defining individual teachers' roles, schools were asked to recognise the importance of job-satisfaction. Clearly, the Authority perceived a risk that junior PNP appointees might be exploited or marginalised, and took steps to prevent this.

What, then, did the very large number of Scale I/MPG teachers (some 267 overall, or 68 per cent of the teachers appointed under PNP) actually do? Our annual surveys yielded a range of roles and activities. Table 6.1 shows the distribution of PNP Scale 1/MPG roles revealed by the survey of all schools over the period 1986–89. It should be noted that the percentage column in the table sums to considerably more than 100 because most staff in this category combined more than one role. Typically, those (the majority) who did not have a full-time class teaching

Table 6.1 PNP Scale I/MPG roles, 1986–89

	Frequency	%
Releasing class teachers	170	88.1
TTT	141	73.1
Special educational needs	93	48.2
Class teaching	87	45.1
Curriculum responsibility	63	32.7
Work with parents	37	19.2
Miscellaneous administrative	14	7.3
Unclassified	6	3.1
Work with outside agencies	5	2.6
Other special needs (not SEN)	1	0.5
Total responses	617	

Note: Number of respondents was 193; mean number of roles was 3.2.

responsibility, might 'float' and cover for an absent colleague one day, act in a support TTT capacity the next, and so on. The average number of such combined roles, across all three phases and over the four years in question, was just over three.

There were, however, significant differences between PNP phases in how such staff were used. Generally, there was more diversity of role in Phase I than later phases – not least, presumably, because the higher staffing complement allowed this. Perhaps more significant is the fact that SEN-related roles were more prominent in Phase I schools than Phase III, and using extra staff to cover for others was a more common use in Phase III than Phase I. This tends to bear out the point raised above about the level of Phase III staffing. With an average staffing enhancement in Phase III schools of 0.9, and with the majority of appointments made at MPG level, many such teachers found the developmental aspects of their job specifications constantly subverted by the need to cover for colleagues.

Disentangling Phase III heads' analysis of their use of PNP staff from their collective sense of outrage at the phasing policy is difficult. Again and again in the responses to our 1989 survey of all heads, those in Phase III schools commented negatively on their PNP staffing: that it had little impact; that it even exacerbated their previous staffing problems; that it was too little too late; that the LEA did not understand the problems which their schools were trying to tackle. Positive responses, very much in the minority in Phase III, therefore, focused mainly on the way PNP appointees freed heads and senior staff for managerial tasks and facilitated classroom collaborative activities, especially TTT.

In contrast, Phase I heads, and to a considerable extent Phase II heads also, listed gains like enhanced management, TTT, curriculum review and development, staff development, and others to do with the quality of professional life in the school: improved morale; increased enthusiasm and vitality; the sharing of ideas and expertise; and the collective appraisal of alternative practices. (It should be noted that the Phase III heads' comments came from a group whose schools had only recently been brought into PNP and that expressions of dissatisfaction were also voiced at equivalent points in Phases I and II. However, these were rarely as vehement or focused as those of their Phase III colleagues.)

In the period leading up to and immediately following the introduction of the National Curriculum, such qualitative gains were in themselves an essential resource. Where schools, aided by PNP resourcing, had lifted their professional climate and decision-making processes out of the slough of low morale, crisis management and paternalism, they were able to confront the next wave of change constructively and with confidence, having the will, expertise and procedures to tackle the very difficult questions about curriculum and assessment which the 1988 Act provoked. This transformation of professional climate may prove to be one of the most important legacies of the Primary Needs Programme.

Although the perception that Phase III schools were under-resourced was widespread, the effectiveness of the PNP staffing enhancement was certainly not a consequence of numbers alone, any more than it is when schools are staffed at the conventional establishment figure. We came across many cases of schools using minimal resourcing to maximum effect; and of schools with a substantial PNP staff enhancement manifestly failing to take advantage of what that enhancement could offer. Many of these problems centred on the way schools deployed their PNP coordinators (see pp. 113–19), but Scale I/MPG staff could also find themselves marginalised or used as supply teachers or even ancillaries in the very way the Authority had warned against. Moreover, given the fact that classes have always been much larger in primary schools than elsewhere, and that primary teachers have persistently urged the need to improve pupil–teacher ratios, it is not surprising that many heads saw the opportunities afforded by PNP only in terms of smaller classes.

For schools fully to exploit the potential of enhanced staffing after a century of working on the basis of n class teachers plus the head, they needed the imagination to conceive of alternatives; a shift in attitudes away from the entrenched belief in the inviolability and supremacy of the traditional twin roles of head and class teacher; and the will to enact such alternatives and live with the discomfort which the changing of professional roles inevitably generates. In some schools these attributes were in short supply, and the PNP staffing enhancement was largely wasted. This problem, too, is still with us: radical changes in professional culture and structure cannot be achieved overnight.

Although advisory staff delivered warnings on this matter, they were not always followed through into the PNP INSET programme. PNP staff attending these courses complained of being told what to do but not how to do it, and of receiving dismissive or baffled responses to their anxieties about coping with colleagues who were reluctant or unable to accommodate to new ways of working. There was also a critical gap in the INSET programme where heads were concerned. Heads' support was cited as the most important factor in the assimilation and success of PNP staff, yet the need to explore with heads, thoroughly and openly, the implications and potential of enhanced staffing, was not addressed at all in the early days of PNP. The Authority responded to our interim statements on this matter and increased its INSET commitment to management issues and leadership roles (including that of the head) as PNP progressed. However, as our reference above to the power of historical habit and precedent indicates, this is a long-term challenge, demanding radical change in the way schools conceive of management and the deployment of staff.

MANAGING CHANGE: THE PNP COORDINATOR

PNP coordinators were perceived and presented as the managerial linchpin of the Primary Needs Programme. The role was an innovative one, and its initial scope was set out in the 1985 job specification (Leeds City Council 1985c). It included working with colleagues and support agencies to further the four PNP aims, a particular brief for special needs provision, and a further injunction to work alongside other teachers to fulfil this brief.

The 1985 specification's emphasis on special needs was consonant with the mixed origins of PNP which we discussed in Chapter 1, and it reinforced initial – and persisting – confusion about whether PNP was a special needs programme or something else. The specification was also very comprehensive, and the 1987 version added the significant message that heads and coordinators should select from and adapt the list rather than seek to implement it in its entirety. In the same year, and in response to these and other difficulties – several of them identified by our project's fifth interim report (Alexander *et al.* 1989: ch. 5) – the Authority circulated *Guidelines for Headteachers in the Use of PNP Staff* (Leeds City Council 1987c). This document made it clear that the responsibility for determining coordinators' roles rested with the heads, who were encouraged to choose from the 1985 specification provided by the Authority. However, the document also emphasised that heads' room for manoeuvre was not unlimited, and that coordinators should be part of a senior management team which would determine and implement school policy. Further, it identified three main ways in which coordinators could expect to contribute to the school's teaching programme:

- taking responsibility for a class;
- working alongside other teachers;
- helping provide non-contact time by covering for colleagues.

In the event, a considerable diversity of roles emerged. On the basis of our initial fieldwork, we were able in our fifth report to group these under five main headings:

- special educational needs;
- curriculum development;
- staff development;
- home–school links;
- whole-class responsibility.

Further, the *curriculum development* role had four main versions:

- curriculum manager;
- curriculum consultant;
- curriculum enhancer;
- curriculum facilitator.

These latter four roles are defined and discussed in some detail in Chapter 3, and are therefore not elaborated here.

The annual questionnaire returns from PNP coordinators confirmed the validity of our initial framework, provided that 'staff development' now subsumes TTT and the release of colleagues, and that 'home–school links' includes working with outside agencies as well as parents. With this proviso, the framework represented, in 1990 as in 1987, the main areas of school life in which PNP coordinators were deployed. In addition, we can now indicate, in Table 6.2, the frequency of each role over the whole evaluation period. Of course, these are not necessarily discrete categories: for example, curriculum development and staff development are intertwined. But the categories and frequencies provide a useful commentary on the ways schools chose to implement the main managerial aspect of PNP policy, as contained in the various documents and courses relating to the coordinator role.

Within these overall figures there were significant phase differences. Special educational needs was always a much more prominent aspect of the work of Phase I coordinators than of those in Phases II or III, and for the first three years of PNP SEN was the dominant coordinator task in Phase I. In contrast, the Phase II list was consistently headed by staff development and support, particularly TTT.

There were also important changes over time. Coordinators' involvement in special needs declined while their full-time class teaching commitments increased, as did their participation in school management, especially curriculum development. TTT, carefully nurtured in the early

Table 6.2 Coordinators' roles, 1986–89

	Frequency	%
Curriculum development	109	68.1
TTT	100	62.5
Special educational needs	97	60.6
Miscellaneous administrative	56	35.0
Class teaching	55	34.4
Releasing class teachers	37	23.1
Work with parents	33	20.6
Unclassified	21	13.1
Work with outside agencies	17	10.6
Other special needs (not SEN)	8	5.0
Total responses	533	

Note: Number of respondents was 160; mean number of roles was 3.3.

days of PNP – especially after our fourth report had provided both a label and a framework for its development – became less prominent as coordinators returned from a collaborative to a solo teaching role. Thus, where the first coordinators fulfilled a brief dominated by special needs, with curriculum development and TTT level-pegging a little way behind, they and their successors in 1989 were as likely to be concerned with curriculum management and teaching, in collaboration or alone.

Our 1985–86 pilot study suggested that coordinators were having to take on more roles than they could cope with. This was confirmed in the 1987 study and was acknowledged by the Authority, as we have seen. Thereafter, the average number of roles (regrouped from the full list of ten above) was between three and four per coordinator, diminishing slightly towards the end of the evaluation period. The growth in curriculum-related roles is particularly significant. It pre-dated the arrival of the National Curriculum, but was without doubt given a considerable boost by the publication of the government's initial National Curriculum proposals in 1987, and the Education Reform Bill and Act, both in 1988. Our data show the generalised and somewhat ambivalent role of PNP coordinator being translated, by 1988–89, into that of *curriculum* coordinator. (For an extended discussion of curriculum coordination and management under PNP, see Chapter 3.)

Judging the impact of PNP coordinators in absolute terms is as problematic as judging the impact of the programme as a whole. Coordinators themselves, in the annual surveys, had no such doubts about the main gains at least. Their league table is headed by *improved attitudes, increased staffing and staff development*; but there was little consensus about the rest:

widespread agreement (in order of frequency):
   improved attitudes
   increased staffing
   staff development

no clear agreement (in order of frequency):
   curriculum change
   collaborative teaching
   better management
   release of staff
   more individual and group work
   improved SEN provision
   more parental involvement.

Heads were asked to rate coordinators' impact on their schools' pursuit of the four PNP aims. Their response is broadly in line with the frequency of the various roles listed above. It should be noted, however, that heads were on the whole reluctant to ascribe much more than moderate success to their coordinators in respect of any of these aims. On the other hand, coordinators were seen as more effective than most other PNP resources.

Coordinators' unanimity about attitude change in their schools is significant for two reasons. First, because it is evident that many of the problems which the Authority identified in 1985 when it established PNP were centred as much on professional attitudes as professional expertise – attitudes to children, to curriculum, to teaching methods, to parents, to ethnic minority groups, to gender issues – and indeed we have picked up and reported the resilience of many of the attitudes which the Authority sought to change. Second, coordinators as a group were acutely conscious of the way their own success depended in large part upon how they and the practices they were promoting were regarded by existing staff in the schools where they were placed. However, 'improved attitudes' is both elusive as a claim and difficult in practice to demonstrate. It is also possible that in some cases 'improved attitudes' is another way of saying that nothing of substance was achieved.

In our fifth report we identified three main areas within which attitude and related attributes like personal manner and professional style were critically important for coordinators' success:

● the influence of the head;
● the attitude of other staff;
● the persona and style of the coordinator.

From their heads, coordinators needed a negotiated version of the Authority's job specification, support for the difficult tasks they were required to undertake, and a preparedness to include them within the team of senior staff involved in the development of policy. All too often these prerequisites were withheld, especially but not exclusively in the early stages of the programme.

Equally influential for most coordinators were the attitudes of other staff. There was an initial suspicion among teachers at all levels, including some heads, that coordinators were agents of the LEA, charged with identifying and reporting on inappropriate practice. As the programme became established, and as coordinators became a part of the staff team, they were increasingly judged on the practice they delivered rather than the power they seemed to represent.

Coordinators themselves were to a greater or lesser extent sensitive to these anxieties: some fuelled them while others quickly or painstakingly dispelled them. But the job was rarely easy, especially where support from the head was withheld or accorded only grudgingly. Coordinators had to acquire skills in leadership and handling people and ideas which the majority of them had not developed in their previous jobs. They felt that the Authority provided too little support here at first, although curriculum leadership courses introduced in the later stages of the programme provided some help subsequently.

As coordinators' roles shifted towards curriculum responsibility, so *curriculum expertise* itself became a further factor in their success, to be added to the three other factors discussed above.

Coordinators operated, as we have seen, in five broad areas – special needs, curriculum development, staff development, home–school links and whole-class teaching. The first four of these were generally school-wide roles, and three broad styles of implementing these emerged:

- *Whole-school manager* involved at a senior level in school policy and decision-making;
- *Enactor* of policy developed by others;
- *Facilitator* to other staff to enable them to undertake initiatives.

These styles represent different levels of power, authority and influence within a school, and therefore different possibilities for action. All coordinators, as we have seen, worked to the same basic job specification, adapted to meet the circumstances of their school. Whatever version of this specification was negotiated, they needed appropriate authority and resources, and access to the decision-making process, to carry it out. Their chances of success were far less where they were relegated to the position of *enactor* or mere *facilitator*, as some were. The tasks identified for coordinators by the Authority could not be carried out with anything less than *enactor* status. The discrepancy between job-specification and status became acute for some coordinators, and remained a problem in some schools, not just for coordinators but also for many other staff with significant cross-school managerial responsibilities. Again, the remedy is largely in the hands of the head.

In our fifth report we compared the Leeds conception of PNP coordinator with other versions: the role of SEN coordinator which emerged after the 1981 Education Act, and that of curriculum coordinator, first tentatively identified by Plowden (CACE 1967), then developed in the 1970s and 1980s by HMI and others (DES 1978b; House of Commons 1986; Campbell 1985; Taylor 1986). The Leeds role was initially, and to some extent remained, broader than either of these, though it tended to become less and less distinguishable from that of curriculum leader. In addition, it lost its uniqueness and force as a result of two developments. One was the extension of school-based curriculum leadership roles across a much wider range of curriculum areas than was covered in the mid-1980s (see Chapter 3): in this sense, nearly every teacher is a curriculum leader (or even a coordinator) now. The other development was budgetary delegation to schools (LMS) under the 1988 Education Reform Act (DES 1988b, 1991d), which appeared to reduce the scope for enhanced staffing, despite the Secretary of State's approval of PNP-style weightings for social disadvantage, ethnic minority groups, special needs, and small schools in the Leeds LMS formula (Leeds City Council 1989c).

However, the idea of a free-wheeling change-agent and catalyst in each school remains a powerful one. It is dependent not so much on the generous staffing levels of PNP Phase I (though that obviously helped a great deal) as on a combination of a degree of staffing flexibility and a basic preparedness to accept that this kind of role is important and needs to be built into a school's staffing arrangements under whatever label is deemed appropriate. There is no reason why schools should not include within their plans for the 1990s the full range of managerial and support roles which emerged from PNP during the 1980s. If it is now less likely, because of LMS, that one member of staff can combine several of these roles, it is certainly practicable for them to be spread across the staff as a whole, or at least its more experienced and talented members. The most unsatisfactory outcome of LMS in this context would be if schools felt obliged to return to the traditional concept, so inimical to professional and curricular development, of there being just two professional roles in primary schools, those of class teacher and head, each confined to and jealously defending his or her territory.

The residual force of this traditional view was one of the main reasons why PNP coordinators so often encountered anxiety and resistance. As we noted in our fifth report:

> The idea of a coordinator ... signals the limits to the generalist class teacher's whole curriculum/whole child capacities. It denotes

different levels in the staff hierarchy. It overlaps (and perhaps threatens) the head's role as traditionally defined. And it raises questions about what, once the division of labour between head and coordinator is determined, there is left for the deputy head to do. . . . Beyond innocent labels like 'coordinator' and the comfortable language of 'working alongside' are some tough realities.

(Alexander *et al*. 1989: 188–9)

The PNP coordinator idea, whatever its problems and imperfections in practice, represents a vision of professional collaboration, development and decision-making which schools can ill afford to abandon, least of all in the era of the National Curriculum.

MANAGEMENT STRUCTURES

Notwithstanding the above, some schools persisted with, or only cosmetically adapted, their existing management structures. Overall, however, our Fieldwork B studies showed schools tending to cluster towards the following main types:

- *Type 1: 'My school/my class'.* The classic division of labour between a head and class teachers, each with clearly defined roles and 'zones of influence' (Taylor *et al*. 1974; Alexander 1984: 161–8). In this situation, the role of the deputy head might be undefined or non-existent, except in a symbolic sense. Type 1 structures were commoner, for obvious reasons, in small schools than large, though there were examples of large schools persisting, despite the arrival of coordinators, with this model. In such cases the tensions were greater than in the smaller schools.
- *Type 2: head, deputy and class teacher.* Still a two-tier structure, but with three rather than two basic roles. Here that of the deputy was clearly defined, and entailed engagement with policy, management and development rather than merely covering in the event of the head's absence.
- *Type 3: senior management team* With the arrival or designation of the PNP coordinator, some heads constituted the three senior posts as a senior management team, meeting regularly to review and agree policy.
- *Type 4: embryonic departmentalism.* As the focus of concern shifted towards curriculum matters, and as HMI, DES and others argued with increasing insistence that each area of the curriculum should be led by a staff member with appropriate expertise, so designated curriculum leaders assumed greater importance in the overall management structure. However, the structure remained essentially two-tier, with curriculum leaders not involved in major policy matters.
- *Type 5: three-tier.* Whereas Types 1–4 are all variants of the basic two-tier model of primary school management, in this type the coordinator

and curriculum leaders represent a significant and formally recognised additional layer in the management structure, running their own meetings and development programmes, reporting back to the head and the staff as a whole, and contributing in a distinctive way to overall school policy.

- *Type 6: management matrix.* In larger primary schools, the roles of head, deputy, coordinator and curriculum leader might be complemented by those of year leader, head of infants/juniors, and indeed by other posts of responsibility. Where the year-group was large, year leadership became a post of some importance, counterbalancing the cross-school role of curriculum leader, and introducing potential tensions over who was responsible for what. These were resolved by the formal recognition that the structure was no longer one of layers or levels, but a curriculum/year-group *matrix*, requiring close collaboration between the parties and the involvement of all of them in policy discussions.

A number of points should be made about this typology. First, like all others, it represents general tendencies rather than exact categories for defining individual schools. Second, although there is a clear relationship between school size and management structure – there is limited scope for extended curriculum leadership roles, let alone year-group responsibilities, in smaller schools – the relationship is not inevitable. Some medium-sized schools had shifted to a three-tier model, while some large schools were still operating a rather unsatisfactory and somewhat stressed version of Type 2 or even Type 1. Generally, however, by the end of the period in question, larger schools tended towards Types 4, 5 and 6. Third, as we monitored our representative sample of schools over a three-year period, we could perceive some of them undergoing a process of structural transition, shifting away from the simple two-tier model towards departmentalism and/or a matrix structure. Finally, although we have represented the senior management team as a particular type or stage, the emergence of a senior team within schools was a more general characteristic of the PNP period. The arrival and ambivalent status of the coordinator forced many heads to look afresh at structures and decision-making, to delegate more extensively than hitherto, and to establish more regular consultation procedures than the traditional combination of informal encounters and unstructured or semi-structured staff meetings.

DEPUTY HEADS

The role of deputy head did not always feature in this process of management review. When we surveyed deputy heads towards the end of the evaluation period, we found a somewhat surprising proportion – over half of those surveyed – without job specifications. Since they were working with coordinators whose jobs were – at LEA insistence – properly specified, their anomalous position in the school could be severely aggravated by PNP. It seems not unreasonable to argue that in a modern primary school all staff, and especially those with formal responsibilities of any kind over and above the class-teacher role, should have clear and properly negotiated job specifications.

Deputy heads undertook very diverse responsibilities. Every one of those surveyed had a class, though some were released from part of their teaching duties to undertake other activities. In order of frequency, deputy heads' responsibilities were as follows:

- class teaching;
- curriculum leadership;
- general managerial responsibilities, delegated by the head;
- staff development and staff pastoral support.

These four were particularly prominent. Some way behind were a more random and idiosyncratic collection of responsibilities, again listed here in order of frequency:

- taking assemblies;
- staff–head liaison;
- pastoral care;
- discipline;
- buildings;
- home–school;
- library;
- odd jobs – tuck shop, festivals, etc.

It should be noted that just as all deputies combined a school-wide responsibility with teaching a class, so most combined a major school-wide responsibility from the first list above with one or more of those from the second list. However, there were some whose role appeared to involve, apart from class teaching and standing in when the head was absent, no more than relatively low-level jobs like reporting on leaking gutters or running a tuck shop.

Although the latter cases are a probably diminishing minority, especially now that budgetary delegation under LMS has made it essential that heads in their turn delegate a greater proportion of their managerial functions to senior staff, our studies indicate a more general need for primary schools to continue to review the role of deputy headship, to define more exactly the range of tasks it is appropriate for someone at that level of seniority to undertake, and to ensure that all deputy heads have appropriate job-specifications.

DECISION-MAKING

To some extent, management structure and decision-making are directly related. Heads develop particular structures in the light of the decisions which have to be made and the people they believe should be involved in making them. The traditional 'my school/my class' model is based on the assumption that there are two sorts of decision: about the school as a whole – its goals and ethos, its children, its staff and its curriculum – and about the translation of these whole-school decisions into day-to-day teaching. The head deals with the first, class teachers with the second, and there is little blurring at the edges. In the three tier model, the head acknowledges that there is a substantial field of decision-making to do with the content and development of specific aspects of the curriculum which requires the expertise and time of others. In the management matrix model there is an even broader conception of the range of decisions calling for specialisation and delegation.

There are three inevitable consequences of these very different approaches. One is that the further from a Type 1 structure a school is, the greater the need for communication and coordination in decision-making. The other is that while all primary school decision-making is dependent upon both formal and informal relations and contacts, the more complex structures require a much greater expenditure of time on formal decision-making processes; at the same time, there is greater risk of divisiveness if groups and individuals feel that they are being excluded from the formal processes or that the latter are less important than informal, behind-closed-doors negotiations. The third consequence is that while in Type 1 structures leadership is synonymous with headship, in the more complex structures leadership is shared among several people.

The development of PNP is in part a story of growing sophistication over such matters in Leeds primary schools. As schools shifted generally from a dependence on informal contacts to role specialisation, delegation and a greater investment in formal procedures, so they were forced to acquire the vocabulary and skills which formal decision-making dictates.

The formalisation of decision-making could have adverse side effects. Coherence in policy could become less easy to achieve where its components were fragmented among different groups and individuals. Sub-groups could become oppositional rather than cooperative. Consensus could not be guaranteed where particular groups had had little or nothing to do with a particular policy.

The more effectively managed schools understood these problems and sought to ensure that sub-groups and delegated roles and responsibilities remained part of a wider collegial culture in which all participated, and within which divergences of opinion were openly explored.

However, these processes – central though they were to the success of PNP – were at first given little attention in the LEA's in-service support programme. Coordinators had their own courses and conferences from the outset, but courses for curriculum leaders started rather later in the programme, as did management courses for heads. Such courses were initially based on the notion of management as something one person does to others; but the management of a school, it is now generally acknowledged, is a process in which all members of the school's staff are, in different ways, engaged: it is a multidirectional process. All staff, not just the 'managers', need skills if they are to participate successfully in delegated or collegial management and decision-making, since every person in such contexts has a managerial role of some kind. Even the newly arrived probationer needs managerial skills – for working with colleagues and participating constructively in meetings, for example.

Management, then, has become a whole-school process, and it should be approached as such in any INSET and support programmes organised by the Authority or its schools. This view was endorsed in the School Management Task Force report (DES 1990f), and by 1991 Leeds LEA had a policy and programme for management training (Leeds City Council 1991a) which sought to address the management needs of all staff – heads, deputies, staff tutors, INSET coordinators, curriculum coordinators and probationers. Some of this activity focused on what were termed 'generic' management issues and skills.

However, the need for whole-school approaches to management is only part of the problem. It is also essential to avoid the historic tendency for management training to concentrate on how schools should be run while neglecting the purposes they serve. Shipman puts the point uncompromisingly: 'Learning is the business of schools. It should be the priority for school management. Yet it is usually ignored in school management training. Means have got confused with ends' (Shipman 1990: v). More generally, bearing in mind this report's observations about some aspects of the thinking behind the Primary Needs Programme:

> Specialisation, consultancy and the streamlining of headship may produce greater efficiency, but in respect of what? Ideas imposed more effectively on children and teachers than in the 1960s, but which remain, as ideas, as ill-conceived as ever? Primary education certainly needs to review its professional procedures, but far more pressing is the need to review the ideas which such procedures seek to implement.

> (Alexander 1984: 209)

As governors, heads and teachers become increasingly enmeshed in the complexities of managing *resources* under LMS (Audit Commission 1991), it is important that they are able to keep the management of *learning* as their central objective. LEAs can offer schools significant support in maintaining the balance, and can provide appropriate frameworks to encourage this. One such might be the school development plan, now a statutory requirement. In Leeds, the LEA's current framework (Leeds City Council 1991b) might usefully be monitored – and modified where appropriate – with this issue of *balance* firmly in mind.

THE HEAD

Notwithstanding the current shift to collegial and whole-school management, the head remains pivotal to the successful management of a primary school. Yet though Leeds LEA understood this from the outset, its approach to heads seems to have been curiously negative. As we saw in Chapter 1, it was believed in the early 1980s that much primary classroom practice in Leeds was outdated, uninspiring or downright bad; that heads bore much of the responsibility for this state of affairs; and, therefore, that the same heads could not be expected to put matters right. In evolving PNP policy, therefore, officers consulted no more than a few carefully chosen heads, leaving the rest ignorant and deeply suspicious of what was going on. A new role was then established, that of coordinator, which bypassed the head and was intended to carry the new vision of good practice directly from Merrion House (the Education Department's offices) to the classroom. Such an approach was bound to backfire. Not only were many primary heads suspicious of and unclear about PNP, but the PNP experience provided further fuel for those who felt that Leeds was an authority which treated its heads badly, neither consulting nor supporting them. Relations between schools and the Authority deteriorated seriously as a result.

All this is now history, and the Authority, to its credit, has done much to try to repair the damage done during this period. However, in the present context it is important to make two points of continuing concern. First, though heads are indeed crucial to the character of a school and the quality of the education it provides, they can never be held entirely to blame if these prove unsatisfactory. The policies pursued by Leeds LEA before 1985 – lower-than-average per capita spending on primary education, higher-than-average pupil–teacher ratios, a stagnant staffing profile exacerbated by the ring-fence policy on new appointments, little investment in advisory support – played their own part in producing the conditions of which the LEA itself became, somewhat belatedly, so critical. Second, the way heads responded to PNP, and with varying degrees of success exploited its opportunities and resources for the children's benefit, must be set firmly against this background.

A number of factors emerged from our studies as bearing particularly significantly on how heads managed PNP, and these we now outline.

For decades it has been a basic tenet of primary headship in England that each school should have a distinct 'ethos', 'philosophy' or set of beliefs and aims to guide and inform its policies and practices. Traditionally, determining this philosophy has been the head's prerogative, and few have contested this. While the 1988 Act requires a greater involvement of governors in such matters, and at the same time preempts many of the curricular aspects, the head's role in shaping the professional and educational culture of a school remains critical, and certainly this was the expectation during the period of PNP.

We gained ready access to heads' thinking on such matters, especially in the sample schools. The recurrent theme was 'informality' or 'progressivism': the same value-orientation which they saw the Authority itself espousing as the touchstone for good practice. However, despite the apparent consensus, there were notable differences in style, presentation and treatment where these values were concerned.

- *Purists and sceptics.* Whereas some heads subscribed wholeheartedly to progressive orthodoxies, others were more doubtful or circumspect. Where the former used the full vocabulary of informality, and seemed unprepared or unable to accommodate the possibility that alternative viewpoints might exist, the latter were more aware of the limitations of progressivism, as idea and as a basis for practice.
- *The influence of context.* Whereas some heads saw progressivism as providing a basic recipe for primary practice in any context, others admitted to having their 'philosophy' shaped more by the particular social and cultural circumstances within which they worked, especially the backgrounds of the children and the attitudes and expectations of their parents. Such realities, as pressing for some heads in the suburbs as in the inner city, presented an agenda which primary orthodoxies addressed only partly, if at all.
- *The influence of other ideas.* Similarly, some heads sought to accommodate to their 'core' philosophy ideas and concerns from other sources – their reading, their membership of award-bearing courses, their out-of-school reference and membership groups, their professional and social networks. Such sources were, to them, more significant than those within the Authority, and often provided a more neutral and open context for sharing and debating ideas.
- *Rhetoric and reality.* The mismatch between a head's espoused values and what was actually going on in the classroom could be startling – and indeed is a recurrent theme in several of our interim reports,

notably 10 and 11. As a general rule, the more purist and dogmatic the value-orientation of the head, the bigger the discrepancy with observed practice. In these cases, a school's philosophy might acquire a life of its own: paraded for governors, advisers, parents and visitors, reflected superficially in those aspects of practice like display and decor that such outsiders tended immediately to note, but not necessarily followed through into the day-to-day conduct of teaching and learning.

These differences were only partly about value-orientations as such. Some heads were temperamentally and intellectually less inclined than others to perceive education in terms of grand statements and ringing slogans. On the other hand, a gap or mismatch between rhetoric and reality might reflect a gulf between head and staff, and indeed the discrepancies were most marked in schools where heads were relatively isolated, where communication was poor, and where class teachers were not involved in policy matters.

Thus there was an intimate connection between heads' philosophies and their views of their role, and between these and school management.

Heads perceived their roles in different ways. Of the many perceptions apparent in our data, four seemed particularly prominent (the earlier caveat about the relationship between typologies and individual cases still applies).

- *Head as 'boss'*, controlling – benignly or otherwise, but at any rate firmly – the character and direction of the school and its staff. Decision-making tended to centre on the issuing of directives and instructions.
- *Head as chief teacher*, believing, and demonstrating, that the teaching function of a school is pre-eminent and that the head must play the leading part, by action and example, in advancing it.
- *Head as managing director.* Where the 'boss' tended to be autocratic or paternalistic/maternalistic, the 'managing director' was more likely to be bureaucratic, delegating specialist roles and responsibilities and instituting formal procedures for decision-making.
- *Head as team leader.* Here there was less social distance between head and staff, though the head accepted the main responsibility for initiating and leading. At the same time, the leadership roles and potential of other staff were valued and developed, and decision-making tended to be collective.

Heads inclining towards a 'chief teacher' or 'team leader' role tended to be more visible and accessible to staff, especially in respect of their need for support and advice on everyday teaching problems: their physical base was the classroom as much as, or more than, the office. Heads adopting the style of 'managing director' or 'boss' were more likely to be office-based and thus to run the risk of appearing remote from everyday classroom concerns, especially in larger schools. However, 'bosses' were less prone to such detachment than 'managing directors', since they tended to place a high value on knowing, and hence controlling, all aspects of school life. To achieve this they needed to keep in touch with the classroom directly rather than through intermediaries. They might spend much time, therefore, patrolling their school and its classrooms, talking with children and offering comment to teachers. However, it should also be pointed out that the 'boss' view of headship manifested itself in a continuum of behaviour ranging from the clubbable to the autocratic or even tyrannical, with various shades of paternalism/maternalism in between.

This issue bears importantly on that of the degree of fit between a school's stated philosophy and its observable classroom practice, as discussed above. The closer a head is to the classroom and the challenges confronting class teachers, the greater his or her opportunities for evolving policies which reconcile ideals with practical circumstances. The more extreme flights of rhetoric we encountered were almost always associated with managerial detachment from the classroom.

The shift towards greater delegation, role specialisation and collective decision-making in primary schools, and the emergence of what we have termed departmental, three-tier and matrix management structures, appears to be an inevitable and necessary consequence of the growing complexity of the work of primary schools and the diminishing currency of the 'jack-of-all-trades' view of the class teacher's and head's roles. However, if staff are to remain in touch with one another, and the head is to remain in touch with all staff, close attention needs to be paid to communication, and to ensuring that managerial procedures, like school philosophies and policy statements, remain rooted in day-to-day needs and realities rather than take on a life of their own. Thus, formal procedures are not so much an alternative as an adjunct to the informal collaboration which is such an important feature of the best primary schools; and the part played by the head in securing the most productive mix of formal procedure and informal consultation/collaboration remains central.

We noted earlier the need for investment in support for heads and in management training, while acknowledging the Authority's recent (that is, post-PNP) initiatives in respect of the latter (Leeds City Council 1991a). We also argued that training should focus on management as a collective, whole-school enterprise rather than on the role of the manager alone. Our fieldwork pointed up two further areas of concern, both of which need close and urgent attention in programmes of professional development for heads.

The first was *staff relationships*. Our survey and interview data revealed a number of heads who appeared to have difficulty in dealing with their colleagues as people (a feature of management in all occupations, it must be acknowledged). Some treated their staff in a high-handed and tyrannical way. Some were less overtly overbearing, but no less effective in undermining their colleagues' confidence. Rather different were those heads who avoided not only confrontation but also contact, taking refuge in their office and resorting to memoranda rather than face-to-face encounters. In between were those heads who dealt much more effectively and constructively with some staff than with others. In such cases, as in all human relationships, the presence or absence of personal rapport was a critical element. Equally, some heads were struggling to deal with colleagues who were challenging by any standards – individuals who were combative, touchy, recalcitrant, bitter, lazy or in any of a variety of other ways uncooperative. The roots of such personal antipathies are notoriously difficult to disentangle, but their effect on a school's professional climate can be very damaging, especially in primary schools, because the small size of the institution and close daily contact of its teaching staff make it virtually impossible for either party to maintain social distance.

The second area of concern was *professional knowledge*. A small minority of heads with whom we came into contact seemed somewhat out of touch with recent developments in primary education. They showed little awareness of, or interest in, official surveys and reports, let alone other published research and writing on primary education. Their grasp of LEA and national policies bearing directly on the task of headship was at best tenuous. Frequently they took refuge in platitudes and rhetoric, delivering as unassailable truths ideas which are elsewhere accepted as very much open to debate. About ideas and practices other than their own they tended to be contemptuous, dismissive or hostile; usually such attitudes were grounded in ignorance, rather than engagement with the ideas in question. Their lack of commitment to extending their own professional knowledge and understanding, and their rampant anti-intellectualism, tended to infect the whole professional climate of their schools, depriving them of the spark of lively discussion about issues which is essential to educational progress, and dampening the enthusiasms of those staff who were otherwise inclined. Such a stance, it has also to be said, was sharply at odds with the educational aims to which their schools were purportedly committed, with their emphasis on engendering open, questioning minds, a love of reading and so on, a contradiction of which such heads seemed unaware. Again, the intimacy of the professional culture of a primary school makes it particularly vulnerable to such attitudes (Nias *et al.* 1989).

These two concerns – staff relationships and heads' professional knowledge – are vital ingredients in effective school management, and in the head's professional credibility. That being so, they should feature prominently both in the selection process for headship and in subsequent management support and training. However, since management courses tend to concentrate on basic tasks and procedures, there is a risk that the much larger matters signalled here will be treated rudimentarily at best. The LEA will need to look at other routes as well. It will also need to be aware that concerns such as these expose a major limitation of the school-controlled model of INSET which Leeds, in common with other LEAs, has adopted, and which is reinforced by current government funding arrangements and LMS. In a school having the professional climate characterised above, the capacity – let alone the will – to identify INSET needs with accuracy and honesty will simply not exist, and a self-generated INSET programme may well merely reinforce a school in its inadequacies. For this reason, LEAs must always maintain a major stake in INSET and professional development, above all where heads are concerned.

CONCLUSION

We noted at the start of this chapter that our study of school management was not intended to be comprehensive: our concern was the management of PNP rather than that of every aspect of a school's professional work. To this end, we devoted particular attention to the contribution of PNP enhanced staffing, to the work undertaken by support staff and PNP coordinators, and to the contexts within such staff were working.

However, we showed that the contribution which PNP appointees were able to make was inseparable from the wider management structures within which they were located, and in particular that the head played a key role in facilitating and supporting their endeavours.

It is a truism that every school is unique. However, it is also the case that schools have a lot in common. Our evaluation identified some of these shared features, and showed how primary schools tended to cluster towards a number of broad types in respect of certain issues bearing on the management of PNP: for example, the roles undertaken by support staff and coordinators, and by deputy heads; the managerial styles of senior staff; the management structures which framed the defining and implementing of school policy; the policies themselves; heads' stances on the ideas and practices which have constituted mainstream primary thinking since Plowden; and heads' leadership styles.

Like other studies (for example, DES 1977, 1987; Rutter *et al.* 1979; Mortimore *et al.* 1988; Nias *et al.* 1989, Sammons *et al.* 1995), ours identified or underlined some of the main factors in effective school management: the style and quality of the head's leadership; the intellectual and professional climate of the school; the explication of the management roles of staff with posts of responsibility – curriculum leaders, year leaders, coordinators and deputy heads; the importance of formal structures and mechanisms for decision-making; the need to strike an appropriate balance between such formal structures and informal processes; and the importance of involving all staff in decision-making.

Such issues are likely to be important in any primary school, anywhere. However, there were others, more distinctively local in their orientation: the gradual demise of the traditional two-tier model of primary school management and its replacement by three-tier and matrix models; the desirability of building on the diversification of staff management roles which PNP has produced, avoiding any contraction of such roles as a consequence of LMS; the need to acknowledge the pivotal role, for good or ill, played by primary heads, and to work with and through rather than round or against them; the need to expand the focus of management training courses to encompass the roles and needs of all staff (not just those of the 'managers' as conventionally defined), to locate management strategies in whole-school analysis, and generally to broaden the concept of 'management' which currently informs such courses; the importance of training, support and INSET for heads, and of ensuring that these give close attention to the broader aspects of the expertise needed for headship, such as professional knowledge and personal relationships, as well as the more obvious tasks, roles and strategies.

The recurrent factor in this analysis has been the inseparability of primary school and classroom practice from the policy, resourcing, support and guidance provided by the LEA. These are the concern of our next chapter.

Our evaluation of PNP caught schools during a period of transition, from *laissez-faire* to the much greater LEA intervention that PNP signalled, and from a largely local orientation to one framed by national policies and directives; by the end of our evaluation period, LEA interventive capacity was itself on the wane, as in the guise of delegation of decision-making to schools central government took more and more power to itself. For all concerned, the agenda by 1991, when our report was published, was substantially different from that of 1985, when PNP started.

For class teachers in primary schools, the National Curriculum and assessment had become preoccupations far more pressing than the pedagogical prescriptions which dominated PNP. Alongside these, heads were now contending with school development plans, changing relationships with parents and governors, the pressures and constraints of budgetary delegation, and an ever-tighter framework of resourcing which was forcing them to confront extremely difficult decisions about staff tenure and replacement – decisions whose sensitivity was exacerbated by the small size and strongly personalised character of primary school professional relationships. Heads' thinking and decision-making had become dominated by market and resource considerations which in their scale and complexity were a long way indeed from the traditional concept of primary headship (Audit Commission 1991). By 1991, Leeds LEA had set up services and procedures to guide and support schools in these novel areas of activity, and there was no shortage of advice from other sources.

However, even when the educational agenda is clarified and the professional tasks are clear, choices still remain at school level as to how the agenda and tasks should be managed. In this matter, the PNP experience, and the diversity of management structures, styles and roles which it produced, are of considerable relevance. The items on the agenda may change, but the questions about management remain the same.

Chapter 7

Supporting reform: the role of the LEA

During the 1980s, Leeds LEA set itself the task of reforming an entire local system of primary education. It diagnosed the main weaknesses in the schools it had inherited from earlier decades and set out its alternative vision, a Primary Needs Programme intended to meet children's needs by transforming schools into exemplars of 'good primary practice'.

The LEA then identified the resource needs of the system as a whole and voted the additional resources to meet them, determining precisely which schools would receive what level and kind of additional resources, and when. It set up mechanisms for coordinating, controlling and servicing the new programme, and expanded its advisory and support staff to ensure that such mechanisms would be effective. It determined the job specifications of the 530 teachers and other staff appointed to the programme, and officers themselves were involved in many of these appointments. It also devised a substantial programme of centralised in-service support for such appointees in order to ensure the successful dissemination of the various strands of the LEA's version of good practice.

Finally, the LEA agreed procedures for monitoring and reviewing the entire programme, and this included an invitation to the University of Leeds to undertake an independent evaluation.

This gives some measure of the boldness and scale of the programme. It also indicates how interventionist it was, especially by comparison with the practices of some other LEAs. In the present chapter we consider some of the main issues of policy and strategy which the Leeds approach raises: the way PNP policy was formulated and communicated; the substance and interpretation of the policy; and the LEA's own strategies for implementing the policy – as opposed to those adopted in the schools which have been considered in previous chapters – with particular reference to the INSET programme.

PNP POLICY: FORMULATION
AND COMMUNICATION

All LEAs have a statutory duty to have policies on the various aspects of the education service for which they are responsible. Leeds LEA took this duty very seriously, especially in respect of primary education. However, on matters of substance and strategy LEAs retain discretion. From the various strategies available, Leeds LEA opted for the one which was simplest to enact quickly but was also most likely to provoke adverse reaction – namely, a centralised approach involving minimal consultation with those most affected.

As a result, while the Authority can justifiably take much of the credit for the transformation of certain aspects of primary education in Leeds which PNP began to yield, it may also need to accept responsibility for some of PNP's manifest weaknesses.

The advantages of a centralised policy are the speed and scale of reform it allows; the disadvantages, particularly in a complex arena like education, are the resistance and disaffection it may generate, and the inevitability that the practice which emerges will be rather different from that intended because those at the receiving end may have insufficient understanding or commitment to secure its implementation. The experience of PNP, as recorded in our eleven interim reports and the previous six chapters, suggests that the extent of LEA centralisation over PNP was excessive, and that in certain crucial respects it was counter-productive. There are important lessons here both for future policy formulation and for the way an LEA's officers work. The lessons apply as much to the policies and strategies of central government as they do to LEAs.

The resentment and resistance generated in many schools by the way PNP was developed and implemented was a prominent theme in our early data, and in some schools it persisted until our last major data-gathering exercises: the 1989 questionnaires sent to primary heads, coordinators and advisory staff, and the 1990 home–school links follow-up study. Our subsequent contacts with school staff in the city indicated that the legacy was a powerful and often negative one, and that it continued to be reinforced because, despite a general loosening of LEA control and a government-sponsored shift to a greater measure of school self-determination, the Authority was perceived by schools as continuing to present itself as the main definer and arbiter of good practice.

What made this situation peculiarly problematic for primary teachers was their sense that the firm stance on good practice taken by the Authority's advisory staff was inseparable from the part they played both in the formal processes of promotion and appointment and in the many informal and subtle ways whereby individual teachers were encouraged and advanced – or discouraged and held back.

In any field of employment a successful application depends to some degree on the applicant's being seen to say and do what is expected during the selection process, and to this extent conventional selection methods can always be faulted for the way they may presume that words uttered on a form or in an interview are reliable indicators of future performance. This much is commonplace. However, the situation in Leeds was felt to reach deeper than this, and there were few other issues on which our questionnaires, interviews and observation between 1986 and 1990 yielded such widespread agreement or such strong expressions of anxiety, cynicism or disaffection. Many teachers and heads felt that getting on in the primary sector required verbal and practical allegiance to certain quite specific canons of 'good primary practice', and that anything less, let alone any open challenging of the orthodoxies in question, could damage their professional prospects. Moreover, this normative process was felt to operate at several levels, from appointments, promotions and other career aspirations to the much more subtle everyday processes whereby individuals come to acquire a sense of their professional worth from the comments and valuations of 'significant others' – advisers, advisory teachers and heads in particular.

The fact that heads and teachers of very differing professional styles and values were working in Leeds throughout this period demonstrates, of course, that other factors were at work and that the wilder accusations of patronage which came our way needed to be treated with considerable caution. Clearly, the service was by no means monolithic. On the other hand, there are different levels and degrees of both conformity and dissent, and in a context where prevailing versions of good practice tended to emphasise the visual and organisational, a strategic surface conformity allowed the more subtle and perhaps significant aspects of practice to be retained and underlying attitudes and assumptions to persist.

It is likely that these findings will be disputed in some quarters: understandably, because no individual or organisation wishes to be depicted in terms other than those of the most scrupulous integrity and open-mindedness where such matters are concerned. However, as with some other issues we have explored, the problem here is centrally one of *perception*. If people believe something to be true, then its consequences are the same, whether or not it is *actually* true. In the present case, the perception seems to have affected adversely both the quality and climate of professional discourse and the credibility of structures, procedures and people at LEA and school level. In any event, we have stressed that the perceptions relate as much or more to the *informal* context within which teachers and advisory staff work as to formal procedures. It is a relatively straightforward matter to sort out guidelines for the conduct of the latter; much more difficult to control the character of the former.

Moreover, agents of the process may be genuinely unaware of what they are doing for as long as they see good professional practice as unitary, consensual and unproblematic. For if there really is only one version of good primary practice then it becomes obvious that everyone should subscribe to it. However, since it is to be hoped that the essentially problematic and contestable nature of good primary practice has by now been adequately demonstrated, the state of affairs described here must give rise to some concern.

We recognise that the shift in the balance of power in appointment matters from LEAs to governing bodies may seem of itself to resolve this issue. It does not: proposals under discussion when this book's first edition went to press made it clear that advisory influence on individual careers would remain highly significant (Leeds City Council 1991c). However, the issues here will now need to be considered by governing bodies as well as advisory staff. It is vital that the teaching profession has full confidence in the processes of career development and advancement. The statutory responsibilities of LEAs and governing bodies in respect of quality control should be exercised with due acknowledgement of teachers' special knowledge and skills and their freedom and right as professionals to adopt those strategies which build on their personal strengths and reflect the unique circumstances of each school and classroom.

PNP POLICY: SUBSTANCE

The four key focuses of PNP, each discussed in detail in Chapters 2–5, were:

- children's needs;
- the curriculum;
- teaching strategies and classroom organisation;
- links between home, school and community.

There is little doubt that these are proper, necessary and central focuses for educational policy and practice. Each of them, however, raises certain basic requirements of a conceptual and empirical kind. The *conceptual* requirements are to be clear and exact in our use of these and subsidiary terms, and to confront and seek to resolve the many and often contentious value issues which each of them raises. The *empirical* requirement is to seek, evaluate and make explicit the evidence upon which claims for particular ideas and practices advocated as policy are based. (We develop this argument, and an analysis of the 'good primary practice' problem, on pages 267–87.)

In formulating and presenting the various PNP policies, neither of these basic requirements appears to have been even entertained. Schools were expected to make sense of ideas which had not always been thought through fully, and to implement practices whose justification frequently consisted of little more than unsubstantiated assertion. The force of such ideas and practices lay partly in their 'progressive' origins, which few teachers would be prepared to gainsay; and partly in the authority of those who devised and presented them, whom few would dare to contradict.

It should be added that the absence of proper justification of the ideas and practices underpinning major aspects of the education experienced by primary school pupils was not unique to Leeds. On the contrary, it seems to have been a common condition in post-war English primary education, and the agents of PNP policy in Leeds were merely conforming to the general tendency – a tendency, we must note, to which central government, and the various agencies it devised from 1988 onwards to regulate curriculum and assessment, seem to have perpetuated.

There is, however, no good reason why Leeds, or any LEA [or NCC, SEAC, SCAA or OFSTED] should follow this particular trend. The only proper way to arrive at sustainable definitions of good educational practice is by sharing, clarifying and debating ideas and values, marshalling and assessing evidence, and applying both processes to the task of formulating principles. Arguments and evidence for and against particular propositions are now abundantly available, both from the growing body of research and analytic study in primary education and the cumulative experience of teachers. Published analysis and research are already in the public domain and are liberally referred to in this report. Teachers' experience, which is at least as valuable a source of insight, is also readily accessible, but only if those responsible for policy are prepared to acknowledge its validity and are willing to make efforts to bring teachers into the debate. The shift is necessary, but it requires a fundamental readjustment in the relationship between the Authority and its schools, and between officers, advisers, heads and teachers. The adjustment needed is towards a partnership of fellow professionals rather than a hierarchy of expert superordinates and inexpert subordinates.

Questions about the *characteristics* of LEA thinking on aspects of primary practice are inseparable from questions about its *focus*. In one sense, the concentration on needs, curriculum, teaching strategies and home–school links is suitably comprehensive: it appears to encompass all the main elements of educational practice. However, our interim reports and previous chapters have shown major omissions and distortions *within* each of these elements. Here are some examples.

The needs policy was generally more concerned with children's problems than with their potential, and it omitted totally certain kinds of needs and therefore certain kinds of children, despite its claim to be comprehensive. With the exception of children with special educational needs, the approach to needs was uneven and sometimes weak in the vital areas of diagnosis, assessment and provision. (See Chapter 2.)

The approach to curriculum was strong on rhetoric about the whole, but weak on detail about specifics. Such specifics appeared to receive attention in a fairly random way, and there were notable omissions from the specifics attended to. Among these, the omission of aspects of language was particularly serious. (See Chapter 3.)

The proper concern with curriculum breadth and balance could be subverted at three levels: the Authority, the school and the classroom. At Authority level, the INSET programme, as later sections of this chapter will show, attended to some areas at the expense of others. At school level, the programmes and strategies for curriculum review, management and development, and the staffing of curriculum leadership posts, could sometimes reinforce such discrepancies. At classroom level, the attention on some areas of the curriculum could sometimes be achieved only by the deliberate neglect of others, the reasons having to do partly with teachers' attempts to conform to other advisory expectations: those relating to classroom organisation. Moreover, at this level, PRINDEP's analysis of the *generic activities* of which all curriculum practice is constituted showed the considerable imbalance discussed in detail in Chapters 3 and 4.

The commended approach to teaching strategies was highly partisan in respect of the particular kinds of practice which were endorsed. Moreover, it tended to present a view of practice as constituted largely of issues to do with the visual appearance of classrooms and matters of organisation relating to children's grouping. There was a general neglect of the teacher–pupil and pupil–pupil interactions on which learning depends, and indeed of learning as such; the message appeared to be that if the 'environment of learning' was correctly established, learning, and appropriate learning at that, would follow. Coupled with the neglect of diagnosis and assessment in the 'needs' part of the programme, this constituted an approach to children's learning which was too generalised and unfocused to have any significant impact. (See Chapter 4.)

The policy on home–school links was never properly defined, despite its prominence in the programme's initial aims. (See Chapter 5.)

The lessons for the future are clear. First, the Authority's approach to each of the elements of practice central to PNP – needs, curriculum, teaching strategies and home–school – can now be strengthened and extended in the light of the material presented in our twelve reports; each of these elements, though specific to PNP, is also a perennial concern in education and the issues therefore remain important. Second, the formulation of the Authority's educational policies and programmes, especially those which teachers are expected to translate into day-to-day practice, should from now on be grounded in prior consultation with teachers and others, together with analysis of relevant conceptual and empirical research, and those devising such policies and programmes should be able to justify them in terms of the considerations which this process will reveal.

PNP POLICY: IMPLEMENTATION

The main strategies for implementing PNP policy can be divided into two groups, LEA-based and school-based:

LEA-based strategies:
- the day-to-day work of advisory and PNP support staff;
- the administrative services of the Education Department;
- the Authority's centrally mounted in-service courses;
- the work of the Primary Schools Centre.

School-based strategies:
- enhanced staffing under PNP;
- the PNP coordinator;
- extra capitation;
- refurbishment.

The various school-based strategies have been considered in Chapters 2–6. In the present chapter we consider aspects of the four LEA-based strategies in greater detail.

Advisory staff

The LEA judged the role of the advisory staff to be pivotal to its attempts to improve the quality of primary education in Leeds. Though not part of the Primary Needs Programme, the parallel expansion of the advisory service needs to be noted in this context, since members of the service became the Authority's chief agents in PNP's interpretation and implementation. Before 1985, there were four specialist primary advisers; the LEA then started to rapidly expand the service, the exercise coinciding with restructuring of the administration as a whole. The result, by 1988, was a separate Department of Primary Education with seven advisers, eight advisory teachers, various support staff based in Merrion House, at the Primary Schools Centre or elsewhere, and an administrative officer and clerks, all headed by a Director of Primary Education. This was another powerful signal that primary education had ceased to be the Cinderella of the education service in Leeds. After the 1988 Education Reform Act, the primary team expanded further to accommodate the additional responsibilities placed on LEAs by the Act.

Because the advisory service was so deeply enmeshed in PNP, it is difficult to divorce its contribution from the many aspects and contexts of the programme which are discussed elsewhere in this report. However, certain general observations are merited.

Advisory staff were tireless in their advocacy of PNP and in their efforts to secure its effective implementation. A careful division of labour within the team sought to ensure that most aspects of the programme (with certain omissions referred to in previous chapters) would be effectively managed.

Though subject to shared procedures, each member of the advisory team worked in a different way, modifying formal responsibility in the light of individual personality and experience. Thus, though our surveys document a generalised view of the service as being only moderately effective, heads and teachers viewed individual members of the advisory team very differently, being unstinting in their praise of some, rather less so of others.

The advisory attributes to which teachers responded most positively were: ready availability, especially in a crisis; visibility, especially in the classroom; credibility at both classroom and managerial levels; preparedness to give a clear lead coupled with a willingness to listen and acknowledge that the schools, too, had expertise; a combination of authoritativeness with humility; an open, friendly and supportive manner. It goes without saying that the attributes which most antagonised teachers were the opposite of these, especially in the context of the perceptions about the need to conform referred to earlier.

One of the main difficulties for the advisory team was the way, particularly following the Education Department's reorganisation, they had to combine their advisory role with considerable administrative responsibilities, both for 'their' schools and across the system as a whole. All members of the central team at Merrion House (the Education Department's offices) were severely stretched in terms of both time and the range of roles they were expected to encompass, and it was therefore inevitable that some aspects of their job could be successfully accomplished only at the expense of others. The need to retain the primacy of the professional advisory function is surely paramount, and the Authority might well wish to find ways of reducing the administrative burden on advisory staff. These matters ought to be included in the 1991 advisory restructuring exercise (Leeds City Council 1991c).

The physical conditions in which Merrion House members of the advisory team had to work were grossly inadequate. They shared a cramped open-plan area in which they were disposed rather in the manner of a traditional typing pool. There was no privacy for the interviews and telephone conversations of a sensitive kind which are part and parcel of an adviser's job. When most or all of the team were present, noise levels and constant interruptions effectively frustrated work which needed sustained thinking. Clerical and administrative backup were provided at only a modest level. The fact that the conditions outlined here seem to be all too common in LEAs nationally (Audit Commission 1989b) does not diminish the need to do something about them. The upgrading of the working environment of advisory staff must be treated as a priority.

Administration

As we have noted above, the administrative arm of PNP acquired a poor image. This judgement – as with that of the advisory service – can be accounted for partly in terms of the traditional antagonism of schools to 'the office' which pervades many LEAs. Such antagonism is often unthinking, is frequently unmerited, and seems in any event a necessary device whereby the professional culture of a school sustains itself. An LEA, then, fulfils a scapegoat function – as, indeed, do other contingent groups like teacher educators and HMI/OFSTED.

However, in our many interviews with teachers and heads in individual schools, this generalised view was sometimes fleshed out by reference to specific instances and frustrations, of which the most common were the following: the difficulty of obtaining vital information; the persistent unavailability of individuals who possessed such information; the lack of departmental awareness about who was responsible for what; the classic 'doctor's receptionist' tendency among clerical staff to prevent heads from gaining access to advisory staff and other officers; the Byzantine complexity of the departmental arrangements at Merrion House; the lack of reciprocity in information flow: schools felt that Merrion House tended to bombard them with directives and requests, many of them urgent, yet was unwilling to reciprocate by supplying the schools with what they, often equally urgently, required; and the failure of Merrion House officers and staff to answer letters.

Our final questionnaire to all Leeds primary heads asked, *inter alia*, for ratings of the effectiveness of the LEA's various mechanisms for supporting its primary schools: the administration at Merrion House; communication and consultation between the LEA and its schools; the work of the advisory service. In view of the points above, it is hardly surprising that none of these was rated as more than moderately effective, and only the advisory staff were rated as significantly better than ineffective. On this there was general agreement between the three PNP Phases, with a tendency for Phase II schools to be most satisfied and Phase III least.

The PNP in-service support programme

This section reverts to a finer level of detail because it includes hitherto unpublished material. We discussed the Authority's INSET provision briefly in Report 1, then in Report 6 we explored the style and initial impact of courses and the assumptions about professional development which they reflected. The present section is more concerned with the facts and figures of PNP INSET between 1985 and 1989. Its basis is systematic monitoring of the full complement of courses over this period, and its direct evaluation of some twenty-five of them.

Centrally provided INSET was an essential and substantial part of the Primary Needs Programme. Most courses were mounted at the Primary Schools Centre, also a PNP innovation. In the early days of the programme, these courses all bore the label 'PNP' and many were for PNP staff only. As the programme expanded, the courses lost their specificity of content and audience and became largely indistinguishable from the rest of the Authority's central INSET programme for primary schools. However, it is important to note that PNP provided the resources and framework for the considerable expansion and diversification of such courses between 1985 and 1990: it was not so much that PNP was submerged as that PNP and primary provision became synonymous. The messages of the new courses were clearly rooted in PNP. In the analysis which follows, we have concentrated on courses mounted at the Primary Schools Centre.

The general diversification of INSET in the later stages of PNP came too late for us to include it in our programme, and in any case our resources were already fully stretched. However, it is important to list these alternative modes and thus acknowledge the variety of provision in the Authority. They included, in addition to the extensive programme at the Primary Schools Centre: programmed school-based INSET; INSET supported by the Authority but provided by external agents; INSET related to school reviews; and the expanding school-led INSET initiative. The programme at the Primary Schools Centre remained by far the largest part of the Authority's central INSET commitment during the evaluation period and an important medium for the transmission of advisory views on good practice.

During the first four years of PNP, the Authority appears to have mounted no fewer than 376 primary in-service courses at the Primary Centre. The courses covered a very wide range in both style and content. In style they ranged from formal talks to intensive workshops and such innovative features as the model classroom to which course participants were invited to return with interested colleagues by appointment to discuss its features with an advisory teacher. A detailed discussion of the implications of the different course styles can be found in our sixth report. The variation in content was enormous, although for the purposes of this analysis the course topics have necessarily been grouped into rather broad categories.

In descending order of frequency:

- 31 per cent of the courses dealt with specific individual areas of the curriculum;
- 18 per cent were concerned with social issues, covering such topics as race, gender, drugs and child abuse;
- 16 per cent were dedicated to specific professional roles, such as those of PNP coordinators, probationers or permanent supply teachers;
- 12 per cent were concerned with the introduction of the National Curriculum;
- 8 per cent dealt with issues of classroom management, including teaching strategies, children's behaviour and so on;
- 8 per cent covered such whole-school issues as management and curriculum leadership;
- 6 per cent dealt with special educational needs;
- a nominal 0 per cent (in fact a quarter of 1 per cent, or one course out of the total of 376) was concerned with home–school links.

It would be dangerous to assume that this balance of topics necessarily reflects the Authority's PNP priorities very accurately. Courses vary a great deal in both their length and the number of people who attend them, and it would clearly be unjustified to assume that a single course on one topic was outweighed by, say, five courses on another if the single course involved fifty teachers in a full day's attendance each week for a term, while each of the five other courses lasted only a couple of hours and catered for half-a-dozen teachers. For a closer indication of the Authority's priorities, we have therefore incorporated the length of each course and the number of participating teachers into an index of *teacher-days*: for example, a three-day course for eight teachers would involve twenty-four teacher-days ($3 \times 8 = 24$), while a half-day course for seventeen teachers would involve eight and a half teacher-days ($\frac{1}{2} \times 17 = 8\frac{1}{2}$). We took half a day as the minimum duration for a course, recording that amount of time even for courses which, for example, took place after school hours.

Figure 7.1 shows the allocation of time (measured in teacher-days) to each of the course themes listed earlier. It is immediately clear that some topics received considerably more, or less, attention than would be suggested by the number of courses allocated to them.

Thus, although material tailored to specific professional roles was delivered in only 16 per cent of courses, it accounted for well over a quarter of all the teacher-days devoted to primary INSET, a proportion of time exactly equal to that spent on all individual areas of the curriculum together.

Social issues, which between them were the subject of almost a fifth of the courses, accounted for only 9 per cent of the total number of teacher-days: they tended to be short, workshop-style courses with few participants. At the other extreme, special educational needs – with only a third as many courses as social issues – accounted for slightly more teacher-days, although still only 11 per cent of the total time.

The National Curriculum, as well as specific curriculum areas, received slightly fewer teacher-days than would be suggested by the number of courses allocated to them.

Home–school links, the promotion of which was originally considered important enough to make it one of the four original aims of PNP, accounted for only one teacher-day in every hundred devoted to primary INSET.

The curriculum areas accorded the greatest number of teacher-days were maths, English and science, with English accounting for more than twice as many as science, and these two areas between them taking up about as many teacher-days as maths on its own. A number of other areas of the curriculum – art and craft, PE, music, CDT, computers, dance and so on – were given comparatively little time, amounting to the same number of teacher-days between them as were spent on science alone.

With the passage of time there were changes in both the overall amount of INSET provision at the Primary Centre and in its priority areas. The 9,714 teacher-days spent in this way during the school year 1988–89 (a threefold increase since 1985–86) reflect a very substantial investment of human and material resources, although it should be added that, with about 2,400 primary teachers in the Authority the figures represent a rise from an average of only just over one day's provision per teacher in 1985–86 to about four days' provision in 1988–89.

The major areas of increased provision during the four years are illustrated in Figure 7.2.

From the beginning of PNP, the recruitment of new staff, often with new and untested areas of responsibility, demanded intensive in-service provision tailored to specific roles. Even in the first year, when fewer than a third of Leeds primary schools were involved in PNP, this requirement accounted for 760 teacher-days; but from year to year, as more and more schools became involved, and as roles proliferated, the investment of time increased until in the fourth year it stood at 2,035 teacher-days.

In-service provision relating to special educational needs, though involving a much more modest investment of time throughout, showed a steady and regular increase from year to year.

During the first three years, very little time was spent on such whole-school issues as management and curriculum leadership, but in 1988 an apparent change of priorities led to a dramatic increase in provision in this area, from an average of 102 teacher-days a year to a somewhat startling 1,280. If to these one adds other emerging initiatives in

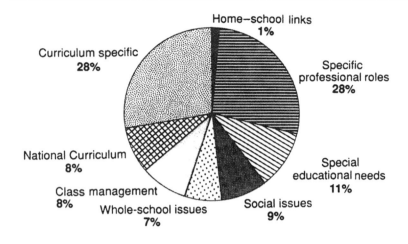

Teacher-days

Figure 7.1   Primary INSET: allocation of time to course themes, 1985–89

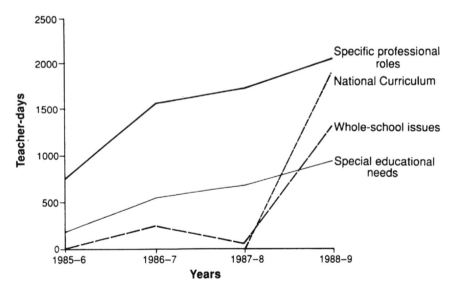

Figure 7.2   Primary INSET: major increases in provision, 1985–89

management INSET – the management training programme now firmly in place (Leeds City Council 1991a), school-led INSET, and external management courses supported by the LEA – then the massive scale of provision for management training by the 1990s becomes very clear.

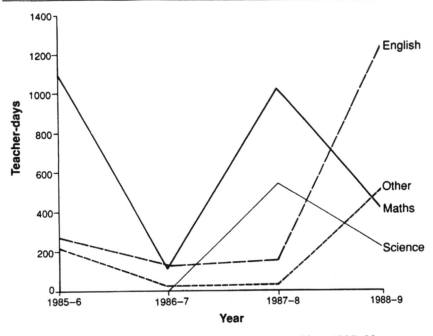

Figure 7.3 Primary INSET: changing curriculum priorities, 1985–89

The impending introduction of the National Curriculum imposed a new demand towards the end of the four-year period, and during the final year 1,813 teacher-days were spent preparing teachers for their new responsibilities.

Within the area of curriculum-specific courses at the Primary Centre there were some marked changes of priority during the four years, and these are illustrated in Figure 7.3.

The graph shows how mathematics courses followed an alternating on-off pattern in which a year of massive time investment in courses was followed by a comparatively quiet year. During the first three years an average of well under 200 teacher-days a year were spent on English courses, a surprisingly modest allocation of time in view of the status of English as a core curriculum area. As if to make up for this, in the fourth year the number of teacher-days shot up to 1,254, an amount of time exceeded only by courses devoted to specific professional roles. No courses at all were devoted to science during the first two years. The third year saw a major initiative in this area, involving 545 teacher-days, while in the fourth year there was something of a reversal as the amount of time was cut back by well over a half. Finally, though the rest of the curriculum was allocated well under 100 teacher-days during the first three years, there was a substantial rise during the fourth year.

In view of the fact that INSET was only one integral aspect of a very large and complex package of PNP resources, it is difficult to pinpoint its unique effect on daily practice in the Authority, although this is precisely the task we undertook in relation to one major series of courses for our sixth and tenth reports. We found that in the long term a little under a third of the participating teachers had been significantly influenced by what they had heard and seen and had made major changes in their classroom practice as a result. Others had made more superficial changes.

To augment this kind of study, in the summer of 1989 we asked all Leeds primary heads to rate the overall effectiveness of the PNP INSET provision in relation to each of the four PNP aims. At best, the programme was rated no more than moderately effective, being considered completely ineffective in respect of home–school links.

In general, our direct evaluation of the sample of courses referred to here showed that a course's effectiveness is closely bound up with the nature and substance of the messages being conveyed. Any tendency to diffuseness or ambiguity led to a wide range of interpretations and allowed teachers and heads to assert in good faith, whatever the nature of their practice, that they were implementing the LEA's policies and principles. They were able to do this partly because some of the messages were generalised enough to allow virtually any interpretation, and partly because messages sometimes combined minute practical detail with broad general principle, allowing teachers to feel they were taking a step in the right direction by changing the surface appearance of their practice without altering its substance. Change at deeper than surface level was maximised as a result of those courses whose messages about practice were clear, unambiguous and precise as to both their substance and their status (as policy, recommendation, suggestion or option).

The effectiveness of courses was also heavily dependent on the degree of consistency and general agreement between the advisers, heads and coordinators who each had a role in the improvement of practice and who each brought their separate influence to bear on the teachers who attended the courses. Where these agents of change were in accord with one another, and where some at least of them were directly engaged in the deeper levels of the everyday classroom practice of the teachers concerned, significant change tended to follow.

During the later stages of the Primary Needs Programme, as we have noted, the Authority started to introduce school-led INSET, first on an experimental basis to some 30 per cent of primary schools, then across the sector as a whole. Since this initiative was financially and administratively separate from PNP, we cannot comment on it here. However, it should be noted that the demands of the National Curriculum, assessment and LMS have been such as to require the Authority to maintain at least as high a centralised INSET profile as previously, and present provision retains, alongside the new agenda of concerns dictated by the 1988 Education Reform Act (ERA), many of the courses and themes established during the PNP period. Moreover, as we argued earlier, the circumstances of particular schools are such as to make it imperative that LEAs maintain a significant stake in centralised INSET. Schools without the quality of leadership or the collective capacity or will to identify and meet their professional development needs are by no means uncommon, and they will always form a problematic minority in any LEA's provision. The current ideology of devolution may favour letting such schools, along with all the others, sort out their own affairs, but that is hardly fair to their teachers, still less to their pupils.

For as long as the Authority retains its commitment to centralised INSET, therefore, the points we raised in our sixth report about the *style* of such courses remain relevant. There we identified and discussed in detail a number of factors critical to the quality and impact of any such course: the clarity and appropriateness of the messages conveyed; the degree of match between messages as intended and as received; the appropriateness of the methods used to convey the messages in question.

We also identified three key questions which need to be addressed as part of the process of devising such courses:

- *General or specific target?* The more precisely a target audience is defined, and the more homogeneous it is, the greater a course's potential for an extended impact.
- *Who defines teachers' professional needs?* Such needs can be defined by others (advisory staff or heads, for example), by teachers themselves, or through a process of discussion and negotiation.
- *Professional training or professional self-development?* An in-service activity can be conceived as something one person does to another, with the assumption that change is most effectively produced from outside; or as a process in which teachers are centrally involved in analysing their own situation and needs and working out the best ways of tackling these.

We showed how, although such questions allowed a wide range of possible approaches to INSET, even within the context of a central provision, and despite the market research which preceded the drawing up of each year's programme, the Authority tended towards a particular combination of imprecise targeting, top-down views of teachers' needs, and external agents adopting training or instructing roles.

It could be argued that centralised INSET has this character of necessity, and that the other possibilities can be achieved through school-based INSET. Our knowledge of approaches to INSET offered by a variety of providing bodies – other LEAs, higher education institutions and so on – shows that the style and quality of INSET have less to do with where they take place than with how those involved stand in relation to questions such as those above, not to mention fundamental prerequisites like their professional knowledge and skill. In this sense, therefore, the now fashionable polarisation of school-led and agency-provided INSET is misplaced and misleading. There is no guarantee at all that the former, simply by taking place in a teacher's place of work, will somehow be more relevant or valuable than the latter (a point made over a decade ago – Alexander 1980 – in the context of a previous incarnation of current debates).

We argue therefore, now as in our sixth report, that among the critical requirements in an INSET programme are the following: the diversity of teachers' needs must be acknowledged and addressed; teachers themselves must be central to the process of defining their needs; and to meet diverse needs there must be diverse INSET programmes: not just as to their *content* and *level*, but also in their *style* and *venue*. A mixed economy of school-led, LEA-provided, and independent-agency provided would seem to be the minimum requirement.

It is clear that the Authority adjusted its approach to INSET quite considerably after the early days of PNP and in the light of our sixth report and feedback from schools. More courses and activities were targeted on specific groups; more attention was paid to consumer opinion; and there was greater diversity within the system as a whole. Preserving such diversity in the context of diminishing INSET budgets and the trend to school-led INSET is going to become increasingly difficult, but since it is very much in the interests of the professional health of the teaching force it must remain a priority.

CONCLUSION

This chapter has made a number of points about the way in which PNP policy was formulated and communicated; about the means and manner of its interpretation; its substance; and the strategies adopted to secure its implementation. We have acknowledged the vital, substantial and positive role played by the LEA in all these matters. However, we have also drawn attention to some less satisfactory features, several of them fundamental.

Among these was the basic stance adopted by the LEA towards its primary heads and teachers, as demonstrated in numerous aspects of the Primary Needs Programme. The shift we commend – from a stance which teachers view as authoritarian and bureaucratic to one founded on professional partnership – is not only preferable in terms of the quality of relationships within the Authority, but is also far more likely to deliver the very improvements in professional practice for which the Primary Needs Programme was established.

In this and other chapters we have discussed the various LEA-based and school-based strategies devised to secure the implementation of PNP. In our tenth interim report we acknowledged that these ought to have been an 'irresistible combination'; yet too often they failed to deliver their potential because of a lack of *linkage* between the key elements, particularly between advisory staff, heads, PNP coordinators and class teachers. It must be clear that improved liaison between these parties will help, but is only part of the requirement. If the basic relationship between LEA and schools is divisive, liaison will remain frustrated by problems of power, status and value. For effective linkage to be achieved between the various elements in the Authority's policies for educational reform, relationships as well as procedures must change.

Throughout the present chapter, and indeed elsewhere in this report, we have intimated that policies too must come in for scrutiny. We have raised many questions about the particular package of policies, recommendations, messages and specifications through which the Authority sought to implement its vision of primary education.

However, beyond the question of the character, quality and impact of such particular ideas are two more fundamental questions about LEA policy in general: how should it be arrived at, and on what should it focus? Is it really appropriate for policy to deal with such matters as classroom display, layout, grouping and teaching methods, to take four by now familiar examples? Should an LEA be telling teachers how to teach? Or should policy concentrate more on clarifying the goals and outcomes of *learning*, and on providing the kind of support which will enable schools to identify for themselves the best possible ways of achieving such goals and outcomes? It could be argued that Leeds LEA sought and expected consensus on aspects of primary education (such as classroom practice) where consensus is neither possible nor appropriate, while at the same time neglecting those other aspects (such as the curriculum and home–school links) where consensus was both desirable and possible.

Just as there are many ways of organising and running an effective school, so there are many ways of running an LEA. It was not part of our brief to undertake a comparative study of policy, strategy and professional roles and relationships in different LEAs, but we strongly commend the study as an adjunct to the appraisal of Authority practices to which Leeds committed itself in response to the recommendations in our final report. Those undertaking it will encounter an extent of diversity which they may find surprising, as well as numerous examples of local authority practice in which members, officers and advisers have successfully managed to reconcile their statutory responsibilities with a commitment to genuine partnership with teachers and parents.

When this report went to press a restructuring of the advisory service was under consideration (Leeds City Council 1991c). The draft proposals tended to emphasise advisory *structures* and *roles*. Perhaps, in the light of our report, the LEA should have given at least equal attention to the *purpose, focus* and *style* of advisory activity, especially as these bear on the day-to-day work of primary teachers and heads.

In the light of the foregoing, it is worth recalling the six tasks commended by the Audit Commission (1989a) for post-ERA LEAs. These include:

- leadership and the articulation of an educational vision;
- partnership and support;
- planning;
- provision of information;
- regulation and quality control;
- channelling funds.

The PNP experience suggests that several of these will need careful thought. LEA leadership is vital, but we have raised questions about the form it might take and the aspects of education with which it should be concerned. Leadership, of course, should be confused neither with autocracy nor omniscience. Partnership should be genuine, rather than paternalism in disguise. As the Audit Commission notes: 'Schools will need support in the new environment. That support should not maintain institutions in a client or subservient role. Rather it should be designed to assist them to achieve autonomy' (1989a). The provision of information presupposes a two-way exchange both as a concomitant of genuine partnership and in order that LEA decisions and information are grounded in an exact and sympathetic understanding of schools' situations and needs. Finally, quality control: it is a complex, sophisticated and highly responsible enterprise, demanding knowledge and skills which cannot be presumed and therefore require proper training, together with a full and open debate with those whose work is under review about the criteria whereby quality is to be judged. Without such a debate, as the PNP experience has amply demonstrated, an LEA's judgements of quality will certainly not lack power: but they may well lack legitimacy.

[In 1996, with LEA power further constrained by government policy in the intervening years, these points should perhaps be addressed with equal force to those quasi-autonomous non-governmental bodies to which much of the power traditionally exercised by LEAs had been transferred: the School Curriculum and Assessment Authority, the Office for Standards in Education, and the Teacher Training Agency. Indeed, the questions are even more pressing now because, unlike LEAs, bodies like SCAA, OFSTED and the TTA are non-elected and non-accountable, except to ministers. This development might also imbue with a certain irony – dare we say hypocrisy – the exploitation by ministers in 1991–92 of the Leeds report's discussion of LEA power and imputed patronage. However, by 1996 too, the imminence of another general election meant that the debate about LEAs was by no means over (Labour Party 1995)].

Chapter 8

Summary of main findings

This chapter presents a summary of the main findings from the evaluation of Leeds City Council's Primary Needs Programme. With a few minor amendments (such as the deletion of paragraph numbers and cross-references to the relevant numbered paragraphs in earlier chapters) they are presented as they appeared in the final report.

AIMS OF PNP

The four aims of the Primary Needs Programme were appropriately focused – on children's needs, teaching strategies, the curriculum and links between school and home – but they were too generalised to provide a secure base-line for a substantial programme of financial investment and structural change.

However, the statement of aims was but one of a large number of written and oral policy statements about primary education which the Authority issued between 1985 and 1991. Some of these, too, suffered from problems of ambiguity and opaqueness. Moreover, heads and teachers were often expected to adopt ideas and practices on the basis of belief and exhortation rather than argument and evidence. This approach does little to help teachers cut through the educational rhetoric and sort out those practices which are most productive in terms of the quality of children's learning.

PHASES OF PNP

There were 71 mainly inner-city schools in PNP Phase I, 56 schools in Phase II, with the remaining 103 schools being in Phase III. Given PNP's commitment to positive discrimination in favour of children and schools with particular needs, the phasing system for introducing schools to the programme was, by and large, appropriate and equitable. There were of course anomalies, but some would have occurred whatever mechanisms for resource allocation had been adopted.

RESOURCES FOR PNP

The Authority allocated £13.75 million pounds to PNP over the four years 1985–89. Most of this money (£11.25 million) was spent on the main strategy of enhanced staffing, with more than 500 additional appointments made during this period. The remainder was divided between increased capitation for all schools, refurbishment of some twenty-five of them, and in-service support. The Phase I schools had the largest share of these resources.

CHILDREN'S NEEDS

The main aim of PNP was 'to meet the identified needs of all children, and in particular those experiencing learning difficulties'. The intention was to address the needs of the majority of children through a combination of the 'broadly-based curriculum' and 'flexible teaching strategies', and to use additional programmes and resources to cater for certain specific categories of need. These included special educational needs, ethnic minority and multicultural needs, equal opportunity and gender-related needs, and social and/or material disadvantage.

We identified four features essential to a properly founded needs policy or programme: a clear *definition* of the categories of needs in question; procedures for the *identification* of children within each category; means for the *diagnosis* of the precise needs of each child so identified; and appropriate educational and curricular *provision* to meet these needs. The four categories of need chosen by the Authority varied considerably in the extent to which they met these conditions, at both LEA and school level. Needs policy in general, despite its centrality to PNP, evolved piecemeal, with some parts not fully thought through.

In terms of resourcing, comprehensiveness of focus and perceived impact, the most extensive and successful part of the needs programme was that designed for children with special educational needs, with well-thought-out and systematic procedures for identification and diagnosis, highly regarded INSET courses, and initially generous provision through a combination of enhanced staffing and central support. However, the provision was concentrated mainly in Phase I schools, and in the later stages of PNP even these schools claimed to be encountering increased difficulty in sustaining their earlier staffing commitments in this area.

Despite the integrative intentions of recent legislation, the Authority continued its administrative separation of special educational needs from primary education. This generated confusion in policy and a certain lack of coherence in practice, which the Authority sought to address in its 1990 advisory restructuring.

The Authority displayed a clear commitment to meeting the needs of children from ethnic minority groups, to combating racism, and to extending multicultural understanding. This commitment was backed by a range of resources, facilities and support staff.

Nevertheless, and notwithstanding the generally good quality of what was provided by the LEA, the actual scale of professional support remained inadequate to the task. Provision was patchy, and professional attitudes ranged from a sensitive understanding of the issues to the blandly ignorant. Some staff failed to distinguish between ethnic minority and multicultural needs, and as a result refused to acknowledge their obligations in respect of the latter.

There is much work to be done here. Professional attitudes and perceptions need to change, and professional knowledge and understanding about societal and cultural matters, as well as about strategies for multicultural education, need to be increased.

Equal opportunities and gender were given a high profile in Authority policy, but again the situation on the ground was uneven and in some cases inadequate. For too many teachers, gender was not taken seriously as an issue. The problem was exacerbated by the way gender inequality was often built into school management structures, and to some extent into the curriculum. Provision was sparse, and often tokenistic. LEA support for developing professional understanding of gender issues was qualitatively good but quantitatively inadequate. However, there were notable exceptions to these trends at the level of individual schools and classrooms.

The larger part of PNP resourcing was concentrated on schools where significant proportions of children were experiencing social and/or material disadvantage. Beyond this, policy offered little. There was no guidance on provision other than the commitments to improving the visual environment and offering a broad curriculum and flexible teaching. While *context* was attended to, therefore, *curriculum content* was largely ignored, and especially those basic areas of the curriculum like reading which are so critical to the improvement of children's educational and career prospects. There was a tendency to acquiesce in low expectations of disadvantaged children and to define their needs in emotional rather than educational terms. Of all aspects of PNP, this one raises the most serious questions about value for money. At the same time, and regardless of the lack of other than financial support from the Authority, certain schools were tirelessly and effectively tackling the needs of these children in the comprehensive way required.

There was no policy for other categories of need. A particularly notable omission was children of high ability, the more serious in view of the widespread evidence nationally that such children underachieve in primary schools, partly because too little is expected of them. The lack of Authority policy was frequently mirrored at school level.

Overall, thinking on children's needs, despite its commendable focus on specific categories, tended to falter on the issue of provision, and it seriously underestimated the extent to which professional attitudes and understanding are vital factors in the improvement of practice. More fundamentally, it was grounded in a *deficit* view of needs. That is to say, it tended to focus on what children *cannot* do rather than what they *can* do, and in (rightly) attending to their *problems* it underplayed or ignored their *potential*. Such an approach can encourage low expectations and a failure to attend properly to the needs of children other than those with 'problems'. In this respect, despite the main PNP goal, PNP was not really about the needs of *all* children. Policy and provision were less well developed in the areas of diagnosis, assessment and curriculum – in other words, the precise points where a policy has its greatest potential to affect the individual child. There is a cycle of low expectations and unchallenging curriculum experiences here, which the Authority itself could help to break – not least by retaining a significant stake in centralised INSET. At the same time all concerned should look carefully for ways of meeting the needs of all children, as well as those minorities for which the Authority demonstrated a proper and necessary concern. We add that this agenda is no less important in the context of the National Curriculum and mandatory assessment: although these seek to raise expectations and improve standards, of themselves they will achieve little unless professional attitudes, knowledge and skill are also attended to.

THE CURRICULUM

Authority policy on the curriculum was contained in various documents. Regrettably, like some of its other statements on primary education, many of these were strong on values and assertion but weaker on substance and justification. They thus combined in a frustrating way a lack of precision and argument with an expectation that they would become the mandatory cornerstones of classroom practice.

More successful in terms of their perceived impact on teachers and children were those programmes associated with certain specific subject initiatives such as PrIME and ESG science.

The Authority's curriculum policies produced various responses from heads and teachers. Whereas some were happy to espouse them without question, others were more critical, the more so because of the Authority's failure to consult any but a small number of heads about their content. But the main problem was that the PNP plank of the 'broadly-based curriculum' turned out to be fairly meaningless. At the same time, PRINDEP data repeatedly showed that the curriculum in action in many schools and classrooms was not, by any of the possible definitions of the phrase, broadly based. The Authority's lead on matters concerning the character, range and balance of the primary curriculum as a whole, therefore, was inadequate.

Schools exploited PNP resources in a variety of ways for reviewing, developing and managing the curriculum. PNP coordinators played a prominent part, whether as *managers, consultants, enhancers* or *facilitators*. Schools made constructive use of the potential of enhanced staffing to secure a collaborative approach to curriculum development in the classroom through teachers teaching together (TTT). The data show a wide range of strategies overall, and we would trust that more of these could enter the management vocabulary of more schools. In some, the potential of TTT was wasted because support teachers were marginalised; in others, highly experienced and qualified coordinators had to be content with a merely facilitating role.

The processes of curriculum review at school level took various forms. Less variable was the tendency to concentrate on reviewing and developing some subjects while neglecting others. The list tended to be dominated by mathematics and language, with science occupying an increasingly important place over the evaluation period. The review process was buttressed by PNP INSET and Development Fund support for the subjects chosen. The neglect of many other curriculum areas was a persistent problem, the more serious in view of the close correspondence between review and development on the one hand and the quality of curriculum provision in the classroom on the other. Certain subjects now in the National Curriculum – notably art, history and geography – were, and remain, particularly vulnerable. We accept that curriculum review and development, and indeed INSET, may have to be selective. However, care should be taken to construct a cycle of attention which eventually includes all aspects of the curriculum. Without this, as has happened in Leeds, certain subjects are perennial losers, and the principles of curricular balance and entitlement are seriously compromised.

There was a significant relationship between curriculum leadership, staff status and gender, and this reinforced discrepancies in the review process and could convey inappropriate messages to staff and children alike. Schools need to be constantly alert to this problem.

Overall, schools used a wide range of strategies for curriculum review and development. These can usefully be viewed as a repertoire from which schools taking a more restricted approach to review could learn a great deal. In particular, we commend attention to the potential (and challenges) of staff meetings. They are a common ingredient in the review and development process, but were handled with widely varying degrees of competence.

One area in which the advisory team made its views on curriculum clear was the way classrooms should be physically disposed to deliver curriculum breadth and flexibility. Some teachers adopted the recommended practices; some found difficulty in doing so; others rejected them. However, while the advisory team's views had the undoubted consequence of making many Leeds primary classrooms seem busier and more attractive, the beneficial consequences for children's learning were less clear; and for some teachers, the claim of 'flexibility' had exactly the opposite effect, strait-jacketing them into practices to which they had no real commitment and which they had difficulty in managing.

We commend close attention to the way time is used in the curriculum. At one level we discovered time being spent on different curriculum areas in similar proportions to those recorded by HMI and by other research projects. However, we also found an inverse relationship between time and efficiency: time was sometimes used least effectively in those subjects to which most time was allocated. We also noted a tendency for some teachers to create time to monitor children's learning in prioritised areas like mathematics and language by treating other areas as time fillers. Such findings have serious implications for curriculum planning and provision: children are entitled to a curriculum which is consistent in its quality across all subjects, not just those accorded most time. Moreover, the findings challenge conventional assumptions about the amounts of time the different subjects should be allocated. Given the time constraints to which primary teachers have felt increasingly subjected since the introduction of the National Curriculum, this set of issues deserves very careful attention.

We uncovered four quite distinct ways in which the curriculum in practice was defined and delivered: first, as *areas or subjects* (mathematics, language, and so on); second, as *organisational strategies* (topic work, thematic inquiry, 'choosing' and so on); third, as *generic activities* (reading, writing, collaboration, construction, drawing/painting and so forth); fourth, as a combination of two or more of these. We found the idea of *generic activities* to be particularly potent as a tool for describing and evaluating curriculum practice. Regardless of subject labels, children's curriculum experiences tended to be dominated by writing, with reading, using task-specific apparatus, and listening to the teacher also prominent; collaborative activity and talking – with the teacher or with other pupils – were a long way behind. Some of these discrepancies were related to children's age, gender and perceived ability. This alternative analysis reveals a pervasive imbalance in children's curriculum experiences and conflicts sharply with primary rhetoric.

In this and other respects, the principle of the 'broadly-based curriculum' appeared not to be reflected in practice. At each level of the system, we found claims to breadth and balance undermined by countervailing policies and practices: by Authority special projects favouring some areas at the expense of others; in central INSET provision; in PNP development fund allocations; in the distribution of posts of responsibility in schools; in school-based INSET; in the status of post-holders and the time they had to undertake their curriculum leadership responsibilities; in the areas of the curriculum subjected to review and development; in teacher expertise; and above all in the quality of children's classroom experiences. In the end, curriculum breadth and balance are less about time allocation than the diversity and challenge of what the child encounters. Moreover, if the goals of breadth and balance are to be achieved in the classroom they must be pursued at every other level of the system as well.

We undertook a comparative study of five areas of the curriculum – English, mathematics, science, humanities/environmental studies and art – and although acknowledging the many examples of stimulating and challenging practice, noted problems of imbalance in each of them. The National Curriculum may introduce a greater degree of consistency in respect of subject content, but quality in the way such content is treated will only be achieved if the anomalies at the various levels – LEA support, school curriculum management and development, classroom provision – are attended to.

The case of English, on which we assembled data relating to talking, listening and reading, was particularly significant. Classroom talk, despite the apparent conversational liveliness of many classrooms, could be shown on closer examination to be somewhat impoverished and unchallenging, with a general tendency to discourage children from asking their own questions and thinking things out for themselves, and a lack of informative feedback. Our analysis of reading scores at 7+ and 9+ from 1983 to 1991 showed no evidence that the injection of extra staff and money into Leeds primary schools, especially those in the inner city, had had a positive impact on children's reading ability, at least as measured by the Authority's tests. On the contrary, scores showed a very slight decline towards the end of the evaluation period, especially in the inner-city schools where PNP resources were concentrated. However, the situation in Leeds needs to be looked at in a national as well as a local context.

We have recommended that the Authority continues to monitor reading standards across the city but that the screening function of its traditional tests be taken over by National Curriculum Assessment at the end of Key Stage 1. It is also clear that reading must be accorded high priority in inner-city schools and that teachers in those schools need support in this endeavour. However, we have also stressed that any decline in reading standards in the inner city must be set firmly within the context of the political and economic circumstances which lead to poverty and social dislocation. Teachers and schools, however well-resourced and staffed, can only do so much to counter the effects of social disadvantage, and it is too easy to use them as scapegoats for the failure of political and economic policy.

Nevertheless, the reading scores analysis does raise important questions about the PNP strategy in general. It seems probable that if the programme had addressed the curriculum in a more direct and sharply focused way, concentrating attention and resources on particular curriculum areas at a time, then the impact on the quality of children's curriculum experiences, and hence on their learning, would have been much greater. In any event, though teachers continued to give reading their attention throughout the PNP period, it received very little attention in the Authority's INSET and support programmes.

The PRINDEP evaluation highlighted the primary curriculum as an area needing attention at three levels: Authority policy, school management and classroom practice. The National Curriculum will undoubtedly change matters to some degree at each of these levels, and indeed the situation in 1991 is already very different from that of 1985–89, but the National Curriculum cannot of itself provide the understanding, skills and commitments which are needed to prevent the weaknesses and inconsistencies we have identified from reappearing in another guise. In place of vague ideological statements and piecemeal policies the primary sector now needs a substantial programme of professional development and support aimed at enhancing the curriculum expertise of all its primary staff, and targeted in the first instance on those aspects of the curriculum where studies like this have identified the greatest problems.

TEACHING STRATEGIES

The Authority rightly identified teachers' classroom practice as a critical factor in children's learning, and gave it considerable prominence in documents, courses and the day-to-day work of its advisory staff in schools. The messages thus transmitted were more precise and sharply focused than those on curriculum. The general conception of 'good primary practice' was a consistent one, with the generation of a 'quality learning environment' accorded high priority.

Given the strongly visual and organisational emphasis, the impact in classrooms was readily apparent, and the Authority and schools can take considerable credit for a general improvement in the physical circumstances in which primary children and teachers work.

However, we expressed certain reservations about the prevailing approach. Though ostensibly child-centred, it paid rather more attention to teachers and classrooms than to children's learning. It presumed that the particular classroom layouts and patterns of organisation commended would promote children's learning more effectively than any others. It made much of 'flexibility', but in a way which implied that only certain versions of flexibility were permitted, and it failed to treat the notion of 'good practice' as the problematic issue it manifestly is.

That being so, teachers felt themselves to be under pressure to adopt practices whose efficacy we have shown to be debatable. The most notable examples were grouping, the practice of having a multiple curriculum focus in teaching sessions, with different groups working in different curriculum areas, and the kinds of teacher–pupil interaction associated with a commitment to discovery learning. The complex patterns of classroom organisation associated with the versions of good practice commended in Leeds require considerable skill on the part of the teacher. They make adequate monitoring of children's learning a particularly demanding task and children themselves may find that such arrangements reduce their opportunities for the quiet, concentrated study required by the reading and writing activities which dominate their curriculum. School and advisory staff need to look very closely at the balance of benefits and costs, for both children and teachers, in the teaching strategies and patterns of classroom organisation which have been so strongly promoted in recent years.

We found the issue of *time* to be revealing and important. While children were spending time on task and on different curriculum areas in similar proportions to those identified in other studies, it was also clear that such figures are by no means inevitable or appropriate. Although the time a child spends on task relates to many factors, including some beyond the teacher's control, the organisational complexity obtaining in many primary classrooms would seem to play a significant part. This underlines our sense that it is a grave mistake to pursue the notion of teaching strategies as somehow disconnected from children's learning on the one hand, and from teachers' intentions and attributes on the other.

Similarly, our analysis of how time was used across the curriculum provoked further challenges to conventional assumptions: that the way to do a subject justice is to give it more time; and that 'balance' is about the proportions of time given to the various subjects. We found it far more instructive to analyse balance in terms of the cross-curricular 'generic activities' of reading, writing, listening/looking, drawing/painting, collaboration and so on which are a universal feature of primary classroom life, regardless of the curriculum labels used. We identified, and questioned, the apparent imbalance in such generic activities. We argued for much greater prominence to be given to the potential of genuine pupil–pupil collaboration, and less to low-level writing, reading and drawing tasks. We noted the mismatch between the mainly solitary activities children were undertaking and the gregarious settings in which they were often expected to undertake them. It would seem to be a basic condition of effective classroom practice that the setting in which children work should be consistent with and supportive of the particular learning tasks they are given.

The quantitative and qualitative analyses of teacher–pupil interaction showed how vital a part it can play in children's learning, yet how easy it is to waste the very limited time teachers have to interact with each child. We argued for a more discriminating balance of questions, statements and instructions; for fewer pseudo-questions and more questions of a kind which encourage children to reason and speculate; for more opportunities for children themselves to ask their own questions and have these addressed; for oral feedback to children which without being negative is more exact and informative than mere praise; for both questioning and feedback to strike a balance between the *retrospective* function of assessing and responding to what has been learned so far, and the *prospective* function of taking the child's learning forward; and for much more use to be made of structured pupil–pupil interaction both as a learning tool and as a means of helping teachers to function in a more considered manner and therefore more effectively.

It is essential that all these issues be addressed openly, free from the sense, powerfully conveyed by some respondents, that pedagogical orthodoxies must not be challenged. The questions are clear: what kinds of learning should primary schools seek to promote, and what are the most effective ways of achieving them? It is here – with learning processes and educational outcomes rather than the 'learning environment' – that policy and planning for classroom practice should start.

Enhanced staffing under PNP enabled schools to break away from the tradition of one teacher per class and experiment with various forms of classroom-based professional collaboration. This proved to be one of the most significant aspects of PNP, and one which had, and has, considerable potential. We identified four essential dimensions of such collaborations, which we – and subsequently others – termed TTT (teachers teaching together): purposes, participants, collaborative style and pupil organisation. Applied to the practices emerging in the period 1985–89, this framework yielded a variety of ways in which TTT can help both children and teachers, and a diversity of forms that such collaborations can take.

However, we also identified problems that needed to be resolved: purposes have to be crystal clear; matters of status, leadership and the division of responsibility have to be negotiated; and all such collaborations have to be jointly planned. We therefore cautioned against seeing TTT as a panacea. If not properly thought through and implemented, it can be disruptive, disorganised and fraught with tensions between the teachers concerned – and therefore considerably less beneficial to children than the solo teaching it replaces.

Since teachers were the main resource in PNP, it is teaching – and hence learning – which should have benefited most from the Council's initiatives. There is little doubt that changes in teaching took place. However, the possibilities and limits of improvement were determined by a number of factors: existing classroom expertise, individual school and classroom circumstances, professional attitudes and commitments; and, framing all of these, the quality of the thinking which informed the appraisal of existing practice and the exploration of alternatives. In these respects, too, there was much variation between schools.

However, the lead given by the Authority in this regard was not a strong one. In an LEA where schools are encouraged to resolve these matters for themselves and in their own ways, the character of official thinking about classroom practice is not particularly important. But Leeds neither was nor is such an LEA, at least where its primary schools are concerned. The models of teaching it commended were expected to be influential, and the Authority saw itself as having a duty to provide a clear lead on the direction and character of primary classroom practice.

We have identified both strengths and achievements where classroom practice is concerned, particularly in the transformation of the physical settings in which teaching and learning take place, and the exploitation of the potential of classroom-based professional collaboration. However, if the Authority is to continue to seek to influence day-to-day classroom practice to this degree (and this itself is a proposition which must now be questioned) then certain fundamental changes are called for.

Thus, 'good primary practice' must cease to be presented as an uncontentious absolute. Good practice is conceptually and empirically problematic, and ought to be treated as such. It is inappropriate to act as though consensus exists (or should exist) over good practice, and doubly inappropriate to expect conformity to a particular version of it.

Much more account should be taken of the individual teacher in discussing classroom practice; the notion that a 'practice' can exist independently of the practitioner and can be imposed without regard for the individual's personality, intentions and preferences is both professionally demeaning and impractical.

Teaching needs to be discussed in a much more rounded and comprehensive way, with far less emphasis on surface aspects like display and resources; far more emphasis should be placed on the character of the minute-to-minute encounters which children have with teachers and one another, on the precise nature and purposes of the tasks they are given and the activities they undertake, and on the relationship of these and other aspects of the practice of teaching to learning.

Classroom organisation and teaching strategies need to be seen as means to an end, not as ends in themselves, and in order to allow this shift the ends or purposes need to be discussed and clarified. The dilemmas and compromises which are inherent to the task of teaching need to be honestly identified and openly confronted.

Above all, the notion that the LEA can be the sole definer, arbiter and guardian of good classroom practice must be abandoned. Expertise in such matters is as likely to be found in schools as in the LEA; but in any event good practice is defined and achieved dialectically and empirically, not by decree.

LINKS WITH PARENTS AND THE COMMUNITY

Although the fostering of links between schools, parents and the community was one of the main aims of PNP, it received notably less attention than the other three. There was no clear policy on this matter, only a series of apparently unrelated initiatives. By the end of PNP, despite PRINDEP findings and recommendations on this matter, policy was still awaited.

We found the lack of apparent commitment to this aim at Authority level reflected in the deployment of PNP resources. There was virtually no INSET, and schools felt that PNP resourcing had very little impact on what they did in the home–school area.

Nevertheless, our surveys showed schools undertaking a wide range of activities in pursuit of home–school rapport and cooperation, particularly where younger children were concerned, and many schools went well beyond the obvious activities like information exchange, open days and social events to pursue more adventurous and long-term programmes.

By the end of PNP, parent–teacher liaison had a higher profile, but this was mainly due to the need to meet the requirements of the 1988 Education Act and undertake consultations over school reorganisation.

There were three specific initiatives: home–school liaison officers, Portage, and the Early Education Support Agency. Of these, only the first was part of PNP and it proved to be the most problematic, partly for administrative reasons and partly because of the delicacy of the issues of culture and status which it raised. In any case, the HSLO initiative was on a very small scale. Nevertheless, in so far as it addressed the complex issue of home–school relationships in multi-ethnic contexts, it was an important initiative which deserves to be extended in some form.

The absence of policy and the paucity of central support and initiatives meant that the majority of schools devised their own home–school policies, strategies and roles. Some exploited PNP resources, especially enhanced staffing, for this purpose. But how they acted, and with what effect, depended mainly on the attitudes and commitments of heads. This is not to say that practice was unsatisfactory: rather that it was highly variable and that it mostly had little to do with PNP, despite the

Authority's intentions and despite its being written into the job specifications of PNP appointees.

We have to conclude that home–school links was the forgotten PNP
aim. Yet, paradoxically, the quality and character of the relationships
which are forged between a school, its parents and its immediate
community seem a much more appropriate focus for LEA policy than,
say, the fine detail of classroom practice. The whole structure and ambience of local government are community-centred: the electoral ward
system produces elected community representatives on councils; elected
members seek to respond to community needs and views and to safe-
guard community interests; and councils have a generous array of other
policies which engage directly with the quality of life which communities experience. Schools, and especially primary schools, have always
been regarded as essential to a concept of a complete community, and
many schools have taken their responsibilities and opportunities in this
regard very seriously.

It might also be argued that despite recent legislation (some would
say because of it) parent–teacher relations are still too often fraught with
fear, suspicion and misunderstanding; that there is still too much teacher
stereotyping of 'good' and 'bad' homes and parents; and that many
parents still lack power in relation to their parental rights and responsibilities. The Authority missed the opportunity to use PNP resources to
bring about change here: it needs now to explore other avenues. As with
classroom practice, it can learn much by attending to the best of what
is taking place in its schools.

MANAGING PNP IN THE SCHOOL

The Authority recognised that the effective management of PNP ideas
and resources within each school was critical to the programme's
success. Its main lever for change was enhanced staffing, and in particular the role of PNP coordinator.

The phase disparities in enhanced staffing were deliberate – the
programme was one of positive discrimination in favour of children and
schools with the greatest needs. However, the low enhancement in Phase
III raised the more general question of minimum effective levels. Though
any help is better than none, it is only when the enhancement is one
extra teacher or more that schools really acquire the flexibility in staffing
that they need if they are to carry through major reforms in curriculum
and classroom practice. Most Phase III schools received enhancement
well below this level. Moreover, the lack of seniority of most Phase III
appointees further reduced their potential to generate change. At the
other end of the scale, some Phase I schools were flooded with PNP
staff yet scarcely knew how to employ them.

It may well have been a more sensible policy, therefore, to make the Phase I/III disparity less extreme, and to use the resources to ensure that *all* schools were staffed on the 1986 Select Committee recommended basis of *n* registration groups plus one, with further pro rata adjustments for school size and specific challenges like those of the inner city. The current LMS formula should be kept under review with these issues in mind.

We identified a wide range of roles undertaken by PNP Scale I/MPG staff, with releasing class teachers and TTT most prominent. Because class size has always been a cause for complaint in primary schools, some heads used their staffing enhancement to create smaller classes. Such reductions might be marginal, and therefore the enhancement tended to have less impact than when it was used for cross-school initiatives. However, many staff deployed in the latter way encountered problems in working with colleagues. The Authority appeared to have underestimated these in its programme of INSET and support. Nevertheless, in many schools enhanced staffing stirred up traditional structures and assumptions to produce a more open and reflective professional climate.

The key role of PNP coordinator was applied to a variety of tasks, of which staff development, curriculum development and special needs were pre-eminent over the evaluation period as a whole. The initially strong emphasis on special educational needs (and the attendant confusion over whether PNP was a special or general needs programme) gave way to a concentration on curriculum development, mainly in response to the shifting national agenda.

Coordinators were initially expected to do far too much. Their success depended on a sensible and achievable role being negotiated with their heads, on heads' support, staff attitudes and their own skills. They were sometimes denied the authority necessary for the fulfilment of their expected role, and it was critically important that they were seen as part of a school's management team rather than being relegated to the position of mere facilitator. Thus empowered, they could achieve a great deal, particularly in the areas of curriculum development and staff support.

Though LMS is widely felt to have reduced the scope for staffing enhancement in primary schools, we believe it to be essential that schools retain the broader managerial repertoire which PNP has encouraged. Under PNP, schools have been able to break away from the traditional conception of primary school professional life centring on just two roles: those of head and class teacher. Although one person may not be able to combine the range of roles and tasks in the way that some coordinators have, it is perfectly possible to spread these across the staff as a whole and thus maintain the momentum of innovation and support. The

PNP coordinator idea, whatever its problems and imperfections in practice, represents a vision of professional collaboration, development and decision-making which primary schools can ill afford to abandon, least of all in the era of the National Curriculum.

New staff roles dictate new management structures. We identified six main types or clusters, and noted the way that recent changes under PNP and ERA have encouraged a shift, particularly in larger schools, towards three-tier and matrix management structures. While each school must evolve its own way of working, it is clear that the traditional two-tier model has limited capacity to cope with change on the scale now being experienced.

The role of deputy head was all too often a marginal one. All deputy heads need a clear job specification and a place in school development and decision-making commensurate with their experience and seniority.

Change challenges a school's capacities for receiving ideas, reviewing practices, and making decisions. During the PNP period, many Leeds primary schools acquired greater sophistication in such matters, and both understood and exploited delegated responsibilities and collegial action. Initially, they found their way by trial and error, as LEA support was concentrated elsewhere. Subsequently, the level of Authority investment in management training expanded considerably.

However, it is important to note and counter the limitations of mainstream approaches to management training, with their top-down assumptions, their tendency to exclude all but the head and senior staff, and their focus on strategies at the expense of educational purposes. Management has become a whole-school process, entailing that every member of staff has a managerial role of some kind, and it should be approached as such in any INSET or support programmes.

The exclusion of many heads from the development of PNP, and the attempt to use PNP coordinators to carry the Authority's versions of good practice directly from Merrion House to the classroom, had unfortunate consequences for both the success of the programme and school–LEA relationships.

Heads responded to advisory views of good practice in different ways, ranging from unthinking conformity to outright rejection. Such variation reflects as much on the Authority's style and the quality of its thinking as it does on the heads, and there is a clear need for much greater dialogue between the two levels. However, it is encouraging to note the recent evidence of greater consultation between school and Authority staff and the increased participation of teachers in Authority working parties.

Equally important was dialogue on matters of purpose and policy *within* each school, especially between head and staff. Without such dialogue, and the associated openness in management and decision-making, there could be a substantial gap between a school's espoused philosophy and its classroom practice. Heads' realisation of the head-ship role tended to fall into four main types. The more successful heads were those who remained in close touch with classroom realities and teachers' everyday concerns, who valued and developed individual staff potential, and encouraged collective decision-making.

However, while current challenges facing primary schools demand greater delegation and role specialisation than hitherto, it is essential that schools avoid the trap of over-bureaucratisation, and that they seek to retain and nurture the close informal collaboration which has always been an essential ingredient in effective school management.

We expressed concern about the poor quality of head–staff relation-ships in a minority of schools, admittedly not always the fault of the head but sometimes a consequence of autocratic behaviour at that level. Equally, we noted the resistance of a few heads to developing their own professional knowledge and awareness. Such characteristics could have a corrosive and debilitating effect on the entire staff of a school, to the obvious detriment of children as well as teachers. In such circumstances, the currently fashionable notion of 'closed-circuit' school-led INSET has clear limitations. The Authority needs to retain a significant stake in INSET run by itself and other institutions in order to prevent schools from simply recycling and reinforcing their own inadequacies.

SUPPORTING REFORM: THE ROLE OF THE LEA

PNP was an ambitious programme of reform, conceived on a large scale. The LEA's role in the programme was an interventionist rather than a facilitating one: it devised PNP's goals and strategy, and sought closely to influence and control the programme's implementation. The success of PNP at school and classroom level, therefore, is closely related to the role adopted by the LEA.

It would seem that in some respects the programme, and indeed wider aspects of the Authority's approach to primary education, were centralised to an excessive degree and that this generated reactions from heads and teachers which were both powerful and counter-productive. Much of their concern centred on what they saw as the imposition from above of particular versions of 'good primary practice' and the rela-tionship between teachers' allegiance to these and their career prospects.

The matter is a complex and delicate one, yet of all the findings from this evaluation it is one of the most pervasive and consistent, recurring in questionnaire responses and interviews, and validated by extensive observation. It also has serious implications for the professional health of the Authority and its schools, since the belief that getting on is merely a matter of saying and doing what significant others wish to hear and see produces not just disaffection and cynicism but also unthinking conformity and the loss of the professional analysis and debate which are essential to educational progress. Having said that, we stress that in some respects the problem may have been one of how the Authority was *perceived* rather than how it actually was.

PNP policy was embedded in the broader framework of Authority-thinking about children's needs, the curriculum, teaching strategies, classroom practice, school management and home–school relationships. These ideas had, and were intended to have, considerable influence at school and classroom levels. Because of this, they needed to be firmly grounded in careful analysis of the issues, and justified in terms of a coherent value-position, argument and evidence. These basic requirements were not often met, and teachers were confronted with, and expected to adopt, ideas which might be little more than expressions of officially endorsed belief.

Those constructing future policies and principles should strive to make them exemplary in this regard, not least because of the encouragement this will give to schools to be rigorous in their own thinking. The particular themes of PNP – needs, curriculum, teaching strategies, home and school – remain areas of central concern, and about each of them there is now a substantial body of conceptual and empirical material to be tapped, some of it in the twelve PRINDEP reports.

In any event, the experience of PNP raises important questions about the proper focus of an LEA's policies. We showed how in certain areas – for example, home–school links, the curriculum, and whole-school management – clear policies can be appropriate and helpful; and how in other areas – notably classroom practice – advisory staff seemed eager to prescribe in some detail how teachers should organise their classrooms and manage their teaching, a focus for policy and action at that level which seemed rather less appropriate. It would seem more apposite for the Authority to concentrate on identifying the goals and aspirations of the service, on raising teachers' educational sights and their expectations of children as high as possible, and on providing the opportunities and facilities for teachers to explore, debate and develop their own ways of achieving such goals, aspirations and expectations.

In the devising and implementing of PNP the Authority's advisory service was pivotal; it did much to raise the profile of primary education in Leeds, and to secure development on a number of significant fronts. Collectively, however, the service was not well regarded in the schools since it was seen to be enacting many of the tendencies referred to earlier. Yet individually, advisers and advisory teachers earned considerable respect for the extent and quality of support they provided. The workloads of advisory staff, and the physical circumstances in which they work at Merrion House, are unsatisfactory and should be reviewed.

The Authority's administrative services at Merrion House acquired a poor reputation, and efforts should be made to make them more accessible and responsive.

The Authority mounted a substantial in-service programme in support of PNP, which later merged with its general primary INSET programme. The range in content and style of these courses was considerable, and over the PNP period they focused on many aspects of the curriculum, on social issues, professional roles, classroom management, curriculum development and school management, and on specific areas of child need. This report has analysed the programme of courses mounted at the Primary Schools Centre, and the teacher-days spent on them. The Centre, developed as part of PNP, made a significant and welcome contribution to professional development in the Authority. Other INSET initiatives, particularly school-led INSET and management training, were being developed towards the end of the evaluation period but they were beyond the reach of PRINDEP's time and resources.

The success of these courses in influencing the quality of school and classroom practice depended on a number of factors, some of them – like the receptiveness of teachers attending them and the willingness of schools to encourage and accommodate change – beyond the control of the course providers. At the same time, there were two recurrent factors within providers' control: the clarity and appropriateness of the messages being conveyed, and the appropriateness of the methods used to convey them. Unfortunately, certain courses were characterised by diffuse or ambiguous messages, or by the tendency to unsubstantiated assertion and prescription referred to earlier.

Our study raised wider questions about INSET, and about professional development in general. We argued that the critical requirements in an INSET programme are that the very diverse needs of different teachers be recognised and addressed, that teachers themselves be central to the process of defining their needs, and that diverse needs be met by diverse provision, in respect of not just content and level, but also style and venue. The move to school-led INSET, in Leeds as elsewhere, has the potential to meet the first two of these requirements, but not necessarily the third. Accordingly, and referring to earlier anxieties about 'closed-circuit' professional development, we expressed certain reservations about the tendency of LEAs, with government encouragement, to put all their eggs in the basket of school-led INSET. Our analysis of the professional climate and management structures of primary schools suggests that such an approach would do more harm than good in some schools, and that it is therefore essential that a mixed economy for INSET be maintained, a minimum combination being provided by the school, the LEA and independent agencies.

The Authority devised a number of strategies for implementing PNP at both school and LEA levels. The key components were, at LEA level, the work of advisory staff, centralised INSET, and central administrative support; and at school level, enhanced staffing, the coordinator role, extra capitation and refurbishment. It is clear that enhanced staffing proved to be the single most potent strategy in the programme, though it was not without its problems, and the potential of some PNP appointments was frustrated by attitudes and decisions at the school level.

Two other points are also clear, however: first that heads ought also to have featured explicitly in the strategy from the outset, since their role proved to be critical; second, that there was a serious lack of *linkage* between the strategy's various components, particularly where advisory staff, heads, PNP coordinators and class teachers were concerned. By treating each of these as a separate constituency, rather than as a team, the Authority exacerbated the problems of communication, understanding and relationship referred to earlier, and reduced the programme's impact.

Although we have raised questions about the Authority's role and style, nothing can detract from the vision of increased educational opportunity and improved classroom practice which PNP represented, and PNP would not have come about unless the Authority had been fairly interventive in respect of the schools for which it was responsible. However, because the success of a policy depends in large measure on the way it is developed and implemented, and because the experience of PNP raised such serious questions in this regard, it became increasingly clear a review of Authority policies and procedures bearing on the work of primary schools was urgently required. The 1991 restructuring of the advisory service provided a timely opportunity to address some of these issues, though whether they were in fact addressed is beyond the scope or timescale of this particular study.

Chapter 9

The Primary Needs Programme: conclusions and recommendations

The summary of findings in the previous chapter has identified the main characteristics, gains and problems of the Primary Needs Programme, taking each of its aims in turn and then considering the framework of school management and LEA policy and action in which these aims were set. In this chapter we offer judgements of a more global kind before setting out some fifty-five specific recommendations to inform future policy, planning and practice in classrooms, schools and the LEA.

THE ACHIEVEMENTS OF THE PRIMARY NEEDS PROGRAMME

It is clear that the Primary Needs Programme had many positive and productive features. We would summarise these as follows:

1   The Authority's reversal of years of neglect, stagnation and under-resourcing by investing in primary education.

2   The commitment to positive discrimination in favour of children and schools having the greatest social and educational need.

3   The policy focus on four central aspects of the educational endeavour: children's needs, the curriculum, teaching strategies and links between school, home and community.

4   The generally equitable formula for distributing resources to those schools having most need of them.

5   The comprehensive programme for identifying, diagnosing and providing for children with special educational needs, and the related in-service support programme.

6   The initiatives taken to meet the needs of children from ethnic minority groups, and the effective, though small-scale, programmes aimed at combating racism and increasing multicultural understanding.

7 The attempt to tackle issues of equal opportunity and gender at every level of the system, from Council staffing policies down to classroom practice.

8 The attention given to improving the physical quality of the environment in which socially and materially disadvantaged children are educated.

9 The abandoning of the 'ring-fence' staffing policy and the introduction to Leeds schools of primary teachers from other parts of the country.

10 The use made of enhanced staffing to promote curriculum review and development at whole-school level through curriculum leadership.

11 The use made of enhanced staffing at classroom level to promote curriculum support and improvement through teachers teaching together (TTT).

12 The impact of TTT on special needs provision and professional development.

13 The use of increased capitation to extend schools' resources for teaching and learning.

14 The positive impact on classrooms of the Authority's concern with the physical environment of learning.

15 The use of enhanced staffing to foster and improve home–school–community relations.

16 The opening up, as a result of enhanced staffing, of new ways for teachers to work together in the classroom and the school.

17 The innovative and often influential role of PNP coordinator.

18 The move to more collaborative and collegial approaches to policy formulation and decision-making in some schools as a result of enhanced staffing in general and coordinator activity in particular.

19 The rationalisation of curriculum-related roles, the increased delegation of curriculum responsibilities, and the attention given to curriculum leadership.

20 The provision of much extended advisory and support teams for primary education.

21 The establishment of the Primary Schools Centre as a major venue for INSET and curriculum development.

22 The extensive and diverse programme of centralised INSET made available to primary teachers.

This list represents a substantial and undeniable achievement. At Authority level, policies were subjected to review, firm commitments were made, and substantial resources were allocated. At school level, the resources, at best, were used to the considerable advantage of both children and teachers.

We were commissioned by Leeds City Council to undertake a formative and summative evaluation of its reforms in primary education. The formative part of our brief was fulfilled in the series of interim reports which were published and disseminated between 1986 and 1990. This final report offers judgements of a summative kind, though not all of them can be as definitive or clear-cut as some readers might wish. However, the one judgement we cannot avoid, and which we must now venture, is a general assessment of the balance of cost and benefit.

On the basis of our evidence and analysis, therefore, we can conclude with confidence that PNP was an initiative well worth the Authority's investment.

Yet our analysis also shows that in conception and practice PNP was something of a curate's egg. Thus, if it were to be asked whether the £13.75 million was well spent, the answer would have to be that a different strategy might have given, in certain particulars, better value for money.

However, to those who will seek to capitalise on this judgement and on the problems which we have identified, we would point out that with a programme of such novelty and complexity the outcome could hardly be otherwise. The important thing is to learn from this experience. The extent to which those involved are prepared to do so is perhaps the most important test of the seriousness of their commitment to the long-term improvement of primary education.

In our view the Primary Needs Programme would have been even more effective if the following conditions had been met:

- The programme should have had a more considered and meaningful rationale, grounded in analysis of the issues and close attention to the national research evidence in respect of the various problems to be tackled.
- If the dominant concern was to be inner-city education, there should have been a full and radical re-assessment, before the programme started, of the needs of the children in question, having particular regard to the kinds of curriculum which would be most likely to counter the adverse effects of disadvantage and maximise these children's educational prospects.
- The extra resources should have been distributed to the city's primary schools in a way which responded to the particular needs and

challenges identified, yet also acknowledged the historical under-staffing of *all* primary schools, avoided the extremes of Phases I and III and ensured that every school had a staffing complement which permitted viable cross-school initiatives. In our view, the minimum enhancement should have been one extra teacher per school.

- To achieve and maintain sharpness of purpose the programme should have concentrated on a succession of carefully targeted aspects of learning, curriculum, teaching and management, putting the combined resources of staffing, capitation and in-service support behind each of these in turn.
- There should have been close consultation and cooperation between class teachers, PNP appointees, heads and advisory staff at every stage and on every aspect of the programme, so as to nurture a professional culture which was collaborative and negotiative rather than coercive, to ensure unity of purpose and the most economic use of resources, and to maximise teachers' sense of ownership of the process of reform.
- The LEA should have encouraged a style of engagement with the issues which was open and analytical, and which sought to develop teachers' and heads' professional knowledge, raise their expectations of their pupils, and extend their repertoire of ways of tackling the problems identified.
- The situations and dilemmas of practitioners – both heads and class teachers – should have been acknowledged, and efforts should have been made to enable these to be articulated and addressed.

THE LESSONS OF THE PRIMARY NEEDS PROGRAMME: RECOMMENDATIONS

Looking ahead now, there are a number of ways in which the Leeds LEA and its schools can build upon the gains of the Primary Needs Programme and learn from its problems. These are set out as recommendations.

1 The Authority should maintain its commitment to addressing the needs of specific groups of children in primary schools, but should extend the range of needs so addressed to include other groups.

2 The Authority should continue to seek ways of integrating its primary and special needs support activities and services.

3 The adequacy of school staffing to meet the needs of SEN and state-mented children in the context of LMS should be carefully monitored during and beyond the transitional period leading to full budgetary delegation.

4   An even greater investment than hitherto should be made in improving teachers' knowledge and understanding in the fields of multicultural education and gender.

5   More attention should be given to identifying appropriate day-to-day curriculum provision and classroom practice in the areas of multicultural education, equal opportunities and gender, and the experience of successful teachers should be more fully exploited.

6   Schools should ensure that they avoid management strategies which convey gender-specific messages about the curriculum.

7   The Authority should continue to acknowledge and meet the particular resource needs of inner-city schools as far as this is possible within the constraints of LMS. At the same time, it should move, and help schools to move, from a *resource*-dominated attack on the problem to a *curriculum*-dominated one.

8   Without reducing the quality of care and concern manifested for children experiencing social and/or material disadvantage, schools should strive to maximise the educational prospects of these children through the expectations teachers hold of them and the curricular experiences they provide.

9   The particular needs of very able children should be acknowledged and systematically addressed.

10   Every effort should be made, at both LEA and school levels, to raise teachers' expectations of what children can achieve. Without diminishing in any way their commitment to supporting children with specific needs and problems, the Authority and schools should now act to focus much more attention on children's *potential*.

11   Teachers should be helped to extend their skills of diagnosis and assessment in relation to all children.

12   The diversity of strategies for curriculum review and development which emerged during PNP should become part of the basic management repertoire of every school. Particular note should be made of the range of cross-school and classroom-based roles undertaken by the more successful PNP coordinators.

13   The skills required for curriculum leadership and development, and in particular those of working with colleagues and conducting and participating in meetings, should feature prominently in INSET.

14   Great care should be taken to ensure that the processes of curriculum review and development are applied to *all* areas of the curriculum, not just to the National Curriculum core subjects.

15 Care should also be taken to secure similar comprehensiveness and balance in the allocation of human and material resources to the various curriculum areas, at both LEA and school levels.

16 Schools should look carefully at the way time is used in the curriculum, adjusting the balance by achieving greater efficiency in the subjects allocated most time, and avoiding the strategy of using certain curriculum areas as time-fillers.

17 In reviewing the quality and balance of the curriculum, schools should also look at the range and balance of *generic activities* which their children experience in the classroom. Overall, it needs to be more clearly understood that curriculum balance is a multilayered problem involving resources, INSET, management, planning, time-tabling, classroom organisation and pupil–teacher interaction, and that to define and attempt to address the problem in terms of time allocations alone is inadequate.

18 The Authority should continue to monitor reading standards across the city, replacing current tests by ones which are more comprehensive in their focus; the screening function of existing Authority tests should be taken over by National Curriculum assessment.

19 While the concern with curriculum breadth and balance is of central importance, the Authority should target future curriculum initiatives more precisely and systematically, grounding their prioritisation in a careful analysis of need. Immediate priorities should include reading and spoken language.

20 The Authority's policies on the curriculum should be thoroughly reviewed, and attention should be given to enhancing the expertise of all staff with curricular responsibilities.

21 Without denying the importance of display, layout, resources and organisation, the emphasis in discussion of classroom practice in the Authority and its schools should now shift from these to *learning*: to its purposes and content; to strategies for diagnosis and assessment; and to extending the professional repertoire of strategies, tasks and activities for making learning happen.

22 The potential of collaborative group work and pupil–pupil discussion should be more fully explored and exploited.

23 The common practice, endorsed in Leeds and elsewhere, of multiple curriculum focus teaching, should be reviewed against two main criteria: its capacity to maximise children's learning and progress; and teachers' ability to manage such strategies successfully without reducing their opportunities for proper monitoring, diagnosis and

assessment. Where multiple curriculum focus teaching falls short on any of these counts, teachers should be encouraged and supported in the adoption of alternative strategies.

24 Attention should be given to ways of improving the quality of classroom talk and using it to stimulate and challenge children's thinking. In particular, more discriminating use should be made of questioning as a classroom strategy.

25 Teachers should maintain their commitment to giving pupils praise and encouragement. However, they should avoid devaluing these by indiscriminate use and should seek always to provide feedback to children which is precise and informative.

26 Teachers should look carefully at the way they invest their time in the classroom, ensuring that it is fairly and appropriately allocated in respect of all their pupils and each area of the curriculum. The 'unequal investment' strategy of neglecting certain pupils and certain curriculum areas in order to concentrate on others should be weighed against the entitlement of all pupils to appropriate attention and a curriculum of consistent quality.

27 Teachers should strive for match between the nature of the learning task and the context in which children undertake it. This is particularly important where solo tasks requiring quiet and concentration are concerned, given the near-universal adoption of group work and an ideology in which physical and verbal 'busyness' are deemed to be among the hallmarks of good practice.

28 The above points notwithstanding, the practice of making specific aspects of teaching and classroom organisation the subject of Authority policy or prescription should be abandoned, as should the Authority's model classroom. However, the amount of attention given to classroom practice in Authority and school INSET and advisory activity should not be reduced; rather, its emphasis and style should change radically. There should be more open discussion, analysis and weighing of evidence; more emphasis on the development of professional understanding and skill. Where a need appears to exist, as in the cases exemplified in the preceding paragraphs, the concern should be to help teachers explore and understand the nature of the problem and hence work out the most appropriate solution, rather than to present them with ready-made solutions to problems left undefined.

29 Though the process may take time (the problem being a historical and national one), all parties should strive to divest discussion of primary curriculum and classroom practice of its ideological and

rhetorical baggage, consciously seeking out a more open and analytical mode of discourse.

30   The Authority should abandon its role of definer, arbiter and keeper of 'good primary practice', opening up the issue to the alternative processes defined above, and placing classroom teachers at the centre of the debate. Class teachers should no longer be expected to conform to particular models of good practice, but should be encouraged and enabled instead to review alternatives, and the arguments and evidence for and against these, before making their own decisions. Good practice should henceforth be treated as problematic, rather than as an uncontentious absolute.

31   The potential of classroom-based professional collaboration (TTT) should continue to be exploited. Particular attention should be given to resolving the division of responsibility in classroom collaborations, to establishing clear agreement about purposes, and to joint planning.

32   Links between school, home and the community are a proper and necessary area for Authority policies, and these should be developed without delay.

33   In addition to the Home–school Liaison Officer experiment, the Authority should identify other roles and strategies to improve the quality of home–school cooperation.

34   The Authority's LMS formula should preserve weightings to support inner-city schools in their particular tasks, but the staffing discrepancies between these and other schools should be kept under close review to ensure that the extra resources are well used, and that other schools are not thereby prevented from undertaking their own developmental and support work.

35   The principle of staffing all but very small primary schools on the basis of one teacher for each registration group plus at least one extra should be pursued, notwithstanding the constraints of LMS.

36   Schools should seek to retain the *range* of managerial roles and strategies made possible by the introduction of PNP coordinators. In the absence of staffing on the PNP scale, such roles and strategies should be spread across the staff as a whole, rather than confined to one or two people.

37   Schools should adopt management structures consistent with the range of tasks they now, in the 1990s, have to undertake, and existing structures, together with roles, responsibilities and procedures, should be reviewed with the new agenda in mind.

38 All deputy heads should have a job specification and a place in school management and development commensurate with their experience and seniority.

39 The management needs of *all* staff, not just heads and senior staff, should be addressed in management INSET. Management should be tackled as a whole-school issue, entailing participation by all staff. Though effective management strategies are needed and must therefore feature prominently in INSET, they should be balanced by, and embedded in, a full exploration of the educational tasks which they exist to promote.

40 The Authority should ensure that it fully involves heads in the development of all future policies for primary education in the city.

41 Heads should likewise ensure that they involve all staff in the development of any school policies which affect their day-to-day work.

42 The Authority should give continued and substantial attention to the professional development of heads, especially those experiencing problems in professional relationships and those out of touch with current educational thinking.

43 The Authority should act to improve relationships with its primary schools.

44 In its approach to future policy-making the Authority should adopt and exemplify the approach it commends for schools: proper consultation, careful analysis of the issues, and full consideration of evidence from a variety of sources.

45 The Authority should provide resources and opportunities to meet the professional development needs of advisory staff as well as staff in schools.

46 Advisory staff should be properly accommodated and serviced, and their administrative burden should be reduced so that they can concentrate more on professional support.

47 The Authority should make its administration more accessible and responsive to the needs of schools.

48 The Authority and school governing bodies should act to maximise teachers' confidence in the processes of appointment and promotion.

49 A mixed economy of school-centred, LEA-provided and independent agency-provided INSET should be achieved. The Authority should ensure that it is always able to ensure externally based forms

of INSET in the case of schools without the professional capacity adequately to generate their own.

50   At the same time, teachers and schools should as far as possible be involved in identifying their own development needs.

51   Future strategies for school improvement should ensure that there is effective linkage and commonality of purpose among the various individuals and bodies concerned.

52   The Authority should take steps to ensure that it has full, up-to-date and readily accessible records on the factual and logistical bases of primary schooling, so as to aid policy-making and facilitate longer-term monitoring of the effectiveness of such policies.

53   Officers of the Authority and heads of all schools should seek to encourage a climate of professional discourse in respect of primary education which is more reflective, analytical and open to new ideas, less doctrinaire and dependent on ideology. The discourse should encompass the entire professional community, teachers being treated as partners in the enterprise rather than as subservient.

54   The Authority should review its roles and responsibilities in respect of children, curriculum, teaching, school management and professional development in primary education. In doing so it should identify those aspects of school life in which it is appropriate for it to invest and intervene, and those aspects which are more properly the concern of individual schools, noting our general conclusions that the current balance is neither appropriate nor conducive to school and staff development and that radical adjustment towards a much greater degree of school self-determination is therefore needed.

55   The 1991 review of advisory structures and roles should be extended to include the issues raised here.

Part II

Classroom practice and national policy: the sequel

Chapter 10

Winter initiative

Ministerial soundbites are nothing if not transitory. Education Minister Michael Fallon's assertion in 1991 that the Leeds report was 'devastating' and 'a parable for our times' could hardly be rated a considered judgement, except in so far as it reflected a sizing-up of political possibilities. Yet it captures well enough the comprehensive way that the Leeds report, and the initiative with which it dealt, were together caught up in the maelstrom of political and journalistic opportunism during the months preceding the 1992 general election. In this and the next chapter I shall show how one city's educational policies and practices became the catalyst for the national policy initiative known by some as the 'three wise men' inquiry which led to the DES primary discussion paper of Alexander *et al.* (1992), and how in turn this fed a broadening tide of concern about the effectiveness of British primary education in relation to the demands of the National Curriculum and in comparison with what is achieved in other countries. I shall also attempt to assess the impact of this initiative.

As I write this, over four years later, another general election is approaching and – in 1996 as in 1987 and 1991–92 – primary education has once again been staked out as a key electoral battleground. The 1991–92 headlines and slogans – word for word in many cases – have been dusted down and recycled. The absence of progress on these matters, in both public discourse and national policy, would be remarkable were it not so predictable. The story of what went on in one LEA between 1985 and 1991 may well have been symptomatic of the condition of primary education nationally at that time; however, the real 'parable for our times' in all this is not so much the Leeds report itself as what was done – and, equally significant, what was not done – with the report by others than the primary teachers who featured so prominently within it.

I need to make clear the nature – and limitations – of the perspective which these final chapters will offer. I am taking the reception and exploitation of the 1991 Leeds report, and the commissioning, writing, publication and reception of the 1992 DES primary discussion paper, both as episodes in recent educational history worthy of analysis in their own right and as useful illustrations of the educational policy process at work. However, while my personal involvement in both initiatives has the attraction of any 'inside story', by the same token it is also fraught with dangers. What the account may gain in terms of access to the unpublished details and private dynamics of the events in question it may lose in terms of the more distanced analysis which such events undoubtedly require. It is difficult for participants in controversial public events to resist the urge to present their own actions in the best possible light. It is hard, where blame is attributed, not to try to avoid it. It is tempting, when the going gets acrimonious, to respond in kind. The more an account gains in personal immediacy from the involvement of its author, the more it necessarily ignores the claims of other participants.

These dangers relate especially to the 1992 DES primary discussion paper. In Leeds, the policy commanding our interest was the Primary Needs Programme. The commissioned evaluation studied the policy, and its implementation, by triangulating many perspectives – those of teachers, heads, advisers, officers and external observers in particular. This book's appendix shows clearly the multiplicity of voices and viewpoints from which the accounts and judgements of PNP in the Leeds report were constructed. The construction process itself was strongly pluralist, since it was undertaken by a research team rather than one individual.

In contrast, when we consider the account in this and the next chapter of the national sequel to Leeds, the 1992 DES primary discussion paper, we have to note that one viewpoint predominates: that of just one of the paper's three authors. The politicians and ministry officials who devised the policy do not speak for themselves, nor do the teachers to whom it was directed, nor of course do the discussion paper's other two authors. All these people appear, and many are quoted, but they are viewed through a single lens, and the quotations are selected by a single hand.

However, an analysis is not necessarily more searching or accurate simply because it is delivered by someone not immediately involved. The external observer may not be in possession of all the facts; his or her perspective, notwithstanding the patina of disinterestedness, may be every bit as partial as that of the insider. Being outside a particular set of events is no guarantee of objectivity. If these problems are familiar territory to the historian, separated from events as he or she is by years or centuries, they bear even more heavily on the analyst of current affairs.

Thus, though readers will inevitably be conscious of the limitations of the perspective offered in these final chapters, they will not necessarily find it easy to adjudicate between the authority of the participant and the authority of the observer.

The three chapters function as follows. The present chapter is an insider's narrative of events surrounding the commissioning and writing of the 1992 primary discussion paper. It simply tells the story (or, rather, provides one version of that story), at this stage providing relatively limited theoretical framing. The chapter takes the story to the point where the 1991–92 national policy initiative on primary education entered the public domain as a published document, offered by government as 'a basis for the debate' about the quality of primary education.

Chapter 11 then shifts from narrative to a consideration of the 'debate' as it most prominently took place in three constituencies critical to its fortunes: in the media; among academics; and in the teaching profession. Thus, in terms of the framework for the policy process formulated by Bowe and Ball (1992), in which there are three policy 'contexts' – of 'influence', 'policy text production' and 'practice' – the present chapter focuses on the contexts of influence and policy text production in respect of the primary discussion paper, while Chapter 11 deals with the context of practice. Since the policy in question was ostensibly directed at influencing discourse as well as school and classroom action, we can legitimately take an eclectic view of what, in this particular case, 'practice' encompasses: not just the actions of teachers and pupils in classrooms, but also the various discourses which bear on those actions, in the media and among academics and politicians, as well as in schools.

However, if we do take this view, our analysis of the context of practice encounters an immediate difficulty. The media and academic debates were conducted in print; the professional debate – random published responses and commentaries from some LEAs and professional associations apart – was conducted by word of mouth and, more often than not, behind the closed doors of individual schools. It was relatively elusive and fragmented. It was constituted in part of countless formal and informal conversations between teachers, in part of private readings and reflections. In turn, in the light of these conversations, readings and reflections, the classroom decisions and actions of individual teachers might or might not be subjected to some degree of modification.

It is therefore easier to engage with the media and academic debates than with the considerably more complex and elusive professional one. Yet if we accept in good faith the claim that the discussion paper was intended to contribute to the improvement of the quality of teaching and learning, the professional debate was far more important than the other two. Moreover, if, as Bowe and Ball argue, educational policies are not so much *implemented* by practitioners as *re-created* by them, then for a policy which explicitly invites such re-creation (in the way that the primary discussion paper did but legislation, typically, does not) what teachers did with the discussion paper is of critical importance to our understanding not just of the policy's success but also its very character. The chapter considers the evidence about the professional debate surrounding the primary discussion paper, while accepting, perforce, that so far this evidence is very limited.

Finally, Chapter 12 sets the two policy/practice 'cases' – Leeds and the primary discussion paper – in a more generalised analytic frame, focusing in particular on the question begged by both studies, how we should define quality, effectiveness or 'good practice' in primary education.

First, however, we return to the events of 1991.

SEIZING THE MOMENT

On 17 April 1991, a Deputy Secretary at the Department of Education and Science (precursor to the Department for Education and Employment) had prepared for ministers and senior officials a memorandum entitled 'Improving Primary Education' (DES 1991i). It contained an assessment of the main weaknesses of England's primary schools, analysed the main obstacles to progress, and set out policy options, drawing heavily on evidence from HMI and the Department itself. It made a particular point of identifying inner-city schools as resistant to the government's post-1988 reforms, deploying the frequently repeated 'stubborn statistic' of 20 per cent to quantify the level of inadequacy, and argued that though the reform programme did not encompass teaching methods, they nevertheless were as much in need of reform as curriculum, assessment, school governance, budgetary delegation and the other matters addressed by legislation. Significantly, however, the paper did not confine its analysis to these politically attractive themes. It also argued that the demographic and financial problems facing primary schools were worse than at any time for twenty years, with class sizes continuing to rise and the long-standing imbalance of resources between secondary and primary schools disadvantaging the latter more than ever.

In attributing the problems of primary education to structural as well as pedagogical deficiencies, the DES paper gave advice which, however well-founded, was also likely to be unacceptable politically. The cue for some kind of inquiry on teaching methods was what the government eventually chose to respond to, while the arguments about class sizes and underfunding were rejected, then and on several occasions subsequently, as we shall see. Indeed, government's refusal to countenance this analysis meant that structure and pedagogy were increasingly presented as mutually exclusive, as if the 'problem' of primary education was either (in the eyes of government) poor teaching or (as seen by the unions) lack of resources, but never a combination of these, let alone the possibility that resourcing might have an impact on teaching quality; similarly, each side caricatured the other's preferred solution as (unions of government) 'teacher bashing' or (government of unions) 'throwing money at the problem'.

That the Leeds initiative combined substantial expenditure with problematic pedagogy was thus bound to offer more of an advantage in this continuing and carefully nurtured stand-off to government than to teachers, unions or LEAs, especially when the LEA in question was Labour-controlled.

Primary education, then, was on the government's policy agenda for some time before the Leeds report was published. For example, during 1990–91, reports on the implementation of the National Curriculum from the inspectorate and the National Curriculum Council (DES 1989i, 1991j, 1991k; NCC 1991) were pointing up problems in curriculum planning and subject expertise in primary schools, especially in Key Stage 2. At about the same time, the Centre for Policy Studies (CPS), a right-wing think tank, was mounting an attack on existing approaches to the training of teachers on the grounds that these delivered irrelevant theory and left-wing ideology rather than practical guidance (Lawlor 1990), and the government itself was intensifying its arguments for shifting training from higher education institutions to schools.

On this matter it might have been advised to tread rather carefully, because the courses in question were being run in accordance with criteria the government itself had laid down (DES 1984, 1989h), and were being policed by a quango (CATE, the Council for the Accreditation of Teacher Education) whose members had been hand-picked by ministers themselves. Indeed, from 1990–91, ministers did not merely approve membership nominations for CATE; they also personally vetted them, subjecting several nominees to the full rigours of a ministerial interview, presumably in order to satisfy themselves that such nominees were ideologically 'one of us'. Whether they succeeded in ensuring the ideological unanimity or purity of CATE is much more doubtful.

Nevertheless, the assault on the higher education wing of what ministers and their advisers called the 'educational establishment' intensified during 1990–91, fuelled by press sensationalising of episodes like that of Annis Garfield, the Cambridge graduate who was rejected for entry to a teacher-training course in her own name, but accepted in the guise of 'Sharon Shrill', an Afro-Caribbean animal rights campaigner – thus ostensibly demonstrating that teacher trainers were more interested in political correctness than talent; and of Culloden Primary School in London, featured in a television programme for its progressive practices and dogged espousal of the 'real books' approach to the teaching of reading, and then heavily criticised for the latter in an HMI report.

The replacement of John MacGregor as Secretary of State for Education by the much more confrontational Kenneth Clarke had already raised the political temperature of the education debate. His track record on applying market theories to the reform of the police and the health service had spread considerable alarm in the education service in advance of his arrival at the DES in place of the relatively emollient MacGregor. What he needed, however, was something more substantial by way of evidence against the educational establishment than isolated cases like Sharon Shrill and Culloden.

The final evaluation report on the Leeds Primary Needs Programme – Part I of this book – was presented to Leeds City Council on 31 July 1991. Its findings, conclusions and recommendations were accepted in full and an action plan was approved which sought to address the latter. A joint Leeds City Council/Leeds University press release was then issued and the usual circulation to schools, governing bodies, libraries and so on – as described in this book's Introduction – was set in train. There was some nervousness about the capacity of sections of the press and the Conservative Party to make mischief whenever there was a conjunction of primary education and Labour LEAs. However, many in Leeds believed that the mischief-makers would be unlikely to stir themselves from their summer retreats in Tuscany and Provence and that by the time they returned the story would be dead.

They were wrong. The press were alert, they had few other stories (though barely two weeks later the Leeds affair would have been eclipsed by the attempted *coup* against Mikhail Gorbachev), and at the DES the ministerial team had left one of its number, Michael Fallon, on watch. Most national newspapers covered the story, the *Times Educational Supplement* gave it extensive treatment, and 2 August being a Friday, the story was still fresh enough for a reprise the following Sunday. The articles in the main sought to present the Leeds initiative as an extravagant failure. Few mentioned the overall conclusion of the report (page 173) – that 'on the basis of our evidence and analysis . . . we can conclude that PNP was an initiative well worth the Authority's investment' or the list of twenty-two 'positive and productive features' (pages 171–3) which preceded it. The recurring themes in the stories, often reduced to caricature, were the same throughout: declining educational standards as indicated by reading scores; the pervasiveness of 'trendy' progressive teaching methods; the baleful and repressive influence of a Labour LEA and its advisers; and, more generally, of an educational establishment of inspectors, teacher-trainers and – the ultimate British insult – intellectuals and theorists.

Thus, a complex and carefully qualified analysis was reduced to a simple pathology. The cure for the condition thus identified was equally straightforward: return to chalk-and-talk methods, introduce subject teaching, abolish inspectors, advisers and teacher-trainers, and train all teachers in the classroom (Burchill 1991; Lawlor 1990). The two glaring contradictions in this supposed cure for the ills of primary education – that the new generation of teachers who would put things right were to be trained by the very people whose practice was deemed so deficient, and that the evidence against the theory-bound educational 'establishment' was itself a prime example of that establishment going about its proper business of conducting educational research – were never addressed.

Attempts to limit the damage caused by this one-sided treatment of the Leeds report were probably doomed from the start, though not for want of trying. Officers and friends of the LEA wrote their own accounts (for example, Johnson 1992; Spooner 1992). Some used a variety of other strategies to contain the fall-out and minimise the damage, including, as a last resort, seeking to discredit the report and its author. Officers of the LEA and I, separately and jointly, undertook interviews with newspapers and on radio and television, though in one case an invitation to write a piece about the report for a national Sunday newspaper was withdrawn at the last moment for fear that what I wrote might be, as the journalist in question put it, 'too balanced'. I had letters published in those newspapers whose accounts were factually inaccurate or loaded beyond the (undefined) bounds of 'fair comment'. I wrote articles for professional weeklies like the *Times Educational Supplement* (Alexander 1991b). I circulated my own summary of the report to every chief education officer in Britain (Alexander 1991c), drawing attention to the discrepancies between the press coverage and what the document actually said and inviting them to copy the summary to advisers, inspectors, elected members, teachers and others in their LEAs as they saw fit. I worked with Routledge to secure the earliest possible publication of the report for readers outside Leeds. I responded to more than 1,200 letters, mainly from teachers, parents and members of the public. Finally, I spoke to groups of primary heads and teachers in a large proportion of these LEAs (including, of course, Leeds itself) during the period covering the publication of the Leeds report in 1991 and the DES primary discussion paper in 1992.

I do not propose to offer a detailed analysis of the press coverage of the Leeds report, or of the important relationship which this episode illustrates about the relationship between the media and the policy process in education. It is almost certainly better that this task be undertaken by someone less directly involved, and indeed a research study is currently (1996) under way on just this theme, using Leeds and the 1992 primary discussion paper as case material (Wallace 1993). But because the way the press handled events like these had such a powerful impact on the climate of educational discourse during this period and subsequently, I shall need to give a few further examples in what follows.

It is important to remind ourselves of the political climate into which
the Leeds report was launched. A Conservative administration was
approaching a general election after an unbroken spell in office of twelve
years but with rather less confidence than it had displayed at equivalent
junctures in 1983 and 1987. The government had recently experienced a
traumatic change of leadership and the eruption of ideological differences which had been kept very much on a leash during the Thatcher
years. In contrast, the main opposition party was displaying unprecedented unity of purpose.

During this period education had featured prominently on the political agenda. In 1988 the government had used its impregnable majority
to force through the Education Reform Act, the most radical piece of
educational legislation since the Butler Act of 1944. After decades of
laissez-faire, control of curriculum content was placed firmly in the hands
of central government. A national curriculum of ten subjects (nine at the
primary stage), together with religious education, was introduced
progressively from September 1989. School accountability to both parents
and government was formalised through a number of measures heralded
in the 1988 Act and consolidated in the 1991 Parents' Charter: open enrol-
ment, or the right of parents to send their child to the school of their
choice; a national system of assessment at ages 7, 11, 14 and 16; mandatory annual reports on each child's progress; regular and public reports
on every school; and area school performance tables. School self-determination was increased through the delegation of budgetary control
from LEAs to individual schools, through a parallel delegation of INSET
budgets, and through the right of schools to seek Grant Maintained
Status or to 'opt out'.

As part of this process the 'educational establishment', as we have
seen, was subjected to considerable pressure. LEA power was diminished, though as agents of quality assurance LEA advisers and inspectors retained far greater influence than many of their opponents
had hoped. Initial teacher training institutions were subjected to an
intense barrage of criticism, including an unprecedentedly vitriolic attack
from the Prime Minister himself, about the supposed inadequacy and
irrelevance of their courses. This did not always square with the rather
more positive reports and surveys on initial training provided by HMI
(DES 1982b, 1988c); but the days of the HMI, too, appeared to be
numbered. After a brief internal inquiry, the government announced in
1991 that the inspectorate would be cut from 480 to 175, the central
inspection function which it had fulfilled for over 150 years would be
taken over by teams of inspectors appointed locally, and in 1992 OFSTED
was born.

For those with reasonably good memories much of the press coverage conveyed a sense of *déjà vu*. Though controversy about reading

standards, progressive primary teaching and the relevance or otherwise of theory have been a familiar part of the educational scene for several decades, the previous time the controversy peaked in the way it did over the Leeds report was in the 1970s. Then the initiative was seized by a group of commentators who were portrayed as uniformly right-wing but who in fact held fairly diverse views. In a series of 'Black Papers' published between 1969 and 1977 (Cox and Dyson 1971, 1974; Cox and Boyson 1975, 1977), they mounted a sustained attack on two targets: the egalitarian principles embodied in the then relatively new comprehensive schools; and progressivism, particularly in primary education. The initiatives which had prompted the developments of which the Black Paper authors were so critical were the Labour government's 1965 circular requesting LEAs to submit plans for replacing selection at age 11 by a comprehensive system, and the 1967 publication of the Plowden report.

Within the second theme, progressivism, the concerns were very similar to those voiced in the wake of the Leeds report. Thus, evidence was cited (Cox and Boyson 1975) for a decline in reading standards; complaints were made about the 'lottery' which allowed one child to experience a broad curriculum, another a curriculum which barely extended beyond the 'basics'; and about 'the progressive shibboleths of reading readiness, free expression, team teaching and integrated days'.

The solutions, too, look familiar. Thus, presaging the 1990s advocacy of school-based teacher training: 'Teachers do not need longer training. . . . They want both a spell as a pupil-teacher apprentice to a skilled teacher and to be taught the techniques of teaching and a body of subject knowledge which they can pass on to their pupils.' And, fore-shadowing key elements in the 1988 legislation:

> National standards . . . could be laid down for the 7, 11 and 14 year old and should be the minimum standards for all pupils of over 70 IQ. . . . The 7+ examination should cover literacy and numeracy and pupils should be expected to pass such a test before they pass to junior school. The 11+ and 14+ tests should also cover a body of minimum geographical, historical, scientific and literary knowledge. Teachers could teach beyond these basic syllabuses and could introduce other subjects; but such syllabuses would ensure that all schools offered a reasonable education, which is not now the case. . . . The enforcement of the 7+, 11+. and 14+ national tests . . . would ensure standards.
>
> (Cox and Boyson 1975: 4)

Evidence which could be used to support such criticisms and recommendations emerged with increasing frequency over the next decade or so: the William Tyndale primary school affair in 1975 which was billed as indissolubly coupling extreme progressivism with wilful or incompetent management and leftist politics (Auld 1976); Neville Bennett's apparent rebuttal of progressive methods (Bennett 1976); the 1978 HMI primary survey (DES 1978b) which for the first time charted the extent of curriculum inconsistency claimed by commentators like those cited above, and similarly targeted follow-up surveys of first and middle schools; the important sequence of primary school and classroom studies of the 1980s from Galton, Bennett, Mortimore, Tizard and others, to which we have already referred at several points and which gave to the debate about primary teaching methods a precision which the earlier rhetoric had lacked; and the questioning by a number of commentators, including the present author, of the conceptual adequacy of the ideas and values by which some of the observed school and classroom practice was sustained (Dearden 1968, 1976; Entwistle 1970; Alexander 1984).

Yet, despite this, the story of post-war primary education has been one of remarkable continuity and consistency. Each new *cause célèbre* has produced discomfort which, though acute, has usually been short-lived. It was this persistence in the face of apparently incontrovertible evidence which fuelled the frustrations of those seeking radical change, and their belief that such change was being blocked by an educational establishment which was far more committed to protecting its members' interests than to educating children.

Hence, with the publication of the Leeds report – which by linking classroom, school and LEA provided ammunition more comprehensive and coherent than that offered in the earlier classroom studies – the charges most characteristically expressed in the *Daily Telegraph*:

> A generation of wasted time. . . . The education of millions of primary school children has been blighted in the name of an anarchic ideology. . . . The 'progressive' theories that have dominated primary school education for the past 25 years have been exposed as a fraud. . . . This anarchic regime was rigorously imposed from the top. Teachers believed that if they did not toe the line they would not be promoted. . . . Equivalent in educational terms to the breaching of the Berlin Wall and the dismantling of the Soviet Empire, the report should pave the way for a long-awaited return to classroom sanity . . . it is clear that it will become a significant landmark in the history of primary education.
>
> Clare 1991

Can one change educational practice by railing against it? Probably not: such attacks engender solidarity rather than self-awareness, defensiveness rather than introspection. As politicians have increasingly come to understand, professions are extremely slow to change of their own volition, and tend particularly to resist change which rides on the back of charges of incompetence or self-interest. Even the more judiciously couched appeals to professional goodwill and expertise may achieve little in a climate of suspicion and antagonism. That being so, a government's more effective strategy is legislation. If change cannot be achieved by consent then it must be mandated. The adversarial encounters then serve a different, softening-up purpose: of marshalling and manipulating public opinion, isolating the professions in question, and creating the climate in which draconian measures seem to offer the only solution.

The National Curriculum effectively exemplifies this process at work, the more so as the evidence for the need for legislated change seemed so convincing. Witness, for example, the long-running and not particularly successful attempts by central government between 1977 and 1988 to persuade LEAs to take seriously their statutory obligation to have coherent policies on the curriculum (DES 1977, 1979, 1983).

The National Curriculum is an important example in another respect: its assumption that to effect genuine change what is mandated needs to penetrate to the deeper levels of educational *structures*: in this case, the character and scope of the subjects of which the new curriculum is constituted. However, the government initially failed to realise what in this book we have constantly emphasised, that content and pedagogy are indissolubly linked. By 1991, as we saw in the DES memorandum quoted on page 186, they had come to recognise that the key to the transformation of curriculum content was the transformation of pedagogy. Yet the 1988 Act and subsequent ministerial pronouncements had explicitly stated – as we ourselves have done in relation to the Leeds initiative – that the important decisions about pedagogy are those taken by teachers at the level of the classroom, and it is therefore with teachers that responsibility for pedagogy should rest. Opening up, therefore, was a vision of the government's commitment to raising educational standards through its reforms of curriculum and assessment being frustrated by primary teachers' continued control of classroom practice.

Indeed, it could be argued that the professional conditions with which government were now coming to terms had already ensured that the impact of progressivism, in its pure form at least, had been rather less than either its proponents hoped or its detractors feared. My own analysis suggests that the progressive revolution – which was centrally about pedagogy – was frustrated in part by the persistence of nineteenth-century assumptions about curriculum content. In its early days the National Curriculum was to some extent domesticated by pressing it as far as possible into the Plowden mould (Alexander 1995: 270–314). Thus – if the analysis is correct – does a culture protect itself.

Ministerial interest in the Leeds report showed itself promptly. Within a fortnight of its appearance, Junior Minister Michael Fallon had indicated that his team would be trawling the report for policy implications. At that stage he highlighted, interestingly, not errant teachers but the report's recommendation that primary schools needed to be staffed more generously in order to give them a better chance of delivering on their statutory obligations: this interest, having cost implications, proved short-lived.

In September, the report was used to buttress a strong assault on progressivism and Labour LEAs by John Major, speaking to his first Conservative Party Conference as Prime Minister:

> We will take no lectures from those who led the long march of medi-ocrity through our schools. What Labour governments did and what all too many Labour councils are still doing is unforgivable. I will fight for my belief. My belief is a return to basics in education. The progressive theorists have had their say and, Mr President, they've had their day.
>
> Major 1992

On cue, the national press, which had flagged but then relinquished the story in August, now scented further mileage and returned to it with gusto: the theme ran, pretty well uninterrupted, until the announcement of the 'three wise men' inquiry in December.

On 16 September, I received two invitations from the Department of Education and Science: first, to address officials and HMI about the Leeds report and its implications 'for national and local policies as well as for practice in primary schools'; second, to meet Minister of State Tim Eggar privately. Both of these meetings took place a month later, on 16 October. At the first meeting, which was also attended by Minister Michael Fallon, I entered caveats about the limits to national generalisations from a local study before selecting five issues for analysis and discussion:

- views and expectations of children in primary classrooms, and the teaching skills and strategies needed for accurate diagnosis and assessment;
- the problem of curriculum breadth and balance, in both the classroom and national policy;
- the quality of teaching of English, and its relationship to classroom organisation and pupil–teacher discourse;
- classroom practice in general, and the need to explore prevailing notions of 'good practice' in particular;
- the staffing of primary schools and its relationship to educational quality.

I then offered comments on a number of wider policy issues, most of them already prefigured in the summary of the report I had by then sent to all LEAs:

- inner city education;
- initial teacher training, especially the need for a twin-track approach to the development of subject knowledge and pedagogic skill and the dangers of a wholesale rush into school-based training;
- inspection and quality assurance;
- the future of LEAs, arguing for a strong and continuing, though modified, role in the provision of state education;
- research priorities, especially in the area of school and classroom effectiveness;
- the class teacher system, and the need both for a debate about how best to staff primary schools and resources to ensure that the best could be delivered;
- a plea for the prevailing blanket assault on educational theory to be replaced by an acknowledgement that theory is an essential prerequisite to intelligent professional action and that the issue was not theory *per se* but the validity of certain theoretical positions.

(Alexander 1991d)

The meeting with Tim Eggar was more sharply focused on action. In the context of the government's reform brief to the Council for the Accreditation of Teacher Education (CATE), of which I was at that time a member, we spent some time on the need for any statement about the reform of primary training – a circular on the reform of secondary training (DFE 1992) had already been published – to avoid pre-empting the review of primary school staffing which I was urging. In this context, too, we also looked at the limited capacity of the funding system, with its sharp discrepancy between funding levels for primary and secondary schools, to deliver the flexibility and expertise which primary schools needed. However, an official advised Eggar that the balance of funding was a matter for LEAs, not government – a line which the government repeated in its response to the 1994 Education Select Committee report on this matter (House of Commons 1994a, b) and several times subsequently. (Remembering this meeting, I attempted to pre-empt such a response in my own evidence to the Select Committee (Alexander 1994c) but to no avail.)

Immediately after the meeting I wrote two papers for ministers and officials. One was a detailed analysis of the relationship between school staffing and educational quality in the primary sector; the other, in the form of a letter to Eggar, was a more compressed version of this analysis which ended with a plea for avoiding the 'quick fix' and argued instead for a proper inquiry into the contingent issues of educational quality, professional expertise, school staffing, initial training and in-service teacher development in the primary sector (Alexander

1991e, 1991f). By this time, informal conversations had started about the possibility of my working with the then Chief Inspector for Primary Education, Jim Rose, on some kind of discussion paper along these lines.

Outside, the fuss about the Leeds report showed no signs of abating. On 1 November, Minister Michael Fallon opened the NAHT primary conference with a strong endorsement of what he took to be the report's attack on prevailing primary practice, offering useful soundbites like 'much happiness and painting but very little learning' (Fallon 1991). As the conference that year took place in Yorkshire, there were a number of Leeds heads present and at least one strenuously challenged Fallon's version of the report. However, NAHT General Secretary David Hart rounded off the conference with his own extrapolation, including, surprisingly, the claim that the report stated that 'on average, children wasted 40 per cent of each school day' (Hart 1991). As we show on pages 75–6, this claim, first made by the *Daily Telegraph* on 19 September, was based on a misreading of the relevant section of the report and an invalid generalisation from a small sub-sample of Leeds teachers to the national teacher population. Nevertheless, this particular version of the report was now so firmly established, notwithstanding my directly challenging it in a letter to the newspaper in question (Alexander 1991g), that the journalist responsible, John Clare, was able to recycle it on several subsequent occasions between 1991 and 1996, when this book went to press. For example:

> [Most primary classrooms] now resemble noisy, aimless nurseries with an emphasis on fun rather than learning. One consequence was vividly described in 1991 by Robin Alexander. ... At the end of a five-year study of what went on in the 'progressive' classrooms of 231 schools, he and his researchers concluded that on average children were wasting 40% of each school day. ... The educational consequences of this nonsense came to light only slowly, not least because local authorities and schools conspired – as they still do – to suppress the evidence, particularly of falling standards in reading.
>
> *Daily Telegraph*, 26 January 1996

Once a myth has taken hold in this way, it is not easily dislodged. By the same token, it is difficult to challenge the gratuitous charge of LEA conspiracy, even though the LEA in question, Leeds, had in fact made its 7+ and 9+ reading scores available throughout the period of our research and had been happy for us to disseminate an interim analysis of these scores three years before the final report and its attendant publicity (PRINDEP 1988c).

THE 'WINTER INITIATIVE' OF 1991–92

Department officials were by now preparing the ground for the annual policy stock-taking at Chevening in November. This was to be the last such meeting – involving the full ministerial team, senior officials and senior members of the inspectorate – before the 1992 general election, and was to delineate the thrust of the government's pre-election education initiatives. Some of the briefing material ranged over what was by now familiar territory: excessive variability in standards of work within and between primary schools; the continuing impact of child-centred rhetoric; the weakness of topic work, especially as a medium for delivering the National Curriculum; the particular problems of primary schools at the geographical, social and demographic extremes in rural areas and the inner cities; curriculum overload and manageability, and the damaging impact of the demands of the National Curriculum on the teaching of basic skills.

Other briefing papers set a rather different agenda. In one, from officials, the arguments for and against the government's authorising a full review of the National Curriculum Orders at Key Stages 1 and 2 were rehearsed (the problems of curriculum overload were not acknowledged until a year later, when in September 1992 NCC Chairman David Pascall promised the review; however, it was not until April 1993 that his successor, Ron Dearing, actually initiated the review procedure). Alongside this acknowledgement of the problems consequent upon government policy were uncompromising references to 'incompetent post-Plowden approaches' and the 'malign influence' of LEA advisers. Much was made of the relevant sections of the Leeds report (chapters 3, 4, 7 and 9 in this version), and phrases with soundbite potential like 'taboo on didacticism' and 'pseudo-questioning' together with the now familiar '40 per cent of lesson time which. . . . on average, is wasted' were highlighted and stored for future use (DES 1991).

In this latter document, too, the idea of a discussion paper was taken further. A package of initiatives was proposed which included

> the publication (by the National Curriculum Council) of a document (based on Alexander's analysis) which reviews current models of curriculum organisation and classroom management in the light of National Curriculum demands. The tone would not be prescriptive, but the aim would be to challenge assumptions and lead towards a serious consideration of alternative possibilities.
>
> (DES 1991l: 3)

Although, naturally, I do not have access to the minutes of discussions at Chevening, I understand that primary education and teacher training were identified as the two main targets for a ministerial 'winter initiative' and that the Secretary of State decided to commission a document, along the lines set out above, from Chief Inspector Rose and myself. The teacher-training part of the initiative was to be a further push towards school-based training and the reform of primary training along similar lines to those proposed under DES Circular 9/92 for secondary. This, however, would need to be deferred until after the publication of the Rose/Alexander document. Immediately after Chevening, on 13 November, the terms of reference for the latter were firmed up as:

> Taking into account available evidence about the delivery of education in primary schools, to make recommendations about curriculum organisation, teaching methods and classroom practice appropriate for the successful implementation of the National Curriculum, particularly at Key Stage 2.
>
> (DES 1991m: 3)

The memorandum containing this recommendation set a time scale of just over two months (to the beginning of February 1992) and even anticipated the press coverage by calling it 'the report of two wise men'. Rose and I, having known each other for several years, were happy to work together, and, in any case, from our conversations since the DES seminar on 16 October it had become clear that an initiative along these lines was a probability. However, we did register some concern, aggravated by the sexism and exclusivity of 'wise men', that there were to be no women working with us: in 1991 over 80 per cent of primary teachers, and an even larger proportion of early-years teachers, not to mention half the pupil population, were female.

In the days which followed, the remit was clarified. One issue which was to prove decisive was the relationship of our work to that of the National Curriculum Council. NCC was preparing the ground for its own foray into pedagogy – which in a sense had now replaced the curriculum as the 'secret garden' of educational practice decried by ministers ever since Sir David Eccles' famous speech in 1960. Like ministers, NCC had pinpointed changed pedagogy as one of the keys to successful delivery of the National Curriculum, and it was made clear in the early briefings on the primary discussion paper that we would need to 'avoid treading on NCC toes'.

Nevertheless, it was without NCC involvement that we went ahead. Rose and I mapped out a structure, timetable and division of labour to take us through to late January 1992. The early drafts included outlines of many of the sections which were to appear in the paper as published, and there was a firm commitment to grounding the entire document in evidence from research and inspection. However, there were two important differences.

First, examination of the problems schools were having in implementing the National Curriculum, and the whole area of curriculum
overload and manageability, featured much more prominently in our
initial plans than they were allowed to in the document's execution.

Second, the document's working title – 'Classroom practice, curriculum expertise and staff deployment' – retained the emphasis of the
October discussions at DES on the need to treat as contingent the questions of educational quality, staffing and resources. However, in the
paper as finally published, though we made strong statements about the
primary/secondary funding differential, the question of National Curriculum manageability was confined to the three paragraphs of Chapter 6
and various brief references scattered elsewhere, and the staff deployment question was made subsidiary to that of professional competence.

From now on events moved very fast, and it became clear that the
stakes in what started as a deliberately low-key, albeit significant, initiative were to be raised considerably. In late November two events
occurred which put the entire initiative on a different footing. In this
tale of media–policy interdependence it was significant that one involved
the government and the other the BBC.

On 26 November, Rose and I attended a final briefing meeting at the
DES. Seated in shirtsleeves and braces behind an intimidating mound
of sandwiches, Secretary of State Kenneth Clarke reminded us of our
timetable and remit, both of which were already well understood. Then,
abruptly casting aside such familiarities, he announced that he was
adding to the team of Rose and myself a third member, NCC Chief
Executive Chris Woodhead.

The problem at that stage, it must be said immediately, concerned the
office of NCC Chief Executive rather than the person of its incumbent.
Changing our terms of reference in this way, I felt, could damage our
credibility as independent commentators on the vital matter of the
impact of the National Curriculum on teachers and teaching in primary
schools, and I said so. I was not alone: senior officials, and Eggar himself,
also challenged Clarke's decision, arguing strenuously against it on
similar grounds. They seemed as startled by his announcement as were
Rose and I. Clarke stood firm, insisting that if the inquiry was to encompass the National Curriculum he could hardly justify to the NCC the
exclusion of one of their senior officers. He hinted that NCC had
subjected him to considerable pressure on this score. It seems reasonable to infer that influence at an even higher level had been brought to
bear, since the then Chairman of NCC, David Pascall, had been a
member of Prime Minister Margaret Thatcher's policy unit and was in
close touch with her successor, John Major.

After the meeting, I informed officials that unless the decision were
reversed I would have to pull out. Early the next morning, Eggar tele-

phoned me at home to urge me to stay in. He indicated that he himself had continued to press for a two-person independent study, but had been overruled by Clarke. He also said that he was particularly concerned that the initiative, which he saw as very much his own, should somehow steer the debate about primary education away from the sterile trading of slogans about 'traditional' and 'progressive' into a mode of discourse more in tune with the complexities of the tasks now confronting primary schools, but that in this he was fighting a losing battle both within the ministerial team and the Conservative Party. Under strong pressure, I agreed to remain on the inquiry, but on three conditions, to which Eggar immediately agreed: first, that our independence should be preserved and respected; second, that we would be writing from individual rather than institutional standpoints; third, that whatever we eventually wrote should be published and disseminated as it stood, without the departmental vetting to which such commissions are normally subjected.

Eggar's apparent disenchantment over the hijacking of the initiative for cruder political purposes than he had intended was confirmed in an interview which he gave subsequently to George Low of *Education* (Low 1992). In this interview Eggar apparently asserted that the harder line adopted by Clarke was the result of intense lobbying by Fallon and right-wing interests within the Conservative Party, and that Fallon's 'much happiness and painting but very little learning' speech at the NAHT primary conference on 1 November (page 196) had caused alarm and dismay among more moderate opinion within the Department, almost destroying the initiative before it had started. My reading of several of the briefing documents prepared by Department officials and HMI in connection with the initiative (some of which are referred to above) indicates that there was no shortage either of moderate opinion or of careful and balanced analysis in the advice which ministers were given at this time.

I suspect that the expansion of our team was only partly to do with preserving good relations between the DES and NCC, as claimed by Clarke. One commonly voiced suggestion was that ministers felt that Rose and I might be in need of a 'minder' to prevent further inflammation of the sensitive issue of National Curriculum manageability and to discourage equivocation on the matter of primary school teaching methods, on which Clarke was to make his own distinctly unequivocal views very clear in his subsequent announcement of this initiative.

THE PANORAMA AFFAIR

A more public confirmation of the way the political temperature of the post-Leeds debate was being raised came with the BBC *Panorama* programme 'Class Wars' on 25 November, the evening before the final briefing with Clarke. In October, I and others in Leeds, including several LEA officers and primary school heads, were approached by a BBC researcher with a view to our participating in a programme which would be devoted, we were told, to a careful and balanced exploration of the issues surrounding the government's assault on progressivism, especially as expressed in Prime Minister Major's recent speech at the Conservative Party Conference (see page 194). The Leeds report, the Language in the National Curriculum (LINC) project and visits to teacher training institutions would provide the main foci, allowing viewers to test government claims that its reforms, and the wider battle to raise educational standards, were being frustrated or subverted by the educational establishment – whether left-wing LEAs, progressive teachers or bag-carrying teacher-trainers. For the Leeds section, the *Panorama* team proposed to combine footage from Leeds primary schools with interviews with me, heads, LEA officers, the Secretary of State and the opposition spokesman on education (Jack Straw).

Anxious about the way media treatment of Leeds and the report seemed by that time to be spinning wildly out of control, I wrote to the LEA to suggest that notwithstanding the high reputation of *Panorama* the programme 'could easily backfire, and my own view [is] that if they want to do a programme about primary education they ought to go anywhere but Leeds, since the political and media risks here are now too high' (Alexander 1991h). The LEA replied that they shared my anxiety but felt that they should participate (Leeds City Council 1991d). The programme was duly put together. It included various interviews together with extensive footage from two Leeds schools, one on the fringes of the city and one inner-city school with a high proportion of children from ethnic minority groups. The latter school had benefited substantially from the Primary Needs Programme.

In view of what followed, Leeds may have had cause to regret its openness, yet this was entirely consistent with its stance since 1985, when it had given our evaluation team unrestrained access to schools, people and documents and had facilitated publication and dissemination of all our reports. The one comment which those who were so critical of Leeds never made was that it was a sound example of that 'open government' which featured so prominently in Conservative Party rhetoric. Would the DES then, or the DFEE now, have opened its doors to researchers in the way that Leeds City Council did in 1996-90, and, after enduring a barrage of adverse publicity, did again in 1991?

A few days before transmission, I was shown a copy of the summary of the *Panorama* programme which had been prepared for the Secretary of State to enable him to judge how best to pitch his own contribution. This was something which, apparently, he had insisted on ever since being embarrassingly 'doorstepped' while in a previous ministry, Health. In my state of possible oversensitivity to such matters, I felt that my anxiety about the likely fall-out from the programme was now justified. On the basis of what this summary conveyed, I also believed that viewers could well be left with the impression that the Leeds report was little more than a crude attack on progressivism and that I was less a researcher than an educational fundamentalist. I immediately told the production team of my concern and asked for my interview footage to be removed. Understandably, since part of the programme revolved round the Leeds report and its author, they were reluctant to do this, but agreed to reduce my contribution to a single brief statement.

It was evident that many in Leeds and beyond were extremely unhappy with the *Panorama* programme as transmitted on 25 November. They believed that the schools footage had been manipulated to confirm the primary school image of 'much happiness and painting but very little learning' which ministers and much of the press were at that time so relentlessly conveying. Such was the force and number of the objections that the BBC commissioned Barraclough Carey Productions to feature the *Panorama* programme in their *Biteback* series, chaired by Julian Pettifer. On this occasion, objectors to the programme would have a chance to air their views and challenge its producer and presenter face-to-face.

I was asked to take part in the programme, but by that time (see below) the primary discussion paper initiative had been launched, and I felt obliged to respond that it would not be proper of me to participate in a discussion which would inevitably spill over into the issues which the Alexander/Rose/Woodhead inquiry was likely to consider. *Biteback* asked me instead to send them any observations about the *Panorama* programme in writing, and I set these down in a brief letter on 11 December (Alexander 1991i). My main complaint was about balance and the selection which had been made from the available footage. The following day a member of the *Panorama* team telephoned me to say that he regarded my comments as defamatory and that unless I withdrew them he would take legal action against me. After receiving advice from various sources, I withdrew not my comments as such, but permission for Barraclough Carey to use them on *Biteback*.

The programme went ahead on 13 December, with contributors from Leeds and elsewhere voicing criticisms at least as trenchant as those contained in my letter. After the transmission, *Biteback* wrote to say that they would be making a formal complaint to the BBC about the *Panorama* member's intervention, which they regarded as unwarranted interference by the BBC in a task which the BBC had itself commissioned.

I include reference to this episode for three reasons. First, to illustrate the central part played by the media in shaping the debate about primary education during this highly charged period. Second – a theme to which we shall return in the analysis of the press treatment of the 1992 primary discussion paper in Chapter 11 – to show the ruthlessness with which news values are pursued, and defended against criticism or erosion. Third, to reinforce this section's general thesis – the 'parable for our times' referred to earlier – that by 1991–92, as again in 1995–96, reasoned public discourse about the quality of state education, of a kind which respects the complexity of evidence and eschews crude sloganising, had become all but impossible. The second and third of these themes are explored more fully by Ball (1990) and Wallace (1993). Wallace's analysis includes a detailed study of the *Panorama* programme referred to above.

LAUNCHING THE PRIMARY INITIATIVE

In between the *Panorama* and *Biteback* programmes, Kenneth Clarke had launched the primary initiative. On 3 December he issued a lengthy statement to the press in which the announcement that he had commissioned the Alexander/Rose/Woodhead discussion paper was embedded in a detailed presentation of his own agenda for a reform of primary school teaching methods which would support the 1988 Education Act's reform of curriculum content.

Clarke's statement stressed that 'questions about how to teach are not for Government to determine' and that he had 'no intention to seek to extend [his] powers in that direction'. He also anticipated the discussion paper's subsequent commendation of a varied and flexible pedagogical repertoire: 'There is no single, magic formula that suits every pupil and every teacher. It is important to move away from fixed notions of teaching methodology' – a view which he would presumably have wished to apply as firmly to the nostrums of the chalk-and-talk tendency as to the Plowdenite 'dogmatic orthodoxy about how children should be taught' which in the same paper he so strongly deplored (DES 1991n). He made much of the Leeds findings, and referred also to other British research and inspection evidence and to HMI's comparative study of primary teachers in England and France (DES 1991o).

On 11 December, Clarke's statement was sent with a covering letter to all heads of primary, special and independent schools in England, and to LEAs and teacher-training institutions. The general view at the time was that in expatiating upon the very topic on which he had commissioned a supposedly independent discussion paper, Clarke was giving a less than gentle steer to the paper's authors, as well as putting down a political marker making absolutely clear his own views on the state of primary education irrespective of what the paper might come up with – insurance, perhaps, against the possibility that the paper might not live up to the hype.

The press, of course, had their by now familiar field-day, ignoring the middle ground which Clarke's statement had in fact included: 'Back to tried and tested methods, Clarke tells teachers' . . . 'Clarke heralds new school era' . . . 'Go back to old ways, Clarke tells teachers' . . . 'The pendulum swings back for teaching . . . the counter-revolution Kenneth Clarke plans for primary schools' . . . 'Back to the blackboard at primaries' . . . 'Clarke backs return to formal lessons' . . . 'Happiness but little learning' . . . 'Schools to end modern lessons . . . Clarke frees pupils from grip of Sixties' . . . 'Dynamo Ken' . . . 'Man of the hour' . . . 'Clarke school probe' . . . 'Clarke shuts the classroom door on 25 years of trendy teaching' . . . and, of course, 'Back to basics'. All this, one needs perhaps to note, before a word of the discussion paper had been written.

Once again, the ground was clearly and simply staked out: the fault lay with the 1967 Plowden report and the thousands of teachers, advisers and teacher trainers who had been influenced by it; the solution was a return to those practices which Plowden was accused of supplanting.

The combined pre-emptive strike by Clarke and the media – more or less repeated as soon as the document was published – had two serious consequences. First, it turned many of those involved in primary education against the initiative from the outset (though I did receive many letters urging me to resist the prevailing line); second, it made extremely difficult the later task of demonstrating that the discussion paper as published was not what it was portrayed as, and indeed of underlining its proper status as a *discussion* paper rather than a definitive report. In a study of this initiative to which I shall refer in greater detail in the next chapter, Woods and Wenham (1995) advance the argument that 'the career of the discussion paper might be conceived of as falling into two stages, the political and the educational', and that only when it had served its political purpose could the paper be reclaimed as the professional document it purported to be. In the winter of 1991 we were firmly locked into the political stage.

WRITING THE DISCUSSION PAPER

The time-scale was tight in the extreme. The initial tasks were to agree the paper's structure, establish and access its base of evidence, and determine a division of labour for extrapolating from and presenting this evidence in draft form. I had been seconded full-time from Leeds University; Rose and Woodhead continued other duties at DES and NCC. It was therefore inevitable that I would take the largest share at the drafting stage.

The structure remained much as Rose and I had mapped it out before our team was expanded to three members. The structural changes were in weight and placing within chapters rather than in theme. Thus, for example, where the first version of the paper's structure had substantive sections on 'Modifying the National Curriculum' and 'Modifying National Curriculum Assessment', the final version had a single, rather generalised section of three paragraphs on National Curriculum matters. However, as significant as these structural adjustments were the considerable changes to the document's *tone*.

Gathering evidence

The evidential base of the paper – about which some academic commentators expressed strong reservations which will be discussed in the next chapter – was substantial. This was not to be an inquiry of the kind which would call witnesses, commission research, make visits and so on in the manner of the great post-war reports like Newsom, Crowther, Robbins, Bullock, Cockcroft and of course Plowden, but an interrogation of evidence which already existed in accessible form. The timetable, and the resources allowed – three individuals, one working entirely on his own, the other two given some degree of support from HMI and NCC – were dramatically different from those available to the inquiries exemplified; in any case, our brief itself – a discussion paper rather than a report – was much more modest.

The sources were listed on pages 55–62 of the paper as published, under three headings: 'Publications', 'Unpublished research material' and 'Other sources'. The ninety-six publications under the first heading include both UK and international material, and a mixture of academic research and reports from agencies like HMI, DES, NCC and SEAC (the initiative preceded the arrival of OFSTED, the DES's change of name to DFE and then DFEE, and the merger of NCC and SEAC into the unitary SCAA).

The 'unpublished research material' and 'other sources' were considerably more extensive as resources and significant in their impact than their brief mention in the discussion paper's second paragraph and its final page might imply. The unpublished material was solicited from two sources: HMI, and academics working in relevant fields. HMI had an extensive database from its programme of inspections of schools and teacher training institutions. Only a proportion of this found its way into the published HMI institutional reports and surveys. The rest was available for calling up in response to specific inquiries by ministers, and much remained unused. We were able to tap this vast pool of material on a number of issues: the discussion of standards of achievement in primary schools in chapter 3; the references to the incidence and character of practices like whole-class teaching, streaming, ability grouping, group work, individual work, topics, matching and so on which featured in chapter 4; the discussion of the expertise and deployment of teachers and heads in chapters 7 and 8; and the material on initial teacher training and in-service professional development in chapter 9. In this matter, a number of HMIs undertook searches of the database on our behalf and drafted summaries.

That this large body of source material is not referenced properly in the discussion paper is the result of one of what I believe were two tactical mistakes we made over the way the evidence should be presented. The first was not to adopt the academic convention of referencing in the body of the text, for fear that it would detract from the paper's concern to speak directly and accessibly to serving teachers (Alexander *et al.* 1992: para. 5); the second, born of a certain sensitivity among HMI about the wisdom of admitting to a vast, useful but unused body of data on important educational matters, was to refer only in the most general terms to the HMI database.

To bring ourselves up to date with available research, and to enable a wider range of expertise to be involved in producing the paper, we not only involved a number of HMI but also deliberately solicited contributions from the academic community. Thus, on 4 December, the day after Clarke launched the initiative, I wrote on behalf of the three discussion paper authors to twenty-five academics known to be undertaking, or to have undertaken, research bearing on the questions of pupil performance, pedagogy, school improvement, National Curriculum implementation and other matters germane to our remit:

> One of the immediate tasks for the group is to assess what the enquiries undertaken by NCC, HMI and academics and researchers like yourself *really* have to say about the pros and cons of particular approaches to curriculum organisation and classroom practice in primary schools, once all the silly rhetoric of the past few months is stripped away. We shall obviously look at the published material, but I wonder if you would be prepared to be drawn more directly into the enquiry, not least in relation to work which you may be at present undertaking in connection with the National Curriculum and which may not yet have seen the light of day.

I then set out nine headings under which we would welcome their comments:

1   Evidence about any rise/decline in standards of achievement in primary schools.

2   The main strengths of primary classroom practice as currently undertaken.

3 The main weaknesses of primary classroom practice as currently undertaken.

4 Evidence about the efficacy or otherwise of particular ways of organising the curriculum – subjects, themes, topics and so on.

5 The key areas of expertise required by primary teachers in order to deliver the National Curriculum and assessment at (a) KS1 and (b) KS2.

6 Ways in which primary classroom practice needs to change in order to become more effective at promoting learning at (a) KS1 and (b) KS2.

7 Ways in which the role of primary teacher itself needs to be modified from the current norm of generalist class teacher with subject specialism for cross-school consultancy. Again, this may need to be subject-specific.

8 Ways in which the expertise identified in (5) and/or the role(s) identified at (7) can best be acquired/trained for in ITT.

9 Any other insights your work offers on improving the quality of primary teaching and the training of primary teachers.

(Alexander 1991j)

Finally, I asked for bibliographic details of those of their publications which informed the responses given, so that these could be included in the paper's list of references.

We received replies from the following: Neville Bennett, Exeter University; Alan Blyth, formerly of Liverpool University; Patricia Broadfoot, Bristol University; Jim Campbell, Warwick University; Paul Croll, Bristol Polytechnic; Charles Desforges, Exeter University; John Elliott, University of East Anglia; Maurice Galton, Leicester University; David Hargreaves, Cambridge University; Wynne Harlen, Scottish Council for Research in Education; Seamus Hegarty, National Foundation for Educational Research; David McNamara, Hull University; Peter Mortimore, London University Institute of Education; Jennifer Nias, Cambridge Institute of Education; Andrew Pollard, Bristol Polytechnic; Diane Shorrocks, Leeds University; Brian Simon, formerly Leicester University; Sally Tomlinson, University of Wales; Peter Woods, Open University; Ted Wragg, Exeter University.

Those familiar with the work of these people will recognise the diversity of interest, methodology and value-orientation which the list encompasses. In particular, it includes the full gamut of attitudes to government educational policy, from broad or partial acceptance through acquiescence or pragmatism to opposition, and there is no sense in which those named here can be defined as representing anything remotely approaching the coherence of outlook implied by terms like 'the educational establishment', whether that establishment is deemed to be of the left, right or centre.

Most of the responses ran to several pages (and, combined, would make an authoritative compendium of research on primary teaching in their own right). Several respondents sent copies of recent articles, some in draft or pre-publication form. Some sent not one but two such submissions. At the same time as offering comments under the headings in my letter, which the majority did, several sounded notes of warning or scepticism, usually along the lines that neither Clarke nor any other Secretary of State would be likely to allow research such as we were surveying to inform policy. In the words of one respondent: 'Policy is decided elsewhere. Research will be used to justify it.'

The material provided by the individuals named above was drawn on extensively in the discussion paper, especially for the chapters on standards of achievement (3), the quality of teaching in primary classrooms (4 and 6) and strengthening curriculum expertise (7). At the same time, we received unsolicited written submissions from several national organisations, including the Campaign for State Education, the National Union of Teachers, the National Association for Primary Education, the British Psychological Society, Teachers of Advanced Courses for Teachers of Young Children, In Education, the Design and Technology Association, the School Natural Science Society, the United Kingdom Reading Association, the Grubb Institute, and the County Education Officers Society; from several LEAs, including Leeds, from many primary schools, and from a large number of individuals. These, too, were scrutinised and incorporated where possible.

The problem with the way in the paper as published our sources were not cited in text was not just the legitimate criticism (Hammersley and Scarth 1993; Dadds 1992) that it prevented readers from checking for themselves that specific statements were as well-grounded in evidence as they needed to be. This strategy also allowed those unsympathetic to the paper or to Clarke's initiative to claim that in a more fundamental way it was empirically weak or at best selective. In fact, the evidential base was extensive and very thoroughly examined; and although, as already noted, the initiative was in no way comparable to a formal commission of inquiry, it was considerably more than a mere literature review, for the procedure outlined above enabled us to draw on the contributions, prepared with this initiative specifically in mind, of a significant number of expert witnesses. The real problem, apart from the strategic error over referencing, was that the careful, qualified style of the early drafts became increasingly overlaid with the tough and uncompromising rhetoric of the political soundbite.

The drafting process

Apart from Christmas Day, we worked non-stop on the paper between early December 1991 and 22 January 1992, when it was launched by Clarke at a press conference. The drafting was done in our separate offices and homes, linked by telephones and faxes, and we met every few days in London, York (the headquarters of NCC) or elsewhere to attempt to resolve the questions of substance and style which became increasingly problematic as we proceeded.

Each of us took responsibility for drafting specific sections. Maurice Galton's critique of the discussion paper speculates with reasonable accuracy on who drafted what (Galton 1995: 89–92). However, the real test of the collaboration which Clarke had engineered came when the drafts were shared, modified and welded into a single text. The natural division of labour – and the one dictated by the acute pressure of time – was for the member of the trio with the lightest drafting load to take on the task of overall editing.

It quickly became evident not only that we had different perspectives on matters of substance – which was to be expected – but that we also differed radically on the vital matter of presentation. The main substantive sticking points were the extent of the problems in primary classrooms which documents like the Leeds report had charted, the causes of these problems, and the most appropriate solutions to them; there was also considerable argument over teacher training.

For example, did low expectations of pupils, over-complex patterns of classroom organisation or inadequate subject knowledge among teachers pervade the entire system or were they confined to a relatively limited part of it? Had standards in pupil attainment in reading and mathematics in the United Kingdom risen or fallen? And in answering these questions how should the research and inspection evidence be interpreted? Or what was the balance of responsibility for such problems and difficulties as between the various constituencies – teachers, LEAs, teacher-trainers, government agencies like NCC, SEAC and HMI, and government itself? Or would the system improve most rapidly through grass-roots reform undertaken, with appropriate support, by the profession itself, through top-down revolutionary measures like transferring teacher training wholesale from higher education to schools, through structural transformation in matters like funding and staffing, or through a combination of these?

Even if these matters could be resolved, there was then the question of presentation. All three of us wanted the document to be straightforward and accessible to its readers, but beyond this point of agreement there were two opposing views. One was to conform to the discussion paper format as originally proposed: a document which would raise questions, respect the limitations as well as the power of the evidence examined, provide a corrective to the polarised rhetoric of the previous few months, and encourage rather than foreclose the intelligent analysis of these matters which was so sorely needed. The alternative was to go for something more decisive, and more in tune with Clarke's own robust manner: no ambiguities, no qualifications, a short, simple and prescriptive document which would define both good and bad teaching, castigate the latter, and come up with clear conclusions and recommendations. In turn, the argument over presentation no doubt reflected differences in perception as to who the audience for the paper really was: the teachers to whom Clarke had written on 11 December, the media, Prime Minister Major and the restive right wing of his party, or the electorate.

The document as eventually published reflects all these tensions, and our failure to resolve them. Given where each of us had come from, the acute pressure to which we were subject, and the fraught political climate in which we were working, this failure was inevitable. As a result, and to an extent which few of its academic critics appear to have registered, the paper is extremely uneven in tone, veering between tough talking and carefully qualified analysis, between blaming and understanding, between defining issues as simple and acknowledging their complexity. After the initial setting out of individual positions, the writing process which these inconsistencies reflect had become a contest: in part, the familiar struggle between the drafter's desire to preserve the substantive and stylistic integrity of what he has drafted, and the editor's wish to modify this material in line with his own imperatives of message, style and audience; in part, a profound and intractable clash of personal agendas and values.

The consequences of the drafting/editing mode we adopted, in terms of the politics of the discussion paper's production, were in fact identified while it was being written. In a letter which I wrote to the other two on 6 January 1992 I noted:

> I had assumed that the person who agreed to do the spadework for each section would be responsible for working that section up into the final version, in the light of the comments offered by the other two. We would then, and only then, need to look at the whole thing to check for continuity, flow, overlap and so on. This procedure would have given us a genuinely collaborative document, whereas what we now seem to be heading for is a managerialist one: x supplies draft material which y refashions into something else. That may seem like a common-sense way to get the job done, but it's actually a critical shift because it puts control of the document into the hands of the person who takes on the editing function.

Expressed like this, the problem may seem somewhat abstract. The example below (a comparison of the second draft and final version of paragraphs 73–75 in the discussion paper, dealing with breadth, balance and consistency in the curriculum) shows how this procedure might not only reduce length and transform style, but could also modify the message:

Whatever pattern of curriculum organisation is chosen, the breadth, balance and consistency of the curriculum as experienced by the child must always be of central concern.

In the 1970s and 1980s, evidence accumulated of major problems in this area. The scope and balance of the primary curriculum varied widely both between schools and within them. Thus, although no school neglected what were then called the 'basics' of language and mathematics, what was covered in these two areas, and more particularly what children experienced in the other subjects, displayed a degree of inconsistency which was generally regarded as unacceptable. There was also the problem of balance *within* subjects – the neglect of reading extension, oral work, and mathematical problem-solving being examples from subjects which in overall terms received ample time, a fact which should remind us that time allocated is not necessarily the best measure of curriculum quality.

Is the National Curriculum the answer to this problem? In a simple sense it is, because it lays down both the overall scope of the curriculum and the requirements for each subject. However, evidence obtained since 1989 by HMI, NCC, Campbell and others suggests that we now have a severe problem of overcrowding in the primary phase. Before 1989 it was the non-core areas which tended to be squeezed, sometimes out of existence. Since then, the situation has become more complicated. Art, music and PE, not to mention aspects of the wider curriculum not covered by the 1988 Act, are being compromised by the pressure to accommodate the considerable demands of the core subjects. At the same time, some aspects of the core subjects themselves, notably reading, are also being squeezed as teachers concentrate their attention on the hitherto less familiar attainment targets.

In other words, there is a need to address now the question of the proper balance of the various attainment targets across the statutory curriculum and to identify the point at which a tightly-specified curriculum becomes counter-productive in terms of overall quality. At the same time, we need to be alert to the possibility that some at least of the problems are in the nature of teething troubles, and that alternative modes of curriculum organisation, coupled with more effective uses of classroom time (see below) would reduce the pressure.

(Alexander *et al.* 1992, second draft of paras 73–5)

73 Whatever the mode of curriculum organisation, the breadth, balance and consistency of the curriculum experienced by pupils must be of central concern.

74 There is considerable evidence that prior to the introduction of the National Curriculum there were significant and unacceptable variations in the curriculum provided between and even within schools. While all schools devoted considerable amounts of time to English and mathematics, some neglected important aspects of these subjects such as reading extension, oral work and mathematical problem-solving. Others failed, moreover, to devote adequate attention to history, geography, art and music. The National Curriculum was introduced, in part, to ensure that all children have access to a broad and balanced curriculum that is consistent country-wide.

75 Concerns are now being expressed over the pressure of time which the core subjects are perceived to be exerting on the time available to teach other curriculum areas. And some aspects of the core subjects themselves, notably reading, appear to be squeezed as teachers concentrate their attention on hitherto less familiar attainment targets. These may well be transitional problems inevitable in a period of radical curriculum change. But the structure of the National Curriculum as a whole and the weight of detail in individual subjects will need to be kept under careful review so that we can be confident that the curriculum experienced by pupils is appropriately broad and balanced, but, nonetheless, rigorous.

(Alexander *et al.* 1992: paras 73–5)

There is scope here for close and illuminating comparison. The stylistic shift, from a relatively discursive and qualified mode to a more condensed, terse and authoritative one, is readily evident. As for the argument, suffice it to say that while, in a sense, the core message of the passage – that curriculum breadth and balance were problems in English primary education after the arrival of the National Curriculum as well as before it, and that the reforms would therefore need to be reviewed – has been retained, the editing has transformed the message's emphasis. In particular, while the draft presented the claimed efficacy of the National Curriculum as an open question, the final version took it as given (a stance for which the discussion paper was widely criticised). In the process, politically inflammatory phrases like 'Evidence . . . suggests that we now have a severe problem of overcrowding in the primary phase' were excised.

I stressed at the beginning of this chapter that it provides but one person's perspective on a collective task. Each of the three authors of the primary discussion paper had a right to ensure that his views were properly represented in the paper as published, and each would no doubt be able to estimate the balance of victory and defeat in attempting to exercise that right. In my own case, for what it is worth, this might be summarised as significant wins on matters of substance and significant defeats on matters of style and tone, leading to modifications which might subtly soften or harden an argument as drafted without necessarily eliminating or reversing it. And with the discussion paper, as so often in the wider political arena, style and tone turned out to be far more important than substance, at least until the document's political capital was exhausted.

Dirty tricks?

The pressures to which the three of us were subject were aggravated when it became clear that the confidentiality of our work had been breached. On 1 January, under the headline 'Educationist demands end to rhetoric on teaching', *The Times* reported the contents of my letter of 4 December to academics undertaking research relevant to our inquiry, quoting its reference to 'the silly rhetoric of the past few months' and pointedly juxtaposing this with Clarke's attacks on 'playschool' classroom practice. It also made a certain amount of the letter's emphasis on our independence, claiming that I had 'let it be known privately that [I was] anxious not to be used by the government'.

This was clearly little more than an attempt to stir the pot during the period of silence but intense speculation between Clarke's December announcement and the discussion paper's release. More serious were pieces in the *Daily Telegraph* on 12 January and the *Independent* the following day. Under the headlines 'School enquiry challenges Clarke's plans', Fran Abrams reported in the *Daily Telegraph* that our inquiry, 'set up by Kenneth Clarke ... to back calls for a return to traditional values in primary schools [had] failed to provide full support for his views'. It went on to say that we would challenge Clarke's call for a return to streaming, recommend 'a mixture of both modern and traditional teaching methods ... anger Right-wingers ... attack extremists from both sides.'

The *Telegraph* piece was clearly based on a leak rather than speculation. It was very close indeed to drafts of sections of the paper on which I myself was working at the time, and it appeared that the newspaper had not only obtained copies of these but also knew which of the three of us had written them, as on another page it took the story further, juxtaposing the headline 'Child-based style chalks up a victory' and a picture of myself working with a group of primary children in a mode which was manifestly 'child-based'. The *Independent*, presumably recycling the *Telegraph* story, repeated the claim that we would come out against the methods Clarke preferred.

It is fruitless to speculate on how the leak occurred. The more interesting question is why this was done. The simplest answer is that there was no intent other than to feed a journalist's need for a story and that someone with access to the drafts was happy to provide this. Alternatively, it was a deliberate attempt to put pressure on the three of us to pull back from any resistance to Clarke's agenda to which we might be inclined. As the member of the team named and depicted in these stories I was presumably believed to be particularly vulnerable to such temptations. In any event, this was the first hint of the marginalisation to which I was to be subjected over the next few months, first by sections of the press, then by academics. Interestingly, however – as Woods and Wenham's analysis shows (1995) – the grounds for such marginalisation were diametrically opposed. Where the press (and those who were monitoring the initiative's political progress) were concerned, I had succumbed to academic equivocation; to academics, I had not been equivocal enough.

THE DISCUSSION PAPER IS LAUNCHED

The discussion paper was launched at a DES press conference on 22 January 1992. Two days earlier, the three of us had met Clarke and Eggar to hear their comments on the final draft. Both of them queried matters of fine detail as well as the broad thrust of the document: Eggar, for example, was particularly concerned to test whether the evidence from international studies of educational achievement really justified the conclusion in our paper's third chapter that there was 'some evidence of downward trends in important aspects of literacy and numeracy'. He was right to raise this, and the paper's use of 'some' was ambiguous. The intended message was that the evidence in 1991–92 was suggestive rather than conclusive, the word 'some' signifying 'a limited amount of'; but seeing the word 'evidence' others took this as a claim that standards had plummeted and that England was lagging catastrophically behind other countries. The situation mirrored that in Leeds, where our report (see pages 59–62) noted a discernible downward trend in reading test scores between 1983 and 1989, but then added careful qualifications about how this finding should, and should not, be interpreted – to no avail, when the press picked it up.

What now began to take place, I suggest, was a battle over the true meaning and significance of the discussion paper. Clarke himself took part, contributing a strong attack on the Plowden legacy in that week's *Sunday Times* ('Education's insane bandwagon finally goes into the ditch') which was coupled, on another page, with a particularly vicious personal attack on Lady Plowden and other members of her committee, under the banner 'The Great Betrayal. ... After affecting our schools for 25 years, the Plowden Report has finally been laid to rest without mourners'. The other protagonists in this battle, which we shall examine in the next chapter, were the media, academics, and two of the discussion paper's authors (Woodhead and myself) – but, significantly, not the teaching profession, for they of course had not seen the document, nor in many cases would they for a further month.

Chapter 11

What paper? Whose discussion?

Woods and Wenham (1995) have identified two main phases in the career of the 1992 primary discussion paper, the political and the educational. In their view, the political phase was dominated by the pre-election agenda of the New Right, supported by most of the press. Only when these political interests were served could the document be reclaimed by the professional constituencies for whom, ostensibly, it had been written. By the time Woods and Wenham completed their case study of the discussion paper's use in seven schools in one LEA (a very small sample, admittedly) they saw it beginning to be used as a resource for professional discussion and decision-making along the lines invited in the paper's introduction and conclusion.

However, Woods and Wenham suggest that this process was complicated by 'a number of competing discourses: the political and the educational, intensification and professionalism, the male and the female, junior (KS2) and early years (KS1), Plowdenism and the move for more traditional approaches, the class teacher and the specialist' (Woods and Wenham 1995: 128). Further, they suggest that such competing discourses can arise within constituencies as well as between them: 'For academics also have their interests – early years learning, child-centred methods, gender equality, higher education based training, rigorous methodology based on scientific procedures etc' (ibid.). Set against experience, this analysis is persuasive. It deserves development, however, and especially the notion of 'competing interests' needs a fuller elucidation.

For example, in the previous chapter's account of the political calculations which seem to have influenced the 1991–92 primary initiative, I hinted at the individual manoeuvrings and ambitions within the ministerial team which lay behind the apparent unity of political purpose, and at some of the differences and indeed conflicts of interest and approach among the discussion paper's three authors.

Similarly, to acknowledge that the interests of academics may compete while listing only those – rigorous methodology, early years learning and so on – which are relatively high-minded, is to underplay the way such interests are rarely, if ever, immune from other values, affiliations and antipathies: professional, personal and political, for example. In the period of New Right ascendancy during the 1980s and early 1990s, much was made of the overt political allegiances of academics like Roger Scruton, John Marks and Anthony O'Hear. Except in the demonology of the New Right itself, which tended to place most other academics within the 'educational establishment', we heard rather less of the politics of the academic opposition – that is to say, of those who objected that figures like those named had allowed their own politics to override academic disinterestedness.

A further line of development on the Woods and Wenham thesis would be to disentangle the political and media interests bearing on how the discussion paper episode was handled and to show how the monolithic implication of 'media interests' is itself unsatisfactory. Thus, though for some newspapers or journalists political and journalistic imperatives may have coincided to yield stories which simultaneously sold newspapers and appealed to those sections of the electorate being targeted by government, in other cases the situation was undoubtedly more complex. On one occasion, a particular section of the press might well respond dutifully to a lead given by politicians and deliver the desired message, but the sometimes fraught relationship of right-wing newspapers to a right-wing government during the 1980s and 1990s suggests that this works only when political and news values coincide. In other situations, as the record of close votes during the last year of the 1992–97 Major administration illustrated, it is probably only backbench members of the party in power who can be relied upon unconditionally and unquestioningly to support the party line: for them, political survival overrides all other considerations.

In the case of the primary discussion paper, the substantial press coverage did not always conform to the expected political affiliations. One right-wing daily newspaper offered relatively neutral reporting and comment while in contrast its Sunday stable-mate took an aggressively pro-government and anti-teacher line. One left-wing newspaper portrayed the discussion paper in rabidly 'back-to-basics' terms which would have delighted the far right, while another – as we shall see – applauded the paper while attacking both its political progenitor and one of its authors.

The media, then, are neither monolithic nor, beyond a certain point, predictable. The blend of corporate political affiliation, news values and (frequently underplayed in analysis of media behaviour) individual journalistic ambition is murky yet volatile.

The story of the post-publication career of the primary discussion paper, as of the Leeds report, is in part an illustration of these processes at work, separately and in interaction. They manifested themselves most obviously as a protracted contest over what the documents said and meant. In this chapter I shall illustrate this battle over meaning by reference to debates in three of the constituencies critical to the paper's fortunes: the media, the academic community, and the teaching profession. My purpose in doing so is not only to complete this account of the government's 1991–92 policy initiative on primary education by exploring events in the 'context of practice' – the third of the three policy 'contexts' identified by Bowe and Ball (1992) and discussed at the beginning of the previous chapter – but also to show something of the acutely problematic and intensely contested power of words when, as in the case of the 1992 primary discussion paper, a text is the *outcome* of policy, rather than merely its instrument or manifestation.

THE MEDIA DEBATE

The handling of the launch of the discussion paper proved controversial. It was also an object-lesson, though a not entirely flawless one, in the management of information. Journalists were given copies of the pre-publication version, together with the DES press release ('Three Wise Men Report calls for big changes in primary education') just fifteen minutes before the press conference. When Clarke and the three authors arrived some were frantically leafing through the paper's fifty-six pages, while others had skimmed the press release and would be working from that and whatever was said at the conference. Clarke's response to this was to tell the journalists, 'Don't bother with the report – read the press release.'

Since the discussion paper itself did not reach the teachers for whom, ostensibly, it had been written until between three and six weeks had elapsed, Bennett's charge (1992) that the delay was 'cynical' may well have been justified. Only the *Times Educational Supplement*, the following Friday, carried a detailed analysis of the paper's text: it had also been almost alone in offering a reasonably balanced account of the Leeds report the previous August. The majority of media reports reflected faithfully some, but rarely all, of the soundbites picked out in the DES press release:

- The progress of primary schools pupils has been hampered by the influence of highly questionable dogmas which have led to excessively complex classroom practices and devalued the place of subjects in the curriculum.

- Much topic work has led to fragmentary and superficial teaching and learning.
- In many schools the benefits of whole-class teaching have been insufficiently exploited.
- Standards of education will not rise until all teachers expect more of their pupils.
- Every primary school should have access to specialist expertise in all nine National Curriculum subjects.
- Primary teaching roles are too rigid; greater flexibility in staff deployment is needed.
- Streaming is a crude device which cannot do justice to the different abilities a pupil may show in different subjects and contexts. Grouping is a more flexible device.
- Decisions about the initial training of primary teachers should be made in the light of a clear understanding of the kinds of teachers which primary schools now need.

(DES 1992)

The usual crop of headlines followed: 'Call for return to traditional school lessons' . . . 'Primary school dogma should be abandoned' . . . 'Clarke backs calls for "common sense" primary teaching' . . . 'Teachers told to rethink methods' . . . 'Let common-sense take over'.

Yet although most of the press reports were clearly steered by the DES press release, the latter was less stark than many of the headlines suggested, and newspapers like the *Independent*, which, like *The Times*, carefully reproduced all of the points listed above, thereby found themselves registering that Clarke's initial call for a return to streaming had not been supported, that primary schools needed greater staffing flexibility but were prevented by tight resourcing from achieving this, and that the government's desire to encourage a wholesale shift to school-based teacher training, which Clarke had announced at the North of England Education Conference on 4 January, was not endorsed.

Altogether, then, despite the undoubted DES efforts at news management, on this occasion the outcome was less than clear-cut. The press release, though selective – the references to topic work and whole-class teaching, for example, ignored the paper's strong emphasis on a mixture of methods and 'fitness for purpose' – also somewhat undercut Clarke's December statement. The paper itself contained a long section on teacher training (chapter 9) which ran strongly counter to Clarke's speech on 4 January. Although newspapers continued to attack the Plowden report, and, in deeply wounding terms, the persons of Lady Plowden and her committee, the discussion paper had actually said something rather different:

It is fashionable to blame the Plowden Report for what are conceived as the current ills of primary education. However, if ill-
conceived practices have been justified by reference to Plowden, this
reflects far more damagingly on those who have used the report in
this way than on Plowden itself. . . . If things have gone wrong – and
the word 'if' is important – then scapegoating is not the answer. All
those responsible for administering and delivering our system of
primary education need to look carefully at the part they may have
played.

(Alexander *et al.* 1992: para 22)

In fact, the press coverage, though extensive, was relatively muted in
comparison with what Clarke's December statement had provoked.
Certainly it was much less consistent, yielding headlines like 'Caution
urged on training reform' and 'Teaching study takes middle line' alongside the familiar calls for 'back to basics'.

More interesting was the way that – the predictable responses of the
tabloids apart – the reporting fault line in the broadsheets did not always
follow the assumed party-political affiliations of the newspapers in question. The *Guardian* episode, which I shall now look at in some detail, is
a useful example.

The *Guardian* coverage of the Leeds report, five months earlier, had
yielded perhaps the starkest headline of all: '£14 million project fails to
improve teaching.' Though it had noted the report's praise for the LEA's
commitment of resources, Stephen Bates' article of 3 August 1991 had
ignored both the report's main conclusion ('On balance, therefore, we can
report with confidence that PNP was an initiative well worth the
Authority's investment') and the appended list of twenty-two 'significant contributions' which PNP had made to the quality of primary education in Leeds. Though I attempted to redress the balance in a letter
which the newspaper published a few days later, on 9 August, a subsequent piece by Melanie Phillips, on 20 December, indicated that the newspaper's initial line was not to be modified. She found the Leeds report
'devastating, not merely about that city but in the bleak truths it relays
about primary education in general' and looked for a similarly 'hard-
headed assessment' from the primary discussion paper (Phillips 1991).

Not surprisingly, therefore, the newspaper's coverage in January and
February 1992 presented the discussion paper as an unremitting attack
on the Plowden legacy. Though he correctly noted the paper's reservations about government teacher training policy, Stephen Bates re-cast its
call for a judicious mixture of teaching methods and professional roles
as an endorsement of 'more subject teaching – and more use of specialists . . . schools should acquire specialist teachers, especially for the upper
years' (Bates 1992). Though noting the paper's rejection of streaming,

Bates turned the paper's suggestions about a flexible pattern of grouping, including ability grouping, into 'streaming for separate subjects' and, using the same partial quotation as several others, he translated the discussion paper's analysis of the pros and cons of whole-class teaching from this:

> Whole class teaching appears to provide the order, control, purpose and concentration which critics believe are lacking in modern primary classrooms. To a significant extent the evidence supports this view. . . . The potential weaknesses of whole class teaching need, however, to be acknowledged [author's note: these are then listed]. . . . Despite these potential weaknesses, whole class teaching is an essential teaching skill, which all primary teachers should be able to deploy as appropriate. . . . Teachers need the skills and judgement to be able to select and apply whichever organisational strategy – class, group and individual – is appropriate to the task in hand. . . . The issue is not one of mathematical proportion. The critical notion is that of fitness for purpose.
>
> (Alexander *et al.* 1992: paras 89–92 and 99–101)

into this:

> [The report] says whole class teaching provides the 'order, control, purpose and concentration which many teachers believe are lacking in modern primary classrooms. . . . It is an essential teaching skill which all teachers should be able to deploy as appropriate'.
>
> (Bates 1992)

The change in words – from 'appears to provide' to 'provides' – is small but critical; taken together with the omission of the discussion paper's references to the 'potential weaknesses of whole class teaching' and the vital qualifying sentences leading up to 'fitness for purpose', the transformation of meaning is profound.

The following day, the Bradford *Telegraph and Argus* published an interview in which I had attempted to show how on the pedagogical issues with which the press were then preoccupied the discussion paper had taken a position which, by being eclectic, was in line with what most independent-thinking teachers would endorse:

> On every issue on which we have been presented as taking a strong and traditional line, we actually argue for a mixture of methods. . . . We specifically say we should get away from the idea of progressive and traditional methods. . . . Teaching is more complicated. . . . Most good teachers use a mixture of methods. We really need to move beyond this simple caricature of what goes on.
>
> (Alexander, quoted in Whitehead 1992)

On the vital question of the document's status, this article also quoted me as stressing that it was a discussion paper 'rather than a report in the conventional sense'. I made similar points in a piece at this time in the *Times Educational Supplement* (Alexander 1992a).

The Bradford article was seen by the *Guardian*, who then commissioned me to write an article outlining my views. At the same time, scenting evidence of the split in the ranks of the discussion paper's authors, which – as we saw in the previous chapter – the *Daily Telegraph* and the *Independent* had registered a month earlier, they commissioned a similar piece from Chris Woodhead. Meanwhile, they had flagged the line they were about to take:

> There seemed to be a degree of confusion at last week's launch of the ... primary teaching report ... about how prevalent 'trendy' methods or the influence of 'highly questionable dogmas' really are. ... Professor Robin Alexander, one of the three wise men at Mr Clarke's side, reckoned that the teaching methods the report castigated were 'far less widespread than you can imagine'.
>
> *Guardian*, 28 January 1992)

The 'far less widespread than you can imagine' was, of course, a reference to the discussion paper's statement that:

> The commonly held belief that primary schools, after 1967, were swept by a tide of progressivism is untrue. HMI in 1978, for example, reported that only 5 per cent of classrooms exhibited wholeheartedly 'exploratory' characteristics and that didactic teaching was still practised in three quarters of them. The reality, then, was rather more complex. The ideas and practices connoted by words like 'progressive' and 'informal' had a profound impact in certain schools and LEAs. Elsewhere, they were either ignored, or – most damagingly in our view – adopted as so much rhetoric to sustain practice which in visual terms might look attractive and busy but which lacked any serious educational rationale. Here they lost their early intellectual excitement and became little more than a passport to professional approval and advancement. The real problem was not so much radical transformation as mediocrity.
>
> (Alexander *et al.* 1992: paras 19–20)

In this matter, the discussion paper was in line not just with the 1978 HMI primary survey, but also with the evidence from projects like ORACLE (Simon 1981, 1991) and indeed the Leeds study reported in this book's first nine chapters. It was Melanie Phillips of the *Guardian* who, at the very beginning of the press conference on 22 January, had asked the question about the prevalence of 'trendy' teaching methods. Since neither she nor any of the journalists present had been given time to do more than glance briefly over the discussion paper's 188 paragraphs before the conference began, her professed sense of confusion on this matter at the conference itself was understandable; for progressive ideology having been presented in the press and ministerial speeches during the preceding months as a major cause of Britain's claimed educational decline, a government-sponsored 'expert' on such matters was now apparently claiming something rather different.

Less understandable was the way that six days later, having by then presumably read the discussion paper in full, *Guardian* journalists could persist with their suggestion that there was confusion over a matter on which the text of the discussion paper, once read, was in fact very clear.

The Woodhead and Alexander articles were published side by side on 11 February, accompanied by a large copy of a photo of the discussion paper's authors which had been torn to symbolise the rift between Woodhead and myself. The pieces were headed:

> The Government's 'Three Wise Men' report on primary teaching methods arrives in schools this week – but the three wise men themselves are at odds over the lesson teachers should draw. Unprecedentedly for an official document, two of the authors are today differing publicly over the report's meaning.
>
> (*Guardian*, 11 February 1992)

Woodhead's article was premised on a view of the discussion paper as definitive report. Prefiguring OFSTED (and perhaps his own subsequent elevation to the leadership of that body), he argued, for example:

> An external review is needed. ... The Government's new arrangements will only work if everyone ... knows exactly what kinds of questions will be asked in the inspection. ... We need a specification for the details of curriculum organisation and classroom management which the inspection must cover. ... Our report should form the basis of that specification.
>
> (Woodhead 1992)

In contrast, my own *Guardian* article made much of the document's explicit discussion paper remit and status, and of the implications of these for how it should be received and used. It summarised the paper's accounts of matters like teaching methods, generalist and specialist teaching, the secondary/primary funding anomaly, the demands of the National Curriculum and teacher training. It also complained – a foolhardy thing to do, as it turned out – about the way the press treatment of the paper had made it difficult for readers, especially teachers, to attend to what it actually said:

The political and media hype, not to mention the ludicrous 'Three
Wise Men' label, have transformed what was commissioned and
presented as a modest discussion paper into a definitive national
enquiry yielding unchallengeable edicts. As a result, many teachers
now view the report, without having read a word of it, with
implacable hostility.

(Alexander 1992b)

This difference of opinion – which was, admittedly, pretty fundamental
in respect of the discussion paper's status at least – gave the *Guardian*
what it needed. On the same day, in another part of the newspaper,
the headline 'Wise men split over teachers' made much of the supposed
'serious divisions between Professor Alexander and his colleagues,
who were generally more prepared to endorse the Government's view'.
This article noted (correctly) that 'the parts understood to have caused
the deepest divisions between the three relate to teacher training.
Mr Woodhead was much keener on the Government's school-based
training plans.'

That might have seemed sufficient. However, the following day the
newspaper consolidated its attack in a long leader headed 'One rather
unwise man'. Referring to the Leeds report and the primary discussion
paper the leader writer asserted:

To write one report and then deny its consequences is unfortunate.
To write two and then deny them both, is unforgivable. . . . Just as
the ship starts to change direction, one of the three navigators declares
. . . that the media has misread the route. This is a crucial issue. It
affects millions of children. . . . Yet . . . Robin Alexander strives to
dilute the report's criticism of present teaching practice – and tries to
present the review as a 'modest discussion paper' rather than a
seminal document commissioned to provide a definitive view on the
present state of primary education. . . . Here was an echo from
Professor Alexander's study of 231 'progressive' primaries in Leeds
. . . which had another uncomfortable conclusion: children were found
to be wasting 40 per cent of each school day.

(*Guardian*, 12 February 1992)

The extent of the conflict over meaning was by now clear. The discussion paper was not a discussion paper; the *Daily Telegraph* version of the
Level Three data from the Leeds classroom practice study (the 40 per
cent myth referred to on page 75) was to be preferred to what the Leeds
report actually said; and anyone who challenged these misrepresenta-
tions was to be accused of 'rewriting the message'. These and other
matters formed the subject of a letter which the *Guardian* published
two days later and in which I itemised five areas of significant factual

inaccuracy in the newspaper's treatment of Leeds and the primary discussion paper. The letter ended:

> Sixth, you castigate me for presenting the primary document as 'a modest discussion paper rather than a seminal document commissioned to provide a definitive view of the present state of primary education'. Read the document's title and introduction and you will see that discussion paper is exactly what it is. Read the Secretary of State's December and January letters to all primary schools and you will see that he too commends discussion rather than unthinking acceptance. A discussion paper may well be seminal, but by its nature it cannot be definitive.
>
> (Alexander 1992c)

But the *Guardian* had no intention of letting go. The same day, Melanie Phillips wrote a long and personalised piece headed 'Rewriting the message'. It began by repeating the newspaper's claim of 28 January (page 222) that there was confusion or contradiction over the extent of the impact of progressivism, a claim which is dealt with above by reference to paragraphs 19–20 of the discussion paper. Phillips ended:

> Why is he so terrified of his own conclusions? ... It must surely be that his fine report swims against current orthodoxy and has upset his peers in the education world. It takes courage to put your head above the parapet – and keep it there. He is therefore saying to teachers: 'Don't trust what you think I wrote; believe instead what I am now telling you I wrote'. But he did write it. Don't trust this revisionist.
>
> (Phillips 1992)

By now, others had entered the fray. A selection of letters on these matters was published on 18, 19 and 25 February. While some used the episode as ammunition for their own attack on the discussion paper, its authors and Kenneth Clarke, others argued that Phillips, Bates and the *Guardian* leader writers had seriously misunderstood and misreported the discussion paper, both in its status *vis-à-vis* the debate about primary education and, more fundamentally, in respect of what it actually said, and asserted that the line I had taken was a necessary and correct response to the press coverage, and was consistent with my obligation as a researcher to identify and respect the limits of the evidence with which the Leeds report and the primary discussion paper had dealt.

As I noted at the beginning of the previous chapter, it is difficult to write about controversial public events in which one has featured without appearing self-justificatory. Yet, judging by the many letters about the *Guardian*'s behaviour which I received, the episode provoked *Schadenfreude* among a few but was viewed by many more with deep disquiet. However, this is not really the issue: as with this entire account of the government's 1991–92 'winter initiative' on primary education, our concern here must be general rather than personal. The important question is how an episode like this is best interpreted in terms of our wider concern with the policy process, educational practice and the relationship between them.

There is no doubt that the media play an important part in the processes of formulating, explaining and 'selling' political policy. In these matters, the relationship between journalists and politicians is one of mutual dependence and considerable complexity. Journalists need stories and for these they must have access to informed sources. Politicians for their part need reliable – or at least predictable – journalistic outlets for ideas which would otherwise remain hidden from much of the population. At the formal level there exists the immense and costly apparatus of government press releases, briefings, interviews and press conferences; at the informal level the perhaps even more significant underworld of spin doctors, intended and unintended leaks of information, off-the-record conversations which, by accident or design, may be nothing of the sort, and the busy exchange, by every human and electronic means possible, of information, misinformation, speculation, gossip and rumour.

But the relationship is not one of simple mutual dependence, with the press in the subservient role of purveyors of political information or of gullible reproducers of the day's political 'spin'. Each group has its own imperatives, and in a given news context these will not necessarily coincide. Indeed, they may override the broader political sympathies or affiliations which, much of the time, make a newspaper's stance on a given political issue fairly predictable.

Such tensions increase as the political stakes are raised, and especially in the run-up to a general election. The period which saw the publication of the two documents with which this book is chiefly concerned was the last few months of the 1987–92 Conservative administration, and indeed it might reasonably be suggested that had a general election not been imminent, neither ministers nor the press would have found the Leeds report as devastatingly significant as they claimed and the primary discussion paper would probably not have been commissioned.

How, against this background, can sense be made of the way the *Guardian* in 1992 dealt with a story in which other newspapers, including those of the political right which might have been expected to exploit its 'trendy teachers' ' potential for as long as possible, had by then begun to lose interest? The following are hypotheses, some of them suggested to me at the time by colleagues.

First, the basic story – of plummeting educational standards in primary schools caused by decades of mindless progressivism – was firmly rooted as both political and media myth, the more so because it was not new (I mentioned its 1970s manifestations in Chapter 10). This story warranted embellishment or further demonstration, but it could not be contradicted. In the context of political and media interests it had the status of incontrovertible fact. Moreover, it provided a recurrent reference point for a succession of other stories, at the time and in the future.

The Leeds report and the primary discussion paper were used to sustain and develop this myth (and indeed to provide entertaining illustrations, like 'Advisers said children should sit on the floor' in the *Daily Telegraph*). But in order to do so, both documents needed to be presented as definitive. The Leeds evidence had to be unimpeachable, and where necessary (as in the case of press treatment of the classroom practice data which I commented upon on pages 75 and 196) the evidence might need to be massaged to guarantee this. Similarly, the 1992 document of Alexander, Rose and Woodhead had to be a report, the outcome of a formal inquiry, not a mere discussion paper offering propositions which its readers were positively invited to question. The authority of its authors had to be unrivalled. The 'three wise men' sobriquet, though facetiously used by some, provided a tag whose reiteration would consolidate this authority.

All these elements had to be protected. However, while the objections of teachers and their unions could be dismissed by both politicians and the press as so much sectional pleading – 'they would say that, wouldn't they?' – for the author of the Leeds report and one of the 'three wise men' to challenge the media/political versions of Leeds and the discussion paper, and indeed actively to resist the authority ascribed to him, was unacceptable, for it threatened to undercut not only the story itself but also the credibility of the journalists who had promulgated it.

There were two ways to handle this unexpected turn of events. One was to exploit it as a story in its own right, giving a tale on which there was perhaps an excess of journalistic unanimity so far a new and lively twist, and setting one 'wise man' against another. The other was to deploy, as a means of both defusing the challenge and marginalising the challenger, the 'discourse of derision' hitherto reserved for teachers, teacher-trainers and Lady Plowden. The *Guardian* used both of these strategies, and continued to do so for as long as the person in question, or others of like mind, challenged either the initial story or its 'wise men split' sequel.

A second area of speculation concerns the complex web of political realignment and the newspaper circulation war. During this period, the *Guardian*, and other 'quality' newspapers like the *Independent*, were in competition for the broad tract of readership in the political centre and left-of-centre. While the *Guardian* purveyed a generally anti-Conservative line, and was certainly seen by the Conservative Party as hostile to its policies, circulation imperatives demanded that it buried for good the fence-sitting, woolly-hatted, liberally ineffectual image which it had managed to acquire during the 1960s and 1970s. Especially, in the educational context, it needed to distance itself from one of that era's central totems, the 1967 Plowden report on primary education. An abrasive and uncompromising line on issues like education was a prerequisite, and indeed was wholly compatible with opposition to government policy, since this was the period when each main political party was seeking to steal a march on the other in the vital electoral battleground of education. Talking tougher than the enemy on educational standards, progressive ideology and incompetent teachers was one way of achieving this, even though on other aspects of education policy the traditional distance might be maintained (policy convergence in education became even more pronounced in the run-up to the 1997 general election). The fact that the *Guardian* team at this time included journalists with known right-wing affiliations would support this hypothesis.

On this theme, Maurice Galton's analysis is pertinent. Relating the discussion paper episode to his own experience of the political and media pressures of membership of a National Curriculum Council committee in 1988–90, he notes:

> What I did not foresee ... was the new alliance between the 'Right' and the new 'middle-class' Left (referred to by some as the 'futon socialists'). At various times, in recent years, both main political parties have called for the reintroduction of streaming at the top end of the junior school. After the publication of the so-called 'Three Wise Men's' report, the quality press, with the exception of the *Independent*, repeatedly criticised Professor Alexander for his attempt to move the debate away from crude denunciations of existing primary practice. The *Guardian*, which throughout the debate in the 1970s and 1980s adopted a balanced view, took a particularly hard line. The paper's editorial team singled out for praise the comments of another member of the three-man team who criticised some primary teachers in language reminiscent of the Black Paper writers of the late 1970s.
>
> (Galton 1995: ix)

Finally, there are the speculations which might seem to border on conspiracy theory but which in relation to what was going on elsewhere at this time may now look entirely plausible. I had been appointed to the Council for the Accreditation of Teacher Education (CATE) in 1989, by Secretary of State John MacGregor. Under his successor, Kenneth Clarke, the attack on the 'educational establishment' in general, and its teacher training wing in particular, had intensified. During 1990–91, the many accusations of left-wing and/or progressive bias in teacher training courses gave way to a concerted drive to remove these courses from higher education institutions altogether and place them in schools. CATE, as the government's advisory body as well as accrediting agency, was asked to draw up the proposals.

To ensure that CATE delivered the right advice, its outgoing members were increasingly replaced by those with perceived right-wing credentials (a process which in most cases backfired, since once appointed the majority of CATE members displayed the independence of judgement which they believed was incumbent upon them and which CATE's chairman, Sir William Taylor, had worked hard to encourage since the council's inception in 1984). CATE first of all drew up proposals for the reform of secondary teacher training. After a rather hasty version of the required consultation process, the government promulgated its response to these as DFE Circular 9/92 (DFE 1992) which, in the case of the Post Graduate Certificate in Education (PGCE) required a considerable shift in the balance of training towards school-based activity.

Next came primary training. However, the commissioning of the primary discussion paper delayed the process, because Clarke wanted the training reforms to relate closely to the school and classroom practices he expected the primary discussion paper to commend. Since I was on both CATE and the discussion paper team, my role in this matter would inevitably be critical. As noted elsewhere, the drafting of the teacher training section (chapter 9) provoked the sharpest divisions and bitterest disputes among the three authors, and by far the most intense sense of pressure to toe the government line.

In the end, the discussion paper supported the call for primary training to be reviewed, but urged a cautious and rational approach to reform. Such reform, the paper argued, should start with a clear analysis of the range of teaching roles needed in primary schools, addressing the vexed question of the balance of generalist, consultant, semi-specialist and specialist teaching examined in the paper's seventh chapter; it should be grounded in the kind of systematic explication of curricular and pedagogic expertise which had informed the paper's fourth and sixth chapters; it should address the increasing problem, exacerbated by the National Curriculum, of course overload, especially in the PGCE; it should grasp the nettle of a proper rationalisation of the relationship of initial training, induction and in-service training and development which successive governments had refused to tackle; and in all these matters it should eschew the simple, school-based apprenticeship models of training which the right was campaigning for and include full and complementary roles for both schools and higher education (Alexander et al. 1992: paras 164–83).

This, clearly, was not what the government wished (or expected) to hear – right-wing bodies like the Centre for Policy Studies even less so. Since the discussion paper, once published, would then be taken as the central piece of evidence in CATE's deliberations on the reform of primary training, if the right wished to have its way on this matter it would need to exert maximum influence within that body. It has been suggested that the press attacks to which I was subjected at this time, including those in the *Guardian*, were in part an attempt by the political right to marginalise and discredit me in the ensuing debate on primary training, in which, as a member of CATE, I would be taking a prominent part. Rose and Woodhead were to be portrayed as the hardliners, unafraid to speak the truth about primary education; I would be presented as the revisionist, capitulating in the end to pressure from my fellow members of the educational establishment, one no longer worthy of the accolade of 'wise man', and one, therefore, whose contribution to the teacher training part of the 1991–92 'winter initiative' could no longer be taken seriously.

I stress that all this is conjecture, though collective rather than private conjecture. However, what is beyond dispute is the considerable power which the media exercised in the matter of the discussion paper, especially during those vital few weeks before it was released to schools when teachers had only the media (and protestations from people like myself) to go on.

In the longer term, we can note simply that little has changed. Whenever the debate about the quality of primary teaching re-surfaced during subsequent months and years, the primary discussion paper (or rather 'the Three Wise Men Report') was referred to as a kind of touchstone. The references were almost always to whole-class teaching, subject teaching, low expectations, dogmas and so on rather than to the paper's more sustained message about the need for teaching decisions to be grounded in professional knowledge, mastery of a broad range of executive skills and strategies, and carefully contexted judgements of 'fitness for purpose'.

Finally, lest it be thought that I am arguing that the press treatment of the primary discussion paper represents a special case, I would stress that this is not the intention. What we have here is merely a specific illustration of a general condition. All summaries of documents, and accounts of events, are necessarily selective and partial, and all selection is a kind of distortion. Journalists and editors, like academics and teachers, have agendas, and these, rather than some kind of disembodied or value-neutral concept of semantic truth, guide the selections and accounts which they provide. One such agenda, inevitably, is to defend the myths which they themselves have created.

Thus the maxim of C. P. Scott, the late and illustrious editor of the *Guardian*'s Manchester forebear, that 'Comment is free but facts are sacred', is either a relic of a more innocent and principled age or so much journalistic humbug.

THE ACADEMIC DEBATE

As soon as the discussion paper was published, it became apparent that academic opinion was sharply divided over its merits. Thus, for example, to take five of the twenty academics who had responded to the invitation to contribute their own research perspectives to the exercise and whose ideas were in fact reflected within the paper (see the list on page 207), Bennett (1992), Campbell (1992) and Simon (1992) broadly commended the paper, while Galton (1995) and Pollard *et al.* (1994) were much more critical.

Counting heads, of course, is not a particularly valuable way to assess critical opinion, except to illustrate that in this case it was divided, but in passing we can note that all of the first three named here explicitly grounded their observations in acknowledgement that the document was a discussion paper rather than a definitive report. Despite the document's subtitle ('A Discussion Paper'), and despite its reiteration of Clarke's remit, several academics, like many journalists, had difficulty accommodating to the fact that the hype of 1991–92 had yielded no more than a set of propositions which were to be regarded as open to debate. The confusion, where it occurred, was exacerbated by the differences between the paper's authors which, as we saw in Chapter 10, newspapers like *The Times* and the *Daily Telegraph* had detected during the weeks preceding publication, and which the *Guardian* made central to its own coverage in January and February 1992. That teachers should have encountered this difficulty was understandable, since the delay over the paper's dissemination meant that they depended entirely on the press for information about its contents.

Among the fullest academic critiques were those of Simon (1992), Dadds (1992), David *et al.* (1992), Hammersley and Scarth (1993), Carr (1994) and Galton (1995). Between them, the critiques illustrate a number of themes. These in turn can be placed under two broad headings: relating to *context, style* and *approach* on the one hand, and to *content* on the other.

Context, style and approach

The highly politicised context of the discussion paper's inception and production was commented on by all. Most found it distasteful. Several, including Hammersley and Scarth, Dadds and Carr, seemed reluctant to disentangle from this context, and their opposition to it, their critiques of the paper's substance. Carr, for example, builds his entire commentary on an entertaining but ultimately counterproductive exploitation of the 'wise men' sobriquet which he uses as springboard for an overworked contrast of the attributes of 'wisdom' and cleverness', while

Dadds begins her piece with a long extract from the Monty Python film *The Life of Brian*. Both (like Galton and Hammersley and Scarth) use pointed titles and sub-titles – 'Wise men and clever tricks' . . . 'Monty Python and the Three Wise Men' . . . 'We three kings of orient are' . . . 'Some talk of Alexander' – to drive home their message that the discussion paper, being in the political arena, is *ipso facto* in the arena of the politics of the absurd.

Simon, writing as a lifelong opponent of Conservative policy yet also as someone with a comprehensive grasp of educational history, argued from the outset that the separation of context and content which some were unable to achieve was an essential prerequisite to clarity of analysis:

> A great deal could be written about the politics of this discussion paper. . . . This is not my intention here. Instead I shall discuss the paper on its merits. . . . In doing so I will extract it as a text (as it were) from all the razzmatazz and hullaballoo surrounding both its inception and, more particularly, its publication. We owe its authors nothing less. . . . They deserve a serious response which need not in any way address the . . . deliberate misrepresentation that followed the report's publication. . . . The discussion should focus on the report itself, its theoretical standpoint, analysis and recommendations.
>
> (Simon 1992)

The failure to separate text from context led some critics to misrepresent the paper's content and argument, for having perceived it as in a fundamental sense politically tainted, they had difficulty in accommodating the paper's many specifics which swam against the (right-wing) political tide. Thus, for example, Galton (1995: 39 and 92) claimed that the paper followed the right in commending a move to specialist teaching in the primary school, when in fact (Alexander *et al.* 1992: ch. 7) it set out a broad continuum of teaching roles, from generalist to specialist, and argued that schools should make their own choices from these on the basis of their particular circumstances and needs. Similarly, Galton (1995: 92), like David *et al.* (1992: 9–10) defined the discussion paper's support for whole-class teaching – another New Right nostrum – as unequivocal. In fact (Alexander *et al.* 1992: paras 89–101) it summarised research and inspection evidence on the pros and cons of whole class, group and individualised strategies before, in a section headed 'Striking the balance', commending a judicious mixture of each:

> The issue is not one of mathematical proportion. The critical notion is fitness for purpose. The teacher must be clear about the goals of learning before deciding on methods of organisation. Whole class

teaching, group work and one-to-one teaching are each particularly suited to certain conditions and objectives. Equally, they can be used in singularly inappropriate ways.

(Alexander *et al.* 1992: 30)

I shall give, below, other examples of the way that some academics followed the press in imputing to the primary discussion paper – as to the Leeds report – statements which it did not make.

The matter of the paper's *style* is more problematic. In the previous chapter I indicated that style was a critical point of difference among the discussion paper's three authors, and one on which I reckoned to have lost many of the arguments. Given the way that this resulted in the paper's offering a fair number of soundbites of the 'highly questionable dogmas' variety, and the way these were exhaustively milked by the press, it is easy to understand how the paper's substantive arguments tended to be submerged and only those commentators with the historical perspective of a Brian Simon could set them in proportion:

> There are two or three unfortunate phrases, naturally seized on by the press, but generally the report presents a clear standpoint – prescriptive at times. But why not? This both offers a challenge and gives us something to bite on – and discuss.
>
> (Simon 1992)

Dadds (1992: 131) detected 'mixed styles, mixed attitudes, mixed purposes, mixed textual devices and mixed logics'. This seems to me a succinct and accurate appraisal, and it reflects the impact on the paper's production of two circumstances: the political agenda which prompted the initiative; and the sharp differences in perspective and purpose, to which I have already alluded, among the paper's three authors. However, Hammersley and Scarth neither acknowledged this unevenness – and its implications for how the paper's arguments should be appraised – nor were prepared to set such infelicities aside. For them, style was all, even to the extent of preventing them from engaging with some of the paper's central arguments:

> We shall not discuss the detailed prescriptions that the 'wise men' make; some seem worthwhile, others not. For us, the manner in which the authors present their arguments is even more significant than what they say.
>
> (Hammersley and Scarth 1993)

Given that the document was commissioned and presented as a discussion paper, this lofty refusal to discuss what it said seems curious. It also presupposes that the discussion paper's manner of presentation is consistent across all ten of its chapters. Yet, as Dadds (above) noted, this

is far from the case, and indeed such basic presentational inconsistencies as she identified may well constitute a much more serious weakness
(though it should be noted that Simon's critique finds that the paper's
theoretical standpoint remains clear, consistent and convincingly argued
despite problems in tone and style).

Perhaps the most interesting aspect of the argument about the discussion paper's manner of presentation was the way that some who
were most critical on this score fell into the same tonal and stylistic
traps as had – in their view – the discussion paper's authors. The most
obvious example was the play – tempting, it must be agreed – on 'wise
men' and 'wisdom'. By 1995, as Drummond pointed out, this had worn
rather thin:

> Galton quite gratuitously . . . goes back over the contemporary press
> attacks on Alexander, quoting at length, and constantly referring
> to the 'Three Wise Men' (who become 'Three Unwise Men?' in
> the chapter title: it is long past time to abandon this feeble little
> joke).

> (Drummond 1995: 14)

If Drummond finds Galton's play on wise/wisdom gratuitous and
feeble, she would presumably have even stronger words for Carr (1994),
whose critique is much diminished by its caustically *ad hominem* stance.
The title of his article ('Wise men and clever tricks'), its subheadings,
the reiteration of the one surname and above all the repeated play on
'wise man/men' do the piece no service. The latter phrase in its singular
or plural form appears no fewer than twenty-three times, 'wise/wisdom'
eleven times, but the more accurate '*so-called* three wise men' only twice
(Alexander 1994a: 107).

What is important about this aspect of some of the academic critiques
of the primary discussion paper is that what starts as mild word-play
becomes, as noted above, an attack less on the discussion paper's arguments than the persons of its authors: as unacceptable, presumably, as
laying all the ills of primary education at the door of Lady Plowden and
her colleagues.

There is one aspect of the paper's approach about which there is probably little room for dispute, though much room for regret. As noted in
Chapter 10, the paper's authors took the decision to list all the sources
at the end of the document rather than as they were drawn upon within
the text, justifying this 'to maintain continuity in the discussion'
(Alexander *et al.* 1992: para 5) and mindful of the fact that the text as
commissioned was intended to speak directly and succinctly to teachers.

I now believe this to have been a mistake, and for three reasons. First,
because it prevented those not reasonably familiar with the literature
(which included unpublished material, so such familiarity would at best

be limited) to check specific claims against the supporting evidence, following the usual academic conventions. Second, because it meant that the sheer weight and range of the evidence which we had consulted might not be appreciated, and as I show on pages 205–8 in the previous chapter, the evidential base was very substantial indeed. Third, because it permitted commentators to level with impunity whatever charges they wished about how the evidence had been used. Here is an example:

> Though the authors list the evidence to which they appeal in a bibliography, there are no specific links provided between their detailed claims and that evidence. . . . The authors . . . clearly believe that they know better than many teachers what facilitates pupil progress, and they . . . expect teachers . . . to accept what they say on the basis of their authority as experts. It seems to us that teachers would be well advised not to do so.
>
> (Hammersley and Scarth 1993: 495)

The first sentence above is factually correct, and, as I have noted, a legitimate criticism. However, what follows is neither correct nor legitimate. The discussion paper makes much of being evidentially based and its judgements and recommendations are presented as stemming from that evidence, not from the 'expert' status, real or imagined, of the paper's authors. However, such was the persistence of the 'wise men' rhetoric and the associated attempt to elevate the discussion paper to the level of a definitive report, that it was easy for the paper's detractors, as well as its supporters, to use this authority, imputed but not claimed, in order to sustain their support or criticism.

In this sense, therefore, there would seem to be a significant connection between the strength of some commentators' opposition to the paper and the authority which they ascribe to it. It seems to me not at all fortuitous, for example, that Galton and Carr, as well as Hammersley and Scarth, press hard the 'wise men' claim in the same context as they reject the paper's arguments. Conversely, it is notable that commentators like Simon, Bennett and Campbell link their generally much more favourable assessments to an acknowledgement of the status of the document as discussion paper.

When we consider Hammersley and Scarth's final observation above, however – the recommendation that teachers should not accept the expert claims of the discussion paper's authors – we see the difficulty in which these two commentators have placed themselves. For on the one hand, the injunction is irrelevant, since the authority of the paper, as we have noted, derives from the evidence on which it draws; on the other, Hammersley and Scarth here do precisely what they accuse the paper's authors of doing: use their authorial status, rather than the evidence (in this case the evidence of the discussion paper as commissioned and written rather than as re-cast by Hammersley and Scarth) to tell teachers how to think and act.

Content

It is not possible to engage systematically with all the criticisms of the primary discussion paper's treatment of matters of substance. Nor is this strictly necessary, given that this chapter is not an author's 'reply to just [or unjust] criticism' but an elaboration on this chapter's thesis that when a text becomes an instrument of policy, everything hangs on who wins the inevitable battle over what that text says and means. In pursuit of the latter objective, therefore, I shall now take a number of themes within the discussion paper around which the battle for meaning raged most fiercely. These – an interesting and perhaps symptomatic list in itself – included the following: standards of achievement in primary schools; the causes of educational decline and the extent of the influence of progressivism; the quality of teaching; and the paper's theoretical basis.

Standards in primary education

The second chapter of the discussion paper reviewed the national and international evidence on standards of achievement in English primary schools, both over time and in relation to other countries, as this evidence stood in 1991. Paragraph 30 lists the main data sources: the now defunct Assessment of Performance Unit (APU), LEAs, the National Foundation for Educational Research (NFER), HMI reports, National Curriculum test results, and the studies conducted by the International Association for the Evaluation of Educational Achievement (IEA). Using cautionary phrases like 'there are reasonable grounds for scepticism' and 'we can conclude tentatively', the chapter nevertheless finds sufficient grounds for concern to register this conclusion:

> Despite the unevenness and gaps in the national and international data on standards, the various sources discussed in this section provide some evidence of downward trends in important aspects of numeracy and literacy. It also suggests that these trends may affect some ability groups and pupils from particular backgrounds more than others.
>
> (Alexander *et al.* 1992: para 50)

Though some commentators noted that the paper's summary (Alexander *et al.* 1992: 1–3) is in places harsher in its judgements than the text it summarises, that criticism does not hold in the present case:

The data on primary pupils' achievement are in many ways inadequate. It is, nevertheless, possible to identify some evidence of downward trends in important aspects of literacy and numeracy. At the same time, there have been improvements in the quality of teaching in, for example, science and information technology.

(Alexander *et al.* 1992: 1)

These judgements bear critically on the political intentions which lay behind the commissioning of the discussion paper, for members of the government from Prime Minister Major downwards had made clear their presumption (1) that standards in primary education were falling and (2) that 'trendy' post-Plowden methods were to blame. If the discussion paper failed to deliver on the first part of this premise, the government's 'winter initiative' would look distinctly shaky.

In the event, as was to be expected, the press (with certain exceptions, the *Times Educational Supplement*, for example) disregarded the qualifications and presented the discussion paper as claiming unequivocally that standards had plummeted. Academic opinion was rather more divided. In her generally hostile critique, Dadds concedes: 'There are sections such as "Standards of achievement in primary schools" that appear to survey research critically, purposefully and with due respect to problems of early closure on inconclusive evidence' (1992: 131). Hammersley and Scarth, however, share the view of the right-wing press that the discussion paper's argument is clear-cut:

The main argument of the report . . . is as follows. First, it is claimed that the current level of pupil progress in primary schools is unsatisfactory. . . . Second, the diagnosis is made that this arises from poor quality teaching, produced by the persistence of elements of progressive doctrine among primary teachers. . . . Finally, recommendations are made proposing the increased use of whole class teaching, subject specialisation etc.

(Hammersley and Scarth 1993: 492)

The matter of cause and effect is taken up below: for now, it is important to register that the chapter of the discussion paper in question does not justify the first of these three interpretations. That Hammersley and Scarth opt for this reading of what is in fact a somewhat equivocal analysis stems, I suggest, from a number of problems, some of them inherent to the discussion paper, others not.

First, as I have noted, the paper's overall inconsistency of tone, and its lapses into the tough, judgemental style whose origins I discussed in the previous chapter, may have engendered an adverse reaction which was not confined – as it was for Simon (and indeed, as I show below, for teachers) – to the sections of the paper in question, but could influence the way the entire document was perceived and interpreted.

Second, the claims being made about the document by ministers and much of the press during 1991–92 must have made it hard for all but the most independent-minded and scrupulous of readers to attend to what it actually said.

Third, both the conclusion of the 'Standards' chapter and the paper's summary contained, in that phrase 'some evidence of downward trends', a dangerous ambiguity. In terms of the evidence and argument up to that point, 'some' clearly signifies 'a certain amount, sufficient to command our attention, but not sufficient to justify a definitive judgement'. In the political climate of 1992, however, there was little room for either presentational ambiguity or academic equivocation, and 'some' meant 'enough to serve our (political or journalistic) purposes'. I noted on page 214 that at one of the final meetings with ministers before the paper's publication, Minister of State Tim Eggar had queried this phrase. One view of his motive for doing so would be that he perceived a crucial window of political opportunity for future exploitation; another would be that he had detected the ambiguity and felt that as authors we should attend to it, in our own interests. Whatever may be said about the political calculations which lay behind the commissioning of the discussion paper, I believe that on this occasion the second of these hypotheses applied.

Who is to blame, and for what?

Hammersley and Scarth, like the press, saw the paper's argument as a simple exercise in cause and effect, or in defining a problem and apportioning blame: falling standards, caused by Plowdenism, reversed by a return to traditional teaching. Repeatedly in their critique, as here, they drive home this characterisation and in doing so lose no opportunity to reinforce their initial premise, essential to the rest of their discussion, about the paper's stance on standards of pupil achievement:

> The main cause that the authors identify as bringing about the claimed decline in standards is the commitment of some primary school teachers to 'highly questionable dogmas', by which they mean those ideas usually listed under the heading of 'progressivism'.
>
> (Hammersley and Scarth 1993: 492)

The phrase 'claimed decline in standards' is repeated at several points in their paper. They then go on to assert:

That the evidence for the authors' causal claim about the relationship between commitment to progressive dogmas on the part of primary school teachers and a decline in levels of literacy and numeracy is weak at all points.

(Hammersley and Scarth 1993: 494)

We have seen that the discussion paper's chapter on standards of pupil achievement is at best cautious, at worst ambiguous, but never as emphatically partisan as Hammersley and Scarth required it to be in order to sustain their critique. That being so, their causal imputations cannot really be justified.

In the same way, the paper is much more circumspect about the impact of the Plowden report and the ideas and practices associated with it than several academic commentators – or, of course, the press – allowed. The paper's second chapter outlines the structural and qualitative diversity of the English system of primary education before quoting the Plowden report's celebrated manifesto ('A school is not a teaching shop, it must transmit values and attitudes') and then attempting to assess its impact. It follows others in concluding:

The commonly held belief that primary schools, after 1967, were swept by a tide of progressivism is untrue. HMI in 1978, for example, reported that only 5 per cent of classrooms exhibited wholeheartedly 'exploratory' characteristics and that didactic teaching was still practised in three quarters of them. The reality, then, was rather more complex. The ideas and practices connoted by words like 'progressive' and 'informal' had a profound impact in certain schools and LEAs. Elsewhere, they were either ignored, or – most damagingly in our view – adopted as so much rhetoric to sustain practice which in visual terms might look attractive and busy but which lacked any serious educational rationale. Here they lost their early intellectual excitement and became little more than a passport to professional approval and advancement. The real problem was not so much radical transformation as mediocrity.

(Alexander *et al.* 1992: paras 19–20)

The paper then goes on (paragraph 21) to cite the warning of Alec Clegg, a strong advocate of the ideas in the Plowden report, of the likelihood of just such a scenario. The clear message here, therefore, is that in 1991 the claims about an entire educational system dominated by 'trendy' teachers and schools – which were central to the political and media accusations in 1991–92, just as they were in the mid 1970s – could not be sustained by the evidence.

Hammersley and Scarth quote the same extract from the discussion paper, but turn it to a different purpose:

A first requirement for this explanation of the claimed decline in standards to be established is, of course, that the authors show that the views they list under the heading of dogmas are indeed widespread among primary school teachers. If this is not the case, these 'dogmas' can hardly serve as the cause of a general decline.

(Hammersley and Scarth 1993: 493)

Exactly so, which is why the discussion paper offers no such 'explanation' for the 'claimed decline', just as it is extremely cautious in its assessment of whether such a 'decline' has taken place.

Equally contentious for some critics of the discussion paper was what followed the references to Plowden and Clegg in paragraphs 19–21:

It is fashionable to blame the Plowden Report for what are perceived as the current ills of primary education. However, if ill-conceived practices have been justified by reference to Plowden, this reflects far more damagingly upon those who have used this report in this way than on Plowden itself. If 'Plowdenism' has become an ideology to which thousands of teachers have unthinkingly subscribed, then it is necessary to ask why the teachers concerned have stopped thinking for themselves and have apparently become so amenable to indoctrination. If things have gone wrong – and the word 'if' is important – then scapegoating is not the answer. All those responsible for administering and delivering our system of primary education need to look carefully at the part they may have played.

(Alexander et al. 1992: para 22)

The meaning of this paragraph eluded several commentators. Despite the repetition, no fewer than four times, of 'if', despite the underscoring of this qualification in 'and the word "if" is important', despite the direct challenge to the prevailing climate of scapegoating, despite the unambiguous transfer of blame from teachers and the Plowden report to 'all those responsible for administering and delivering our system of primary education', Dadds judged the paragraph offensive:

This insult was no less distasteful for having been directed towards teachers and their supposed 'indoctrinators' than towards the good Lady Plowden.

(Dadds 1992: 130)

Similarly, Drummond:

Perhaps the most serious allegation, in terms of teachers' professionalism, was made, albeit in the conditional sense [in this paragraph of the discussion paper].

(Drummond 1993: 106)

Again, we need to ask why the discussion paper could be so thoroughly misread on a matter on which its argument was pretty clear. Perhaps the irony which carries the paragraph forward was out of kilter with both the document and the times. Perhaps the heavy use of the conditional form sowed confusion. It seems to have done so for Drummond: the idea that a statement can be at the same time 'in the conditional sense' and a 'most serious allegation' is curious – a statement is either an allegation or it isn't. Perhaps the understandable desire to defend a profession and a set of beliefs under strong attack from politicians and the press blinded some readers to the possibility that a document commissioned by the attackers might fail to echo their views.

Whatever the hypothesis, the consequences of misreading this part of the discussion paper could be unfortunate. Thus, after quoting the middle sentence above from paragraph 22 ('If "Plowdenism" ... amenable to indoctrination'), but ignoring the preceding and following sentences which with the middle one combine as a single line of argument, Hammersley and Scarth assert:

> We know of no evidence which establishes that this has occurred, and drawing this conclusion would rely on complex and uncertain judgements about how much reflection is desirable and of what kinds. Here as in some other areas the authors seem to be passing off their own opinions as established facts, and doing so on the basis of a spurious appeal to the findings of educational research.
>
> (Hammersley and Scarth 1993: 495)

Again, the paragraph in question makes none of the claims which Hammersley and Scarth attribute to it. The 'conclusion' to which they refer is nothing of the sort: it is a clear condemnation of those who draw such a conclusion; and only such a fundamental misreading of the paragraph, if even that, would justify the accusation made by Hammersley and Scarth in the second sentence above.

Having said all this, it must be acknowledged that one of the 'mixed messages' to which Dadds refers (1992: 131) concerns this vital question of causality. The 'highly questionable dogmas' phrase originated in the body of the paper as this (my italics):

> In recent decades *much teaching has suffered from* highly questionable dogmas which have generated excessively complex classroom practice and have devalued the role of subjects in the curriculum.
>
> (Alexander *et al.* (1992): para 118)

In the summary, however, this was subjected to a crucial modification (my italics again):

Over the last few decades *the progress of primary pupils has been hampered by the influence of* highly questionable dogmas which have led to excessively complex classroom practices and devalued the place of subjects in the curriculum.

(Alexander *et al.* (1992): summary, para 3.2)

It was the wording in the summary, rather than the paper itself, which found its way into the press release and thence into the media coverage. Given that the phrase which, probably above all others in the discussion paper, delighted right-wingers and dismayed the teaching profession, was 'highly questionable dogmas', and that this appeared in both versions, to draw attention to this discrepancy may seem like splitting hairs. Nevertheless, as a matter of record it is worth noting that the link in the causal chain – between dogmas and pupil progress – was forged not by the analysis in the discussion paper but by the hastily-prepared summary of that analysis.

The final point to make on this matter is more fundamental. Hammersley's and Scarth's critique of specific matters in the discussion paper is framed by their view that its overall argument, if not sustainable, is at least coherent. As we have seen however, while the paper's stance is certainly problem-centred, the relationship it posits between problems and solutions, let alone problems and causes, is far less tight than Hammersley and Scarth claim.

Instead, the paper catalogues a wide range of conditions in English primary education which are indicated by the evidence from research and inspection, and operates less on the basis of simple belief that specific problem x is caused by specific condition y and will be solved by specific solution z, than a more generalised faith that attending to a wide range of problems at the levels of the system as a whole, the school and the classroom, and in teacher training and development, must produce improvements in the quality and outcomes of teaching and learning.

The paper's weakness, or strength, therefore, is plural rather than singular. There are many issues to which a critical reading of the paper should attend – the notion of a discussion paper demands nothing less – but undermining the argument on one or even several of these does not – as Hammersley and Scarth would have us believe – demolish the entire document, because its construction does not allow this. Nor could it, given that the paper was written by a somewhat disparate trio, among whom a fragile consensus on some issues and implacable disagreement on others was probably the best that could be achieved. This being so, the discussion paper is perhaps best read as a sequence of essays on a selection of themes bearing on the broad topic heralded by the paper's title, rather than as a single and unfolding strand of argument.

The quality of teaching and learning

One such theme, and the one to which the largest share of the document is devoted (the fourth and sixth chapters), is the quality of teaching and learning in primary classrooms.

Chapter 4 starts by identifying three UK research traditions, or evidential strands, which bear on this theme: children's development and learning, social factors in educational achievement, and the dynamics of the classroom. The chapter then opens up a number of issues bearing especially on the latter: the changing character of primary teaching; planning; the debate about subjects and topics; the problem of curriculum breadth, balance and consistency; curricular expertise; mixed and single age-group classes; streaming; the pros, cons and balance of the three main organisational strategies of one-to-one teaching, group work and whole-class teaching; the generic teaching techniques of questioning, explaining, observing, giving feedback and so on; matching task to pupil; assessing and recording progress.

Chapter 6 takes the issues arising from the earlier chapters, especially the fourth, and sets them out as 'a number of propositions about aspects of classroom practice to which the evidence suggests particular attention should be devoted ... intended not as a definitive checklist but as the basis for open and constructive discussion' (Alexander *et al.* 1992: para 132). It is perhaps worth recording that this chapter's final bullet-point format emerged from lengthy discussion about whether it should list propositions or questions. Thus, in the second draft (8 January 1992) we had bullet-pointed propositions; three days later (11 January 1992), the third draft presented these as questions; these survived into the fourth draft (13 January 1992); but in the fifth and final draft they had reverted to propositions. To exemplify from one sub-section:

How can we most effectively:
• establish clear ground-rules for work and behaviour;
• deploy techniques for ensuring that these are acted on;
• train children in the ways if working to be adopted, and in the various skills of study, enquiry, collaboration, discussion and so on?

(Alexander *et al.* 1992: fourth draft of ch. 6)

It is important that teachers:
• establish clear ground rules for work and behaviour;
• ensure that these are acted on consistently;
• train pupils in the ways of working to be adopted, and in the various skills of study, enquiry, collaboration, discussion and so on.

(Alexander *et al.* 1992: 40)

The change is significant, and in line with the process, which I described in Chapter 10, of rendering the paper's messages tougher and more prescriptive as we moved from early drafts to final publication. There is also an implied shift from a sense that the normative context of classroom learning is problematic ('How can we most effectively . . .?') to a view that success resides in implementing procedures ('It is important that teachers . . .'), and in this respect the criticism of Carr (1994) is well founded: only up to a point, however, for the initial line is maintained by prefacing the entire list (Alexander *et al.* 1992: para 132, quoted above) with a rejection of a checklist approach and an endorsement of the contribution of the propositions to 'open and constructive discussion'. The message, then, is that tough-sounding though some of the propositions have become, it is for teachers to decide whether they should be accepted, modified or rejected.

The same process can be followed in respect of Chapter 4. The second draft of the much-publicised section on whole-class teaching, for example, reads as follows:

> Commentators look wistfully across the Channel, or back into their own childhood, and see in whole-class teaching the order, control, purpose and concentration which they find lacking in many primary classrooms.
>
> To some extent, the evidence from HMI, Galton, Mortimore, Tizard, Croll, Broadfoot, Osborne and others supports them. Whole-class teaching is associated with the highest rates of pupil time on task, and with a greater incidence of higher-order questioning, explanations and statements, and all these in turn correlate with pupil performance. Teachers with a substantial commitment to whole-class teaching appear to be particularly effective in teaching the basic subjects.
>
> Critics' tendency to caricature whole-class teaching as mere telling, copying and regurgitating, may seriously understate the potential of this approach, for in fact much of the evidence shows whole-class teaching to be strong on open-ended questioning, explanation and exposition, all of them, in the hands of a competent and knowledgeable teacher, ways of engaging children's thinking to a high degree.
>
> Yet here, too, things are not necessarily what they seem. The teacher may tend to pitch matters somewhere towards the perceived middle of the ability range, thus risking losing the less able and boring the brightest. Observational study shows that children pay attention and remain on task, but in fact slow down the rate of working to meet the teacher's norm, or what they would like that norm to be, thus controlling events to an extent which advocates of whole-class teaching might find uncomfortable.
>
> Moreover, the French evidence confirms both the pedagogic power of whole-class teaching and the dangers of over-reliance upon it, as

upon any one teaching strategy. The particular risk is the alienation of children at the extremes of the perceived ability range, especially the less able, for whom a more individualised pedagogy may be appropriate.

Whole-class teaching is an important and essential teaching tool, which all primary teachers should have the skills to exploit and the judgement to deploy as appropriate. It is not, however, a panacea. It should also be noted that structured whole-class teaching requires an array of interactive skills and a firm and comprehensive grasp of subject-matter; without these it becomes everything its critics most deplore.

(Alexander *et al.* 1992: second draft of ch. 4)

In the discussion paper as published this became:

89 Whole class teaching appears to provide the order, control, purpose and concentration which many critics believe are lacking in modern primary classrooms.

90 To a significant extent, the evidence supports this view of whole class teaching. Whole class teaching is associated with higher-order questioning, explanations and statements, and these in turn correlate with higher levels of pupil performance. Teachers with a substantial commitment to whole class teaching appear, more-over, to be particularly effective in teaching the basic subjects.

91 The potential weaknesses of whole class teaching need, however, to be acknowledged. There is a tendency for the teaching to be pitched too much towards the middle of the ability range, and thus to risk losing the most able and boring the brightest. Observational studies show that pupils pay attention and remain on task when being taught as a class, but may, in fact, slow down their rate of working to meet the teacher's norm, thus narrowing the challenge of what is taught to an extent which advocates of whole class teaching might well find uncomfortable.

92 Despite these potential weaknesses, whole class teaching is an essential teaching skill, which all primary school teachers should be able to deploy as appropriate. Provided that the teacher has a firm grasp of the subject matter to be taught and the skills to involve the class, pupils' thinking can be advanced very effectively.

(Alexander *et al.* 1992: paras 89–92)

Clearly, more has happened here than the shortening and tightening up which the second draft undoubtedly needed. The last vestiges of specific referencing of the source material (an issue we discussed earlier in this chapter) have been removed. The references to nostalgia and caricature, although applied fairly to both proponents and opponents of whole class teaching alike, have been excised. The important reservations about the international evidence (in this case from France – DES 1991o) have gone; so too has the caveat, in the final paragraph of the draft, about the dangers of seeing whole-class teaching as a panacea. And yet, the critical question to ask is whether the core messages of the section as drafted – that whole-class teaching is an essential professional tool, that it has disadvantages as well as advantages, and that its effective deployment requires considerable skill – have been damaged by the editing process. A close comparison of the two versions will show that they have not.

The section on whole-class teaching can be regarded as a paradigm for much of this part of the discussion paper: succinct, abrupt, yet nevertheless working against the prevailing political and journalistic preference for the simple solution. Yet, equally, what has been removed might be regarded as anything but peripheral to the case being made: to acknowledge that nostalgia is a powerful element in the debate is necessary; so, too, is the reminder that the endorsement of continental teaching methods (a growing trend in 1991–92, by 1996 an unstoppable flood) may be as uncritical as the earlier espousal of neo-Plowden approaches.

However, I suspect that it was the *tone* of some parts of these two central sections of the discussion paper which desensitised some commentators to the balance in argument which it actually offered on politically high-profile issues like streaming, whole-class teaching, specialisation, subjects and topics. Indeed, of these examples, only streaming produced an unequivocal stance one way or the other, and that, significantly, was against the government's preference. On the other matters the paper argued for teachers to have a broad repertoire of skills, strategies and approaches – including single-subject teaching, different kinds of topic work, whole-class teaching, both teacher-led and collaborative group work, and one-to-one individual teaching – and to select from these on the basis of 'fitness for purpose'.

The paper also argued, *pace* the claims of Galton (1995: 39 and 92) and Hammersley and Scarth (1993: 492 and so on), not for 'the use of more specialist teachers' (Galton) or 'the increased use of subject specialisation' (Hammersley and Scarth) but for the introduction of a new continuum of teaching roles for the primary school, from *generalist* through *generalist/consultant* and *semi-specialist* to *specialist* (Alexander *et al.* 1992: para 146), to inform school-level decisions about staffing:

> We do not think that any one of these possibilities is the answer on its own and we recommend that every school should work out its particular combination of teaching roles in the light of two principles.

The first is that the pattern of staff deployment must serve pupils' needs. ... The second is that the strategy must work from the professional strengths of the staff.

(Alexander *et al.* 1992: para 147)

The discussion paper's theoretical stance

Apart from the charge that the primary discussion paper endorsed the New Right nostrums of whole-class teaching, specialisation and so on, which can readily be refuted by referring to the paper's actual text as above, academic opinion also divided on the more fundamental question of the paper's underlying theoretical stance.

There were three to some extent opposing judgements made on this matter. First, that the discussion paper is anti-theory:

The report does make some attempt to introduce a theoretical perspective to learning, based on an alternative to Piaget's model of child development, but this is not carried through in any detail. Instead, the 'Three Wise Men' criticise the over-reliance on theory (by implications Piaget's) in the development of contemporary practice. Throughout this book it has been argued that this view is wrong.

(Galton 1995: 125)

Second, it is claimed that this theoretical vacuum is to be filled by a technicist/pragmatic perspective which reduces all teaching to the enacting of supposedly value-neutral skills:

The notion that teachers do not ultimately need theory but only the techniques which theory establishes as the *sine qua non* of 'good' professional practice. ... A single-minded preoccupation with causal efficiency and effectiveness which interprets the business of education and learning largely in terms of the instrumental manipulation of learners by teachers.

(Carr 1994: 99–100)

Third, and in sharp contrast to the first two characterisations, there is the view that the paper is firmly grounded in a theoretical position which is both explicated in the text and sustainable:

The outlook which underlies the whole thrust of this report relates to the emphasis put upon children's cognitive and linguistic competence. This view, based on recent research into children's learning ... provides a firm theoretical base. ... But there is another theoretical standpoint ... the need to start from what children have in common as members of the human species, to establish the general principles of teaching and, in the light of these, to determine what modifications of practice are necessary to meet specific individual needs. . . . The paper emphasises the latent educability of the normal child, . . . it stresses that the goals and procedures of teaching need to be founded on characteristics which children share rather than on those which differentiate them one from the other. . . . The paper emphasises the need for children to experience a sustained intellectual challenge within (and outside) the classroom. . . . These ideas are very close to those of Lev Vygotski.

(Simon 1992)

Again, it is symptomatic of the climate within which the primary discussion paper was commissioned and published that it should have evinced such contradictory assessments.

Galton's 'anti-theory' claim, repeated by Carr, is without foundation. The paper nowhere makes or implies the rejection of theory (Galton goes on, as he does elsewhere in his critique, to use this misrepresentation as the springboard for his own 'correct' view). Nor, as both Dadds (1992) and Galton (above) claim, does the discussion paper reject Piagetian theory, though it does (Alexander *et al.* 1992: paras 22 and 53) criticise the reduction of Piaget's stage theory to 'chronologically fixed notions of readiness'. That, however, is consistent with the paper's rejection of the prevailing tendency to blame the 1967 Plowden report for the 1991/92 ills of primary education. It is teachers, not reports or research studies, who determine the everyday direction and character of teaching and learning in primary classrooms; and in any event, as we have noted above, 'If things have gone wrong – and the word "if" is important – then scapegoating is not the answer. All those responsible for administering and delivering our system of primary education need to look carefully at the part they may have played' (Alexander *et al.* 1992: para 22).

The pragmatic/technicist claim of Carr (echoed by Drummond 1993) is examined in detail in Alexander (1994a), and I do not propose to repeat the analysis here. My main criticisms of Carr's claim, in which he links the primary discussion paper with my analysis of the 'good practice' problem in the first edition of this book, are twofold. First, because he objects to the narrow, dualist definition of words like 'skill' and 'technique' as these are frequently applied to teaching, he presumes that all who use such words do so in the narrow sense that he deplores. Since much of my own writing on teaching (and on teacher education) is devoted to advancing the inseparability of the executive acts of teaching from knowledge, understanding and judgement, this charge is misplaced. Second, Carr takes my 'good practice' analysis (Alexander 1992d, 1996, and this book's next chapter) as an argument that in teaching there is a stark choice to be made, in determining the most appropriate course of action to be followed in the classroom, between what is ethically defensible and what works. The polarisation is his, not mine: what the 'good practice' analysis tried to do, in isolating conceptual, pragmatic, political, empirical and evaluative considerations bearing on educational decision-making, was

> to construct a framework which acknowledges the paramountcy of the ethical criterion while giving due weight to the competing imperatives of circumstance. To legitimate a perennial tension experienced by teachers seemed a necessary first step in the search for ways of resolving it.
>
> (Alexander 1994a: 109)

This takes us to the characterisation offered by Brian Simon. In respect of the paper's longest chapter (the fourth), which Simon sees as the document's core, his inferences about the paper's theoretical position are correct. So too is his suggestion that in arguing that 'good teaching does not merely keep step with the pupils but challenges and stretches their thinking' (Alexander *et al.* 1992: para 128), the paper deliberately paraphrases Vygotsky's view that 'the only good teaching is that which outpaces development' and thus provides a counterpoint to the 1960s/1970s preoccupation with 'readiness'. Simon, after all, was explicating Vygotsky's work and advocating its pedagogic applications in Britain long before it was more generally adopted as the basis for 'constructivist' views of learning and teaching (Simon and Simon 1963).

However, what must also be acknowledged – in fairness to those commentators like Galton, Carr and Hammersley and Scarth of whom I have been rather critical, as well as to Simon himself – is that the primary discussion paper is not consistent *theoretically*, any more than it is consistent in tone, style or depth of argument. The reasons for this have already been explained, and do not need repeating. Suffice it to say that though the long central section of the paper, to which Simon's review chiefly refers, is theoretically and empirically grounded, the compression and tonal modification to which the drafts of this section were subjected – a process which I illustrated above – tended partly to obscure this element. Simon's own work, in respect of Vygotsky, as director of the ORACLE project, and as long-standing critic of the weakness of British pedagogic theory and research, made him particularly receptive to ideas in the discussion paper of which others may have been unaware. It must also be said that there are parts of the discussion paper which are as pragmatic as Carr and Drummond claim.

The battle over the meaning of the discussion paper which took place in the academic world, therefore, took the form it did partly because the paper's unevenness permitted this. At the same time, when we consider

the misquotation and decontextualising to which offending sections of
the text were sometimes subjected, it is hard to avoid the conclusion
that some commentators were responding less to what the discussion
paper said than to what, politically and educationally, they judged
Clarke's initiative to be about, and indeed to individual motives about
which it is pointless to speculate: for, as Woods and Wenham (1995: 128)
note, 'academics also have their interests'. In this climate, the precision
and justice of proper academic critique may sometimes have been lost
and the necessary distinctions between text, sub-text, fact, inference,
public purpose and private motive may have been blurred.

THE PROFESSIONAL DEBATE

The last of the three constituencies within which the meaning and significance of the education policy enshrined in the discussion paper had to
be resolved was, strictly speaking, the most important. Teachers and
teaching were its focus – and political sub-texts apart – teachers were
intended to be its main readers. To underline this, the DES sent no fewer
than six copies to every primary school in England.

Writing about how teachers received and responded to the paper is
both more complicated and yet more straightforward than dealing with
the media and academic responses. It is complicated because we are
talking here of a professional community of over 200,000, spread across
20,000 schools. Moreover, whereas the media and academic debates were
conducted in the public domain of print – in newspapers, television/
radio programmes, conference proceedings, journals and books – the
professional debates took place mainly behind the closed doors of
staffrooms, in-service courses and LEA conferences. There is very little
published evidence about the large number of events and encounters of
this kind.

Having said that, such evidence as has emerged about the professional
aftermath of the discussion paper's publication suggests that after the
initial period of hype and anxiety teachers dealt with it in a relatively
pragmatic and low-key manner.

The LEA contribution

In their case study of 'Melshire', Woods and Wenham (1995) show how
the discussion paper provided LEAs with an opportunity to maintain
their status and influence in the face of government attacks by taking
the lead in promoting the discussion which the Secretary of State had
invited. Woods and Wenham describe events in just one LEA, showing
how it was able to defuse much of the initial suspicion, hostility and
anxiety which Clarke's letters and the media coverage had generated,

and reclaim the document for professional use. In this process, the medi-
ating roles of advisers, inspectors and heads were critical, but at the
same time the teachers interviewed by Woods and Wenham exhibited
considerable independence of judgement as they weighed the paper's
arguments, accepted some parts, rejected others, or found ways of using
it to support and legitimise their professional actions.

Adapting to this particular policy initiative the framework of Bowe
and Ball to which we have already referred, Woods and Wenham
identify six contexts or stages in the discussion paper's career:

1 the context of general influence;
2 the context of opportunity and mediation;
3 the context of text production;
4 the context of immediate reception;
5 the context of mediation;
6 the context of implementation.

(Woods and Wenham 1995: 119–20)

The account in these two chapters has focused on the first four of these.
By the summer of 1993, Woods and Wenham suggest,

as the discussion paper proceeded to the mediation and implementation contexts, and as the media and politicians lost the force of their
interest (which peaks and then subsides on these issues in a regular
cycle), it had an effect more in line with Alexander's original hopes
and intentions – modulation, debate, discussion, 'bottom-up' decision
making – teachers using the document as resource, appropriating it
for their purposes as others had done for theirs earlier.

(Woods and Wenham 1995: 138–9)

'Melshire' was not alone. Many LEAs initiated programmes for studying
and responding to the discussion paper, and indeed a longer-term
analysis of this period may well show that LEA intervention in the
debate about primary teaching was crucial. Frequently, these programmes started with a conference at which one of the paper's three
authors would be invited to deliver a keynote conference address (it
would be instructive to compare their substance and consequences).
These conferences seem to have been mainly for heads, thus supporting
the Woods/Wenham contention that in this matter, as in so many other
policy areas, the primary head's 'gatekeeper' role is a critical one;
however, this may have been modified by the fact that teachers, as well
as heads, had direct access to the document in question. Often, the
conference would lead to a longer-term programme, typically centred
on working groups. These in turn might produce their own reports
on how the discussion paper might be, or had been used. All this
consolidated professional ownership of the discussion paper.

We might also note, in passing, that the LEA strategy of promoting discussion of the paper and critical examination of the issues and problems it raised, and of encouraging teachers to identify these issues as their own, was the antithesis of the approach adopted in Leeds some years earlier in connection with the Primary Needs Programme. The publicity surrounding the Leeds report would have made LEAs very conscious of this. However, it is not clear how far in their responses to the discussion paper LEAs were consciously exploring the tension between 'top-down' initiation and 'bottom-up' ownership which the Leeds experiment had highlighted, as opposed to merely tailoring their strategies to the changing contexts of power and finance.

One of the most striking features of the forty or so LEA-sponsored events with which I was associated during this period was their receptiveness to the notion that the substance of the document was more important than the tone. It is true that some teachers, like some academics, were antagonised by the paper's much-publicised excursions into the rhetoric of 'highly questionable dogmas', but many more seemed ready to set these in perspective and examine the arguments for what they were. Indeed, the problem in the professional response was sometimes not so much outright opposition as over-ready identification: 'We do all this already.' This might represent anything from considered and critical acceptance of the paper's arguments to a reluctance to accept the challenge which these posed.

Running in parallel with the LEA conferences were those organised by local associations of headteachers and deputy headteachers, often, but not always, under the aegis of the National Association of Head Teachers (NAHT). The growing influence of local heads' groups in the 1990s was related directly to the declining influence of LEAs, and their impact on collective consciousness and solidarity, as well as on professional action in schools, deserves study. For now we can note that the format adopted for many of these conferences was similar to that of the LEA events.

By way of footnote, it can be added that from comparing experiences among the discussion paper's three authors it is apparent that between us we addressed heads and/or teachers in the majority of LEAs in England during the first two years after the discussion paper's publication. It might be interesting to know why which LEA opted for which author; and in how many of those to which none of us were invited this was by accident or design. In one LEA the chief education officer vetoed the recommendation of heads and advisers that I be invited to speak at their conference on the grounds of my supposedly extreme right-wing beliefs. However, as I noted earlier, the more typical stance of LEAs at this time was pragmatic rather than ideological.

LEAs and unions: summaries, digests and commentaries

Alongside, or occasionally in place of, the conferences for heads and teachers, some LEAs circulated their own summaries of the discussion paper, and indeed this effort was matched by several professional organisations and teachers' journals. This practice is a traditional response to the assumption that primary teachers do not have the time (or, possibly, the inclination) to obtain and study publications other than those which they see as relating directly to their day-to-day planning and teaching – a view which was supported by some, but by no means all, of the teacher interview data from the Leeds classroom practice study (Alexander 1995: 66–87). When one considers the length and price of some of the major reports on education which have been published during the last few decades, and the sheer quantity of documentation spawned by the National Curriculum in particular, the urge to help teachers in this regard is understandable. However, it may also have the undesirable consequence of increasing that professional dependency on which we commented, in respect of the Leeds Primary Needs Programme, in Part I. In any event, to presume that primary teachers are unable and unwilling to engage either with educational texts or educational ideas is unjust to those many teachers who do so engage, and perhaps somewhat patronising to the profession as a whole.

In fact, the discussion paper's brevity, and the large numbers of (free) copies circulated to schools, should have made such mediation unnecessary, on this occasion at least. In any event, the process of summarising a document like the primary discussion paper is no less selective for being undertaken by the professionals inside the education service than the journalists outside it (though each group will tend to make rather different selections), and a reading of some of the digests indicates that most reflect quite strongly the personal stance, or (in the case of institutional responses) the collective interest of their authors. Thus, to take one example, the Association of Mathematics Education Teachers (AMET) not only focused mainly on the mathematical applications of the document but also castigated it for not saying more about mathematics than it did (Furby et al. 1992). This, like several commentaries prepared while what Brian Simon called the 'razzmatazz and hullabaloo' generated by ministers and the media were at their height, also responded vigorously to what it saw as the paper's excessively critical tone. Like AMET, the National Children's Bureau (NCB) also criticised the paper's lack of emphasis on NCB concerns (Pugh 1992). Since these were identified as the needs of 3- and 4-year olds, and the discussion paper's remit was to concentrate on Key Stage 2 (7–11), the NCB critique might fairly be regarded as in this respect rather misplaced.

The LEA digests and responses were highly variable as to length and tone. Some were simply summaries (though, as I have noted, none the less selective for that), while others either combined summary with commentary or presumed teacher familiarity with the document and offered commentary alone. Most of these responses revealed two significant characteristics: first, a concern to bypass the public noise surrounding the discussion paper and encourage engagement with its content; second, a concern to defend established values and practices. Thus, in the Tameside 'version' sent to all school heads in that LEA, the discussion paper's warning about the misuse of Piagetian theory ('In the 60s and 70s, Piagetian theories about developmental ages and stages led to chronologically fixed notions of "readiness", thus depressing expectations and discouraging teacher intervention' Alexander et al. 1992: para 53) produced this riposte: 'Readiness is such an important factor that schools have to work vigorously towards it, and then build upon it' (Tameside MBC 1992: para 9) – thus closing down the debate in Tameside, on this extremely important issue at least, before it had started.

It is therefore possible to see some of the LEA digests as fulfilling two purposes: first to provide a service to schools of the kind which was both proper and helpful; second, by putting their own spin on the discussion paper and the debate, to maintain – or after a period of declining influence to re-assert – the kind of ideological hegemony which we explored in Part I.

The most detailed professional responses – and they were unambiguously responses rather than commentaries disguised as digests – came from the teaching unions. A fairly typical example is the contribution from the Assistant Masters and Mistresses Association (AMMA – now the Association of Teachers and Lecturers, or ATL). AMMA took the plea for a debate as an invitation not merely to comment on the specific issues raised by the discussion paper but also as a chance to set these in a much broader context. This context was partly educational – for example, their very proper reminder that the discussion paper's National Curriculum remit had begged important questions about the wider aims of primary education (AMMA 1992: 5) – and partly professional. Thus, a leitmotif of the AMMA response is the conditions within which primary teachers work and which bear on the issues of standards and teaching quality which the discussion paper highlighted: manageability and overload in the National Curriculum, the government's National Curriculum assessment programme, the physical condition of school buildings, the length of the working day, class size, the absence of non-contact time, and funding.

The disparity in funding between primary and secondary education was criticised in the discussion paper in very direct terms (Alexander et al. 1992: paras 4, 149, 187), and this criticism helped persuade the House of Commons Education Select Committee to undertake its 1993 inquiry (House of Commons 1994a, 1994b). As a union with members from secondary and primary schools, however, AMMA had to tread carefully. It supported the analysis that the primary/secondary disparity was excessive, but argued that this should be rectified not by 'robbing the budgets of secondary schools to increase funding for the primary sector' but that 'more money is needed overall' (AMMA 1992: 33–4).

Individual responses

A further insight into how teachers viewed and used the discussion paper is provided by the hundreds of letters sent to myself (and, presumably, to the other two authors). This mailbag constituted a sample of professional opinion which was entirely self-selected and therefore unrepresentative, yet the four groups into which the letters fall are of more than passing interest.

First, there were those teachers who expressed outright opposition to what they saw as the report's attack on much or most that they held dear. Second, matching these, there were those who expressed enthusiastic support for what they generally defined as its 'return to common-sense'. In between were two groups whose reaction was more qualified: a group of respondents who supported much of what the paper said but were deeply anxious about the threat to traditional professional values (curriculum breadth, whole-class teaching, child-centredness) which they believed could be read into the document and which they saw as the government's main agenda; and finally, constituting the largest group of the four – and matching a similar batch of letters received in the wake of the Leeds report – there were the teachers who did not necessarily agree with everything within the discussion paper but wished to celebrate what they saw – in the paper's questioning of established practice and its emphasis on the class teacher as the key decision-maker in matters of pedagogy – as its liberation of professional thought and action from the control of LEAs, advisers, inspectors and heads. Some of these echoed the perceptions of the Leeds teachers (page 134) and wrote tellingly of careers frustrated by pressure to conform to the prevailing educational orthodoxy.

The latter condition would appear not to be unique to England. On 5 March 1993, the Toronto *Globe and Mail* reported:

> In British Columbia, . . . parents and teachers have started to pass around an underground document on schooling that is hotly subversive. . . . Titled *Curriculum Organisation and Classroom Practice in Primary Schools* the British report is a government-ordered review of 'available evidence about the delivery of education' in elementary

schools. ... Unlike British Columbia's *Year 2000* mountain or, say, Ontario's *Common Curriculum*, ... the document calls into question a lot of the educational enthusiasms – particularly the complex patterns of classroom organisation – that educators in Ontario and British Columbia are now introducing. ... What makes the passing around of this document such a radical act is the *Year 2000* claim that its 'programs are based on many years of success with the British primary system.' As a consequence, many parents and teachers have clearly learned from the report that the province's educators have chosen to follow the path the British have plainly abandoned.

(Nikiforuk 1993)

The OFSTED contribution

In 1991 the government announced its intention of abolishing HMI and replacing it by a system of school inspection which would be undertaken by teams of specially trained registered inspectors. The Office for Standards in Education (OFSTED), the body which was to coordinate the new inspection programme, was set up under a part-time Chief Inspector, Professor Stewart Sutherland, in the summer of 1992, shortly after the primary discussion paper was published.

Meanwhile, one of the last acts of the outgoing regime was to set in train a survey of schools' responses to the discussion paper. HMI surveyed more than seventy primary schools, specifically on this theme, in the summer term of 1992. At the same time, HMI incorporated analysis of school response to the discussion paper in all its 1992 inspections, and hosted nine regional conferences for LEAs and schools in September of that year. In parallel, HMI had already embarked on a study of forty primary school classes 'which they judged to be well managed and ... soundly taught in terms of fostering children's learning of National Curriculum subjects but also in the wide terms of Section 1 of ERA' (OFSTED 1993a). The latter reference is to the Education Reform Act's requirement that schools should provide 'a balanced and broadly based curriculum' of which the National Curriculum is but a part, not the whole – a principle which was quickly forgotten in official circles (Alexander 1994b).

This first stage of the OFSTED follow-up yielded two reports, which are the nearest we have to a systematic national analysis of professional response at school and classroom level in the immediate wake of the discussion paper's publication. In their account of the 1992 survey and regional conferences, OFSTED (1993b) identified a generally favourable reaction to the paper's main thrust, together with an emerging consensus on a number of issues which the paper had flagged: support for the

class teacher's generalist role combined with increasing receptiveness to
the idea of semi-specialist variants; anxiety about the particular problems of small schools; support for the principle of a 'mixed economy'
of subject teaching and topic work and of a diverse pedagogical repertoire selected from on the basis of 'fitness for purpose'.

At the same time, the OFSTED report recorded strong professional
concern on the manageability of the National Curriculum, especially
in Years 5 and 6, on funding levels for primary education, and on the
increasing tension in primary headship between the traditional commitment to leadership in curriculum and pedagogy and the administrative
load dictated by the National Curriculum and budgetary delegation.

OFSTED felt able to claim, on the basis of the 1992 survey and conferences, that the discussion paper 'has done much to stimulate a long
overdue debate about pedagogy and classroom organisation in primary
schools' (OFSTED 1993b: 19) and that the National Curriculum provided
an ideal opportunity to give the idea of 'fitness for purpose' precise
application as schools appraised the best ways to implement in their
classrooms the statutory requirements on curriculum content.

Perhaps more significant than these assertions was the way that both
OFSTED documents contained appendices offering what were presented
as descriptions but would inevitably come to be regarded as alternative
prescriptions on good practice: six 'factors associated with successful
topic work' and twenty-one 'factors associated with better classroom
practice' (OFSTED 1993b: 21–3), together with a substantial compendium
of fifty-five 'characteristics of well-managed classes' drawn from the 1991
study of forty classes and 'complemented by the list in section 6 of
Curriculum Organisation and Classroom Practice in Primary Schools'
(OFSTED 1993a: 29–32).

What is significant about these lists is the closeness of their fit with
the discussion paper's fourth and sixth chapters. In the survey report,
the factors are framed by the discussion paper's distinction between
'organisational strategies' and 'teaching techniques' and under those
headings essentially reinforce the paper's messages on these aspects of
teaching, while in the other paper HMI findings are explicitly merged
with the discussion paper's analysis.

A year later, OFSTED published a further follow-up document
(OFSTED 1994). This was based on a survey of forty-nine schools undertaken during the spring and summer terms of 1993. This document tied
its comments on teaching methods to analysis of standards of attainment,
especially in numeracy and literacy, in a much more explicit
and focused way than either of its predecessors, and instead of the
somewhat tautologous 'factors associated with better practice' from the
1992 survey, it offered five major and six subsidiary 'factors associated
with high standards of attainment', four 'factors associated with poor

standards of achievement' and – reflecting a continuing preoccupation –
six 'factors associated with successful topic work' (OFSTED 1994: 14–16).

The 1994 positive factors highlighted subject knowledge, the skills of
direct teaching, a mix of teaching strategies and grouping by ability; the
negative factors included an excess of non-instructional 'facilitative'
teaching, poor management of time, an overuse of undifferentiated
worksheets, and learning tasks which were 'underchallenging or dull'.

Thus, by 1995, what HMI in 1992–93 had identified as an emerging
consensus on primary pedagogy and contingent aspects of curriculum
organisation and staff expertise and deployment had become consolidated as official quasi-orthodoxy. Its most prominent and influential
manifestation was the revised OFSTED inspection criteria for primary
schools (OFSTED 1995a). For example, with the exception of the reference to homework (which was not mentioned in the primary discussion
paper), the list below of OFSTED inspection criteria in respect of teaching
is very close to the main propositions in chapter 6 of the primary
discussion paper:

Judgements should be based on the extent to which teachers:
- have a secure knowledge and understanding of the subjects they teach;
- set high expectations so as to challenge pupils and deepen their knowledge and understanding;
- plan effectively;
- employ methods and organisational strategies which match curricular
  objectives and the needs of all pupils;
- manage pupils well and achieve high standards of discipline;
- use time and resources effectively;
- assess pupils' work thoroughly and constructively, and use assessments to inform teaching;
- use homework effectively to reinforce and/or extend what is learned
  in school.

(OFSTED 1995a: 66)

The OFSTED handbook's elaboration of several of these demonstrates
even more strongly their discussion paper antecedents: there are familiar
references to maximising pupil time on task, making the best use of
whole-class teaching, and deploying the generic skills of questioning,
explaining, instructing and giving formative feedback.

By this time, primary discussion paper co-author and NCC/SCAA
Chief Executive Chris Woodhead had been appointed head of OFSTED
and Her Majesty's Chief Inspector (HMCI). He opted for a personal
profile which was markedly higher than that taken by Stewart
Sutherland and indeed one which was in the sharpest possible contrast
to the guarded utterances and inscrutable demeanour of most of his
HMI predecessors.

Since HMI had frequently been accused – by its supporters no less than its critics – of blandness, this change was not wholly unwelcome, but it had two less happy consequences. First, Woodhead's style of intervention transformed what had from early 1992 been an ever-widening professional debate back from the discussion paper's emphasis on the 'bottom-up' resolution of pedgagogical issues by teachers to the *ex cathedra* interventions of the Clarke/Patten era. Second, whereas the primary discussion paper, for all its imperfections, had sought to break away from the simplistic pathology of 'traditional versus progressive' and to replace this by a multidimensional and multicausal account of pedagogy, the Woodhead interventions once more contracted the analysis to the shibboleths of subject knowledge, whole-class teaching and the malign influence of progressivism and the educational establishment.

A symptom of the shift was OFSTED's 1995 report on its continuing follow-up to the 1992 primary discussion paper. Whereas the three previous OFSTED documents in this series had consisted of deperson-alised presentations of findings and issues, the 1995 report, written round eight conferences for heads and advisers held in the summer of that year, was dominated by Woodhead's personal statement (OFSTED 1995b: 5–20) and by his decision to require conference members to discuss not just the OFSTED reports and evidence but also his personal views as presented at the 1995 RSA lecture (Woodhead 1995a). Opening each conference he said:

> We have organised these conferences as a further contribution to the debate about teaching quality begun in *Curriculum Organisation and Classroom Practice in Primary Schools: a Discussion Paper* (1992) and continued in *Primary Matters* (1994), and, in particular, to develop some of the issues raised in my Annual Lecture and 1993–4 Annual Report.
>
> (Woodhead, in OFSTED 1995b: 7)

The selection from the inspection and research evidence made by Woodhead at the 1995 conferences, and again in the report, was criticised in the educational press. In the section of the lecture headed 'The evidence base', for example, he cited just four publications: OFSTED's *Primary Matters* (OFSTED 1994), Maurice Galton's *Crisis in the Primary Classroom* (Galton 1995), the briefing/summary of the Leeds report (Alexander 1991c) – rather than the report itself – and Harold Stevenson's controversial comparative study of primary education in China, Japan and the United States (Stevenson and Stigler 1992). Compounding this initial selectivity, he focused on the advocacy by *Primary Matters* of subject knowledge, direct instruction and grouping by ability, on the arguments for whole-class teaching in Galton's book, on the questioning of 'good practice' orthodoxies in the Leeds report, and, again, on whole-class teaching in the Stevenson study.

Woodhead's use of conferences like these, and of the traditional platform of the Chief Inspector's annual report, was augmented by the initiation, coinciding with the beginning of his term of office, of the Royal Society of Arts annual HMCI lecture, the first of which (Woodhead 1995a) attracted considerable media publicity of a by now depressingly familiar kind: 'Dogma teachers are danger says schools chief' ... 'Inspector attacks woolly teachers' ... 'Schools chief attacks progressive methods' ... 'Timewarp teachers – sixties dogma is failing youngsters of the Nineties' ... 'Trendies in class who harm pupils' ... 'Woodhead castigates progressives' ... 'Progressive teaching gets a caning'. Woodhead also exploited other platforms for the presentation of his views, notably the right-wing forum Politeia (Woodhead 1995c) and his frequent appearances on radio and television.

Ten contexts of professional influence

Thus, by 1996 the 1991–92 'winter initiative' on primary education had impacted on teachers and schools, directly and indirectly, through three main constituencies of debate (the media, academic and professional) and, more specifically, in the following ten contexts of influence.

First, teachers' initial perceptions of the discussion paper, prior to its distribution to schools, were strongly influenced by the polarised and somewhat confrontational treatment which it (and they) received from the press.

Second, conferences, courses and other activities organised by LEAs and the local associations of heads and deputies marked the beginning of the process of professional intervention in the debate and re-appropriation of the document for the purposes to which, ostensibly, it had been directed.

Third, the printed summaries, digests and commentaries prepared by both LEAs and the professional associations consolidated this process by providing rather different accounts of the discussion paper from those which had appeared in the media.

Fourth, discussion and activity at the level of the individual school, facilitated by the document's wide distribution, gave teachers the opportunity to engage directly with its arguments.

Fifth, random references, accounts and correspondence in the professional literature of primary education provided teachers with a base of interpretation and commentary to supplement that which they themselves had generated.

Sixth, the debate among academics conducted through the medium of journal articles and conference papers provided a parallel resource for commentary and critique, though not one, by and large, to which most teachers will have had or sought access. Its influence was less direct.

Seventh, the OFSTED follow-up conferences and reports fulfilled the dual though not necessarily compatible function of enabling the profession to voice its opinions of the discussion paper and the problems its arguments had raised and generated, while giving OFSTED itself a lever on how the paper should be interpreted and applied.

Eighth, the teacher training courses planned in accordance with the government's 1993 criteria were defined with specific reference to the discussion paper, especially its fourth, sixth and ninth chapters, and they thus consolidated its influence for the longer term.

Ninth, and another potentially powerful longer-term normative influence, the 1995 OFSTED inspection criteria also reflected the discussion paper's messages, particularly on classroom practice.

Finally, however, the interventions by the second head of OFSTED seem to have signalled a perception that domestication of the discussion paper had gone far enough and that the debate about primary education needed to return to the simple and traditional formulae with which Prime Minister Major had opened it in his Conservative Party Conference speech of September 1991. Put another way, if, as Woods and Wenham suggest, the primary 'debate' had been first appropriated by politicians and the media, then re-appropriated by teachers, LEAs, professional associations and academics, the run-up to another general election was the time when it needed to be reclaimed by the politicians.

This brings us to the question of what, having initiated the debate in 1991, politicians had contributed to it after their first flurry of interest.

THE POLITICAL NON-DEBATE

The answer is regrettably simple. The political debate, apart from a couple of lack-lustre and ill-prepared radio interviews, a few jibes exchanged across the floor of the House of Commons and, in a slightly more genteel fashion, the Lords, simply failed to take place.

Among the explanations for this lacuna, three seem particularly persuasive. The first is that, despite the rhetoric of 'stimulating a debate' a real debate on these matters at the political level was the last thing a government heading for a general election wished to provoke, and that their interest was simply in making and reinforcing a public judgement about the state of primary education, deflecting blame away from themselves, and directing it back on teachers and the educational establishment. The second is that the arguments – to which I referred earlier – first among ministers (especially Eggar and Fallon) and then between Woodhead and myself, compromised the initiative to an extent that its political edge was blunted and it was necessary to downgrade it on the pre-election agenda.

The third explanation is that the political system as a whole, debilitated from years of Conservative dominance and Labour conflict, was incapable of responding. The government threw down the gauntlet, but the opposition did not pick it up. Despite having ample warning (six weeks is an eternity in politics) and despite presumably recognising the pre-election advantage which the government had sought to gain from its 'winter initiative', the opposition parties failed to exploit the political opportunities which the government's initiative had so amply offered and for which the discussion paper itself had provided the cue:

> If things have gone wrong – and the word 'if' is important – then scapegoating is not the answer. All those responsible for administering and delivering our system of primary education need to look carefully at the part they may have played.
>
> (Alexander *et al.* 1992: para 22)

For example, if in 1992 judgements were being made about problems in primary education and their causes, the government's own record could hardly escape scrutiny since by that time they had been responsible for the country's education system for thirteen years. The structural and resourcing questions signalled in the paper represented another point of vulnerability for the government, as did the issue of the manageability of the National Curriculum. Both offered considerable political and electoral mileage there for the taking. The government's manipulation of documents like the Leeds report and the primary discussion paper, and its relentless criticism of teachers and the 'educational establishment', could easily have been exposed as the diversionary tactic which it probably was.

Instead, the opposition parties remained silent, or in disarray, on primary education, and the counterbalancing impact in the national debate of a robust political exchange was never provided: that was left to teachers, unions and academics, whose views not only received less attention than those of politicians, but could also be dismissed by them as representing vested interests.

Ironically, one of the most effective political interventions came from a member of the Conservative Party itself. In a speech in Leicester in December 1992, Sir Malcolm Thornton, Chairman of the Commons Education Committee, strongly attacked the culture which the government and its advisers had created:

> If only we could have drawn breath after the passing of the 1988 Act. There was a brief moment . . . when it looked as though that might

happen. But that glimmer of light was snuffed out before most people realised it was there. From that point on, I believe that both the wider debate and the ears of Ministers have been disproportionately influenced by extremists. . . . And who are they to foist upon the children of this country ideas which will only take them backwards? What hard evidence do they have to support their assertions? How often do they go into schools and see for themselves what is really happening? What possible authority can they claim for representing the views of 'the overwhelming majority of parents'? I believe that in all their answers to these – and many more – questions, they are found wanting. Their insidious propaganda must be challenged. . . . The extreme right-wing think-tanks – representing, I believe, the remnants of a group of people who, quite rightly, challenged many of the assumptions which had become entrenched in our education system – are the spindle and loom of chaos; the offspring of bigoted minds and muddy understandings. Sadly, whole sections of our nation . . . have been brainwashed into an acceptance of their dogma. Scarcely a day goes by without yet another newspaper article giving them credibility.

(Thornton 1993: 172–3)

Other challenges to government thinking came from former government servants and advisers: Eric Bolton, HM Senior Chief Inspector from 1983 to 1991; Paul Black, Chair of the Task Group on Assessment and Testing which had drawn up the original model and specifications for National Curriculum assessment; and Duncan Graham, former Chairman and Chief Executive of the National Curriculum Council. Each recounted different versions of the same experience: having a principled and well-founded educational initiative hijacked for narrow party-political purposes (Chitty and Simon 1993; Graham and Tytler 1993). But like the comments of teachers, these, too, could be marginalised as being from the 'educational establishment'.

People like Thornton, Bolton, Black and Graham, however eminent and persuasive, could hardly fill the political vacuum caused by the opposition parties' failure to engage at the political level with the primary initiative. Nor even could former NUT General Secretary Fred Jarvis, whose relentless hounding of Prime Minister Major in correspondence with Downing Street between July 1991 and February 1993 exposed both the cruder ideological aspects of education policy at that time and the misuse of evidence on which it was frequently based. Jarvis's correspondence, remarkably illuminating for its insight into the policy process, contains several specific confrontations on the government's handling of both the Leeds report and the primary discussion paper (Jarvis 1993).

I suspect that Jarvis's published correspondence is the tip of an iceberg of unpublished and perhaps very revealing encounters between members of the teaching profession and politicians or political servants. Thus, before me as this book goes to press is a collection of letters between a Norfolk primary head and OFSTED's Chris Woodhead which skilfully undermines the latter's claim that in 1995 there were 15,000 'failing teachers' in the state schools of England and Wales (Foot 1996). Simultaneously, a recently retired senior member of OFSTED with a distinguished track record in primary education, Colin Richards, broke with the unwritten convention of studied inspectoral silence and publicly disputed Woodhead's claim, on the grounds of allegedly misused evidence, that in 1995 half of the country's primary schools needed improvement (Richards 1996).

CONCLUSION

I have illustrated and examined the debate about the primary discussion paper within three constituencies which were critical to its reception and use, and have noted the relative absence of debate in a fourth constituency, the political one within which the discussion paper originated. All three discourses were to an extent contests over what the discussion paper said and meant, but this element seems to have been less pronounced in the professional constituency. That is to say, while among journalists and academics it was understood, as it is by politicians, that in matters of policy presentation is all, or almost all, teachers seemed less inclined to contest the discussion paper's tone and meaning than to consider how they stood in relation to its substance.

In this matter, it would appear that some academic commentators misjudged the professional response. For though several focused on those statements in the paper which they found professionally 'offensive' or 'insulting' and presumed that such passages effectively invalidated the document as a whole, teachers themselves, and the LEA advisers and inspectors through whom professional discussion of the paper was often mediated, seemed ready to set questions of tone on one side, once the initial period of media dominance was over, and concentrate on the underlying arguments.

Perhaps, in this, the LEA role was particularly significant; for historically, LEA advisers and inspectors have been occupationally closer and more vulnerable than academics to the language and manoeuvrings of politicians, and have needed to learn not just how to survive in such a context but also how to turn political initiatives to their own advantage.

The arguments in the discussion paper to which the professional constituency chose to respond, again, were not, by and large, those which preoccupied the academic critics. Teachers, their unions, advisers and inspectors seized on the criticism of the primary/secondary funding anomaly, welcomed the endorsement of eclecticism in respect of matters like topic work and subject teaching, the balance of whole-class, group and individual work, and the deployment of generalist and specialist expertise. To an extent which some academics may have viewed with surprise or even dismay, teachers seem to have found that much of the primary discussion paper spoke to their condition. To them, recognition that teaching demands a well-developed sense of the pragmatic was admirable rather than demeaning, while some academic commentators viewed the paper's apparent appeal to pragmatism as a rejection of the ethical and theoretical considerations which are the essence of educational judgements. And among teachers nationally, as among the teachers in Leeds, the exposure of the prevalence and dangers of political correctness seems to have evoked a relieved resonance rather than a sense of outrage.

Thus, if we take the line of academic opposition to the discussion paper most characteristically and succinctly expressed by Ball –

> In effect, the debate was opened, judged and closed in the same document. Progressive child-centred methods and the Plowden report were subjected to a public deconstruction, progressive teachers were disciplined and the groundwork was laid for a thoroughgoing reintroduction of traditional teaching methods.
>
> (Ball 1994: 44)

– we might now suggest not only that on these matters this judgement misrepresents the discussion paper's arguments in ways I have demonstrated, but also that within the professional constituency of primary teachers, advisers and inspectors, the discussion paper did the opposite of what Ball claimed: it opened the debate and encouraged it to remain open. The weakness of some of the commentary to which I have referred is that it fails to take account of the history and culture within which primary teachers were operating during the two decades before the paper's publication. Neither as uniformly repressive as portrayed by its opponents, nor as intellectually open as portrayed by its advocates, it was nevertheless a culture in which, for many teachers, there were certain never-to-be-contested 'givens' of professional belief and practice.

It was also a culture in which adaptation and improvisation were cardinal virtues, whether in respect of teaching materials or educational documents. Primary teachers, historically, have always expected to turn whatever materials they have at hand to their own particular purposes, in one context accumulating scrap materials for craft and science, in another cheerfully disregarding the carefully formulated rationales of published schemes and treating them as classroom resources rather than as prescriptive texts. This characteristic frustrated a generation of project directors and publishers responsible for Schools Council materials in the 1960s and 1970s, not to mention officers of NCC and SCAA in the 1980s and 1990s, but it meant that a document like the discussion paper was much more likely to be used selectively and eclectically in primary schools than to be wholeheartedly accepted or rejected.

By 1996, one might have concluded that the 1992 primary discussion paper, flawed though it undoubtedly was, had become more or less institutionalised within the professional culture of primary education, mediated in the three constituencies and the ten contexts discussed above. However, one might also argue that after a period of relatively restrained discussion the pendulum of discourse had once more swung back towards the sharp polarisation of views which had surrounded the paper's inception and publication.

It is true that by 1996 few argued any longer about what the discussion paper said, or indeed whether it was a discussion paper or something else. Events had moved on, and though it – and the 'three wise men' – were frequently invoked to legitimate specific standpoints, this particular document was now part of history. Each constituency had used the paper to serve its own purposes: politicians had exploited it; journalists had mythologised it; academics (some of them) had demonised it; and teachers had domesticated it. However, the arguments about educational standards, the causes of educational success and failure, the conditions for effective teaching and learning, and indeed the nature of teaching itself – issues whose treatment in the discussion paper had, as we saw earlier in this chapter, provoked such controversy among academics – these arguments remained, and remain, very much alive.

Chapter 12

Politics of good practice

In this book we have tracked the progress and impact of two significant policy initiatives in the field of primary education. Though linked – in as far as the 1991 Leeds report is generally regarded as the catalyst for the government's 1991–92 primary initiative, and the present author provided continuity from one to the other – they were also very different.

The Leeds programme was devised, sponsored and funded by a local education authority. It was ambitious, organisationally complex and expensive. It was phased over several years and had in view an even longer-term agenda of professional development and school reform. It sought to marshal a complete system of education, from policy-makers, officials and advisers to heads, teachers and support staff, behind a corporate vision of educational quality and entitlement. Though devised by one political party, it enjoyed the support of the parties in opposition, and – as is often the case in local government in the United Kingdom, though rarely at Westminster – represented a genuine attempt at consensus politics.

In contrast, the primary discussion paper arose from a policy decision of national government, and was speedily devised and cheaply enacted. Its form was simple: no elaborate programme, no commitment of resources, but merely the commissioning, writing and dissemination of a document, a sequence which took barely four months. By this action the government sought to influence school and classroom practice in two ways: at the espoused professional level by using the findings of inspection and research to promote discussion and debate; at the political level by exposing teachers and schools to attention and pressure from the media, parents and the public. Since government must have realised that no professional group is likely to respond other than negatively or defensively to a 'discourse of derision', it is tempting to assume that the motives for giving the initiative such a high media profile had mainly to do with the imminence of the 1992 general election. Whatever the tenor of the discussion paper itself, the postures of those who commissioned it were unambiguously confrontational: cross-party consensus, in the run-up to a general election, was the last thing they looked for.

Both initiatives arose from a deficit view of primary education, though the perceived causes and solutions were diametrically opposed. At the risk of oversimplification one might suggest that in each of the initiating groups – Leeds City Council in 1984/85 and the national Conservative government in 1991/92 – there were those whose images of good and bad practice were rooted in idealised views of the same stages in the development of post-war English primary education, the 1950s and the 1960s/1970s; in Leeds some saw the 1950s as the nadir, the 1960s/1970s as the zenith; in Downing Street and Smith Square, inevitably, it was the other way round.

Though both ventures originated against a backdrop of competing collective agendas and personal ambitions, the government's 1991-92 'winter initiative' was, as we have seen, much more overtly political and short-term than Leeds LEA's Primary Needs Programme. This is not to say that Clarke's intervention in primary education was nothing more than a cynical pre-election stunt; or, conversely, that the Leeds programme was entirely free of political calculation. Though we have uncovered something of the ministerial and departmental manoeuvring which took place in the summer and autumn of 1991, we also found, in some quarters at least, evidence of a serious and longer-term concern with educational quality, informed by a careful sifting of evidence from inspection and research even before the discussion paper was commissioned. Equally, the extent to which the devising of the Leeds programme was bound up with the career ambitions of its key actors can readily be demonstrated, and both its rationale and early history bore witness to their competing agendas. Beyond these mixed motives and origins, however, we have to acknowledge that electoral survival and the demonstration of political machismo played a much more prominent part in the case of the discussion paper than they did in Leeds.

Did this greater degree of overt politicisation lessen the discussion paper's educational validity or weaken its impact? When we remind ourselves of the way political, professional and media forces were marshalled to try to ensure that the paper delivered the hoped-for political message we might be inclined to conclude that it did. However, this is to reckon without the many other influences which intervened between the inception of the discussion paper as a political idea and its reception by teachers as an educational statement. Equally, it seems dangerous to presume that one can predict the outcomes of a policy by evaluating its origins. Policy, as Bowe and Ball (1992) argue, is less a linear or managerialist sequence of production and implementation than a cycle of creation and re-creation in which the policy only comes alive and acquires meaning in the hands of those who enact it; to which one might add – staying for a moment with the implicit dramatic metaphor here – that a policy 'script', however legalistically framed or tightly annotated, is still capable of many different interpretations and performances. In the case of the primary discussion paper, not only did its title positively invite such catholicity in reading and use, but its content – for reasons we have explored – unwittingly reinforced the invitation by conveying mixed and sometimes conflicting messages.

Thus, when Low (1992) argues that the ministerial and authorial arguments surrounding the inception and production of the discussion paper ensured that it 'failed absolutely to spark serious thinking among . . . professionals', he not only ignores the strong evidence to the contrary which we discussed in the previous chapter, but also admirably exemplifies the managerialist fallacy that policy starts and ends with the actions of policy-makers and that the arena which they and the media share is the only one which matters.

Thus too, in both of the cases examined in this book – the Leeds programme and the primary discussion paper – we have ample demonstration of the proposition that the relationship between policy and practice in education is a complex and frequently wayward one. Once policy enters the arena of practice it acquires a life of its own.

This is not to say that the versions of educational practice which inform an educational policy have no bearing on what teachers do with the policy in the classroom. The Leeds evidence showed how the impact of the LEA's view of 'good practice' on teachers' professional consciousness and actions was neither monolithic nor predictable in its outcomes, but powerful none the less; similarly, the evidence from studies of the impact of the National Curriculum shows that, though the balance of intended and unintended consequences in respect of the government's curriculum prescriptions, and of change and continuity, has been complex, sensitive and sometimes unpredictable, the force of those prescriptions has nevertheless been considerable (Pollard *et al.* 1994; Webb and Vulliamy 1996; Alexander 1995). Policy does not determine practice, but it certainly conditions it.

That being so, it is important to analyse policy not just in terms of its mode of generation and its impact, or – in Bowe's and Ball's terms – its contexts of 'influence', 'text production' and 'practice', but also in terms of its intellectual and educational substance. This, indeed, is what we sought to do in our evaluation of the Leeds initiative.

THREE APPROACHES TO DEFINING GOOD PRACTICE

The ultimate test of educational policy initiatives like the two discussed in this book must be their capacity to improve educational practice in schools and classrooms, and hence to enhance the quality of children's learning. The phrase 'good primary practice' was frequently used in connection with both initiatives – to defend, to attack, to rally the troops, or merely to legitimate their actions, but rarely without implying that its meaning was explicit and understood.

In each case, 'good primary practice' indicated not only a substantive package of propositions about teaching and learning – high expectations, group work, thematic inquiry, focused questions, informative feedback and so on – but also a more general posture on how such propositions are to be defined and validated. In this book we have explored in detail many of these propositions, as translated into the day-to-day decisions and actions of teachers and children. I would like to end by attempting a more generalised analysis not of specific educational practices which we might define as 'good' or 'bad' but of the term 'good primary practice' itself, and the postures with which its different usages are associated. This kind of analysis is necessary partly because, while being manifestly problematic, the term is often treated as wholly uncontentious; and partly because the problems it generates have to be resolved, in the end, by teachers in classrooms. Unpacking the phrase 'good primary practice', therefore, may enhance understanding of the situation in which teachers work and support them in their resolution of the day-to-day challenges of teaching.

We can start by identifying three basic postures on, or approaches to, the good practice question readily evident in professional and political discourse during the 1980s and 1990s.

Good practice as ideological conflict

The first, which we can term the *adversarial* approach, perceives educational quality as the outcome of a necessary struggle between conflicting ideologies. The struggle is as much a moral as an intellectual or practical one. Victory is secured by the exercise of persuasion, and, if necessary, power. The language is simple, direct and confrontational. Much use is made of shibboleths and slogans. Complexity is eschewed and issues are presented as simply as possible. The focus of the resulting prescriptions is highly selective and formulaic, and good practice is presented as the mastery and demonstration of a single package of skills and attributes. The stance is firmly dualist: good/bad, for/against, traditional/progressive, subjects/ topics, whole-class teaching/group work, specialists/generalists, one of us/one of them, and so on.

Good practice as fitness for purpose

While the adversarial stance assumes the similarity of schools and classrooms, *fitness for purpose* emphasises their diversity and complexity.

These characteristics are seen to demand teachers who possess an extensive repertoire of strategies and techniques, together with the judgement to deploy them as appropriate and the flexibility to adjust rapidly to changing circumstances and needs. The stance is pluralist: there are many versions of good practice, not just one or a few, and these are defined not away from the classroom but within it, since they arise directly from the decisions of teachers as they seek to match professional practice with educational purpose, and from the unique contexts and dynamics which have influenced these decisions.

Good practice as effectiveness

In this view, good practice is a distillation of research evidence about the capacity of particular strategies, techniques, attributes or circumstances to deliver specific educational outcomes. Classrooms, though recognised as different, are also seen as having many fundamental characteristics in common. These make the exercise of collating and generalising from disparate research findings a legitimate and helpful one. The stance is purportedly scientific rather than moral or pragmatic, with a careful emphasis on the explication and analysis of inputs, processes and outcomes. The watchword is *effectiveness*, with which quality becomes synonymous. The stance is ultimately neither dualist nor pluralist, but singular – having in view the construction of if not a single model of good practice then at least an all-purpose, statistically validated set of factors or indicators which can in turn steer policies of school improvement.

It will be readily apparent that the political and media contexts of the 1992 primary discussion paper favoured the adversarial model of good practice. Two other matters are clear, however. First, that the balance of argument in the discussion paper itself strongly endorsed the opposing and pluralist 'fitness for purpose' view; second, that the discussion paper's authors were not united in their endorsement of this stance, with the result that the document as published contained evidence of their failure to resolve the conflict between the two approaches. By endorsing 'fitness for purpose', the paper partly frustrated the initiative's political objectives; it also appeared to have wrong-footed a number of academics. But by compromising this message with lapses into a confrontational tone and specific phrases with strong soundbite potential, the paper provided sufficient to sustain the political, media and academic claim that it was an adversarial, and especially an anti-progressive, manifesto.

When we attempt to place the Leeds initiative within this spectrum, we find that in certain respects it had a much closer affinity with the first version of good practice than the other two, even though there was none of the aggressive posturing and heightened language of the national debate as it took place during 1991 and 1992. For in Leeds, a specific version of good practice was on offer, physically embodied in the model classroom, and legitimated by reference to the ideology of child-centredness. Moreover, though in the report (pages 133–5) we were careful to emphasise that judgements about the exercise of power and patronage in the LEA were made by the programme's participating teachers, not ourselves, the power context of the preferred version of good practice, for many teachers in Leeds, was an undeniable reality.

In this respect, therefore, it is important to acknowledge that the political and professional constituencies in primary education at this time may have had more in common with each other than either constituency would wish to acknowledge. If the political culture promoted by the right wing of the Conservative Party was strongly adversarial, the professional culture was, in some respects and manifestations, almost as normative, if not as strident, in its advocacy of particular values and practices, and almost as intolerant of those who espoused alternatives. 'Primaryspeak', as I show elsewhere (Alexander 1984, 1995) was not the language of plurality or compromise, and during the 1970s and 1980s consensus was perhaps too readily assumed on the central ethical and practical questions with which primary teachers – indeed, all teachers – were confronted.

This element was eagerly exploited by ministers and sections of the press in 1991–92, and again in 1995–96. In this, they were aided by the 'expert' judgements of the Chief Inspector of Schools, whose frequent claim that primary teachers were implacably opposed to whole-class teaching and subjects (Woodhead 1995a, 1995c; OFSTED 1995b) had some historical justification even if by the mid-1990s it was somewhat overstated.

How far has the situation changed since the two initiatives which form the subject of this book? Adversarialism in respect of notions of quality and good practice is still a dominant feature, and will be for as long as we have a government which prefers confrontation to consensus. But in two other respects there is evidence of a shift in thinking. First, as we saw in Chapter 11, the idea of 'fitness for purpose' appears to have resonated strongly within the teaching profession. While we may need to acknowledge that in part this is because 'fitness for purpose' can be taken to invite not just rigour of situational analysis but also a *laissez-faire* endorsement of pragmatism, it is also clear that the phrase served to liberate many teachers from the real or imagined hegemony of the one-dimensional view of good practice implied by the adversarial model, inviting them instead to see classroom decision-making as the independent application of their own knowledge, judgement and skill rather than as the implementation of the prescriptions of others.

Second, the research-based quest for universal indicators of school and classroom effectiveness became, in the late 1980s and 1990s, one of education's major growth industries, spawning a national and international network of centres, projects and publications, and earning the approval of official bodies as diverse as OFSTED, the Labour Party, the Organisation for Economic Cooperation and Development, and the World Bank (for example, Sammons *et al.* 1995; Lockheed and Verspoor 1991; Reynolds *et al.* 1994; OFSTED 1996b; Labour Party 1995). In these latter manifestations, therefore, notions of 'effectiveness' provided a more respectable obverse to the confrontational public face of educational policy.

The problems of the effectiveness approach deserve a book to themselves, but for the moment we should be content with noting just three.

First, there are obvious dangers in aggregating and extrapolating from data from research studies which have used different methods and have dealt with highly disparate educational contexts and practices.

Second, there is a tempting but spurious absolutism about notions like 'success', 'failure' and 'improvement' with which the literature of school effectiveness abounds. The absolutism is spurious partly because even the most sophisticated statistical techniques are only as good as the raw data upon which they operate, and the range of variables fed into this kind of analysis is bound to be incomplete. In a more commonsense vein, these terms are vulnerable to the accusation that they presume homogeneity in respect of the level of the educational system – national, local, school, classroom – to which they are applied, when in reality in any 'successful' schools there are unsuccessful teachers and pupils, and in any 'failing' schools there are almost certainly tales of professional and educational triumph. In this respect, the notion of school 'improvement' at least incorporates the possibility of a continuum of success or failure, within one school, over time, and in relation to social context.

Third, most of the effectiveness studies take insufficient account of the cultural and ethical contexts within which the observed practices are embedded, and many ignore such contexts altogether. This tendency, in the mid-1990s, was a particular characteristic of those studies which purported to show that schooling, as judged by outcomes such as test scores in science and mathematics, was more effectively conducted in selected countries of mainland Europe and the Pacific Rim than in England; and that by importing the classroom methods used in these countries teachers in England would also import the levels of pupil performance with which, elsewhere, they were associated.

The international effectiveness movement is an extremely important development. It raises critical questions about educational goals and practices; it provides a significant corrective to the sterility of traditional/progressive adversarialism; and it has the potential vastly to extend our vocabulary of educational and professional possibilities. Nevertheless, its failure to accommodate to cultural and ethical questions – an inherent consequence of the methodology adopted – must be counted a serious weakness (Alexander 1966b).

Though appeals to 'fitness for purpose' and 'effectiveness' have far more to commend them as approaches to defining good practice than the political and professional adversarialism which has been such a prominent feature of this country's discourse about primary education during the last twenty years, it is still worth asking whether they go far enough. What follows does not claim to supplant either 'fitness for purpose' or 'effectiveness', but it does place both in a somewhat wider frame of reference.

GOOD PRACTICE: THE TRIUMPH OF VALUES IN A CONTEXT OF COMPETING IMPERATIVES?

Let us start this quest for an alternative approach by returning to Leeds and the primary discussion paper:

> Why do we do it this way? Well, it's good primary practice, isn't it?

> We apply all the basic principles of good practice here – a stimulating environment with high quality display and plenty of material for first-hand exploration; a flexible day in which children can move freely from one activity to the next without the artificial barriers of subjects; plenty of individual and group work.

> We don't believe in teaching here. The job of the teacher is to create the environment in which children can find things out for themselves, not to tell them what they should know.

> Plowden is still my Bible, whatever the government or any airy-fairy academics say. They are not the practitioners – I am!

> I have terrible problems planning, because we're all supposed to use topic webs and show them to the head, and I'm not very good at them, and find them impossible to use, especially as now I have to add all the attainment targets. So what I do is a topic web to satisfy the head, and my own planning for me.

> If you don't have drapes and triple mounting, you won't get on here.

and:

> Child-centred education ... part of a deliberate political project to undermine the respect the young should have for the achievements of those who went before them.
>
> (Anthony O'Hear in the *Daily Telegraph*, 12 February 1991)

A generation of wasted time. . . . The education of millions of children has been blighted in the name of an anarchic ideology, says a new study.

(*Daily Telegraph*, 19 September 1991).

Children spend more time with paint pots than mastering the three Rs, said Schools Minister Michael Fallon. . . . They should get back to basics and teach the whole class in an organised way.

(*Daily Mail*, 2 November 1991)

At its worst, current practice hinders concentration, disguises time-wasting, lack of real learning and superficial questioning; and provides little useful contact between the teacher and the individual pupil.

(Former Secretary of State Kenneth Clarke, in a circular to all primary schools, 3 December 1991)

We will take no lectures from those who led the long march of mediocrity through our schools. . . . I will fight for my belief. My belief is a return to basics in education. The progressive theorists have had their say and, Mr President, they've had their day.

(Prime Minister John Major, Conservative Party Conference, October 1991)

Look on your works, Lady Plowden, and despair.

(*Daily Telegraph*, 7 November 1991)

In essence, these are all variations on the same theme: the pervasiveness and limitations of the adversarial approach to good practice.

A rather different style of pronouncement on the good practice question, more extended and descriptive though no less suffused by values, can be found in official reports. Thus, for example, the 1967 Plowden report portrayed three schools 'run successfully on modern lines', whose characteristics are captured in these extracts:

The children . . . spread into the hall, the corridors and the playground. The nursery class has its own quarters and the children are playing with sand, water, paint, clay, dolls, rocking horses and big push toys under the supervision of their teacher. This is how they learn. . . . Learning is going on all the time, but there is not much direct teaching. . . . The class of sevens to nines had spread into the corridor and were engaged in a variety of occupations. One group were gathered round their teacher for some extra reading practice, another was at work on an extraordinary structure of wood and metal which they said was a sputnik, a third was collecting a number of objects and testing them to find out which could be picked up by a magnet and two boys were at work on an immense painting of St Michael defeating Satan. They seemed to be working harmoniously according to an unfolding rather than a pre-conceived plan. . . . As he leaves the school and turns into the grubby and unlovely street onto which it abuts, the visitor passes a class who, seated in a quiet, sunny corner, are listening to their teacher telling them the story of Rumplestiltskin.

(CACE 1967: 103–5)

Twenty years later, the agenda had changed somewhat, though its antecedents were still discernible, as the following extracts from HMI's direct encounter with the good practice problem show.

First impressions were of an informality which typifies many primary classrooms. Closer investigation revealed that the freedoms were not there merely by chance. . . . The children were keenly interested in their work. Their commitment to what they were doing extended beyond the more obviously enjoyable aspects of their practical activities. . . . The children were being taught to listen carefully and speak clearly and articulately. . . . Their written work caused them to use a variety of styles. . . . The high quality of teaching was the strongest feature common to all the examples . . . there were variations in the teaching styles reflecting the needs of the situation and the personality of individual teachers. . . . Teachers had a sound knowledge of their pupils' social and cultural backgrounds. . . . A dominant factor in the achievement of high standards was the strength of commitment on the part of the teachers to ensure that pupils were making progress. . . . Challenges were set so that the work was neither too difficult not too easy. . . . The overriding characteristic is that of agreed, clear aims and purposeful teaching.

(DES 1987: 32–4)

Thus, the appearance might be that of a Plowden classroom, but the teacher had by now become considerably more prominent, and the organic model of an unfolding sequence of intrinsically educative experiences had been replaced by a firm emphasis upon detailed prior planning. This theme was also taken up at school level, underscoring the way that serendipity was to be replaced by management, and individualism by collective endeavour:

In each school the head and staff had agreed aims . . . a shared sense of purpose . . . curricular guidelines which had been carefully thought out. . . . These guidelines had been written after staff discussions. . . . Schools were exploring ways of deploying the staff so that more effective use was made of their abilities and curricular strengths. . . . Schools were making positive efforts to strike the delicate balance which is involved in making the best use of the curricular expertise of a primary school staff as a combined teaching unit.

(DES 1987: 31–2)

September 1989 saw the start of the phased introduction of the National Curriculum, which carried its own clear messages about good practice, at least where conceptions of curriculum and assessment were concerned. Yet the National Curriculum Council at that point felt it important to combine the reassertion of traditional values with a synthesis of Plowden and HMI:

> The aims of the National Curriculum are more likely to be achieved where ... pupils are properly equipped with the basic tools of learning. In particular, where numeracy, literacy and oracy are given highest priority by teachers and are soundly taught. These skills form the basis of a proper and rigorous education to the highest standards which parents and public expect. ... Due recognition is given to the importance of first-hand experience and practical tasks. ... Pupils are led to ask questions and seek answers. ... Teachers' expectations of what pupils are capable of achieving are high and pupils' learning is structured, relevant and stimulating. ... Pupils are encouraged to become self-confident, self-disciplined and courteous.
>
> (NCC 1989: 2)

With the debate about the content of the curriculum apparently closed, the focus of concern shifted to pedagogy, especially during the highly charged period 1991–92 which saw the publication of the Leeds report and the commissioning and publication of the DES primary discussion paper. The latter, as we have seen, trawled the by then extensive body of research on teaching and learning in primary schools, much of it grounded in systematic classroom observation and, under the heading 'Improving classroom practice', offered a set of 'propositions about aspects of classroom practice to which the evidence suggests particular attention should be devoted ... not as a definitive checklist but as the basis for open and constructive discussion' (Alexander *et al.* 1992: 37). The propositions related to the themes of teacher knowledge, planning, curriculum balance, the classroom context, teacher expectations of pupils, the management of classroom time, differentiation in learning tasks, assessment and diagnosis, feedback, teaching strategies and techniques.

In respect of all of these, and of the many alternative possibilities for action which they suggest, the document identified 'fitness for purpose' as the key principle for deciding what course of action to take in particular circumstances. Good practice, the document suggested, resides in the teacher having a clear sense of educational purpose, reflected in his or her planning and the context in which teaching and learning are to take place; a well-developed range of pedagogical skills, firmly grounded in appropriate knowledge of children, curriculum and pedagogy; and the capacity to judge how and when this repertoire should be exploited.

The specific research on which the 1992 primary discussion paper drew included several studies which themselves had addressed the good practice question, albeit from the rather different standpoint of a concern with 'effectiveness'. Thus, Mortimore *et al.* (1988: 250–6) identified 'twelve key factors for effective junior schooling', several of which accorded with the conclusions of the earlier studies of Galton and Simon (1980), Galton *et al.* (1980), Bennett *et al.* (1984) and others. The Leeds project highlighted fifty-five issues arising from the initiative which merited local attention, and twenty-four priorities for improving educational practice which were deemed to have national relevance (Alexander 1992d: 195–6).

The 1992 primary discussion paper led to follow-up reports from OFSTED which identified six 'factors associated with better topic work' and twenty-one 'factors associated with better classroom practice' (OFSTED 1993b), then six 'factors associated with high standards of achievement', eight which in contrast were 'associated with poor standards of achievement' and a further six 'associated with successful topic work' (OFSTED 1994). Thus:

> In virtually all the lessons with high standards teachers had satisfactory or good knowledge of the subject they were teaching.

> In more than half (58 per cent) of lessons where pupils achieved high standards teachers demonstrated good questioning skills to assess pupils' knowledge and challenge their thinking.

> In 54 per cent of the better lessons teachers made effective use of exposition, instruction and direct teaching.

> In 31 per cent of the better lessons teachers used a good balance of grouping strategies including whole-class, small group or individual work as appropriate.

> In 19 per cent of the better lessons teachers used ability group work effectively.

Several other factors were evident though less frequently highlighted than those listed above:

> clear objectives for the lesson;
> good management of lesson time;
> effective use of other adults in the classroom;

appropriate range of teacher assessment techniques;
well-established classroom routines providing minimal disruption to
  tasks and teaching;
good classroom organisation of resources and materials;
effective planning of the pupils' work.

(OFSTED 1994:14)

Finally, OFSTED offered what it deemed the definitive judgement of
good practice at the level of the whole school:

OFSTED judges a school effective according to the success it meets
in four aspects of its work: its pupils' standards of achievement, the
quality of education it provides, the efficiency with which it manages
its resources, and its contribution to pupils' spiritual, moral, social
and cultural development.

(OFSTED 1996b: 58)

Whatever the limits of each such study, collectively they did at least
offer clearly enunciated propositions helpful in the quest for good
primary practice, and, it must be said, a fair degree of consensus arrived
at by different methodological routes. But was this enough?

The most important point to make, and the most obvious, is that any
notion of good practice presupposes criteria for judgement. Although
some of the published extracts above make criteria explicit, they remain
tacit or only partly explicated in others, and in some of the statements
above from teachers, the press and politicians there is a clear assumption that criteria are not needed at all – either because good practice is
about belief rather than justification, or because the presumed consensus
makes their explication unnecessary. In general, good primary practice
discourse has tended to be strong on assertion and weak on justification. As a result, the necessary task of defining and defending criteria
for judgement has been somewhat neglected.

When we say of teaching which we do, see or commend 'this is good
practice', what are we really asserting? There seem to be four main
possibilities:

- This teaching is in line with what x defines as good practice and the
  status of x is such that his/her views must be heeded.
- This teaching works, in as far as teachers and children seem to be
  appropriately and gainfully occupied.
- This teaching produces specific and recognisable kinds of learning,
  and a causal relationship between the teaching methods and learning
  outcomes can be demonstrated.
- This teaching is consistent with my/our values and beliefs about the
  proper purposes and conduct of education.

Though there is inevitable overlap between the statements, their status is nevertheless somewhat different. Thus, the first, being about the exercise of power, is a *political* statement. The second is essentially a *pragmatic* statement. The third, being grounded in experience and observation and being concerned with verification, is an *empirical* statement. The fourth is *evaluative* in the sense of expressing, and being explicitly validated by, values and beliefs.

If we now return to the quotations and extracts above, it is possible to classify them in terms of these categories. Sometimes the classification is clear-cut, as in the case of several of the assertions by teachers and politicians, where a firm value-stance is adopted, but no justification, evidential, ethical or otherwise, is offered. Sometimes the exercise of classification shows, notwithstanding the apparent certainty of the judgement being offered, how the ostensible neutrality of the empirical statement is usually nothing of the sort, being on the one hand necessarily and inevitably underpinned by values, and on the other sustained by a sense of its own (methodological or academic) authority.

This classification begins to unravel the 'good' in 'good practice': it is anything but the absolute many claim or wish. What of the notion of 'practice' itself? Is it reasonable to assume that when we speak of good primary practice we are all talking of the same phenomena, and the only problem concerns the basis on which we rate them as good, bad or indifferent? Though we readily acknowledge that 'education' is a pluralistic concept, is 'teaching' significantly less so?

The quotations above indicate that it is not. Of course, none of the statements made by teachers, journalists or politicians was intended to be anything other than selective in its focus, though the nature of that selectivity is of considerable interest. However, even the ostensibly more comprehensive statements display somewhat different conceptions of, as well as different values about, teaching. Thus, the Plowden extracts are preoccupied with the use of time and space, relationships, children's motivation, attitude and behaviour, the school and classroom context, pedagogic processes, the whole rather than the parts, evolution rather than structure, and especially with the needs of the child, defined developmentally and motivationally. In contrast, the 1987 HMI extracts imply a very different agenda: aims, planning, curriculum content, staff expertise and deployment, challenge in learning experiences, diagnosis and assessment, matching of child and curriculum task, structure, progression and continuity, the parts as well as the whole, and the needs of the child, defined in relation to societal realities and expectations. In turn, and with a narrower focus still, the 1994 OFSTED list highlights the attributes of the teacher, especially subject knowledge and classroom strategies. Or consider this statement from an HMI report on an initial teacher-training institution:

The college declares publicly its philosophy of good primary practice. This is stated in all substantial course documents. The philosophy has several key elements. These are stated to include: the recognition of the uniqueness of the individual child; the importance of first-hand experience; the value of an attractive and stimulating learning environment.

The problem here is not so much the substance as the scope of this statement. Few would dissent from the three principles thus enunciated – except those on the political right who would probably view them as outrageously provocative – and many would applaud them. But as a philosophy of good primary practice this is surely deficient. It is rather like a play with scenery but no actors or text, or a concert with orchestra but no music, or the National Gallery bereft of its pictures. It provides the context for education and gently hints at its conduct, but it indicates nothing of its purposes, scope, content or outcomes.

The problem with many such everyday accounts or definitions of good practice is that not only do they leave unexplored vital questions of justification, but they also focus in a frequently arbitrary way upon particular aspects of practice which are then elevated to the status of a complete and coherent 'philosophy'. More often than not, they are merely philosophical fragments or preliminary clearings of the throat. In its everyday usage, therefore, the phrase 'good primary practice' is deeply flawed, both ethically and conceptually. Some who use the phrase are intuitively aware that this is so, and in writing adopt the apologetic device of placing the words in inverted commas, providing the digital equivalent in conversation. This is rarely more than a tic, since having made this passing acknowledgement that the phrase is problematic they invariably go on to treat it as though it were not.

In order to judge the adequacy of a good practice claim, therefore, we need not only to examine the criteria by which practice is judged to be good, but also to be clear about which aspects of practice are defined in this way and which aspects are ignored. There is of course no reason why a good practice statement should not be selective and sharply focused, and indeed every reason why sharpness of focus is desirable, for it is difficult to talk meaningfully about teaching unless we engage with its specifics. The problem comes when over time, or within a statement purporting to stand as a complete educational rationale, some aspects of practice are consistently emphasised while other aspects are consistently ignored. The underlying message of selectivity in this context is that what is emphasised is all that matters, whether it be – to draw on contrasting selections – display, group work, thematic inquiry, the subject-based curriculum, whole-class teaching or the basics.

	ASPECTS		CENTRAL EDUCATIONAL QUESTIONS
OBSERVABLE PRACTICE	CONTEXT	physical interpersonal	
	CONTENT	whole curriculum subjects/areas	WHAT should children learn?
	PEDAGOGY	teaching methods pupil organization	and
	MANAGEMENT	planning operation assessment of learning evaluation of teaching	HOW should children learn and teachers teach?
IDEAS VALUES BELIEFS	CHILDREN	development needs learning	WHY should children be educated in this way?
	SOCIETY	needs of society needs of the individual	and
	KNOWLEDGE	children's ways of knowing culturally evolved ways of knowing	WHAT is an educated person?

Figure 12.1   Educational practice: a framework

Figure 12.1 attempts to provide a framework for approaching this aspect of the good practice question in a more rounded way. The two main dimensions reflect a view of teaching as educational ideas in action, or as classroom actions and events which both manifest and are informed by ideas, values and beliefs. The seven aspects of teaching so defined arise from observation of teaching as it happens and from analysis of ideas about teaching which have been articulated by practitioners. The resulting categories are of course not discrete, but are presented separately for analytical purposes. Similarly, the two dimensions, here presented as a sequential list, interact: each aspect of practice is to a greater or lesser extent informed by one, two or all of the areas of ideas, values and assumptions. Armed with such a framework we can return to any good practice statement, test its emphasis and scope, and examine the thrust and genealogy of the ideas, values and beliefs in which it is rooted.

Applying the framework to the various examples given earlier, and to the wider context of the National Curriculum, we can venture some basic propositions. Plowden, for example, tended to focus on context and pedagogy rather than content and management. Its vision was firmly grounded in views of the child, especially the child's development and learning. About society and its needs it had relatively little to say, while its view of knowledge was an extension of its analysis of the nature and needs of childhood. In contrast, HMI from 1978 onwards began to develop a view of practice which dealt with all four elements or practice in the framework, but focused particularly on content and management, with a relatively subsidiary interest in pedagogy. The justificatory basis had less to do with children's inherent characteristics as learners than with a quasi-legal notion of entitlement to breadth, balance and challenge in the curriculum, and was firmly guided by a sense of knowledge as cultural artefact, handed on from one generation to the next and providing an essential tool for the individual to make sense of, participate in, and act upon society and to respond to its needs. In turn, the National Curriculum is even more distant from Plowden. The emphasis here (at least until the interventionist rumblings about pedagogy in late 1991) is almost exclusively on content and management – or rather those aspects of management which are concerned with delivery of content and proof of such delivery, planning and assessment. (The postal nuances of the language of the National Curriculum are startlingly pervasive, and have built remorselessly on former Secretary of State Keith Joseph's initial concept of the curriculum as educational package.) The justificatory basis is unambiguously societal or, rather, economic.

To take stock. 'Good practice' statements come in different forms. Some are statements of value or belief; some are pragmatic statements; some are empirical statements; some are political statements; most combine more than one of these characteristics, which are themselves neither discrete nor one-dimensional; and all presuppose a concept of practice itself. Pursuing our quest for good primary practice in this way, therefore, we can see that while in a physical sense it resides in primary schools and classrooms, in order to know what we are looking for and to begin to understand how we might define and judge it, we need to recognise that it lies, conceptually, somewhere at the intersection of the five considerations or dimensions which have been identified so far: evaluative, pragmatic, empirical, political and conceptual. Figure 12.2 represents this relationship.

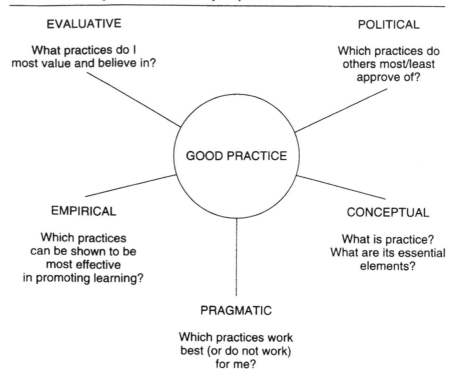

EVALUATIVE

What practices do I
most value and believe in?

POLITICAL

Which practices do
others most/least
approve of?

GOOD PRACTICE

EMPIRICAL

Which practices
can be shown to be
most effective
in promoting learning?

CONCEPTUAL

What is practice?
What are its essential
elements?

PRAGMATIC

Which practices work
best (or do not work)
for me?

Figure 12.2   Good practice 1: reconciling competing imperatives?

The quest for good primary practice, then, is as much a conceptual as an empirical one. However, the point at which the various overlapping considerations meet is an arena of conflict as much as of resolution. Primary practice – any educational practice – requires us to come to terms with and do our best to reconcile competing values, pressures and constraints. It is about dilemma no less than certainty. If this is so of practice in general, it must also be the case, *a fortiori*, with practice we wish to define as 'good'.

However, there has to be a qualitative difference between practice and good practice if the latter notion is not to become redundant. Or is it the case that good practice is no more than the best we can do in the circumstances? Is our quest for educational quality to run into the morass of relativism? I believe not. Though in Figure 12.2 the five considerations or dimensions appear to have equal weight, the pursuit of good practice has to move beyond a mere balancing of competing imperatives. There have to be superordinate reasons for preferring one course of action to another, which enable education to rise above the level of the merely pragmatic. For education is inherently about values: it reflects a vision of the kind of world we want our children to inherit; a vision of the kinds of people we hope they will become; a vision of what it is to be an educated person. Whatever the other ingredients of good practice may be, they should enable a coherent and sustainable value-position to be pursued. Values, then, are central.

Yet, in teaching, values have to be made manifest rather than merely held or voiced. They are manifested as learning contexts, tasks and encounters. While, clearly, such activities must be congruent with the values they seek to realise, such congruence is of itself no guarantee of success in terms of the specific learning goals which give the broader vision practical meaning. We need to go one step further, therefore, and to couple with the commitment to values and value-congruence a clear awareness of evidence, published or experiential, concerning the strengths and weaknesses of the various teaching strategies open to us, in order that we can construct, ideally, learning tasks and contexts which are not just consistent with the values but will also translate them into meaningful learning for the child. It is for this reason that the empirical dimension is so critical an adjunct to matters of value, belief and purpose.

It is also clear that the pursuit of 'effectiveness' *per se*, a currently popular quest among educational researchers and policy-makers as we have seen, can produce versions of good practice which are incomplete or even untenable in the same way that value-statements detached from empirical understanding may be inoperable. Those who presume that the inconveniently untidy cultural and ethical problems in the good practice question are resolved at a stroke by talking of 'effective' practice (or the 'effective' teacher/'effective' school) are engaging in mere sleight of hand: practice, we must ask, which is effective in relation to what? In relation, of course, to a notion of what it is to be educated. Good practice, then, justifies its approbation by being both intrinsically educative and operationally effective. In the educational arena, effectiveness as a criterion existing on its own is meaningless.

We are now in a position to sum up. Figure 12.2 represented good practice as existing at the intersection of the five considerations and as a matter of reconciling competing imperatives. However, I then suggested that this approach does not take sufficient note of what the 'good' in 'good practice' might dictate, and that although all the considerations are important, they are not equivalent. The pursuit of good practice sets the considerations in a hierarchical relationship, with evaluative and empirical questions pre-eminent, and with both dependent on a prior conceptualisation of the nature of educational practice itself. This alternative relationship, a development of the initial idea, is shown in Figure 12.3.

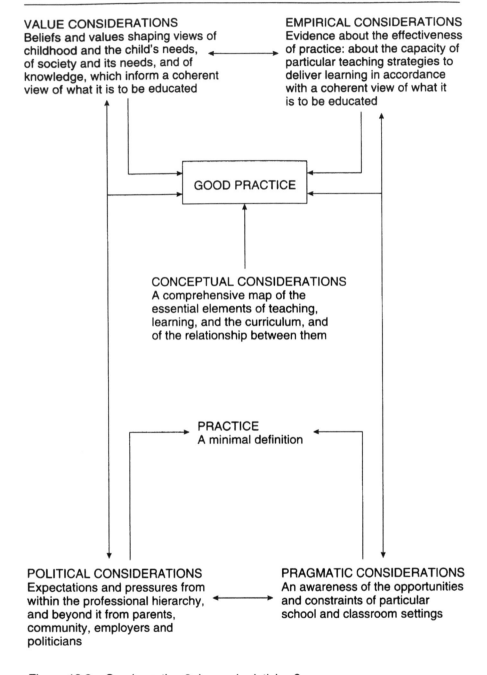

VALUE CONSIDERATIONS
Beliefs and values shaping views of
childhood and the child's needs,
of society and its needs, and of
knowledge, which inform a coherent
view of what it is to be educated

EMPIRICAL CONSIDERATIONS
Evidence about the effectiveness
of practice: about the capacity of
particular teaching strategies to
deliver learning in accordance
with a coherent view of what it
is to be educated

GOOD PRACTICE

CONCEPTUAL CONSIDERATIONS
A comprehensive map of the
essential elements of teaching,
learning, and the curriculum, and
of the relationship between them

PRACTICE
A minimal definition

POLITICAL CONSIDERATIONS
Expectations and pressures from
within the professional hierarchy,
and beyond it from parents,
community, employers and
politicians

PRAGMATIC CONSIDERATIONS
An awareness of the opportunities
and constraints of particular
school and classroom settings

Figure 12.3   Good practice 2: beyond relativism?

When this approach to the good practice question was first presented (in Alexander 1992d) some took it to espouse a narrowly technicist view of teaching, in which the identified considerations bearing on the good practice question – evaluative, empirical and so on – were seen as discrete, mutually exclusive and equivalent (Drummond 1993; Carr 1994). This misreading I find inexplicable, except perhaps as a casualty of the polarised political climate of the time. But because the misreading exists I must emphasise again that the intention was precisely the opposite: to argue for more comprehensive versions of both practice and good practice than some of those on offer; and to insist that, however hard the task of reconciling the various competing demands, pressures and considerations to which the teacher is subject, the primacy of values and a clear and explicit value-orientation in teaching must always be asserted, for without them all notions of being educated, let alone any versions of good educational practice, become meaningless.

Similarly, to appeal to 'fitness for purpose' was not, as some suggested, to invite the bald pragmatism of 'anything goes'. It represented a different kind of attempt to underline the importance of the quest for congruence between classroom action and educational values. It is the challenge of attaining this congruence which makes the notion of good primary practice, like education itself, as much an aspiration as an achievement. But the other message of 'fitness for purpose' is that good practice, created as it is in the unique setting of the classroom by the ideas and actions of teachers and pupils, can never be singular, fixed or absolute, a specification handed down or imposed from above in the manner charted in several contexts within this book.

When in the Leeds report (page 163) we asserted that 'good practice is achieved dialectically and empirically, not by decree', there were those who were happy to take this simply as an attack on LEAs. In fact, the judgement was a general response to the problematic nature of teaching and the contestable notion of good practice, and it therefore applied as much to schools, teacher-training institutions, governments, government agencies and political think-tanks as to LEAs. By 1996 it had become clear that government and its triumvirate of non-elected agencies – OFSTED, SCAA and TTA – had taken over the mantle of those 'definers, arbiters and guardians of good practice' to which the same paragraph of the Leeds report referred. The centralisation of education experienced during the 1980s had produced intellectual hegemony as well as administrative control. The pronouncements of OFSTED, in particular, laid it open to the charge that it was operating on the basis not just of decree but also of a highly selective use of evidence.

Good educational practice is provisional, dynamic – and plural. In a democracy any attempt to monopolise the task of defining what it means to be well taught and well educated must be strenuously resisted.

Appendix: the Leeds evaluation – themes, evidence and methods

THEMES AND METHODOLOGICAL STRANDS

The background to the evaluation of Leeds City Council's Primary Needs Programme is described on pages xvii–xxii, as are ethical and procedural matters such as access and reporting. The six foci or themes for the evaluation related to the main aims of PNP and contingent enabling aspects of the work of schools and the LEA. They were:

- children's needs: identification, diagnosis and provision;
- the curriculum: content, development, management and evaluation;
- teaching strategies and classroom practice, including collaborative teaching;
- links between home, school and community;
- staff roles and relationships, and the management context of PNP schools;
- professional support and development, with particular reference to the LEA.

There were seven methodological strands:

- annual questionnaire surveys of the main groups of participants in all schools in the LEA: heads, PNP appointees, non-PNP appointees, advisory staff and various other groups;
- a longitudinal analysis of change and development in a representative sample of thirty schools, ten from each of the three phases of PNP and incorporating a combination of interview and observation in respect of all six themes (the PNP sample schools);
- a three-level observational study of classroom practice in sixty schools, ten of them from the PNP school sample, the remainder from the group of schools ostensibly most affected by PNP in terms of additional resourcing and involvement in in-service courses;
- fieldwork involving observation and/or interviews in a further ten schools (making a combined fieldwork total of ninety schools)

identified by advisers or the schools themselves as displaying interesting or significant practice as a consequence of PNP;
- observation of and/or interviews with participants involved in contingent activities such as in-service courses, LEA meetings, support
services and so on, and with leading LEA players like advisers;
- examination of a large range and quantity of documentary material
from both schools and the LEA;
- collection and analysis of all 7+ and 9+ reading scores over a six-year
period, starting two years before the Primary Needs Programme's
introduction.

These procedures are now listed in greater detail.

QUESTIONNAIRES

Q01   All Phase I Scale I appointees, 1986
Q02   All Phase I probationers, 1986
Q03   Phase I post-holders, 1986.

These three preliminary questionnaires covered (1) general aspects of
the first year of PNP and (2) the first stage of the PNP INSET programme.
Together with the 1986 coordinators' and heads' questionnaires (Q04
and Q13), their purpose was to identify issues and starting points for
the evaluation.

Q04   All Phase I coordinators, 1986
Q05   All Phase I coordinators, 1987
Q06   All Phase I coordinators, 1988
Q07   All Phase I coordinators, 1989
Q08   All Phase II coordinators, 1987
Q09   All Phase II coordinators, 1988
Q10   All Phase II coordinators, 1989
Q11   All Phase III coordinators, 1988
Q12   All Phase III coordinators, 1989.

Coordinators' questionnaires covered job specifications, roles, changes
in roles, successes, problems, influences, INSET, support and resources.
The range of questions from one year to the next was consistent so as
to permit longitudinal analysis of change and development between 1985
and 1989.

Q13   All Phase I heads, 1986
Q14   All Phase I heads, 1987
Q15   All Phase I heads, 1988
Q16   All Phase I heads, 1989
Q17   All Phase II heads, 1987

Q18   All Phase II heads, 1988
Q19   All Phase II heads, 1989
Q20   All Phase III heads, 1988
Q21   All Phase III heads, 1989
Q22   Heads of middle schools fed by Phase I primary schools, 1989
Q23   Heads of 11–16 secondary schools fed by Phase I primary
       schools, 1989.

The 1986–88 PNP heads' questionnaires covered PNP resources, their
use and impact, successes, problems, LEA INSET and support, and year-
by-year changes. The range of questions from one year to the next was
consistent so as to permit longitudinal analysis of change and development between 1985 and 1989. The 1989 heads' questionnaire was much
more comprehensive and detailed than those in the previous three years.
It focused on the implementation and success of each of the PNP aims
and strategies in turn. The survey of middle and 11–16 school heads
gathered views on the impact of PNP from staff in the schools to which
PNP Phase I pupils had transferred.

Q24   Members of the LEA's advisory and support staff, 1989
Q25   Participants at 25 LEA INSET courses formally monitored during
       1986–89.

The advisory and support staff questionnaires covered the roles, responsibilities and experiences of these staff within the LEA and its schools. It
also reviewed the whole PNP initiative, seeking respondents' views on
the impact of the programme in terms of the four PNP aims, and inviting
them to identify examples of good practice in respect of each.
    Taking all twenty-five questionnaire surveys together, we find a vari-
able response rate. Those distributed during school and INSET fieldwork
achieved a high response (95–100 per cent). Postal questionnaires to the
thirty schools in the representative sample achieved a 90 per-cent
response rate. The overall average response rate for the postal surveys
was 65 per cent.

INTERVIEWS

In the thirty schools in the PNP sample:

I01   Preliminary interviews with heads, 1987
I02   Preliminary interviews with PNP coordinators, 1987
I03   Preliminary interviews with selected non-PNP staff, 1987.

These preliminary interviews covered in turn each of the six themes of
*children's needs, curriculum, teaching strategies, home–school links, manage-
ment* and *professional development*, and in relation to each of them explored
policy, support, priorities, management and emerging issues.

I04   Heads' interviews on needs definition, identification, diagnosis and provision, in respect of the LEA's categories of children's needs, 1987

I05   Coordinators' interviews on needs definition, identification, diagnosis and provision, in respect of the LEA's categories of children's needs, 1987

I06   Heads' interviews on curriculum policy and management, 1987

I07   Coordinators' interviews on curriculum policy and management, 1987 (see Ob05)

I08   Post-holders' interviews on curriculum policy and management, 1987

I09   Heads' interviews, 1988 (follow-up to 1987 interviews, I04)

I10   Coordinators' interviews, 1988 (follow-up to 1987 interviews, I05; see Ob06)

I11   Heads' interviews, 1989 (follow-up to I09)

I12   Coordinators' interviews, 1989 (follow-up to I10; see Ob07)

I13   Deputy heads' interviews on roles and responsibilities, 1988

I14   Pre-observation interviews with ten teachers as part of Level Two of the classroom practice study, 1988 (see Ob11)

I15   Post-observation interviews with ten teachers as part of Level Two of the classroom practice study (see Ob 11).

In other schools:

I16   Heads' interviews on home–school links, 1987

I17   Heads' follow-up interviews on home–school links, 1989 and 1990

I18   Interviews with home–school liaison officers, 1987 and 1989

I19   Interviews with class and support teachers in schools selected for the 1987 TTT study (see Ob02)

I20   Interviews with class and support teachers in schools selected for the 1989 TTT follow-up study (see Ob04)

I21   Pre-observation interviews with forty teachers as part of Level One of the classroom practice study, 1988 (see Ob10)

I22   Post-observation interviews with forty teachers as part of Level One of the classroom practice study, 1988 (see Ob10)

I23   Interviews with heads in the ten schools from the PNP sample chosen for Level Two of the classroom practice study, 1988 (see I14, I15, Ob11)

I24   Initial interviews, at the start of the two-week observation period, with heads in the ten schools at Level Three of the classroom practice study, 1988 (see I25–30 and Ob12–14)

I25   Initial interviews, at the start of the two-week observation period, with class and support teachers in the ten schools at Level Three of the classroom practice study, 1988 (See I24, I26–30 and Ob12–14)

I26   Daily pre-observation interviews with ten class teachers throughout the two-week period of Level Three of the classroom practice study, 1988 (see I24–25, I27–30 and Ob12–14)

I27   Daily post-observation interviews with class teachers throughout the two-week period of Level Three of the classroom practice study, 1988 (see I24–26, I28–30 and Ob12–14)

I28   Final interviews with support teachers at the end of the Level Three classroom practice study, 1988 (see I24–27, I29–30 and Ob12–14)

I29   Final interviews with class teachers at the end of the Level Three classroom practice study, 1988 (see I14–28, I30 and Ob12–14)

I30   Final interviews with heads at the end of the Level Three classroom practice study, 1988 (see I24–29 and Ob12–14).

Other interviews:

I31   Providers of twenty-five LEA INSET courses, 1987, 1988 and 1989 (see I32, Q25, Ob08, DT12)

I32   Teachers attending twenty-five LEA INSET courses, 1987, 1988 and 1989 (see I31, Q25, Ob08, DT12)

I33   LEA advisory and support staff, including staff concerned with special educational needs, gender, multicultural education, the Primary Schools Centre, home–school links, the PNP refurbishment programme, ERA implementation, National Curriculum support, and LMS, 1986–90

I34   The Director of Primary Education, Director of Special Services and other key LEA staff concerned with PNP and related Authority policy, 1986–90.

OBSERVATION

Ob01   Observation of TTT collaborations in the thirty PNP sample schools, using semi-structured schedule, 1987 (see I06–8)

Ob02   Observation of TTT collaborations in selected other schools, using semi-structured schedule, 1987 (see I19–20)

Ob03   Follow-up observation of TTT collaborations in the thirty PNP sample schools, using semi-structured schedule, 1988 (see I06–8)

Ob04   Follow-up observation of TTT collaborations in other schools, using semi-structured schedule, 1988 (see I19–20)

Ob05   Observation of PNP coordinators at work in the thirty PNP sample schools, using semi-structured schedule, 1987 (see I07)

Ob06   Follow-up observation of PNP coordinators at work in the thirty PNP schools, using semi-structured schedule, 1988 (see I10)

Ob07   Follow-up observation of PNP coordinators at work in the thirty

PNP sample schools, using semi-structured schedule, 1989 (see I12)

Ob08 Observation of twenty-five INSET courses, using semi-structured schedule, 1987–90 (see I31, I32, Q25, DT12)

Ob09 Observation of curriculum and staff meetings in the thirty PNP sample schools, using semi-structured schedule, 1988 (see I09 and I10)

Ob10 Observation of forty classrooms, using a structured observation schedule and one observer, as part of Level One of the classroom practice study, 1988 (see I21, I22)

Ob11 Observation of teachers and children at work in classrooms in ten of the PNP sample schools, using a more comprehensive structured observation schedule and one observer, as part of Level Two of the classroom practice study, 1988 (see I14, I15, I23)

Ob12 Systematic observation of teachers in ten classrooms as part of Level Three of the classroom practice study, 1988. Using the PRINDEP Teacher Observation Schedule, one of a pair of observers noted aspects of teacher–pupil interaction and classroom organisation during each of two daily observation sessions over a two-week period. The data were then coded for computer analysis (see I 24–30)

Ob13 Systematic observation of pupils in ten classrooms as part of Level Three of the classroom practice study, 1989. Using the PRINDEP Pupil Observation Schedule, the second of a pair of observers noted aspects of the task-related behaviour and interactions of sixty target pupils during each of two daily observations sessions over a two-week period, The data were then coded for computer analysis (see I24–30)

Ob14 At the same time as the systematic observations of teachers and pupils (see Ob12 and Ob13), all teacher–pupil interactions during each observation session over the two-week period were recorded, using radio microphones worn by the teacher, for later qualitative analysis (see I24–30).

DOCUMENTARY AND TEST MATERIAL

DT01 All LEA policy documents relating to PNP, 1985–89

DT02 LEA policy documents on primary education, 1985–91

DT03 Other LEA policy documents, 1985–91

DT04 Minutes and papers of Leeds City Council's Education Committee, the Primary Needs Monitoring and Evaluation Committee, and the Special Programmes Steering Group, 1985–90

DT05 DES Form 7 from every primary school in Leeds, 1985, 1986. 1987, 1988 and 1989

DT06 Staffing data, gathered by PRINDEP, from the thirty PNP sample schools, 1985, 1986, 1987, 1988 and 1989

DT07 PNP Development Fund bids, 1985, 1986, 1987, 1988 and 1989

DT08 HMI reports on inspections of PNP schools undertaken between 1985 and 1990

DT09 7+ reading scores (Young's Group Reading Test), from all schools, 1983, 1984, 1985, 1986, 1987, 1988 and 1989

DT10 9+ reading scores (NFER Reading Test AD), from all schools, 1983, 1984, 1985, 1986, 1987, 1988 and 1989

DT11 Supplementary LEA reading test score data, analysed by the LEA, for 1990 and 1991

DT12 Course material presented at twenty-five LEA INSET courses, 1987–89 (see Q25, I31, I32, Ob08)

DT13 Lists of all courses and teacher attendances at the Primary Schools Centre, 1985–89

DT14 Miscellaneous school policy documents and guidelines on aspects of the curriculum, classroom practice, home–school relations, meeting special and other needs, from the PNP sample schools, 1985–89

DT15 LEA job specifications for PNP appointees, 1985–89

DT16 School job specifications for PNP and other staff in PNP sample schools, 1985–89.

Bibliography

Alexander. R. J. (1980) 'Towards a conceptual framework for school-focused INSET', *British Journal of In-Service Education* 6(3).
—— (1984) *Primary Teaching*, London: Cassell.
—— (1988) 'Garden or jungle? Teacher development and informal primary education', in W. A. L. Blyth (ed.) *Informal Primary Education Today: Essays and Studies*, London: Falmer Press.
—— (1989) 'Core subjects and autumn leaves: the National Curriculum and the languages of primary education', *Education 3–13* 17(1).
—— (1991a) *Primary Education in Leeds: Twelfth and Final Report from the Primary Needs Independent Evaluation Project*, Leeds: University of Leeds.
—— (1991b) 'Politics of good practice', *Times Educational Supplement*, 9 August.
—— (1991c) *Primary Education in Leeds: Briefing and Summary*, Leeds: University of Leeds.
—— (1991d) *Primary Education in Leeds: Implications for Practice and Policy*, Paper given at the Department of Education and Science, 16 October.
—— (1991e) *Educational Standards and Primary School Staffing*, Paper prepared for internal DES discussion, 17 October.
—— (1991f) Letter to Minister of State T. Eggar, 4 November.
—— (1991g) Letter to the *Daily Telegraph*, 2 October.
—— (1991h) Letter to Director, Advisory, Leeds LEA, 11 October.
—— (1991i) Letter to Barraclough Carey Productions, 11 December.
—— (1991j) Letter to fellow academics, 4 December.
—— (1992a) 'Holding the middle ground', *Times Educational Supplement*, 31 January.
—— (1992b) 'Floodlights, fanfares and facile factors', *Guardian*, 11 February.
—— (1992c) Letter to *Guardian*, 14 February.
—— (1992d) *Policy and Practice in Primary Education*, London: Routledge.
—— (1994a) 'Wise men and clever tricks: a response', *Cambridge Journal of Education* 24(1).
—— (1994b) 'What primary curriculum? Dearing and beyond', *Education 3–13* 22(1).
—— (1994c) Memorandum submitted to the Education Committee, in House of Commons, *The Disparity in Funding Between Primary and Secondary Schools*, London: HMSO, Vol. II: 224–7.
—— (1995) *Versions of Primary Education*, London: Routledge.
—— (1996a) 'In search of good primary practice', in P. Woods (ed.) *Contemporary Issues in Teaching and Learning*, London: Routledge.

—— (1996b) *Other Primary Schools and Ours: Hazards of international Comparison*, Warwick: Centre for Research in Elementary and Primary Education.

Alexander, R. J., Broadhead, P., Driver, R. H., Hannaford, P., Hodgson, J. and Squires, A. (1990) 'Understanding our world: towards a framework for curriculum planning in the primary school', Leeds: University of Leeds.

Alexander, R. J., Rose, A. J. and Woodhead, C. (1992) *Curriculum Organisation and Classroom Practice in Primary Schools: a Discussion Paper*, London: DES.

Alexander, R. J., Willocks, J. and Kinder, K. M. (1989) *Changing Primary Practice*, London: Falmer Press.

Alexander, R. J., Willcocks, J. and Nelson, N. (1996) 'Discourse, pedagogy and the National Curriculum: change and continuity in primary schools', *Research Papers in Education* 11(1).

Assistant Masters and Mistresses Association (1992) *Primary Education: a Contribution to the Debate*, London: AMMA.

Audit Commission (1989a) 'Losing an empire, finding a role: the LEA of the future', Occasional Paper No. 10, London: HMSO.

—— (1989b) *Assuring Quality in Education: the Role of Local Education Authority Inspectors and Advisers*, London: HMSO.

—— (1991) *Management Within Primary Schools*, London: HMSO.

Auld, R. (1976) *The William Tyndale Junior and Infants Schools: Report of the Public Enquiry*, London ILEA.

Ball, S. J. (1990) *Politics and Policy-making in Education*, London: Routledge.

—— (1994) *Education Reform: a Critical and Post-structural Approach*, Buckingham: Open University Press.

Bates, S. (1992) 'Teachers told to rethink methods', *Guardian*, 23 January.

Bennett, S. N. (1976) *Teaching Styles and Pupil Progress*, London: Open Books.

—— (1978) 'Recent research on teaching: a dream, a belief and a model', *British Journal of Educational Psychology* 48.

—— (1987) 'The search for the effective primary teacher', in S. Delamont (ed.) *The Primary School Teacher*, London: Falmer Press.

—— (1991) *Managing Learning in the Primary School*, Association for the Study of Primary Education.

—— (1992) 'Never mind the sophistry', *Times Educational Supplement*, 14 February.

—— (1994) *Class Size in Primary Schools: Perceptions of Headteachers, Chairs of Governors, Teachers and Parents*, Exeter: University of Exeter.

Bennett, S. N., Desforges, C., Cockburn, A. and Wilkinson, B. (1984) *The Quality of Pupil Learning Experiences*, Hove: Lawrence Erlbaum.

Bennett, S. N. and Dunne, E. (1992) *Managing Classroom Groups*, Hemel Hempstead: Simon & Schuster.

Berlak, A. and Berlak, H. (1981) *Dilemmas of Schooling: Teaching and Social Change*, London: Methuen.

Board of Education (1931) *Report of the Consultative Committee on the Primary School* (Hadow report), London: HMSO.

Bowe, R. and Ball, S. J., with Gold, A. (1992) *Reforming Education and Changing Schools: Case Studies in Policy Sociology*, London: Routledge.

Brooks, G., Gorman, T., Kendall, L. and Tate, A. (1992) *What Teachers in Training are Taught about Reading: Report to the Council for the Accreditation of Teacher Education*, Slough: NFER.

Burchill, J. (1991) *Inspecting Schools: Breaking the Monopoly*, London: Centre for Policy Studies.

Campbell, R. J. (1985) *Developing the Primary School Curriculum*, London: Cassell.

—— (1992) 'Scapegoats and the education debate', *Guardian*, 19 February.
—— (1993) 'A dream at conception: a nightmare at delivery', in R. J. Campbell (ed.) *Breadth and Balance in the Primary Curriculum*, London: Falmer Press.
Campbell, R. J. and Neill, S. R. StJ. (1994a) *Curriculum Reform at Key Stage I: Teacher Commitment and Policy Failure*, London: Longman.
—— (1994b) *Primary Teachers at Work*, London: Routledge.
Carr, D. (1994) 'Wise men and clever tricks', *Cambridge Journal of Education* 24(1).
Cato, V. and Whetton, C. (1990) *An Enquiry into LEA Evidence on Standards of Reading of Seven Year Old Children*, Slough: NFER.
Central Advisory Council for Education (England) (CACE) (1967) *Children and Their Primary Schools* (Plowden report) London: HMSO.
Chitty, C. and Simon, B. (eds) (1993) *Education Answers Back: Critical Responses to Government Policy*, London: Lawrence & Wishart.
Clare, J. (1991) 'A generation of wasted time', *Daily Telegraph*, 19 September.
Clark, C. M. and Yinger, P. J. (1987) 'Teacher planning', in J. Calderhead (ed.) *Exploring Teachers' Thinking*, London: Cassell.
Council for the Accreditation of Teacher Education (1992) *Training Teachers to Teach Reading: a Review*, London: CATE.
Cox, C. B. and Boyson, R. (eds) (1975) *The Fight for Education*, London: Dent.
—— (1977) *Black Paper 1977*, London: Temple Smith.
Cox, C. B. and Dyson, A. E. (eds) (1971) *The Black Papers on Education 1–3*, London: Davis-Poynter.
—— (1974) *Black Paper Four*, London: Dent.
Cunningham, P. (1988) *Curriculum Change in the Primary School Since 1945: Dissemination of the Progressive Ideal*, London: Falmer Press.
Dadds, M. (1992) 'Monty Python and the Three Wise Men', *Cambridge Journal of Education* 22(2).
David, T., Curtis, A. and Siraj-Blatchford, I. (1992) *Effective Teaching in the Early Years: Fostering Children's Learning in Nurseries and in Infant Classes*, Stoke-on-Trent: Trentham Books.
Dearden, R. F. (1968) *The Philosophy of Primary Education*, London: Routledge.
—— (1976) *Problems in Primary Education*, London: Routledge.
Dearing, R. (1993a) *The National Curriculum and its Assessment: Interim Report*, York and London: NCC and SEAC.
—— (1993b) *The National Curriculum and its Assessment: Final Report*, London: SCAA.
Delamont, S. (ed.) (1987) *The Primary School Teacher*, London: Falmer Press.
Department for Education (DFE) (1992) *Initial Teacher Training (Secondary Phase)* (Circular 9/92), London: DFE.
—— (1993) *The Initial Training of Primary School Teachers: Criteria for Courses*, (Circular 14/93) London: DFE.
—— (1995a) *English in the National Curriculum*, London: DFE.
—— (1995b) *Mathematics in the National Curriculum*, London: DFE.
—— (1995c) *Science in the National Curriculum*, London: DFE.
—— (1995d) *History in the National Curriculum*, London: DFE.
—— (1995e) *Geography in the National Curriculum*, London: DFE.
—— (1995f) *Information Technology in the National Curriculum*, London: DFE.
—— (1995g) *Design and Technology in the National Curriculum*, London: DFE.
—— (1995h) *Art in the National Curriculum*, London: DFE.
—— (1995i) *Music in the National Curriculum*, London: DFE.
—— (1995j) *Physical Education in the National Curriculum*, London: DFE.

Department of Education and Science (DES) (1972) *Educational Priority, Vol. 1, EPA Problems and Practices*, London: HMSO.

—— (1977) *Local Authority Arrangements for the School Curriculum* (Circular 14/77), London: DES.

—— (1978a) *Special Educational Needs: Report of the Committee of Enquiry into the Education of Handicapped Children* (Warnock report), London: HMSO.

—— (1978b) *Primary Education in England: A survey by HM Inspectors of Schools*, London: HMSO.

—— (1979) *Local Authority Arrangements for the School Curriculum: Report of the 14/77 Review*, London: HMSO.

—— (1982a) *Education 5–9: an Illustrative Survey of 80 First Schools in England*, London: HMSO.

—— (1982b) *The New Teacher in School: a Report by HM Inspectors*, London: HMSO.

—— (1983) *Local Authority Policies on the School Curriculum* (Circular 8/83), London: DES.

—— (1984) *Initial Teacher Training: Approval of Courses* (Circular 3/84), London: DES.

—— (1985) *Education 8–12 in Combined and Middle Schools: an HMI Survey*, London: HMSO.

—— (1987) *Primary Schools: Some Aspects of Good Practice*, London: HMSO.

—— (1988a) *Report by HMI on a Survey of Parent–School Liaison in Primary and Secondary Schools Serving Ethnically Diverse Areas within Three LEAs*, London: HMSO.

—— (1988b) *Education Reform Act: Local Management of Schools* (Circular 7/88), London: HMSO.

—— (1988c) *The New Teacher in School: a Survey by HM Inspectors of Schools 1987*, London: HMSO.

—— (1989a) *Report by HM Inspectorate on a Survey of Support Services for Special Educational Needs*, London: DES.

—— (1989b) *Mathematics in the National Curriculum*, London: HMSO.

—— (1989c) *Science in the National Curriculum*, London: HMSO.

—— (1989d) *Aspects of Primary Education: the Teaching and Learning of Science*, London: HMSO.

—— (1989e) *Aspects of Primary Education: the Teaching and Learning of Mathematics*, London: HMSO.

—— (1989f) *Aspects of Primary Education: the Teaching and Learning of History and Geography*, London: HMSO.

—— (1989g) *Standards in Education 1987: the Annual Report of the Senior Chief Inspector Based on the Work of HMI in England*, London: DES.

—— (1989h) *Initial Teacher Training: Approval of Courses* (Circular 24/89), London: DES.

—— (1989i) *The Implementation of the National Curriculum in Primary Schools*, London: HMSO.

—— (1990a) *English in the National Curriculum (No. 2)*, London: HMSO.

—— (1990b) *Technology in the National Curriculum*, London: HMSO.

—— (1990c) *The Teaching and Learning of Reading in Primary Schools: a Report by HMI*, London: DES.

—— (1990d) *Aspects of Primary Education: the Teaching and Learning of Language and Literacy*, London: HMSO.

—— (1990e) *Standards in Education 1988–9: the Annual Report of HM Senior Chief Inspector of Schools*, London: DES.

—— (1990f) *Developing School Management: the Way Forward: a Report by the School Management Task Force*, London: HMSO.

—— (1991a) *Standards in Education 1989–90: the Annual Report of HM Senior Chief Inspector of Schools*, London: HMSO.

—— (1991b) *History in the National Curriculum*, London: HMSO.

—— (1991c) *Geography in the National Curriculum*, London: HMSO.

—— (1991d) *Local Management of Schools: Further Guidance* (Circular 7/91), London: HMSO.

—— (1991e) *Department of Education and Science News* 142/91, London: HMSO.

—— (1991f) *Art for Ages 5–14: Proposals of the Secretary of State*, London: HMSO.

—— (1991g) *Music for Ages 5–14: Proposals of the Secretary of State*, London: HMSO.

—— (1991h) *Physical Education for Ages 5–16: Proposals of the Secretary of State*, London: HMSO.

—— (1991i) 'Improving Primary Education', Departmental memorandum, 17 April.

—— (1991j) *The Implementation of the Curricular Requirements of ERA: an Overview by HM Inspectorate on the First Year, 1989–90*, London: HMSO.

—— (1991k) *Assessment, Recording and Reporting: a Report by HM Inspectorate on the First Year, 1989–90*, London: HMSO.

—— (1991l) 'Primary education: how can standards be raised?', Departmental memorandum, September.

—— (1991m) 'Follow-up to Chevening/Primary Education', Departmental memorandum, 13 November.

—— (1991n) *Primary Education: Statement by the Secretary of State for Education and Science*, London: DES.

—— (1991o) *Aspects of Primary Education in France: a Report by HMI*, London: DES.

—— (1992) 'Three Wise Men Report Calls for Big Changes in Primary Education', *Department of Education and Science News* 20/92 London: DES.

Department of Education and Science and Department of Health and Social Security (1983) *Assessments and Statements of Special Needs* (Circular 1/83), London: HMSO.

Drummond M J (1993) *Assessing Children's Learning*, London: David Fulton.

—— (1995) 'Lessons of experience', *Times Educational Supplement*, 13 January.

Entwistle, H. (1970) *Child Centred Education*, London: Methuen.

Evans, L., Packwood, A., Neill, S. R. StJ. and Campbell, R. J. (1994) *The Meaning of Infant Teachers' Work*, London: Routledge.

Fallon, M. (1991) Speech to the National Primary Conference of the National Association of Head Teachers, 1 November.

Foot, M. (1996) *Who's Failing? Doubts about the Statistical Basis of OFSTED's/Chris Woodhead's Estimated Numbers of Failing Teachers*, Mimeo.

Furby, L., Haylock, D. and Morgan, C. (1992) *Mathematics in Primary Schools: a Response on behalf of the Association of Mathematics Education Teachers to the Alexander, Rose and Woodhead discussion paper 'Curriculum Organisation and Classroom Practice in Primary Schools*, Norwich: AMET.

Galton, M. (1989) *Teaching in the Primary School*, London: David Fulton.

—— (1995) *Crisis in the Primary Classroom*, London: David Fulton.

Galton, M. and Simon, B. (eds) (1980) *Progress and Performance in the Primary Classroom*, London: Routledge.

Galton, M., Simon, B. and Croll, P. (1980) *Inside the Primary Classroom*, London: Routledge.

Gipps, C., Gross, H. and Goldstein, H. (1987) *Warnock's Eighteen Per Cent: Children with Special Needs in Primary Schools*, London: Falmer Press.
Graham, D. and Tytler, D. (1993) *A Lesson for Us All: the Making of the National Curriculum*, London: Routledge.
Hammersley, M. and Scarth, J. (1993) 'Beware of wise men bearing gifts: a case study in the misuse of educational research', *British Educational Research Journal* 19(5).
Hart, D. (1991) *An Agenda for Primary Education* (Speech to the National Primary Conference of NAHT), Haywards Heath: National Association of Head Teachers.
House of Commons (1986) *Achievement in Primary Schools: Third Report from the Education, Science and Arts Select Committee*, London: HMSO.
—— (1994a) *The Disparity in Funding between Primary and Secondary Schools: Education Committee Second Report*, London: HMSO.
—— (1994b) *Education Committee Third Special Report: Government Response to the Second Report from the Committee, Session 1993–4 (The Disparity of Funding Between Primary and Secondary Schools)*, London: HMSO.
Jarvis, F. (1993) *Education and Mr Major*, London: Tufnell Press.
Johnson, S. (1992) 'Missing the point', *Education*, 9 August.
Kelly, A. V. (1990) *The National Curriculum: a Critical Review*, London: Paul Chapman,
King, R. A. (1978) *All Things Bright and Beautiful: a Sociological Study of Infants' Classrooms*, Chichester: John Wiley.
—— (1989) *The Best of Primary Education? A Sociological Study of Junior Middle Schools*, London: Falmer Press.
Labour Party (1995) *Excellence for Everyone: Labour's Crusade to Raise Standards*, London: Labour Party.
Lake, M. (1991) 'Surveying all the factors: reading research', *Language and Learning* 6.
Lawler, S. M. (1988) *The Education Support Grant (Urban Primary Schools) Leeds Project: Interim Report*, Leeds: Leeds City Council.
Lawlor, S. (1990) *Teachers Mistaught*, London: Centre for Policy Studies.
Leeds City Council (1984a) *Submission to the Department of Education and Science for a Grant Under ESG Scheme F: Improving the Quality of Education Provided in Primary Schools in Urban Areas*, Leeds: Leeds City Council.
—— (1984b) *Special Educational Needs: a Handbook for Schools*, Leeds: Leeds City Council.
—— (1985a) *Primary Needs Programme* (Education Committee Document), Leeds: Leeds City Council.
—— (1985b) *Leeds In-service for Special Educational Needs: Course Manual*, Leeds: Leeds City Council.
—— (1985c) *PNP Co-ordinator: Job Specification*, Leeds: Leeds City Council.
—— (1986) *Primary Needs Programme: Equal Opportunities for Girls*, Leeds: Leeds City Council.
—— (1987a) *Anti-racist Education: a Policy Statement*, Leeds: Leeds City Council.
—— (1987b) *Early Education Support Agency: a Letter to Headteachers*, Leeds: Leeds City Council.
—— (1987c) *Guidelines for Headteachers in the Use of PNP Staff*, Leeds: Leeds City Council.
—— (1988) *Primary Education: a Policy Statement*, Leeds: Leeds City Council.
—— (1989a) *PNP Conference Report*, Leeds: Leeds City Council.
—— (1989b) *Early Education Support Agency: Report 5*, Leeds: Leeds City Council.

—— (1989c) *The Leeds Scheme for Local Management of Schools*, Leeds: Leeds City Council.
—— (1989d) *A Quality Learning Environment: Display*, Leeds: Leeds City Council.
—— (1989e) *The Primary School: A Guide for Parents*, Leeds: Leeds City Council.
—— (1989f) *Equal Opportunities: Guidelines for Primary Schools*, Leeds: Leeds City Council.
—— (1990a) *The Curriculum 5–16: a Statement of Policy*, Leeds: Leeds City Council.
—— (1990b) *Assessment, Recording and Reporting: a Support File*, Leeds: Leeds City Council.
—— (1990c) *A Survey of Year 1 Pupils in Leeds Primary Schools*, Leeds: Leeds City Council.
—— (1990d) *Primary Detail: Design and Technology*, Leeds: Leeds City Council.
—— (1991a) *Towards a Coherent Management Policy: Leeds LEA*, Leeds: Leeds City Council.
—— (1991b) *School Development Plan 1991–2*, Leeds: Leeds City Council.
—— (1991c) *Advisory Division Review and Structure*, Leeds: Leeds City Council.
—— (1991d) Letter to author from Director, Advisory, Leeds LEA, 16 October.
Lockheed, M. E. and Verspoor, A. M. (1991) *Improving Primary Education in Developing Countries*, Washington, DC: World Bank.
Low, G. (1992) 'Ministerial row botched primary campaign', *Education*, 8 May.
Lynch, J. (1983) *The Multicultural Curriculum*, London: Batsford.
McMahon, A., Bolam, R., Abbott, R. and Holly, P. (1984) *Guidelines for Internal Review and Development in Schools: Primary Schools Handbook*, London: Longman/Schools Council.
Major, J. (1992) Speech to the Conservative Party Conference, September.
Maltby, F. (1984) *Gifted Children and Teachers in Primary Schools 5–12*, London: Falmer Press.
Merson, M. and Campbell, R. J. (1974) 'Community education: instruction for inequality', *Education for Teaching* 93.
Mortimore, P. and Blatchford, P. (1993) *The Issue of Class Size*, NCE Briefing No. 12, London: National Commission on Education.
Mortimore, P., Sammons, P., Stoll, L., Lewis, D. and Ecob, R. (1988) *School Matters: the Junior Years*, London: Open Books.
Nash, R. (1976) *Teacher Expectations and Pupil Learning*. London: Routledge.
National Commission on Education (1993) *Learning to Succeed: a Radical Look at Education Today and a Strategy for the Future*, London: Heinemann.
—— (1995) *Learning to Succeed: the Way Ahead*, London: NCE.
National Curriculum Council (1989) *Curriculum Guidance 1: a Framework for the Primary Curriculum*, York: NCC.
—— (1991) *Report on Monitoring the Implementation of the National Curriculum Core Subjects 1989–90*, York: NCC.
Nias, J. (1989) *Primary Teachers Talking: a Study of Teaching as Work*, London: Routledge.
Nias, J., Southworth, G. and Yeomans, R. (1989) *Staff Relationships in the Primary School: a Study of Organisational Cultures*, London: Cassell.
Nikiforuk, A. (1993) 'Fifth column', *Toronto Globe and Mail*, 5 March.
Office for Standards in Education (OFSTED) (1993a) *Well-managed Classes in Primary Schools: Case Studies of Six Teachers*, London: OFSTED.
—— (1993b) *Curriculum Organisation and Classroom Practice in Primary Schools: a Follow-Up report*, London: OFSTED.

—— (1994) *Primary Matters: a Discussion on Teaching and Learning in Primary Schools*, London: OFSTED.
—— (1995a) *Guidance on the Inspection of Nursery and Primary Schools*, London: HMSO.
—— (1995b) *Teaching Quality: the Primary Debate*, London: OFSTED.
—— (1995c) *Class Size and the Quality of Education*, London: OFSTED.
—— (1996a) *The Teaching of Reading in 45 Inner London Primary Schools*, London: OFSTED.
—— (1996b) *The Annual Report of Her Majesty's Chief Inspector of Schools 1994–5*, London: HMSO.
Peters, R. S. (ed.) (1969) *Perspectives on Plowden*, London: Routledge.
Phillips, M. (1991) 'The lessons ministers refuse to learn', *Guardian*, 20 December.
—— (1992) 'Rewriting the message', *Guardian*, 14 February.
Pollard, A. (1985) *The Social World of the Primary School*, London: Cassell.
Pollard, A., Broadfoot, P., Croll, P., Osborn, M. and Abbot D (1994) *Changing English Primary Schools: the Impact of the Education Reform Act at Key Stage One*, London: Cassell.
Primary Needs Independent Evaluation Project (PRINDEP) (1986a) *Reactions to the PNP In-service Support Programme* (PRINDEP Report 1), Leeds: University of Leeds.
—— (1986b) *One Year into PNP: the View from Phase I Schools* (PRINDEP Report 2), Leeds: University of Leeds.
—— (1987a) *Home–School Links: First Findings* (PRINDEP Report 3), Leeds: University of Leeds.
—— (1987b) *Teachers Teaching Together: Emerging Issues* (PRINDEP Report 4), Leeds: University of Leeds.
—— (1987c) *The PNP Co-ordinator: Opportunities and Ambiguities* (PRINDEP Report 5), Leeds: University of Leeds.
—— (1987d) *PNP INSET: a Closer Look* (PRINDEP Report 6), Leeds: University of Leeds.
—— (1988a) *Children in Primary Schools: Defining and Meeting Needs* (PRINDEP Report 7), Leeds: University of Leeds.
—— (1988b) *The PNP Curriculum: Policy and Management* (PRINDEP Report 8), Leeds: University of Leeds.
—— (1988c) *Reading Standards in PNP Schools* (PRINDEP Report 9), Leeds: University of Leeds.
—— (1989) *Changing Classroom Practice: Decisions and Dilemmas* (PRINDEP Report 10), Leeds: University of Leeds.
—— (1990) *Teachers and Children in PNP Classrooms* (PRINDEP Report 11), Leeds: University of Leeds.
Pugh, G. (1992) *Curriculum Organisation and Classroom Practice in Primary Schools* (Letter to the Secretary of State), London: National Children's Bureau, 9 March.
Reynolds, D., Creemers, B. P. M., Nesselrodt, R. S., Schaffer, E. C., Stringfield, S. and Teddlie, C. (1994) *Advances in School Effectiveness Research and Practice*, Oxford: Pergamon.
Richards, C. (1996) 'At a hinge of history', *Times Educational Supplement*, 19 April.
Rutter, M., Maughan, B., Mortimore, P. and Ouston, J. (1979) *Fifteen Thousand Hours: Secondary Schools and their Effects on Children*, London: Open Books.
Sammons, P., Hillman, J. and Mortimore, P. (1995) *Key Characteristics of Effective Schools: a Review of School Effectiveness Research*, London: OFSTED.
Sharp, P. and Green, A. (1975) *Education and Social Control: a Study in Progressive Primary Education*, London: Routledge.

Shipman, M. D. (1990) *In Search of Learning: a New Approach to School Management*, Oxford: Blackwell.

Shorrocks, D., Frobisher, L., Nelson, N., Turner, L. and Waterson, A. (1993) *National Curriculum Assessment in the Primary School*. London: Hodder and Stoughton.

Simon, B. (1981) 'The primary school revolution: myth or reality?', in B. Simon and J. Willcocks (eds) *Research and Practice in the Primary Classroom*, London: Routledge.

—— (1991) *Education and the Social Order 1940–1990*, London: Lawrence & Wishart.

—— (1992) 'Curriculum organisation and classroom practice: a discussion paper', (Review article) *Curriculum Journal* 3(1).

Simon, B. and Simon, J. (eds) (1963) *Educational Psychology in the USSR*, London: Routledge & Kegan Paul.

Spooner, R. (1992) 'For failure, read success', *Times Educational Supplement*, 16 August.

Stevenson, H. and Stigler, J. (1992) *The Learning Gap*, New York: Summit Books.

Tameside MBC (1992) *A summary of 'Curriculum Organisation and Classroom Practice in Primary Schools'*, Ashton-under-Lyme: Tameside MBC Education Department.

Taylor, P. H. (1986) *Expertise and the Primary School Teacher*, Slough: NFER.

Taylor, P. H., Reid, W. A., Holley, B. J. and Exon, G. (1974) *Purpose, Power and Constraint in the Primary School Curriculum*, London: Macmillan.

Thornton, M. (1993) 'The role of the government in education', in C. Chitty and B. Simon (eds) *Education Answers Back: Critical Responses to Government Policy*, London: Lawrence & Wishart.

Tizard, B., Blatchford, P., Burke, J., Farquahar, C. and Plewis, I. (1988) *Young Children at School in the Inner City*, Hove: Lawrence Erlbaum.

Turner, M. (1990) *Sponsored Reading Failure*, Warlingham: Education Unit.

Wallace, M. (1993) 'Discourse of decision: the role of the mass media within the educational policy process', *Journal of Educational Policy*, 8(4).

Webb, R. and Vulliamy, G. (1996) *Roles and Responsibilities in the Primary School: Changing Demands, Changing Practices*, Buckingham: Open University Press.

Whitehead, M. (1992) 'Wise man follows the middle route to schooling', *Bradford Telegraph and Argus*, 24 January.

Wolfendale, S. (1987) *Primary Schools and Special Needs: Policy, Planning and Provision*, London: Cassell.

Woodhead, C. (1992) 'Raise the standard bearers', *Guardian*, 11 February.

—— (1995a) *Education: the Elusive Engagement and the Continuing Frustration*, (Annual HMCI Lecture, Royal Society of Arts), London: OFSTED.

—— (1995b) 'Teaching quality: the issues and the evidence', in OFSTED *Teaching Quality: the Primary Debate*, London: OFSTED.

—— (1995c) *A Question of Standards: Finding the Balance*, London: Politeia.

Woods, P. and Wenham, P. (1995) 'Politics and pedagogy: a case study in appropriation', *Journal of Education Policy*, 10(2).

Wragg, E. C. and Bennett, S. N. (1990) 'Leverhulme Primary Project Occasional Paper', Spring 1990, Exeter: University of Exeter School of Education.

Index

Printed in the United Kingdom by
Lightning Source UK Ltd., Milton Keynes
138351UK00003B/68/A